CANADA

A STORY OF CHALLENGE

CANADA
A Story of Challenge

BY

J. M. S. CARELESS

Department of History
University of Toronto

Laurentian Library 30

MACMILLAN OF CANADA
TORONTO

ST. MARTIN'S PRESS
NEW YORK

First published 1953
Revised and enlarged edition 1963
Third edition 1970
First published in the Laurentian Library 1974
Reprinted 1976, 1979
ISBN 0 7705 1253 4

Printed in Canada for
The Macmillan Company of Canada Ltd.,
70 Bond Street, Toronto, Ont. M5B 1X3

AUTHOR'S PREFACE

This is a revised and enlarged edition of a book first published in
1953. The preface to the original work outlined its frame of
reference and the author's general attitude to its theme of
Canadian history. That preface still seems worth repeating in
part, as expressing the nature of this volume.

'In the following pages I have tried to present the major facts of
Canada's history and the main forces that have shaped it; the
pressures and promises of Canadian geography, the pull of the
United States, the influences stemming from Britain and France,
and the interrelations of the French- and English-speaking communities in Canada. The book's main theme, however, is the
emergence of a Canadian nation out of scattered colonies, in
response to the challenge of the vast Canadian land and the forces
that have played on its inhabitants. Without overestimating this
national growth, one may claim that there has indeed been a
distinctive Canadian achievement, the product of long and
enduring efforts to build a community in the northern half of the
North American continent separate from the United States.

'There is no attempt here to ignore the obvious limitations of
partly developed Canadian nationalism – nor to view nationalism
as a supremely worthy development in itself. Yet this study
finds the very core of Canadian history in the fact that a separate
Canadian community has always survived in North America, and
still continues to grow. The problems of creating a continent-
wide Canadian unity have been immense; and yet a degree of
unity has been created, maintained, and gradually strengthened.
Hence the general tone of the book is neither typical Canadian
pessimism concerning Canada's shortcomings as a self-conscious
nation, nor equally typical optimism regarding the country's
"limitless resources" and all-excusing "youth". It is, rather, a

surprised and measured satisfaction that so much has been accomplished in the face of such grave difficulties.'

By now, these words themselves have become a tiny bit of history, reflecting perhaps some of the sense of achievement in Canada during the booming 1950's. Yet, in the strained 1970's, the author would not greatly wish to alter them. His satisfaction at Canadian achievement might be still more qualified, his belief in the strengthening of Canadian unity considerably less certain. Nevertheless, his consciousness of Canada's historic record of accomplishments gives him grounds for hope that they will still continue.

J. M. S. CARELESS

Toronto,
  March, 1970

CONTENTS

CONTENTS

CONTENTS

CONTENTS

ILLUSTRATIONS

ACKNOWLEDGMENTS

For permission to reproduce copyright illustrations listed above, the publishers express their thanks to the following:

Confederation Life Association (nos. 1, 5, 9, 10, 13, 15, 16, 22, 23); Sigmund Samuel Gallery, Royal Ontario Museum (nos. 2, 4, 6, 8, 11, 17); Public Archives of Canada (nos. 3, 7, 14, 18, 26, 27, 29, 30, 31, 32); John Ross Robertson Collection, Toronto Public Library (nos. 12, 19, 20, 25); Provincial Archives of British Columbia (nos. 21, 28); National Film Board of Canada (nos. 24, 33, 36); Ontario Department of Highways (nos 34, 41); Toronto Star Syndicate (no. 35); Royal Canadian Navy (no. 37); Canadian Army Photographs (no. 38); Man and His World (no. 39); Ontario Department of Tourism and Information (no. 40).

MAPS AND DIAGRAMS

PART I
BACKGROUND

CHAPTER I

GEOGRAPHY SETS THE STAGE

1 *The Challenge of the Land*

What is Canada? It is a vast land-mass over three thousand miles wide, larger than the United States and Alaska put together, a little bigger than Europe, nearly a third larger than the island-continent of Australia. It extends from the temperate climate of the lower Great Lakes, from tobacco fields, peach orchards and grape vineyards, to the coldest Arctic regions, where the granite-hard subsoil never thaws. To east and west this massive land is flanked as well by great islands in the sea, Newfoundland and Vancouver Island. To the north so much empty space remains that, even since the second World War, aerial surveys could find unknown territories at the top of Hudson Bay as big as the province of Prince Edward Island to add to the map of Canada. Sometimes full of warm colour and contrast, sometimes bleak, monotonous and unfriendly, the Canadian land stretches in all its immensity from ocean to ocean and to the polar ice-cap.

There is no virtue in mere size, however. As in Canada's case, it can raise many different problems in a country's development. And Canada above all has been affected by its geography: there is so much of it. Geography, of course, does much to influence the history of any nation. But this is particularly true of a land as sprawling and spread out as Canada, composed of a number of different geographic regions, often with natural barriers between them, regions which in Europe might have contained a whole patchwork of separate countries. Thus Canadian history largely records a struggle to build a nation in the face of stern geographic difficulties. That struggle still goes on.

The difficulties arise from the very extent and variety of the Canadian landscape: the range on range of far western mountains,

3

the rough tracts of forest and bush, the Arctic and sub-Arctic wastes, and the infertile belt of ancient rock nearly a thousand miles wide, called the Canadian Shield, which runs through the very heart of Canada. Barriers such as the mountains and the Shield exact a heavy price in scattering the population. They make for sectional divisions and high transportation charges. They weaken national unity and retard national development. Since, moreover, so much of Canada lies outside the limits set by soil and climate for successful farming, merely numbering the thousands of empty or almost empty square miles in the country does not necessarily indicate the amount of room left for growth. It may equally point out the size of a problem of development that has been, and still is, slow and expensive of solution. These are some of the costs of geography that have had to be borne throughout the course of Canadian history.

Yet geography has offered Canada much as well. This giant land has held rich rewards for those ready to meet its challenge. The challenge of the land steadily led men across it, from east to west. In the east, the old sunken coastline of the continent formed great fishing banks off shore that first beckoned to the hardy fishermen of Europe who were willing to dare the stormy northern passage across the Atlantic. Beyond the Atlantic fishing shores the gateway of the St Lawrence gulf and river stood wide, inviting the venturesome to thrust boldly into the middle of an unknown continent. Adventurers who pressed up the St Lawrence and on to the Great Lakes would find a broad water highway stretching nearly half-way across Canada and by-passing the inhospitable Shield. From the St Lawrence system other waterways, easily reached, led to the Gulf of Mexico, to the Arctic, even to the Pacific. The St Lawrence rewarded daring by unlocking the interior of North America to those who sought the meaning of the great river.

West of the Great Lakes the great plains spread out, easy to travel, and deep-layered in black topsoil that promised the future

4

golden treasury of Canadian wheat. The Shield itself, in the long run, would prove a treasure-house; first of furs, then of timber, and finally of pulpwood, minerals and water-power. More mineral riches were sealed in the mountain walls west of the plains. Beyond these mountains, the Pacific coast could furnish stands of giant timber and more teeming fisheries. To-day the sub-Arctic 'wastes' are the latest land of promise. Their mineral resources are only now being tapped. If Canada is a hard country, it has indeed been a rewarding one for those who have met its challenge.

2 *Sectionalism and the St Lawrence*

Not all Canada is hard, however, and the bulk of its people do not live in regions that are difficult to develop. In the southern parts of the country long fertile valleys or rich garden lands have come to support a fairly dense population within a comparatively small area. This is the Canada that most Canadians themselves know: a land of dairying and mixed farming, of orchards and grain fields. This too, is the Canada of large cities and factories that have made the nation a notable industrial power in the world. As a result, the country which is often thought of abroad as the realm of frontiers and wide horizons, to-day has over three quarters of its population in urban centres and two thirds of it in large metropolitan areas.

From the start the more fertile areas in southern Canada, chiefly along the valley of the St Lawrence or in the maritime regions beside the Atlantic, provided the bases for settlement. From here expansion was made into the harder northern zones. By this process Canada grew. But because the areas of relatively easy conditions across the continent were cut off from one another by geographic barriers and more difficult country, Canada tended to develop in separated communities or sections.

The populated parts grew like separate melons on one long vine, strung out across the continent close to Canada's southern

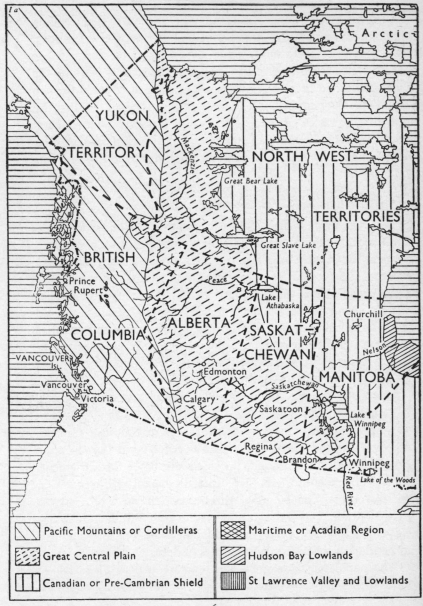

▨ Pacific Mountains or Cordilleras	▨ Maritime or Acadian Region
▨ Great Central Plain	▨ Hudson Bay Lowlands
‖ Canadian or Pre-Cambrian Shield	‖ St Lawrence Valley and Lowlands

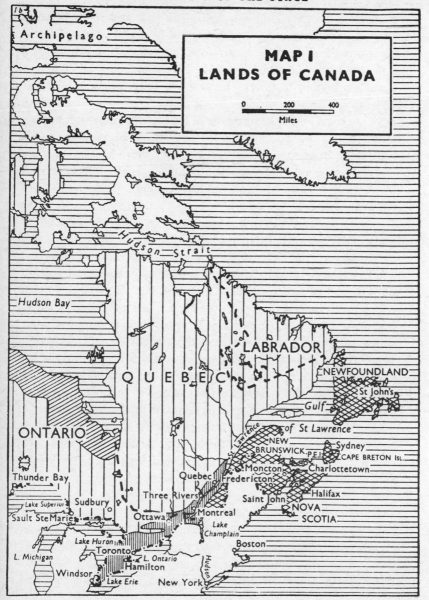

1b

Archipelago

MAP I
LANDS OF CANADA

0   200   400

Miles

Hudson Strait

Hudson Bay

LABRADOR

QUEBEC

NEWFOUNDLAND

St John's

Gulf

ONTARIO

Lawrence   of St Lawrence

NEW
BRUNSWICK   P.E.I.

Sydney

CAPE BRETON Isl.

Thunder Bay

Quebec

Fredericton

Moncton

Charlottetown

Lake Superior   Sudbury

Three Rivers

Sault Ste Marie

Ottawa

Montreal

Saint John

Halifax

NOVA

SCOTIA

Lake
Champlain

Lake Huron

Toronto

L. Michigan

L. Ontario

Boston

Windsor

Hamilton

Lake Erie

New York

Hudson

boundary. To-day, although costly railways and roads link the heavily populated areas together, only in the western plains is there any great depth of continuous settlement, and Canada still falls into a number of distinct sections. In consequence, much of Canadian history has been the story of individual sections and provinces. Because of their somewhat different interests they have not combined in a complete, or legislative, union in founding a nation, but have adopted the looser form of federal union. This federation, moreover, has turned out to be more loosely knit than that of the United States, where a much larger and more continuous population, not so hindered by geography, has fused more fully together.

Furthermore, because the lines of geographic division that mark off the regions of Canada tend to run north and south across the continent, and because so much of the Canadian population lies near the American boundary line, Canadians in one section have often had easier contacts with the neighbouring American region to the south than with the other parts of Canada that lie east or west. Hence the 'north-south pull', heightening sectionalism, has played a significant role throughout Canadian history. Nevertheless there have also been powerful forces pulling in an east-to-west direction that work to bind the parts of Canada together. Indeed, they brought the sections to form one country, almost despite geography, and certainly in the face of its costs.

Some of these forces have come from the people rather than the land; they have been historic rather than geographic. For example, they include the centuries-old resistance of French Canada to the American pull to the south, and the traditional desire of later English-speaking settlers to remain linked with Britain and independent of the United States. But perhaps the most powerful force that has helped to bind Canada from east to west as one country is geographic in origin. It is the influence of the St Lawrence system of rivers and lakes, and the east-west trade that grew up along that water route. The Canadian nation itself, in fact, developed along the St Lawrence highway, as trade and settlement advanced from east to west by that path, from the lands about the gulf to posts up the river and on the Great Lakes.

First came the fur-trader's canoe. Short 'carries' or portages overland from the St Lawrence headwaters brought the fur trader to western rivers, and finally to the Pacific. That the breadth of the North American continent was first crossed in its northern, Canadian half indicates the early usefulness of the St Lawrence and its connections as a transcontinental route. Next came the canal boat, to bring the increasing grain crops of the interior to the Atlantic for shipment to European markets. Then the railway stretched through the St Lawrence valley, and reached out east and west to two oceans, tying all Canada together with gleaming steel.

All through these stages the trading and financial interests which developed with the St Lawrence system had been competing with the other trade routes spanning the continent that led to American ports. The Canadian interests strove to build their half of North America into one secure trading empire from sea to sea, to make Canada an economic unit apart from the United States. The influence of the great east-west Canadian trade route, therefore, throughout history has worked against the north-south pulls in each region of Canada. It has supplied a core about which the modern nation could grow, despite the cross-currents of sectionalism. This much, again, geography has done for Canada.

3 *Influences by Land and Sea*

Geography has done still more by land and sea; to link Canada's destinies by land, with the United States; by sea, with Britain. The easy access to Canada by land from what is now the United States has been of great significance in Canadian history. Since the main geographic barriers in North America run north and south they do not block the way into the various parts of Canada from the United States, and the boundary between the

9

two countries is on the whole simply a man-made line. Conditions of every-day life may be much the same on either side of the border. The common problems that are met in living in the same kinds of land, the similar outlooks thereby produced, and the constant movement of trade and people to and fro across the border result in Canada being readily open to American influences, and Canadian history being closely tied to that of the United States.

The stronger nation tends usually to influence the weaker. And geography has decreed that the United States should be much stronger. Geography, that is, has divided and scattered the Canadian people, made the cost of developing their country higher than that of the American republic and given them far fewer men and less money to work with. It has declared that Canada should be rich, but not endowed with the variety of the United States; and it has sharply restricted the northern nation in regard to soil and climate. Geography has placed the barren Shield across the heart of Canada and the populous Mississippi valley, containing some of the finest land in the world, in the midst of the United States. The result, indeed, may be read in the populations of the two nations to-day: some twenty million people as compared with well over two hundred million. Canada's achievements may be great, especially for a relatively small population, but the mighty American neighbour still towers above the northern nation.

No other Commonwealth country has had to grow up beside a tremendously powerful foreign state. This is a special problem for Canadian history. It has meant in Canada both a tendency to copy American ways and a suspicion of American influence and power to dominate. It has meant in the more remote past two wars to repel American conquest and many periods of alarm. More recently, it has also come to mean a striking record of close co-operation between nations, a long era of peace and an unfortified American-Canadian border. But in general, the presence of the United States has involved Canada in a struggle for survival as an independent nation in North America—a struggle, first, against superior force and later against the process of gradual and peaceful absorption.

Yet a powerful counter-weight against the American influence by land has been supplied in Canada's past through the British tie by sea, which is no less grounded in geography. The modern Canadian nation, of course, has grown out of former colonies of the great British oceanic empire. In Britain lay a source of protection against the power of the rising young republic in the dangerous days. From Britain came ideas and influences to modify those received from the United States. And from Britain as well there flowed the main stream of population that made the former French possession of Canada a British colony in content as well as name.

The Canadians of to-day are a little less than half of British stock, about thirty per cent French, and the rest very largely of other European origins, who have generally joined the English-speaking majority. The British immigrant group, however, loomed especially large in the nineteenth century in Canada. To a great extent it was because of their strong traditions that Canada advanced to self-government without leaving the empire, and thus to-day remains a partner in the Commonwealth. Canadian history has therefore been deeply affected by British influences. They did much to shape the modern nation and to keep it independent in North America.

All this again goes back to geography, to the sea. Canadian history began by sea as Europe expanded over the oceans. First came French overseas enterprise. The building of New France left an enduring element in the life of Canada, making the present nation a partnership of two peoples, languages and cultures. But British sea power wrested Canada from French control and kept it in British hands. The new British colony grew and flourished within the sea-trading empire. It was easily accessible by the oceans and could be effectively tied to the imperial islands of

Great Britain. To-day the trade with Britain still remains important to Canada's well-being. Geography, in sum, has set the stage for Canada by sea no less than it has fixed conditions by land for Canadian development.

The great St Lawrence system, key to the whole course of Canadian history, was linked by the sea to Britain. If one end of that long trade route lay deep in the continent, the other lay in London. It formed a broad funnel through which trade, people and ideas could pour from Britain into the North American heart of Canada. Then, too, the Atlantic regions of Canada, to be known as the Maritime provinces, faced out to sea and turned their backs on the continent; Newfoundland was virtually a British fishing ship anchored off America, and for long years was actually governed by British naval officers.

The Pacific coast of Canada was first opened by sea. The long fingers of British sea power stretched to Vancouver Island from around Cape Horn and across the Pacific. Even the interior western plains were early reached by sea, for the English Hudson's Bay Company developed the cold northern gateway to Canada as the way to the western fur trade. The sea touches all the regions of Canada and sounds through all its history.

4 The Regions of Canada

Despite the common influences which reached Canada by sea, it remained a land of distinct regions, each with its own history. They formed the moulds in which Canada gradually took shape, as successive generations flowed into each one in the course of moving across the continent. From east to west there are five main geographic divisions in Canada. North of them, in addition, lie the sub-Arctic and Arctic areas, consisting of the Hudson Bay Lowlands, bush country and tundra about the vast Bay, and the Arctic Archipelago, bleak rocky hills and islands extending to the polar seas.

The easternmost of the five main divisions is the Acadian or

Maritime region. It contains the Atlantic provinces of Nova Scotia, New Brunswick and Prince Edward Island, and the newest Canadian province, though oldest British colony, the massive island of Newfoundland, which joined the Canadian union in 1949. The Acadian region is a northward extension of hilly New England: an area backed by the long line of the Appalachian mountains that parallel the whole coast and formed the first main geographic barrier to the settlement of North America. The rounded Appalachians, rising only to 4,000 feet in Canada, are low mountains by the standard of the western Rockies, but their forested wilds long presented a serious obstacle, and still restrict easy passage by road or rail between the Maritime provinces and the neighbouring province of Quebec.

The Atlantic shores of the Acadian region are deeply indented with coves and buttressed with rugged headlands. This is particularly true of Newfoundland. But the many excellent harbours thus provided and the nearby shallows or banks made seafaring and fishing flourish in this region from the start. There are also sheltered green valleys in Nova Scotia and New Brunswick, and Prince Edward Island is a quiet garden in the Gulf of St Lawrence. Farming, therefore, has also been important in the Acadian region; and lumbering too, particularly where the river valleys rise against the Appalachian ridges in New Brunswick.

On the other side of the Appalachians the broad St Lawrence river begins its thousand-mile passage into Canada from the Gulf to the Great Lakes. At first the Appalachians to the south and the rim of the Shield on its northern bank hem in the St Lawrence. But so wide is the stream in its lower course that each high wall above its margin appears only as a faint blue line when seen from the opposite shore. By the time the river reaches the city of Quebec, however, the walls have moved back, and now there begins a fertile valley, nine hundred miles in length, that gradually broadens into a gently rolling, park-like plain. This St Lawrence valley, that ends amid the Lower Lakes, has always been the heart of settled Canada. To-day it contains over sixty per cent of the population. Its farmland is rich; so are its industrial resources. The two greatest Canadian cities, Montreal and Toronto, and many others, are set in the long St Lawrence plain.

The St Lawrence valley region includes the southern portion of Quebec province and the broad triangle of southern Ontario, that lies between the inland seas known as the Great Lakes. If the valley, however, is geographically and economically one unit, historically it has been two, for the French Canadians who settled in Lower Canada, now Quebec, and the English Canadians who settled chiefly in Upper Canada, now the province of Ontario, divided it into two strong sections.

Yet the larger portions of Ontario and Quebec, their northern areas, fall within the region of the Canadian Shield, the most prominent geographic feature in the whole of Canada. This huge mass of rock is a plateau worn down by prehistoric glaciers from a range of ancient mountains. It sweeps in a mighty arc about Hudson Bay, extending from the Atlantic edge of Quebec and Labrador across northern Ontario and northern Manitoba into the Northwest Territories, until it touches the Arctic ocean. The southern edge of the Shield thrusts down on the fertile St Lawrence valley, and places a thousand miles of rolling granite hills, bush, and muskeg swamp between the farms of southern Ontario and those of the western plains.

It would be wrong, however, to think of the Shield as a fearsome badlands of rock, scrub and muskeg. Some of it is; but much as well is evergreen forest, one of Canada's richest resources. Large fertile pockets of soil are also found within it, and the whole Shield is pitted and scored by countless lakes and streams. First formed by the melting glaciers, they provided a network of waterways for easy travel by canoe. The same eroding glaciers, moreover, that ground off the good top soil, made almost incalculable mineral wealth available for 'hard rock' mining.

To-day busy cities may be found deep in the silence of the

Shield, developing the mines and the hydro-electric power to be obtained from its streams, linked by rail and aeroplane with the rest of Canada. Besides being a vast source of wealth for Ontario and Quebec, the Shield is now a sporting and vacation paradise. It seems far from inhospitable on a summer day, the blue lakes sparkling, the keen air spiced with the scent of evergreens. Still the Shield has long been a barrier. The best through highway across it was only opened in 1943, although three transcontinental railway lines had spanned it earlier.

Beyond the lands of central Canada, beyond the St Lawrence valley and the Shield, the true West begins. Across the prairie provinces of Manitoba, Saskatchewan and Alberta the richly fertile plains stretch out to the Rocky Mountains, and run north-west to reach the Arctic. Not all this region is flat, treeless prairie. It rises gradually towards the foothills of the Rockies in western Alberta, park-lands run through central Saskatchewan, and Manitoba has large lakes and, of course, its share of the Shield. Not all the plains region is good farming country. There is a dry belt in the south where Alberta meets Saskatchewan, which is better suited for grazing land. Cattle-ranching is important here, and in the Alberta foothills.

But, in general, despite more recent developments in industry, northern lumbering and mining—and, above all, in Alberta oil— the region of the plains remains the home of one great enterprise; grain-producing for the markets of the world. The farms to-day are measured in square miles and involve much mechanized farming and complicated financing. Mile on mile their waving wheat fields sweep to the flat horizon, broken only by the lonely shafts of grain elevators that have become the very symbol of the prairie West.

The westernmost, or Cordilleran region of Canada, between the great plains and the Pacific, contains some of the highest mountains in North America. It really consists of four mountain chains rising parallel to one another. They run north out of the

United States through the Pacific province of British Columbia, and on to the Yukon territory. They represent an extension of the American western ranges, as the Canadian plains represent the northward extension of the interior plain of North America. This sea of mountains four hundred miles wide has its largest range, the Rockies, on the side next to the plains, where they rear a tremendous snow-capped wall above the flatlands. Good passes from east to west through the Rockies and other ranges are few, and were hard to find for railways or roads. Nor were the cold mountain rivers, rushing through deep, twisted canyons, easy for the early fur traders to navigate.

Between the ranges, however, there are often long, peaceful valleys running north and south, such as the lovely Okanagan, where placid lakes reflect the blossoming apple orchards and the distant silvery line of peaks. Where the valleys slope up to the mountains there may be good ranching land, or great mineral deposits that have produced some of the world's largest mining developments in the thriving province of British Columbia. There is no coastal plain beyond the ranges on the Pacific shore, but the deltas of the mountain rivers, especially the Fraser, widen out to afford some room for towns and farms. Vancouver, Canada's third city, lies here, a sea port growing steadily with the expanding Canadian Pacific trade; while on beautiful Vancouver Island, really part of a half submerged mountain range, flower-filled Victoria basks in the mild Pacific climate.

These then are the main regions of the Canadian land, each providing a distinct section within which the Canadian people took form, yet all of them bound together by forces of geography and history. And, in a sense, the Canadian people took shape in history in response to the challenge of their mighty land: the challenge of the rugged eastern coastline, the wide water gates of the St Lawrence, and Hudson Bay, the dark, wintry forests and endless, sunlit prairie—the grim fortress of the Rockies, the roaring mountain torrents, and the icy stillness of the Arctic night.

CHAPTER 2

THE ACTORS APPEAR

1 *The Indians and the Land*

Before Europeans came to Canada, prehistoric man had worked out his own way of life in the American continent. The Indian was the Canadian prehistoric man. The description does not seem surprising when one realizes that it refers only to people who lived prior to the age of recorded history. Thus, since the written records only begin for eastern Canada with the sixteenth and seventeenth centuries, A.D., the prehistoric period extended this far, and for much of western Canada until the eighteenth century. Indeed, some of the Eskimo tribes of the far north belonged to prehistory until the last century brought white men into contact with them.

But the Eskimos and Canadian Indians had their own learning and skills even if they did not have the art of writing. To-day the life of their descendants has been transformed, in greater or lesser degree, by the impact of the white man's world, but the original knowledge and abilities of these native races was all-important both in enabling them to exist in North America and in teaching European peoples ways to meet the challenge of the continent. The Eskimos, who represent a particular branch of the Indian people adapted to Arctic life, were of relatively minor importance in the story of Canada since they occupied only the cold northern fringes of the continent. The other Indian groups were of much greater significance.

It is held that the Indian race is related to the Mongol peoples of Asia, and that its ancestors must have crossed to the American continent by way of Alaska in the dim recesses of time. The tip of Alaska, the north-western corner of the continent, is only fifty miles from Siberia. The opposite shore can even be seen on a clear day. This is a gap narrow enough for a primitive people to have bridged in crude boats. Untold centuries later, such a people could have spread by slow wandering all over America, to form the Indian groups that the discoverers from Europe found.

The Indians were never very numerous—supposedly only about 220,000 in all Canada at the time when Europeans first arrived. This sparse population was fairly well fixed in size by the Indians' inability to feed many more mouths, despite the vastness of the continent. For the northern Indian, in particular, was primarily a hunter, and he needed wide, empty areas to range in search of food. Though some Indian groups did plant crops and scratched a living from the soil, the primitive Canadian Indian depended largely on hunting and fishing. Hence prehistoric Canada generally remained a wilderness hunting-ground, a silent world of forests in the east and far west and of untilled grasslands on the interior plains.

The Indians of Canada were divided into four main groups, apart from the Eskimos in the Arctic. Each contained many tribes. The groups were distinguished, basically, by the regions they lived in and the ways of life they had adopted to meet their surroundings. There were the Indians of the Pacific coast and mountains, the Plains Indians, those of the St Lawrence valley, and, finally, a broad group that may be called the Indians of the North-east Woodlands. In other words, while some of the divisions of the native people conformed to those of the land, in the east of Canada the same sort of Indian roamed the woods of the Shield and those of the Maritime region, from the Atlantic to the tree-line in the Arctic north.

The northernmost tribes of these woodland Indians, west of Hudson Bay, spoke the Athabaskan tongue, but the main group is termed Algonquian, from the name given to their language. They included Algonquins proper of the Ottawa-St Lawrence region, Micmacs of the Maritimes, Montagnais of Quebec and Cree and Ojibwa of northern Ontario and Manitoba. They were above all nomad hunters, moving over their tribal hunting grounds in search of the animals that supplied them with both food and clothing, though fish was also an important article of diet. They lived in birch-bark wigwams, and used this paper-like but strong bark to cover their light canoes. In these they made long journeys with remarkable ease.

In winter they moved almost as easily over snow-covered land and frozen stream by means of the snow-shoe, while fur robes replaced their deerskin summer garments. As well as using the bow and arrow these able hunters made skilful traps. But their weapons and implements were contrived of wood, bone and stone, because, like all the other Canadian Indians, these prehistoric people were in the stone age until the white men introduced metal articles among them.

The Algonquins moved into parts of the St Lawrence valley from time to time, but in general the fertile land of this region was held by the next Indian group, the Iroquois, who fought frequently with the Algonquins. The Iroquois language-family was centered in the country about the lower Great Lakes, and included the Hurons of central Ontario and the League of the Five Nations (later six) who lived south of Lake Ontario in what is now the United States. The Five Nations, as the most powerful Iroquois group, have acquired in history the name 'Iroquois' for themselves, but it is well to remember that they were really tribes of the same stock as the Huron people with whom they waged relentless war.

The Iroquois group, unlike the Algonquins, were farmers. They hunted and fished as well, but their dependence on fields and crops made theirs a settled life. They lived in stockaded villages, around which lay the fields they had cleared from the forests. Within the stockade were a number of large lodges, wood-framed, bark-covered, with arched roofs. Each housed several families of Iroquois. This was a much more social and complex existence than that of the wandering Algonquin families, dwelling in scattered wigwams. The Iroquois grew tobacco, squash and pumpkins, but their chief crop was Indian corn or maize. Life itself could depend on the corn crop being safely harvested, or the storehouses being saved from burning in an enemy raid.

The Iroquois made pottery and did beadwork, engaged in trade with other tribes and used worked bead belts, or wampum, as money. Their canoes were elm-bark covered or heavy dug-outs, hollowed-out tree-trunks, and not the more efficient Algonquin birch-bark type. But in government organization and military power they surpassed all the Canadian Indians. The secret lay in their settled life, which made the tribe a much tighter, stronger unit, and in the co-operation between tribes in the case of the Five Nations. This was a primitive international body, with a central council containing representatives from each elected tribal council. The League's ability to keep the Iroquois a unit, and to wield their power in war, is shown by the persistence of the Five Nations, as a power to be feared, long after the coming of the white man.

The other two Indian groups had much later contacts with the white man than the Algonquins and Iroquois, and taught him less. The Plains Indians were wandering hunters like the Algonquins; but their chief quarry was not the beaver, deer, and other forest animals but the great buffalo herds of the grasslands; and their chief means of transport was not the canoe but the horse. The horse, in reality, was not native to America but had been introduced by the early Spanish explorers far to the south in Mexico. By the time the prehistoric period ended for the Canadian west, however, the Indians of the plains had long since captured and tamed wild horses from the herds that had spread up the continental interior. Earlier, the Plains Indians had hunted the buffalo on foot, and used dogs to carry the tribal baggage. Dogs, of course, were also used by Indians and Eskimos to draw sleighs in the frozen north.

The plains Indians included the Sioux, the Blackfeet, the

Plains-Cree and the Plains-Ojibwa. They lived in tepis similar to Algonquin wigwams, but skin-covered. Great men among them wore the huge feathered headdresses often regarded as typical of all American Indians. The eastern tribes wore only a few feathers. The only crop cultivated by these people, who lived on some of the world's richest soil, was tobacco for smoking on occasions of ceremony. Buffalo meat, fresh or smoked as pemmican, supplied their chief article of diet, buffalo skins their clothes and robes.

The Pacific Indians, among them the Haida, Nootka and Salish tribes, made good use of the plentiful supply of fish in mountain streams and coastal waters, and also of the long, straight timber of the Pacific region. They were capable fishermen, and though they gathered roots and berries, chiefly lived on fish, especially the Pacific salmon. Their canoes were long dug-outs. They lived in villages in great box-like houses built of evenly split planks, split by stone and wooden tools. These were the Indians who raised the lofty totem poles. also often attributed to all Indians, which were carved from the giant trees of the area. Yet actually this practice did not begin till the prehistoric era was over in the nineteenth century. The life of the Pacific Indians was quite as settled and social as that of the Iroquois. Their village units were as closely knit, although, far from electing a tribal government, their hereditary chiefs had much power, while men of wealth also had great influence among them.

2   The Red Man and the White

What could Indian society teach the white man? The use of the canoe and the waterways to surmount the trackless distances of the continent; the forest craft to keep him sheltered, properly clothed and fed in the wilderness; the value of Indian corn as a quick-growing, large-yielding crop, once settlement had begun. It could show him too the skills of trapping, the art of the snow-shoe for winter travelling, and how to make long journeys on a basic diet of pemmican in the western, buffalo country. In short, the Indians could teach the Europeans how to survive in the empty continent; and how, indeed, to conquer it. For thanks to their superior civilization and tools, the white men could go forward to master and transform the raw land, as the Indians had never really done.

At the same time, the coming of Europeans sooner or later spelled death to Indian society. It was too weak to prevent the spread of the invader across the continent, although from time to time in history the Indians made attempts to block his further advance. Nor was it simply the white man's iron and guns that won the day for him. His diseases did more. Whole Indian tribes not used to European illnesses were ravaged by epidemics. Even measles became a killer of multitudes. The weakened remnants were further ravaged by the intruder's 'fire water', since the Indians had not known the use of alcohol before.

Tribal wars, more destructive with the introduction of guns, further reduced the Indians. Yet the chief weakness really lay in Indian society itself. Quite apart from good or evil designs of the Europeans, the weaker, more primitive Indian tribal life simply collapsed and fell apart as it met a more advanced civilization. As long as the Europeans in Canada were chiefly concerned with fur trading, so that the forests were not harmed, Indian life might seem to be unthreatened. But actually its collapse had already begun. Seeking the white men's superior weapons and goods, whether guns, iron traps, or kettles, Indians became dependent upon them. They forgot their old skills, and had to engage among themselves in a grim struggle for these goods, or die. Tribes that had guns, steel knives, and iron traps could drive out those that had not and gain the furs which would bring them more of the all-important trade goods. A bitter fight to survive developed, increasing in extent as the links between white and red men spread westward.

Tribal organization and customs decayed. The tide of settlement spread over their remnants; until in the end some of the old

Indian hunting life was only preserved in the fur-trapping far North, or on the reservations, the tracts of land guaranteed at last to the remaining tribes by white governments. And even here, on eastern reservations, the Indians have largely adopted the same ways as neighbouring white farmers. Thus, for better or worse (for remember that the 'noble red man' had often lived a life of squalor and near-starvation) the Indian world gradually but inevitably collapsed, as Europeans entered the Canadian scene.

3   The Europeans Enter

Why did they come? Why should nations of western Europe suddenly interest themselves, in the sixteenth century, in a New World, and in the Canadian portion of it? Before that time there had been visitors from Europe to the Canadian shores but they had not led to the opening of the continent to white men. Their journeys, instead, had been forgotten, save in a few tales and folk ballads. Only strange legends of mysterious isles beyond the western seas had remained in Europe to suggest that new lands might lie far over the Atlantic.

The first white visitors had been the Norsemen, the great sea-rovers of the tenth and eleventh centuries, who built an empire in the northern oceans extending from Scandinavia to Iceland. From Iceland bold discoverers had reached out to the cold forbidding shores of so-called 'Greenland'. About the year 1000, Lief Ericson, 'the Lucky', was blown south of his course for Greenland and came upon the coast of North America proper, probably touching at some point in Labrador. Further voyaging south brought him to a land of wild grapes, 'Vineland' he called it, that perhaps lay in Nova Scotia. Here the Norsemen even planted a colony, but fighting among its members and with the Indians soon destroyed it.

The Norsemen still continued to visit America, ranging along its eastern coasts. There are claims, indeed, that they penetrated Hudson Bay and reached the interior, claims based on strangely inscribed metal plates found there and the rusted fragments of weapons. But whether they did or not, their discoveries did not result in occupation. As Norse sea power faded, America sank again into the unknown. Medieval Europe was not far enough advanced, had problems enough of its own, and too many frontiers at home to develop, to pay heed to the sailors' tales of Norse wanderers. Behind the Atlantic mists, America lay forgotten.

But towards the year 1500 Europe was changing greatly. Powerful nation-states were emerging. Strong at home, they were ready to look for imperial power abroad. A new wealthy middle class of traders and business men was eagerly seeking to extend the limits of European commerce, to reach out over the oceans to other parts of the world. And the learning and energy of the Renaissance was bringing increased scientific knowledge and enthusiasm to that cause. In particular, efforts were being devoted to finding new routes by sea to the fabulous riches of the East. Portugal and Spain, two rising nation-states that jutted out into the ocean, led in these attempts. The Portuguese were pressing south-east around Africa towards India. Christopher Columbus, in the service of Spain, sought to girdle the globe and reach Asia by sailing west. In so doing he rediscovered the forgotten continents of America.

Columbus, for all his greatness, was only part of a mighty wave of expansion that now swept west as well as east from Europe. As the sixteenth century began, the age of discovery was well under way. Gradually the whole eastern coast of North America was disclosed to white men. Realizing that this was not Asia but a continent in itself, they began to come to America for its own sake, and not because it lay athwart the way to the East. Yet the hope of finding passages through the land mass continued to invite the discoverers, and led to further explorations.

A south-west passage to the East was found, through the Straits of Magellan at the southern tip of the Americas. A north-west passage was not; but the dream of it continued to haunt men and to send them further and further north into ice-filled Arctic waters. Only in 1906, in fact, was the dangerous north-west passage above America finally navigated, and not until 1969 was a serious attempt made to exploit it commercially.

The search for the north-west passage, however, the hopes of unknown riches, the enterprise of business men and seafarers and the dreams of national power, brought men from a newly aggressive Europe to America in the sixteenth century. And so the real history of Canada began. Another motive was the desire to carry Christianity to the pagan Indians who were found in the New World. When, in the course of the sixteenth century, the Reformation split Christian Europe into armed Protestant and Catholic camps, then the religious motive received new force. Men came to America either to gain souls for the Catholic or Protestant faiths, or to escape religious persecution at home. Yet though zeal for religion, riches or power, and sheer curiosity and love of adventure all played their parts, two humbler instruments were also significant in opening up Canada. They were the codfish and the beaver.

4   *The Codfish and the Beaver*

Shortly before the sixteenth century began, on a summer's day in 1497, the ship 'Matthew' of Bristol, under Master John Cabot, made an all-important discovery. It was not Cipangu, or Japan, which Cabot was seeking in sailing west, in imitation of Columbus's voyage of five years earlier. It was not 'the Newfoundland' which he did discover, and for which King Henry VII of England rewarded him with the generous gift of ten pounds. It was a sea so thickly swarming with fish that it seemed almost solid, and baskets let down on ropes from the deck of the ship could be taken up crammed full. Cabot had come upon the great fishing banks off North America, that would bring fishermen from Europe in increasing numbers, and would finally lead them to set up fishing stations on the nearby shores.

Cabot's voyage, and those which he and his son Sebastian made later, had further significance. They showed that England, newly strengthened under the Tudor kings, was also entering on overseas expansion, and that English trading enterprise as well was turning in this direction; for though, like Columbus, Cabot was Italian, he sailed for the merchants of the port of Bristol. These voyages, moreover, uncovered much of the north-eastern coasts of America and provided the basis for English claims in the continent. But it was the fisheries that Cabot found which did most to teach Europeans the American shoreline, and to acquaint them first with the northern part of this New World.

As reports of the new fishing grounds spread, fishermen along the Atlantic coasts of Europe began to make voyages each summer to the coasts and banks of Newfoundland. They came from Brittany and Normandy in France, and from Spain and Portugal as well as England. From 1500 on, the waters around Newfoundland and its harbours gradually became familiar to these unknown seamen of the summer fishing fleets. The fishermen also came close to the mainland shores along the lower reaches of the Gulf of St Lawrence, to fish off Cape Breton Island and Nova Scotia proper.

The large and abundant codfish was the main catch. At first the cod were heavily salted and carried back 'green' to Europe in the holds of the ships. But the practice of drying the fish on shore also came into use. There was less spoilage this way, in the days before refrigeration, and the dried cod needed only a light salting to keep them during the long voyage home. But as the 'dry' fishery began to replace the 'green' fishery it led also to the first occupation of the new land, since drying racks, or 'flakes', had to be built on shore, and huts and storehouses for the men who tended them during the summer.

In this way French and English fishing stations were established around the coasts of Newfoundland during the sixteenth century. The English stations were chiefly concentrated in the eastern Avalon peninusla. The French were scattered along the northern and southern coasts, or even on Cape Breton and the mainland shore. The Spanish and Portuguese had kept to the green fishery and did not need the same kind of shore establishments. Their fisheries, moreover, began to decline in the later sixteenth century as Portugal's interests turned more to the Indian Ocean and Spanish sea-power began to collapse under the attacks of the English Elizabethan sea-dogs.

At English or French fishing stations, Indians might gather to investigate the strange white men and admire their knives and metal goods, their clothes and blankets, for which they had little to offer in exchange except furs or beaver robes. But furs were expensive luxuries in Europe, while the North American forest held a plentiful supply of fur-bearing animals, especially of the beaver. It was soon apparent to the fishermen that they could reap a large profit by trading a few knives or trinkets for pelts to be sold in Europe.

An important side-line in fur trading developed at points along the Atlantic shores among tne fishermen established there for the summer. It was only a matter of time before some men would decide to engage only in the profitable fur trade, to fill their ships wholly with furs, and perhaps to set up permanent posts in America to which Indians could bring a constant supply. From the fish of the sea, the white men had advanced to think of the furs of the land. They were being drawn into the continent.

The milder climate of the more southerly regions of North America had invited settlement almost from the start. Thus before the sixteenth century was out the Spanish had built whole towns in Mexico and central America. But the colder northern half of the continent, with its heavy forests, was not so inviting. Yet in that same northern forest lay one easily available source of wealth —fur. Hence the fur trade first brought white men to occupy Canada and long remained the chief reason behind any colonies established within its bounds.

Furthermore, about the end of the sixteenth century, the felt hat came into widespread use in Europe, and it was discovered that beaver fur made excellent felt for hats. The beaver hat became the fashion, and remained so until the middle of the nineteenth century. The fur trade of the beaver-rich northern forests of America took on new importance. The beaver to-day is rightly a national Canadian symbol, but perhaps the beaver hat would have been quite as symbolic. At any rate, to a great extent Canada was built on the back of the beaver. The fisheries kept their importance, but the fur trade expanded steadily, and spread westward into the interior as the regions close to the coast were exhausted of their supply of furs. As the fur trade moved west, so did the line of European occupation, until finally a vast fur empire stretched across Canada to the Pacific.

It was the French who reared the first fur-trade empire within what is now Canada. The first period of Canadian history is thus that of the French regime. But before turning to the story of New France, it is well to recall the factors that lay behind it: the Indians, the first fur hunters, who showed white men how to live in the Canadian wilds; the age of discovery, which turned the eyes of Europe to this continent; and the codfish and the beaver which first brought Europeans in numbers to Canada and led them to stay and seek to possess the land.

PART II
NEW FRANCE

CHAPTER 3

THE BUILDING OF NEW FRANCE, 1534-1663

1 *A Century of Exploration without Occupation*

No successful colony was founded in Canada until after 1600. During the previous century, however, while the coastal fisheries were thriving and the fur trade beginning, a good deal of exploration and preparatory efforts paved the way for the colonies that were to come. The voyages of Cabot had been followed by further expeditions, Portuguese and French as well as English, to the north-eastern coasts of the American continent. Yet England's interest in discovery only rose to its peak in the latter half of the sixteenth century. Then, during the great reign of Elizabeth, the growth of English sea-enterprise showed itself in Canadian waters in renewed attempts to find the north-west passage: a way to the East that would not be blocked by the Spanish or Portuguese foe.

Frobisher, Davis, and other English seamen penetrated into the sub-Arctic regions, working their way up the perilous seas between Greenland and the Canadian shores, only to be stopped by ice-fields. Early in the next century, Henry Hudson, perhaps the last of the great Elizabethan discoverers, thought that he had finally found the passage to Asia when he turned westward through the gap of Hudson Strait into the broad, land-locked Bay that also bears his name. But he perished in its icy waters in 1611, set adrift in an open boat by a mutinous crew. The English were not to find the north-west passage, though Hudson's discovery had really opened a seaway for them into the heart of North America.

English interest in Newfoundland had meanwhile continued. In 1583 Sir Humphrey Gilbert took formal possession of the eastern part of the island in the name of his queen. A permanent

31

English settlement, however, was not attempted until 1610. Besides, England was increasingly turning its attention south of the limits of Canada, to the coastline of the present United States. Gilbert's half-brother, Sir Walter Raleigh, had tried to place a colony on this coast at Roanoke Island, during Elizabeth's reign; but its inhabitants had mysteriously vanished, leaving only a name carved on a tree.

Soon after 1600 a new English attempt succeeded in founding Jamestown, Virginia, and thenceforward England's colonial enterprise was chiefly directed to the areas from Virginia to New England. Jamestown was established in 1607; the first colony in New England, that of the Pilgrims, in 1620. The Dutch, another rising maritime people, had meanwhile begun a settlement at the mouth of the Hudson River, between New England and Virginia. But both English and Dutch had left the harder, more northerly coasts of Canada alone.

It was the French instead who chiefly concerned themselves with the region of Canada. Their fishermen had early ventured into the Gulf of St Lawrence and to the mainland shores, while the English had remained based in Newfoundland. In the first part of the sixteenth century, moreover, the newly powerful French monarchy under Francis I was dreaming of a New World empire that would match that of its rival, Spain. Accordingly, Francis sent out expeditions to survey the American coast north of the Spanish possessions, to claim land, discover treasure, and perhaps find the true north-west passage. A hard-bitten Breton sailor served King Francis best: Jacques Cartier was his name. He discovered the St Lawrence river, and unlocked the northern half of the continent to France.

Cartier made his first voyage in the King's service in 1534. He sailed into the broad Gulf of St Lawrence and pushed on across it, beyond where fishermen had gone before. He reached the Gaspé peninsula, at the tip of the present province of Quebec, in a hot July of blue skies, wild roses and strawberries, and there erected a thirty-foot cross claiming all the land for France. He had done more as well. He had shown that behind the rocks and fog of the Atlantic coast and the lower Gulf shores lay a smiling country of great trees and grassy meadows. This new land far to the west seemed much more suitable for settlement.

The next year Cartier returned and this time sailed on beyond Gaspé, entering the mouth of the St Lawrence river. While he voyaged upstream in the early autumn of 1535, he might well have thought that here at last was the passage to India, as the river stretched its mighty length into the hazy distance, and days of sailing along a shore crowned with golden ash, reddening maples and wild grapes brought no sign of the channel's end. At length he reached narrows in the river, between a bold promontory and a broad, beautiful island, where he stopped to visit the Iroquois Indian village of Stadacona. This would be the site of Quebec. And Cartier, misunderstanding an Iroquois word, perhaps a reference to the Indian corn fields, thought that the country's name was Canada. 'The river of Canada', he named the broad St Lawrence.

The river channel once more spread before him beyond the Quebec narrows, and he sailed on, until at last, near the Indian village of Hochelaga, rapids barred his ship from proceeding further. Yet Cartier climbed a nearby crest and gazed on into the west at the broad silver stream that wound through the unknown forests. Was it the way to India? Reluctantly he turned back, having named the mountain crest Mount Royal. It would give its name to Canada's chief city, Montreal, which grew up where the rapids in the river halted ocean-going ships, as they had Cartier's vessel.

Autumn was passing, and at Stadacona Cartier halted his expedition to wait for spring, rather than dare the dangerous winter Atlantic crossing. But the smiling land now turned a cold and frowning face to the inexperienced Frenchmen. Many fell sick and died that winter, penned up in their makeshift little encampment. Nevertheless, Cartier returned to France with glowing tales of the wonders of Canada: of the river that might lead to Asia, of the gold and diamonds that might be found, and the mysterious Kingdom of the Saguenay, a land of jewels and spices, perhaps a part of India, that the Indians had described. They had, indeed; but it had been an artistic invention of the Indian story-tellers to please the credulous French.

In any case, the French king was convinced, and this time ordered a large expedition fitted out, in order to found a colony. A court favourite, the Sieur de Roberval, was placed in command, with Cartier as his chief pilot. The expedition was delayed until 1541, however. Cartier and five ships then left for Canada, expecting Roberval to follow. But Roberval delayed further, until the spring of 1542. By this time Cartier, having wintered in the new land again, had set out back to France, discouraged by now from believing that the St Lawrence was the way to India, that the kingdom of the Saguenay existed, or that any gold was to be found in Canada. Roberval's colony merely proved the same things, and the next year, in 1543, after a hard winter at Cap Rouge above Quebec, the colonists returned home. Canada and Cartier had failed them.

Yet, had they known it, in the river itself that Cartier had found, and in the furs that the Indians of the river were so eager to trade for European goods lay real wealth, and the future of France in America. Later French adventurers were to build New France on these foundations. It was only a matter of time, once more, before Cartier's work as a forerunner would lead to the permanent French occupation of Canada.

2   The Day of Champlain

The failure of Roberval's colony and renewed war with Spain discouraged the French monarchy after 1543 from further attempts to build an empire in America. Then came the most bitter kind of war—civil and religious conflict—to distract France for nearly

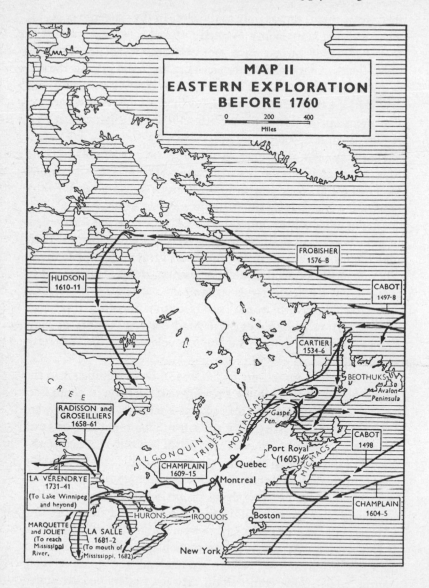

MAP II
EASTERN EXPLORATION
BEFORE 1760

0   200   400
Miles

FROBISHER
1576–8

HUDSON
1610–11

CABOT
1497–8

CARTIER
1534–6

BEOTHUKS
Avalon
Peninsula

C R E E

RADISSON and
GROSEILLIERS
1658–61

Gaspé
Pen.

CABOT
1498

A L G O N Q U I N   TRIBES   MONTAGNAIS   MICMACS

Port Royal
(1605)

LA VÉRENDRYE
1731–41
(To Lake Winnipeg
and beyond)

CHAMPLAIN
1609–15

Quebec

Montreal

CHAMPLAIN
1604–5

MARQUETTE
and JOLIET
(To reach
Mississippi
River,

LA SALLE
1681–2
(To mouth of
Mississippi, 1682)

HURONS   IROQUOIS

Boston

New York

forty years more. It was only at the close of the sixteenth century, when a strong king, Henry IV, had restored order to his country, that the French turned once more towards colonizing Canada. Nevertheless, in the years between 1543 and 1600 private French ships had continued to visit Cartier's river of Canada and had extended the fur trade to the St Lawrence. The feeling was rising that great opportunities for wealth and power might lie in that region, if France would only act.

Henry IV, accordingly, was ready to grant a monopoly of trade in order to establish colonies in America. The practice of colonial monopolies was widely accepted in Europe at the time. Wealthy nobles and merchants, singly or in groups, would seek a royal charter of monopoly granting them sole rights of trade and control in some portion of the new world overseas, in exchange for their undertaking to develop the country and plant a settlement there. The monopoly protected the adventuring group from having to struggle against trade rivals as well as against the wilderness. The crown in return would see its colonial holdings built up. This pattern of monopolies lay behind the early history of New France, as well as that of the English colonies on the American mainland.

The fur trade, moreover, which was to be so significant in the case of New France, lent itself readily to monopoly. Although its profits might be high, the market was uncertain, since furs were a luxury, not a necessity; and though profits might not be sure, costs were inevitably heavy. Trade goods had to be carried across the width of the ocean and the furs transported as far back to the uncertain market. Hence a struggle between competing traders might easily wipe out the shaky profits. It seemed that only a group with a monopoly could afford the burden of transportation and stand the risk of bad markets by avoiding the ruinous drain of competition. At any rate, throughout the history of the fur trade in Canada there was a constant tendency towards monopoly control, while strong competition between traders usually ended in the ruin of some and the merging of the survivors in a single organization.

Though the granting of fur-trade monopolies accompanied revived French interest in Canada at the close of the sixteenth century, the first monopolists failed in their efforts to found colonies. But when at length monopolists succeeded, the credit was not due to the merchants or noblemen in France but to their agent in America: to Samuel de Champlain, the true founder of New France.

Champlain was an ardent Catholic, an able geographer, and a soldier and seaman who had already voyaged to the Spanish possessions in the New World. He made his first voyage to Canada in 1603, when he sailed for the French monopolists of the day to trade for furs in the St Lawrence. Champlain must have been struck by the possibilities of planting a French colony on the river to control the trade. On his return to France he found that the Sieur de Monts, the new monopolist, was planning a colonial venture, and the next year de Monts and Champlain left for America with a royal patent and 120 colonists.

They first tried to found a colony on the more accessible Atlantic shores of Canada rather than in the distant St Lawrence valley. The first site, on the island of St Croix in the Bay of Fundy, proved an unwise choice, the island lacking water and wood. In 1605, after a disastrous winter, the colony was moved across the Bay to the Nova Scotian side, to Port Royal, now Annapolis Royal. Port Royal, set in the fertile Annapolis valley, proved an excellent site, and the first crops planted in Canada by white men were harvested there. Cultivated fields began to spread by Fundy side, and within the log buildings of Port Royal the settlers enlivened winter's evenings with the first social club in Canada, the Order of Good Cheer, dedicated to feasting and enjoyment.

Port Royal grew slowly, however, and there were quarrels over the fur-trade monopoly in this maritime region, now becoming known as Acadia. De Monts, in fact, lost his monopoly in 1607. His settlers returned to France. For a few years Port Royal was deserted. Acadia was empty except for fishing stations. A new grant and new colonists then re-established the settlement, but its troubles were only beginning. Meanwhile de Monts, largely through Champlain's persuasion, had transferred his interest from Acadia to the St Lawrence valley, and had gained a new trade monopoly for this region. Accordingly, Champlain was sent out again by de Monts' company, this time to the St Lawrence. There, in 1608, where the river narrows by the bluffs of Quebec, a natural fortress commanding the river, Champlain built a trading post. Thus the capital of New France, the oldest city in Canada, came into existence.

In the next few years from his post at Quebec, Champlain pushed on up-river in the canoes of friendly Indians until he had explored much of the unknown country that Cartier had viewed from the top of Mount Royal. Champlain's purposes were several: zeal to spread French claims and Catholic Christianity, the hope still that the St Lawrence might lead to the western sea, and a good agent's concern for the fur trade. There promised to be a rich harvest of furs if Champlain could bring the French into contact with western Indians. This motive was never far from mind in the exploring ventures of Champlain and his successors.

Furthermore, the Montagnais, Algonquin Indians who had replaced the Iroquois on the St Lawrence since Cartier's time, urged the French to accompany them in raids against their Iroquois enemies to the south and west. Champlain went with them, since the French had to keep the friendship of the Algonquins of the St Lawrence in order to obtain the necessary supply of furs. In 1609, on Lake Champlain to the south, a few shots from French muskets easily scattered an Iroquois war party, who had never seen guns before. But those shots were to be answered in fire and bloodshed about New France in years to come, for the Iroquois proved a powerful and relentless foe.

The raiding and exploring missions with Indian allies taught Champlain and his few French companions the art of the canoe and the life of the forest. At the same time these journeys disclosed to white men the Richelieu river and Lake Champlain to the south of the St Lawrence and the Ottawa river on the northern side. The Ottawa would become a great fur trade highway to the West. In 1615, Champlain travelled up the Ottawa and west to Lake Huron, where broad horizons of water in the middle of a continent met his astonished gaze. The 'freshwater sea' he called it. The French had reached the Great Lakes.

From Lake Huron Champlain went southward to Lake Ontario through the country of the Hurons, which lay in the centre of what is now southern Ontario. Although of Iroquois stock, the Hurons were also enemies of the Five Nations Iroquois, and Champlain accompanied a Huron war party on a raid south of Lake Ontario that was none too successful. The French, it is true, had made an important alliance, since the Hurons became their chief suppliers of western furs. Yet the quarrel with the Iroquois had gone a stage further. And in the long run it would result in the Hurons themselves being wiped out.

This consequence was still far in the future, and in the meantime Champlain had laid the basis of the French inland fur trade. His 'young men', lieutenants like Brulé and Nicolet, who lived with the Indians, carried on the work of exploring the Great Lakes basin. As men like these ranged freely over the wilderness, there began to emerge the type of French fur-hunter and half-savage forest-dweller to be known as the *coureur de bois*.

At the same time settlers were beginning to arrive at Quebec from France, to make New France something more than a wilderness fur preserve. Louis Hébert, a retired Paris chemist, was the first to come. He arrived with his family in 1617 and began farming outside the stockades of Quebec. Under Champlain's earnest guidance as governor of the settlement, lands were cleared and crops planted. But there were still only sixty-five colonists in New France ten years later, and the following year, 1628, the feeble settlement was threatened with destruction by an English attack.

The English attack by sea, under David Kirke and his two brothers, was largely a private buccaneering venture, although war had broken out between France and England in Europe. The English did not actually sail up the river to Quebec until 1629, but when they did, Champlain, now an elderly man, was forced to surrender his weak little settlement. Yet because of the delay in the attack, the war in Europe was actually over when this first English conquest of Canada occurred. Champlain, who had gone back to France, therefore pressed the French Government to demand the return of Quebec, and in 1632 Canada was restored to French rule.

Champlain returned to his beloved New France as governor, to die there in 1635 as the settlement at last was forging ahead. In his day he had served his country well. Not only had he explored much of the St Lawrence water-system, not only had he planted a permanent colony in Canada, but he had as well founded a great French fur empire in the heart of North America.

3   *For the Glory of God*

Despite the advance of the fur traders into the interior, the settled heart of New France grew very slowly. Champlain had brought out colonists in his last years to spread settlements along the St Lawrence, and had founded Three Rivers upstream from Quebec in 1634. Yet whatever he and his successors as governors of the colony attempted in trying to encourage its growth, the unfortunate fact was that the fur trade tended to discourage settlement. The enterprise which had virtually created New France also held it back.

Settlement was the foe of the forest; but it was on the forest that the fur trade lived. The fur monopolists in France could not help but be lukewarm in carrying out the terms of their royal grant, that committed them to plant colonies in Canada. Bringing out settlers was expensive, moreover, and would cut into fur profits. And in Canada itself, the dream of a quick fortune made in the fur trade, and the free life of the forest, tended to lure men from the stern task of hacking out a pioneer farm. While the fur trade led New France to reach far into the interior, it also diffused its strength and delayed the growth of concentrated settlement.

Despite the best efforts of Champlain in Canada, the monopoly changed hands several times, because of the repeated failure of monopolists in France to fulfil their obligations to colonize. Then in 1627, the great Cardinal Richelieu, chief minister of France, formed a new organization, the Company of New France, made up of a select group of a hundred wealthy associates who were to hold the monopoly and to make France as strong in America as Richelieu sought to make her in Europe. But in 1628 the Kirkes captured the first large convoy of supplies and settlers sent out by the Company on its way to Canada. This nearly ruined the Company of a Hundred Associates at the start. It never really recovered, and hence its obligation to bring out 4,000 settlers in fifteen years was never fulfilled. In 1645, in fact, the nearly bankrupt company handed over its fur trade monopoly to a group in Canada, the Company of the Habitants, for an annual rent. France's attention was now taken up with the Thirty Years' War in Europe, and Canada was left much to itself. The fur trade continued to extend westward, the company granted lands, which usually remained empty, but New France stagnated in neglect.

In this case, when the state and business enterprise had largely failed the colony, it was the Catholic Church that stepped in, that supplied enthusiasm, stimulated some settlement, at least, and left an enduring mark on the character of New France. In old France at this time, the zeal of the Catholic Counter-Reformation was running high. What better task for the Catholic than to win new lands to the faith, especially the pagan wilds of America?

Priests, religious orders and some laymen all shared the grand ideal. Out of it, indeed, the city of Montreal was born.

The island of Montreal, where Cartier's Mount Royal stood, was already becoming an important trading centre, since it was situated at the crossroads of great water routes, the Richelieu from the south and the Ottawa and upper St Lawrence from the west. It was, in fact, the gateway to the west; then and now the key to a continent-wide trade. This same commanding position was an exposed one, open to Indian attack from many angles. It lay on a dangerous frontier, far upstream from Quebec. Yet despite this perilous location, and indeed because of it, a devoted group of Catholic laymen decided to found a mission and hospital for the Indians there—'though every tree should be an Iroquois.' Led by a pious soldier, Maisonneuve, almost a latter-day Crusader in spirit, and a brave woman, Jeanne Mance, Canada's first nurse, a party of fifty-four set out from France. In 1642 they founded Ville-Marie, the ancestor of modern Montreal.

Churchmen, meanwhile, were also active. The warmly Catholic Champlain had early appealed for missionaries to be sent to Christianize Canada, and four Récollet fathers had come out in 1615. Realizing the size of the task, however, the Récollets had sought the aid of the powerful Society of Jesus, that was dedicated to the work of conversion in particular and had already sent missions as far as India and China. Three Jesuits arrived in Canada in 1625. The power and influence of the order in New France rose rapidly in the following years, until, in fact, they almost came to dominate the colony.

Jesuit power did much for Canada. The Jesuits' interest in the country and their influence in France helped keep the colony from complete neglect. They sought to encourage settlement, for they warmly believed in New France. To this end the Jesuit *Relations*, annual reports on their activities in Canada, enthusiastically set forth the merits of life in the new country. Besides being an invaluable and fascinating source of information on early Canadian history, the *Relations* are in a way an interesting example of emigration propaganda. And they did attain wide publicity for New France.

The Jesuits also sought to restrain the evils of trading liquor to the Indians. They tried to teach, guide and protect the native. For the settler's guidance as well, they secured the appointment of the first bishop of New France, François de Montmorency-Laval. The new bishop did a great deal to fill out the structure of the church in order to meet the needs of the ordinary Canadian colonist, until it became part of the very fabric of his daily life. And Laval, the friend of the Jesuits, was as devoted to the Papacy as they were. He established a Catholic Church in Canada directly linked to Rome rather than to France. This has remained an enduring tie in French Canada.

Yet the unbending discipline of the Jesuits and their sweeping views on the extent of their religious powers caused trouble in New France. They clashed with merchants, governors and the other clergy, and many resented their control over ideas and society, or feared that they sought absolute power. But the Jesuits' efforts outside the colony, among the Indians, aroused less questioning, and earned them lasting honour for tireless courage and high devotion to their ideals.

There were others besides Jesuits who established missions and schools for the Indians, among them brave and diligent nuns. Yet the Jesuit missions among the far-off Hurons have rightly captured more attention in history. To begin with, they were important for French imperial power and the fur trade. The mission centres in Huron villages served to cement the French alliance with the chief tribe of the Great Lakes country and strengthened the trading partnership that brought the French on the St Lawrence so many western furs. But beyond this, the labours of the Jesuit fathers, that ended in martyrdom, were a tremendous effort to win a savage, half-comprehending people to Christianity and civilization. They were no less outstanding because they finally failed.

The mission to the Hurons had really begun in 1634 when the Jesuit father Brébeuf and two companions were at last permitted by the suspicious natives to return with them to their country. Conversions were slow, because of the strangeness to the Indians of the white man's teachings, and because of the active hostility of tribal medicine men. A permanent central mission, called Ste Marie, was established in 1639, however, and others were gradually planted in Huron villages and even among neighbouring tribes. Ste Marie was really the first civilized site in the present province of Ontario. Archaelogists to-day can trace here the first canal built in Canada.

The mission to the Hurons was doomed even as it seemed at last to be succeeding. By 1640, the Iroquois torrent was rising to sweep it away. Yet though that torrent raged about New France in the years thereafter, the courageous example of the men who had worked for the glory of God remained to strengthen the colony in its struggle for survival.

4 *The Peril of the Iroquois*

From 1640 on mounting waves of Indian war threatened the very life of New France. The Indian allies of the French were involved first, but before the conflict was over the colony was almost living under siege. Its development was further held back. Murderous raids out of the forest were a constant threat. It took the might of the crown of France, stepping into the neglected colony, before the Indian menace was finally checked after 1660.

Those who had raised the danger were the Five Nation Iroquois, the most powerful Indian confederacy in America. The conflict had been long developing, and it had not been caused merely by Champlain's unwise skirmishing with the Iroquois, nor by their desire for revenge. The whole pattern of the fur trade, and of the relations of red men and white, had been far more significant in bringing on war.

The fact was that the Iroquois had become engaged in the fur trade, too, but they bartered not with the French but with the Dutch who had established posts in the Hudson River valley running north from their main base, New Amsterdam, now New York. Like other Indian tribes in contact with white men, the Iroquois had become dependent on European goods for their very survival—steel knives and traps, and the arms to meet those that their enemies were obtaining from the French. Lack of guns could mean the end of the Five Nations.

When the Iroquois, who lay south of Lake Ontario and the St Lawrence and north of the Hudson valley, had exhausted the furs of their own area in trade, they had to reach out to other regions in order to keep up the vital traffic in European goods. They became 'middlemen', obtaining furs from other tribes to trade to the Dutch, as the Hurons became middlemen for the French, passing on western furs. But here the Iroquois lines of trade clashed with those of the Hurons and French. The latter allies sought to drain the furs of the Great Lakes and the west down the St Lawrence river to Montreal and Quebec. The Iroquois sought to divert this trade to the Hudson river and to the Dutch. It was the St Lawrence versus the Hudson: the struggle of two great trading systems.

Accordingly the Iroquois' old struggles with the Hurons mounted in intensity as it became a war to control the fur supply and to maintain the flow of precious European trade goods. European arms made the fight much more deadly. The Iroquois were well organized and desperate. They determined that the Hurons must go. In 1648 they turned their full force on the Huron enemy, and on the Jesuit missions which they regarded as the centres of Huron-French power. The mission village of St Joseph was razed to the ground. The next year St Ignace and St Louis followed; and heroic Jesuits like Brébeuf and Lalemant were put to death by the Iroquois with all the cruelty of Indian warfare. No longer safe, Ste Marie was left deserted. The proud Huron tribe was shattered into fragments of panic-stricken refugees, some fleeing to the west, some to the protection of French settlements, never again to form a nation. The Iroquois ravaged the neighbouring tribes and then turned on the French, for they now felt strong enough to attack the real foe behind the Hurons.

They set about cutting the St Lawrence trade, till no Algonquin or remaining Huron canoe dared to go down to Montreal. The fur traffic almost came to a stop. Montreal itself was repeatedly menaced and raids even came near Quebec. Although the larger settlements were generally safe from direct attack the outlying colonists worked with guns at hand, and the business life of New France was at a standstill. Despite breathing spells during the 1650's the colony's future was gloomy in the extreme.

The turning point was slow in coming. A large-scale assault on Montreal in 1660 was only prevented by the gallant fight-to-the-last of Adam Dollard and sixteen comrades at Long Sault, some miles west of Montreal. The damage they wrought discouraged the Iroquois from attacking the well-defended town. Yet the danger of raids and the trade blockade continued, until aid at last came from France, and the feeble control of Canada by a company was replaced by direct royal government in 1663. By 1663, therefore, New France stood at the end of an age, although at a critical point in its history. In its first period it had been mapped out and its foundations painfully but successfully laid. Now the colony was not only to survive the Iroquois peril but to begin its greatest period of growth and expansion.

CHAPTER 4

ROYAL GOVERNMENT AND EXPANSION,
1663–1702

1 *The French Crown takes Command*

By 1660 the French colony on the St Lawrence was in desperate straits. The thin trickle of settlement under company rule had brought its population only to about 2,000. It was too weak to end the Iroquois peril by itself, and until that was done the colony could not prosper. The settlement was even dependent on France for much of its food supply, so slowly had farming developed in face of the fur trade. To add to all this, the governors appointed for the company quarrelled with the bishop and clergy, the clergy among themselves, and the merchants, fur traders, and farmers with the authorities generally. Help had to come from the homeland to end the sad confusion, and, indeed, to save New France.

It was fortunate for French Canada that no foreign enemy as well threatened it at this point. Dutch power was declining. In fact, in 1664, the English were to end it in North America by capturing the Dutch citadel of New Amsterdam, which they renamed New York. England itself had long been busy with the struggles of king and parliament at home, and for some years after 1660 the newly restored king, Charles II, was on friendly terms with France. As for the old French rival, Spain, the Thirty Years' War had resulted in exhaustion and defeat for the Spanish, and had left France the strongest nation in Europe.

Hence at this critical moment in Canada's history the French motherland stood at a peak of strength, under an all-powerful crown. In 1661, Louis XIV, the Sun King, came of age and took over absolute rule of a rich and orderly France from his earlier advisers. Louis had grand designs for his country, both in Europe and beyond. France should be the centre of a mighty empire, reflecting glory on its royal master, who should reign over all with a sway wise and fatherly—but always absolute.

Pleas for help from New France were now to receive a ready hearing, though the French crown would equally insist on complete control over the colony. Men, money, and supplies began to flow as the crown set out to protect and develop Canada. It was not Louis alone, however, who turned to save New France by the use of royal paternalism. The king's chief instrument was his great minister Colbert, an architect of French empire.

As minister of finance, Colbert sought to apply the prevailing doctrines of mercantilism to increase the wealth and power of France. Mercantilism taught that, to achieve these ends, a country should sell more abroad than it bought, should build up its shipping and develop its own sources of necessary raw materials. Colonies would supply raw materials and cut down dependence on foreign sources. They would increase external trade, and this would encourage shipping. A self-sufficient empire could be constructed, closed to foreign competitors, enriching the homeland in peace and securing her in war. Under Colbert the French began to create such an empire in seas both east and west. In particular, New France received attention as an important part of the imperial scheme.

First of all the unsuccessful company rule over Canada was brought to a close. The Company of New France, a complete failure, itself surrendered its charter in 1663. The royal government that replaced it in authority was to remain the same in general outlines until New France fell to the British in 1760. All officials were now directly appointed by the Crown, and the king's court at Versailles kept a tight hand over them. Three main officers carried on the royal government in New France: the governor, the bishop, and the intendant. Together with a few lesser councillors, these three composed the Sovereign or Superior Council, the official ruling body of the colony.

The governor, the nominal head of government, was responsible chiefly for the military affairs and the external relations of the colony. He was most powerful in time of war, and could exercise much control over the fur trade. The bishop, thanks to the prestige and influence of the Church in the colony, had been an important authority even under company rule, and now, as a member of the Sovereign Council, he could wield power in far more than church affairs. The intendant was a new official in Canada. He was modelled on the intendants of old France, the agents of the central government in each province. In New France the intendant looked after justice, finance and economic development, and the general routine duties of administration.

This new form of government was stronger than the old, and centralized power in the three chief members of the Superior Council. Yet it also made for friction between the three and quarrels over the extent of their authority. Sometimes an able governor or intendant might win the upper hand, while the strong-minded Laval, bishop until his retirement in 1684, in particular made his office a force to be reckoned with. Quarrels might arise between governor and bishop over the use of brandy in the fur trade with the Indians; governor and intendant might countermand each other's orders. The whole machinery of government might seem to be working at cross purposes. Furthermore, the all-embracing supervision from Versailles could bring delays, interference and contradictions to add to the problems of governing New France. Nevertheless, in its early years at least, the new system worked fairly well, and the colony began to advance at last, thanks to able leaders and ample royal support.

The Indian menace was now dealt with. Over a thousand regular French troops were sent to Canada in 1665, battle-hardened soldiers of the Carignan-Salières regiment. Accompanied by colonial militia this force—a large one for America in those days —invaded the Iroquois country the next year and ravaged the lands of the Mohawks, the most dangerous of the Five Nations. In 1667 the severely shaken Mohawks made peace. The power of the Iroquois was not yet broken and there was no general peace for some years, but the Indian threat to New France had been blunted, and the colony could proceed to develop itself with a fair degree of security.

2 The Work of Talon

The fur trade revived and New France began to prosper. But it needed more than the fur trade to make it strong and more self-reliant. It needed to establish other lines of enterprise, to increase farming. Above all it needed settlers. And now there came the man to meet these demands: Jean Talon, the great intendant, the brilliant servant of Colbert's imperial designs.

In the ordinary course of affairs, the intendant was the most important official in New France. He was the business manager for the colony while the governor was the imposing figurehead. The intendant was the main link between Canada and the central officialdom in France. Thus a talented man in this position could exercise a great deal of power. Talon was such a man. He had been trained in the royal administration in France, and, like his master Colbert at home, worked in the colony for the wealth and power of the imperial French monarchy. He spent less than seven years in Canada, between 1665 and 1672. But in those years Talon's vision, energy, and determination virtually transformed New France from a feeble little settlement struggling for survival to a flourishing, expanding colony that might be conquered in future but could never be destroyed. To a large degree the vigour and permanence of French Canada to-day is the mark of the success of Talon.

His first task was settlement. The crown had undertaken to send out groups of colonists each year, but Talon sought in every way to increase the flow. He managed to have the Carignan-Salières regiment kept in Canada and settled along the Richelieu river, both as a defensive barrier against the Iroquois and to increase the farming population. Free passage and cheap land were

CARTIER AT PERCE ROCK, GASPE, 1534

CHAMPLAIN AND ALLIES ATTACK AN IROQUOIS VILLAGE, 1615

offered to other immigrants, who came largely from Normandy. To supply colonists, especially the soldiers, with wives, Talon suggested that suitable girls be found in the country villages of Normandy. Parties of young women, the 'filles du roi', properly recommended and chaperoned, soon began to arrive at Quebec, where they were eagerly sought in marriage by the waiting bachelors.

Furthermore, laws were put into effect rewarding early marriages and fining those who hung back. Large families also received annual grants—the ancestor of the present system in Canada of government family allowances. And it might be noted that the tradition of early marriage and families of ten or more children established in Talon's day still remains in French Canada. The result of these various measures could be seen in the rising population, which had reached well over 6,000 by the time of Talon's departure. Meanwhile settlement was spreading out, especially on the south bank of the St Lawrence. Assuredly New France had at last begun to thrive as an agricultural settlement.

Talon tried to do more than build a farming colony, however. He and Colbert wanted to develop other resources in Canada, to give the colony something else to trade with Europe besides furs, to make it less dependent on French manufactured goods, and to fit it into the schemes of mercantilist empire. He sought to open mines, to start an iron industry, to encourage lumbering and shipbuilding. His efforts in these directions were none too successful, because the colony lacked the necessary money and labour supply for industry. Still, local tanning and weaving helped to reduce the dependence on France for clothing; shipbuilding and iron founding did finally develop in the next century; and lumbering gradually grew up along the edges of settlement. Talon's work here was useful. Yet Canada remained tied to the fur trade as its main or staple export. Sending furs to France paid for the goods New France had to have. Though now it could feed itself more fully, a flourishing fur trade still meant the difference between prosperity or deep depression for the colony.

Accordingly, the newly invigorated colony soon found itself engaged on a further expansion of the fur trade, now that the Iroquois menace had been removed—or at least held in check by the military power of the royal government. In this expansion, which carried the bounds of New France far to the west and south, another great name emerges: that of the Comte de Frontenac, governor of the colony from 1672 to 1682 and from 1689 to 1698. If Talon had consolidated New France in time of peace, Frontenac carried it far forward, and defended it successfully in time of war.

3 *Expansion, Conflict and the Rule of Frontenac*

The spreading of French empire in America in the later seventeenth and early eighteenth centuries was chiefly due to the demands of the fur trade. The French fur kingdom did not only grow because the Iroquois no longer barred the way. It had to advance. The fur supply of the St Lawrence valley and lower Great Lakes was becoming exhausted. In its usual way, the fur trade had to march west. Besides, the Iroquois wars had destroyed the Hurons, who had been the chief suppliers of the French. To maintain the flow of pelts the French had to seek contacts themselves with tribes further west. These western Indians, moreover, were eager to trade for white man's goods. They almost drew the fur trade onward.

The consequence was renewed French exploration and claims, followed by the establishment of forts and trading posts deep in the interior. In this way French America by 1700 had come to stretch south to the Gulf of Mexico, north to James Bay and west beyond Lake Superior to the Lake of the Woods. Thanks to the pressing demands of the fur trade, so vital to New France, and the easy access to the interior supplied by the St Lawrence water system, the French had occupied the heart of North America while the English still held only the Atlantic coast.

To the south-west, much of the French expansion came with finding the way from the St Lawrence system to the vast Mississippi basin. In 1673, Joliet and Marquette—a fur trader and a Jesuit, typical of the men who built New France—crossed from Green Bay on Lake Michigan to the upper Mississippi and journeyed down the 'father of waters' as far as the Arkansas river. In 1682 the Sieur de la Salle went on further, to reach the mouth of the Mississippi.

There he was murdered in 1687, while trying to establish a French colony; but one was successfully founded in 1699 by Pierre le Moyne, Sieur d'Iberville. Aristocrat, fur trader and explorer, the first to build a ship that sailed the upper Great Lakes, La Salle was one of the great French imperial figures. His efforts helped to give France an arc of empire stretching across America between the mouths of the two greatest water routes into the continent. D'Iberville was another towering figure of the French expansion, who worked for French empire not only in the far south-west but in regions as distant from there as Hudson Bay and Newfoundland.

To the north-west, the French made Sault Ste Marie, Michilimackinac, and Green Bay their chief posts. At the first-named they had claimed the interior of the continent with great display of ceremony in 1671. From the Sault on the upper Great Lakes, the route to Montreal and Quebec ran by way of the Ottawa. West from the Sault, Green Bay opened the road to the Mississippi. North from the Sault across Lake Superior lay more excellent fur country, for the northern forests of the Shield and its colder climate produced the finest furs. Du Lhut penetrated here in 1684, and five years later the French went on westwards to the Lake of the Woods. But meanwhile two adventurers, Radisson and Groseilliers, had crossed north to salt water at James Bay. They were to spell much trouble for New France.

Radisson and Groseilliers had first struck into the rich fur lands near James Bay and Hudson Bay in the troubled 1650's, during the period of company rule. In 1661 they had been refused a licence to trade unless they would share half their profits with the greedy governor of the day. On their return to the colony, the two adventurers had been severely fined and charged with heavy dues to the Company of New France. They carried their case to France, but failing redress there, turned angrily to England. Here their tales of the wealth to be had in the northern regions aroused interest at the Court of Charles II. An expedition sent by sea to the Bay in 1669 proved most rewarding. In 1670 an English company was chartered under the governorship of Prince Rupert, with a monopoly of the Hudson Bay trade. It gradually set up a number of trading posts on the shores of Hudson and James Bays. Thus the work of Henry Hudson and Radisson and Groseilliers had combined. The Hudson's Bay Company was on the great Bay, claiming all the land that drained into it, using Hudson's northern gateway to the continent, and competing with France for the western fur trade.

Competition further stimulated French expansion. There was an increasing need to press west and reach the Indians first, before the English rivals did, for the natives preferred the cheaper English trade goods. On the south, the English had replaced the Dutch fur traders in the Hudson valley and the Iroquois had become their middlemen, trading to the west. French expansion into the Mississippi valley was in part an effort to get behind this English line of trade. Now the English were cutting into the French western fur empire from the north as well, seeking to drain it into Hudson Bay. The French had to keep the Indians from the English posts. They founded a French Hudson Bay Company to carry on the contest.

Expansion thus led to conflict. The Iroquois, moreover, now tied to the English, were again deciding to war on tribes that traded with the French. The French in their turn wanted to force the English from the Bay on the north and to drive in their frontiers to the south. The English were dreaming of capturing Quebec again, the foundation of the whole St Lawrence western French empire, without which the entire structure would surely collapse. As spheres of the expanding fur trade clashed, war drew close. And at this time New France gained a new leader in its governor, Frontenac, for the approaching hour of danger.

The Comte de Frontenac had arrived in New France in the year of Talon's departure. He shared Talon's hopes for empire, carried on his plans for explorations, and certainly became the new strong man in the government. But he was a courtier and soldier, not a statesman. He quarrelled mightily with the other officers of state, his projects were often rash, and he probably showed too much concern for the growth of the fur trade, defending the use of brandy, and extending the colony too fast for its own good. At the same time he backed the efforts of La Salle and other explorers, and even in his private hopes for trade returns helped win and guard the French empire.

To guard that empire—indeed, to protect the fur trade and overawe the Iroquois—Frontenac built a fort at the point where Lake Ontario runs into the St. Lawrence. At Fort Frontenac, now Kingston, he held solemn council with the Iroquois in 1673, with ceremonial firing of guns and splendid pageantry. With a fine taste for the dramatic, he sought to impress the Iroquois at their own game of ceremony and oratory. But this success of the 'Great Onontio', as they called him, only delayed their outburst. Iroquois discontent over the French trade with western Indians led to an effort to destroy these tribes as the Hurons had been destroyed. In 1680, as Frontenac's term of office was closing, the Iroquois attacked Indian allies of New France.

Frontenac's successors were unable to check the Iroquois. In fact, in 1689, the Iroquois boldly attacked the village of Lachine, near Montreal, and massacred its inhabitants. Then the Indian war became merged with a European struggle. England and France had finally come to blows in Europe in the War of the League of Augsburg. It had its echoes in America; or rather, it provided the occasion for all the simmering trouble between the

French and English possessions on the continent to boil into open war. Frontenac was at once recalled to meet the emergency.

He planned a daring stroke to capture New York by means of an invasion from Canada down the Hudson valley coupled with a French naval attack. But lack of sufficient French naval power reduced the plan merely to a series of raids on English frontier settlements. They were carried out with the savagery of Indian war, though often the French could not restrain their Indian allies. Meanwhile the English settlements sought to reply, and in their turn the colonists tried to take Quebec by land and sea. In 1690 the land force made a raid near Montreal, and the sea force sailed up to Quebec. But Frontenac's bold front and the cannon fire from ramparts high on Cape Diamond turned them away disheartened. New France had been saved from the English. Now Frontenac turned to the Iroquois. Carrying the war into their own country he struck them hard and repeatedly. The grim old campaigner died in 1698 at Quebec, before the fighting was over. Nevertheless he had lived to see the Iroquois seriously weakened. Peace between England and France in 1697 had left them fighting a lone battle, and in 1701 they came to terms, never again to be a threat to New France in themselves alone.

In Hudson Bay, meanwhile, the French led by d'Iberville had taken most of the English posts. The Hudson's Bay Company barely kept a foothold. Moreover, the French had also laid waste English settlements in Newfoundland. By the close of the seventeenth century, therefore, it seemed that France had saved its enlarged American empire during the struggle, and could even look forward to further imperial growth. To a considerable extent Frontenac had left his mark on these years of expansion and conflict, as Talon had on the previous work of consolidating New France. Only in the region of Acadia had there been real defeat. But Acadia had always been a backward colony.

4 *Acadia: a Backward Colony*

While the main French possession in America centred on the St Lawrence had faced a difficult career of ups and downs during the seventeenth century, the settlements in Acadia, the Atlantic maritime region, had had a much more stormy time. From the day in 1605 when Port Royal was founded, Acadia had changed hands several times, from French to English and back again, and there had been quarrels quite as bitter between rival French leaders. Nevertheless the colony had managed to remain in being, though it had grown very slowly.

From the start Acadia had been neglected. It lay between the main French area of interest on the St Lawrence and the English on the coast to the south. France showed it little concern. Yet Acadia was also in an exposed position between the chief French and English holdings. Because of this, and its own weakness, it was readily captured by the English in the event of a war, or sometimes even without one. Thus it was that in 1613, in time of peace, an expedition by sea from the new English colony in Virginia took the settlement at Port Royal, on the grounds that the English claim in America extended that far up the coast.

The French were removed and Acadia was left empty, except for a few fishermen and fur traders. In 1621 Sir William Alexander, a Scotsman, secured a grant to all the lands of Acadia—the present three Maritime provinces—under the name of Nova Scotia. Little remains from this except the name and Nova Scotia's own flag, which is still flown. A new colony at Port Royal, begun in 1628, was ended when the treaty of 1632 gave Acadia as well as Quebec back to France. The following years looked bright at last, as two hundred colonists from France reestablished Port Royal. But this was still a private settlement, not a royal colony, and a quarrel soon broke out between two rival claimants to Acadia that turned to virtual civil war around the Bay of Fundy.

The struggles of the rivals, La Tour and D'Aulnay, finally

ended with the latter's death in 1650. La Tour secured the governorship of Acadia. Now, however, the English stepped in again, still without a declaration of war. This time New England forces captured Port Royal, and from 1654 to 1667 Acadia was in English hands. Returned once more to France, Acadia had reason to hope that royal government would at last bring it aid, as it had New France.

Talon, indeed, did want to develop the Acadian outpost and to tie it into an imperial trade with Quebec and the French West Indies. Yet the French crown would do no more than send out a few settlers. Acadia was again left on its own. Accordingly, in 1690, during the War of the League of Augsburg, Port Royal fell once more an easy prey to attack from New England—only to be given back to France in the peace of 1697. It seemed that France did not care enough to defend Acadia, nor England to keep it when conquered. Yet it is also true that both countries, feeling other areas in America were more vital, were devoting their energy and attention to these, and not to the Acadian lands beside the Atlantic.

Nevertheless, Acadia in the later seventeenth century managed to develop on its own. The rate of growth was slow, but considering the conquests and lack of help, that was hardly surprising. By 1698 there were over a thousand colonists, chiefly farmers, spread along the fertile tidal flats and marshlands at the head of the Bay of Fundy and in the Annapolis valley. The soil was good and farming easy. Thus there emerged a quiet but sturdy people, the Acadians, living a simple country life, despite the momentary upheavals of war. Content in their isolation, philosophic about other people's quarrels, they did not reckon on the great conflict of empires that would one day dislodge them from their 'backward' state.

CHAPTER 5

THE LIFE OF NEW FRANCE, 1663–1760

1 *The Structure of Society*

In the time of New France, and particularly after 1663 when the colony began to thrive, a distinctive way of life was worked out in Canada. It still leaves its mark on French Canada to-day. A glance at the society of New France not only reveals the world of the seventeenth-century colonists but throws light on the life and outlook of the modern French Canadians, who form nearly one-third of the present Canadian population.

To begin with, life in New France was fashioned on authoritarian lines: that is, power was concentrated at the top of society, and the mass of the colonists were used to obeying authority, not to governing their own lives. This did not necessarily mean an attitude of dependence or meek docility. The people of New France showed their sturdy self-reliance in other ways. Yet in matters of religion, government, and relations between classes of people, French Canada readily accepted direction from above. There was little of the demand for religious independence and self-government, or the levelling of social distinctions which generally marked the English colonies to the south. In these unruly provinces the trend was toward democracy and the emphasis was on liberty. New France instead put its faith in ordered authority, not disorderly freedom, and stressed duties, not rights.

The forms of government helped shape this attitude in New France. All power depended finally on the King. He and his ministers at Versailles supervised even the minor details of government in the colony, and little could be done without their direction. Their control might have been well-intentioned, kindly, or even wise; but it was absolute. This was paternal absolutism at its best and worst. It developed in New France the habit of looking beyond herself for guidance and leadership. Similarly, the government within New France was absolute and paternal as far as the inhabitants were concerned. Except for the popularly chosen captains of militia in each parish, there were no agencies of local self-government, nor elected bodies voicing public opinion. A few attempts to include elected representatives in the councils of government were soon cut short. New France never learned to manage its own affairs—or even to ask to do so.

The society of French Canada was also hierarchical in structure: it was graded into distinctly separate upper and lower layers. The bulk of the colonists, or habitants, were farmers and formed the broad lower order. On the upper levels were the government officials, the large landholders, or seigneurs, and the principal clergy. In between the two main groups the wealthy fur-trade merchants and the ordinary fur traders did, in a sense, represent a commercial or middle class. In reality, however, New France had virtually no middle class. The big fur merchants tended to be closely linked with the government officials; and since there was little commerce in the colony apart from the fur trade, and no industry to speak of, there were very few tradesmen and only a handful of artisans. They did not form an effective middle class.

As for the ordinary fur trader, he hardly belonged to the colony at all. His world lay far beyond in the forest. He visited the settled areas only occasionally to obtain his earnings, spent his money on a wild spree, and disappeared again into the woods. The life of the independent fur trader, the *coureur de bois*, seemed glamorous and free (actually it might be bitterly hard) and it attracted many reckless spirits away from the farmlands. But, far from the fur trader forming a real part of the society of the colony, he almost represented a minus quantity, a subtraction from it.

Accordingly, with hardly any middle class between upper and lower orders in French Canada, the division in society was clearcut, indeed. Furthermore, the system of land-holding established definite social distinctions. Land was held according to the seigneurial system. It was granted in large blocks to the seigneurs, who rented it in smaller holdings to the habitant farmers. The habitants paid their seigneur various forms of rent and performed certain services for him. The result was to create two groups on the land: the seigneurs, who were landlords with special privileges and authority, and the habitants, tenant farmers, who owed not only rent and services but honour and respect as well. In the English colonies, on the other hand, while there might be large and small farmers, and sometimes landlords and tenants, there were not the same class divisions fixed by law, and most farmers owned their own land.

The seigneurial system, therefore, was a major factor in making the society of New France authoritarian and hierarchical in character. It entered widely into the life of the colony, and so deserves more investigation.

2 *The Seigneurial System*

The seigneurial system in New France represented the importation of feudalism into America. Feudalism was dead in England by the seventeenth century, but particularly on the lower, or seigneurial, level it was very much alive in France; and survived, indeed, until the French Revolution. It was natural that the French should bring their prevailing mode of holding land with them to Canada. Besides, feudalism had been a system concerned with government and defence as well as land, and it seemed well suited to meet the problems of building a colony in the North American wilderness.

According to the workings of feudalism, the lord owed duties of government and military leadership to his tenants, and they owed obedience and armed support to him. Hence the seigneurs in Canada might serve as a military order, their holdings, or seig-neuries, as units of local government or defence. Furthermore, the seigneurial system provided a means of settling the land. Large tracts were granted to seigneurs on condition that they brought out settlers, who would be their tenants, to clear and develop these grants. Thus block by block, in orderly fashion, New France would be built up by the seigneurial system. Unfortunately it did not work out as planned.

Seigneuries were early granted under company rule, but not many of them were taken up. Court favourites and land speculators acquired large amounts of land and either failed to bring out settlers or did not try, preferring to hold their large pieces of wilderness for sale to others more honest, or more foolish, in their purposes. Seigneuries granted to religious orders tended more usually to be taken up, populated, and developed; yet in general the seigneurial system failed as a means of bringing about private colonization.

The system was maintained under royal government, but the seigneuries only really developed while the crown itself was bringing out colonists after 1663. Then, indeed, the seigneurs' agents would meet the ships arriving at Quebec to compete with each other to secure settlers. While the tide of immigration was running to populate New France, so, too, many seigneuries were populated. But when the crown turned away much of its interest towards the end of the seventeenth century, because of wars in Europe, the immigrant stream again slowed to a trickle. It remained only a trickle during the eighteenth century until the fall of New France, which in the meantime grew chiefly through its own high birthrate. The seigneurs again failed to bring many new immigrants, although the seigneurial system remained in being, and lasted, in fact, until the middle of the nineteenth century.

The seigneuries did serve, however, as units of local government and community life; and their role in defence was shown by the establishment of military seigneuries along the Richelieu, as a barrier to the Iroquois, where the tenants, who were ex-soldiers, still owed military service. Much of the life of French Canada was that of the seigneury. It was the habitant's little world.

Nor were the conditions of seigneurialism really burdensome

to him. The system was far less oppressive in Canada than in France. With the wilds close at hand, promising freedom and fortune in the fur trade, and with the need always to gain farmers, it would not have been possible to place heavy obligations on the habitants. They owed *corvées*, the obligation to work a few days a year on the land the seigneur kept for his own farm; they had to pay rent in the form of *cens et rentes*, the former a small annual payment in money, the latter often paid in produce; and when land was sold or passed on by other than direct inheritance sums called *lods et ventes* were due. But all these obligations were slight; and as for the *banalité*, the requirement to use the lord's mill for grinding grain, often the expense of building the mill far outweighed the tolls that were charged.

Furthermore, relations between habitant and seigneur were far closer and more friendly than in Old France. After all, both were working together against a wilderness. Though larger, the seigneur's house might not be more comfortable than the habitant's; it was no ancient castle or luxurious palace. The seigneur himself was not usually of an old noble family. He might often have sprung from the trading classes. The habitant was better off, the seigneur not as well off as their counterparts in France. Moreover, the conditions of pioneer life in America produced some of the open, independent atmosphere that was found on the frontiers in the English colonies. The habitant was no downtrodden peasant but a self-sufficient, self-respecting farmer. In his prosperity, he was not even a great distance from the seigneur in wealth.

Nevertheless, if relations were good and no heavy burden of dues came between habitant and seigneur, there was still a broad distance of dignity and privilege to separate them. The seigneur was shown much respect. His word carried weight throughout the countryside. And seigneurialism embraced the countryside in what was, above all, a farming community. Hence that system played so large a part in shaping the outlook of the French colonists. But quite as important was the part played by the Church.

3 The Role of the Church

One of the most significant features of New France was that it was solidly Catholic. It was orthodox: there were no heretics or questioners of the Catholic faith in the colony. Once, indeed, there had been Protestants in French Canada. The Huguenots, a Protestant minority in Catholic France, had been specially strong in western French seaports, and from there had entered actively into the fur trade of the St Lawrence during the later sixteenth and early seventeenth centuries. But the earnestly Catholic Champlain had urged that the new land be kept free from heresy, and the king's minister, Cardinal Richelieu, had listened. He wanted no such difficulties with Huguenots in New France as the crown was facing in Old France. He ordered that the colony should admit Catholics only; and henceforth New France was a Catholic preserve, its people faithful to that Church.

Furthermore, while New France was being built in the seventeenth century, a high tide of religious enthusiasm was running in the Catholic Church. Devoted priests, nuns and missionaries came to Canada and entered into the task of shaping New France. They left their mark on the colony. Its Catholicism was more devout and the power of the Church greater than in Old France. Thanks both to the energy and determination of the religious leaders, and to their early hold in New France, the Church came to occupy a place of great authority in the colony. Much of that authority was unquestioned.

The Church's religious teachings, indeed, were unquestioned in this Catholic domain. But its hold extended beyond religion to matters of government, to education, and to the land. With regard to government, the zeal and organization of the Jesuits had given them almost the power to rule the colony in the days of weak company control. Laval, the Jesuit's ally, bishop in New France from 1659 to 1688, maintained the dominant place of the Church even when strong royal government was introduced. Far from letting the Church fall under the power of the state, he insisted on a large share in shaping policies of government. Overcoming Gallican opposition, he built a strongly ultramontane Church in New France.

An ultramontane Catholic Church was one that stressed absolute obedience to the Pope at Rome, denying the power of any national state to control or limit the Church. In France, however, the state had acquired considerable power over the clergy, and a kind of national Catholic Church had emerged. Supporters of such a Church, that was limited by the power of the state—and certainly did not direct policies of government—were known as Gallicans in France.

But thanks largely to the Jesuits and Laval, Gallicanism did not become established in Canada. The Church there turned its eyes only to Rome, and maintained considerable influence over policies of government. French Canada became and remained an ultramontane citadel. After Laval, quarrels continued in the government of the colony as the claims of church and state to control clashed repeatedly. By the eighteenth century a compromise was gradually reached. In fact, the Church ceased to press for as much influence in state affairs. Nevertheless, although in the latter days of New France the state was in the ascendant, the Church was still in a strong position. Not only was its religious hold unchallenged, but its share in government remained, because the bishop continued to be one of the three chief officials in the Superior Council that ruled the colony.

The Church also exercised power over men's minds through controlling teaching and the institutions of learning. The close connection between religion and education was, of course, a deep-rooted Catholic idea, and it was not surprising that the Church, not the state, should found and direct schools in New France. Because of the wholly orthodox Catholic atmosphere in the colony, however, there was no development of learning apart from the Church, as in Old France. There was no secular education, no attempt to inquire into and certainly no attempt to criticize the authority of Church teachings. The Church, moreover, carefully censored thought and reading for laymen, and no newspapers or other organs of public opinion developed. Once more this air of quiet and obedience to authority was very different from the free and lively mental climate of the English colonies to the south. The ordinary Canadian habitant was cheerfully uninformed, though simple, straightforward, and contented.

Yet the ignorance among the masses was no worse than in many other countries of the age. And certainly the Church laboured hard to reduce it. Religious orders sought to establish schools as well as missions and hospitals, and several famous schools were founded that still endure. The names of Mother Marie de l'Incarnation and Marguerite Bourgeouys, two great nuns who worked to educate young girls, will never be forgotten in Quebec. The teaching provided, however, was largely religious or classical, and the lore of Greece and Rome did not filter down to the ordinary habitants. Still, this was the usual form of education in the seventeenth and eighteenth centuries, and there was no belief in that time in general popular education.

Hence ignorance in New France did not follow from the Church's control of education. The nature of that education, however, theoretical and classical rather than practical or scientific, remained firmly fixed in French Canada, to affect the thinking and outlook of its people for centuries thereafter.

One of the chief teaching institutions founded by the Church was the Seminary at Quebec, which has come down to the present in Laval University. Laval himself began it in 1663, to train Canadians for the priesthood. The religious orders had their teachers or their missionaries to the Indians, but there was a need for ordinary parish priests among the colonists. A native Canadian parish clergy was thus built up. They came to have great influence among the habitants. A seigneury would constitute a parish of the Church as well, though as population increased it might be divided into several parishes. In each parish the priest or curé became the representative of the great and powerful Church and, at the same time, the beloved leader of his flock: a man of Canadian background who knew their problems—their friend, adviser and protector. As a result, the ties between the people and their Church were knit even tighter.

The parish priests, consequently, extended the Church's hold over the land. But it grew in other ways as well. As was mentioned, seigneuries were often granted to religious orders, and generally these clerics made the best landlords, developing their holdings and watching carefully over their tenants. As more land grants were made, the clergy came finally to be landlord for about half the population, which again added greatly to the power of the Church in New France. This meant wealth, besides, for a large share of the total seigneurial dues would go to the clergy. Furthermore, in order to support the parish priests, tithes were established throughout the colony by royal order in 1663. A fraction of the habitant's income from his crops henceforth belonged to the Church in each parish. Yet for all the colonists' Catholicism, protests were made at the amount of the tithe, and it was finally reduced to one-twenty-sixth of the value of the grain crop. With this tithe, seigneurial dues as well on much of the land, and royal subsidies also, the Church was made financially secure.

It should be abundantly plain how large a part the Church played in New France. Besides reigning over the religion of a staunchly Catholic colony, it had power over government, education, and the life of the countryside. Like the seigneurial system it helped shape the society of New France, and it was thoroughly authoritarian and hierarchical in character. The Church entered deeply into the ordinary life of the people. But it remains to see just what ordinary life was like.

4 The Life of the People

How did the inhabitants of New France live? They knew three kinds of life: that of the forests, that of the town, and that of the countryside. The life of the forests was the fur trader's, and he lived mainly as the Indians had done, beyond the settlements, outside white civilization. He travelled by canoe and snowshoe, wore deerskin and moccasins, slept in bark shelters or bough-covered lean-tos. Often he lived with the Indians, and raised a half-breed family. His life was almost a savage one, and but for, say, a European shirt or hat and an inexhaustible and un-Indian cheeriness, he might have been taken for a native.

As fur-trading posts grew up in the interior, with log houses and tilled fields around them to supply the post, the fur trader might see a few traces of European civilization in his world. But generally, except for his yearly trip to Montreal for a grand orgy, he spent a lonely life trapping in the dark forest or paddling mile on mile down empty sunlit rivers. But as he journeyed, the folk songs of his childhood kept him company, and he freely added to them. The songs of the French fur traders have come down across the years, telling of the warm good humour, dauntless will and simple faith of the men of the forests.

These were the men who spread the bounds of New France, explored the unknown, and gathered the wealth of furs so vital to the very existence of the colony. They were the roamers of the woods, the *coureurs de bois*, often unlicensed traders, frowned on by the state for trading illegally, and by the Church for their pagan wildness and brandy-drinking. In many ways they were a drain on New France, a waste of settlers and a source of vice and immorality. And yet they were necessary. On their energy, daring and knowledge of the Indians depended the success of the far-flung fur trade in the growing competition with the English. The authorities might not like them—this one group of Canadians who defied authority—but the fate of New France was in their hands.

In total contrast to the life of the vast wilderness was that of the little towns of New France, nestled beside the broad St Lawrence. Montreal, Three Rivers, and Quebec were the only real towns, and the main centre of urban life was in the capital. Here the government officials, the rich merchants, and the seigneurs in town from their estates carried on a gay and colourful social life: a far-off colonial miniature of the great doings of Versailles. Courtly balls with cavaliers in lace and plumes were held in the candle-lit Chateau St Louis, the governor's residence on the heights at Quebec. In the town below, a jumbled pile of little stone houses and cobbled streets, the busy market place or the dockside were centres of activity.

Here, until the river froze, the ships came in from France with the cargoes the colony must have to exist, or they might arrive with tropical goods from the French West Indies. The furs that paid for the colony were loaded for France; but sometimes most of the colony's money also was drained out to meet the costs. Then indeed, one intendent hit on the device of dividing playing-cards in four, signing them, and circulating them within New France as money to meet the problem of shortage.

But while Quebec bustled with the affairs of government or the sea trade, while guns boomed as the great brigades of canoes arrived at Montreal laden with furs from the west, or the bells of churches, convents, and seminaries clanged over the towns, the real life of the colony was lived in the quiet, peaceful countryside. There, spread out along the banks of the St Lawrence like an endless village street, were the little whitewashed cottages of the habitants, the fields behind them, and rising not far beyond, the dark green wall of the forest.

The sparkling St Lawrence was the main highway of New France, whether by boat in the summer or by sleigh when frozen in the winter. Hence the cottages clustered beside it. Moreover, the practice of dividing land equally among the family's sons, giving each a piece of river frontage, multiplied the houses along the river. It made for long narrow strip-farms, inconvenient to work; but during the life of New France there was still enough room along the shores, and on the whole the population had not yet been forced to move into the back lots to open up lands away from the water.

The life of the habitant was thus a very social one. He was no lonely bush farmer but a member of a compact village community, further held together by the ties of his parish and his seigneury. In general, his was a good life. The land was easy to farm and his burdens light. He was not rich, but he had enough to keep himself—good bread, milk and vegetables, game and fish from the forest and river, sugar from his maple trees, and a tobacco patch on which to raise the rank 'tabac Canadien'.

He dressed in warm homespun, tied with the long woollen sash, *la ceinture flèche*, a woollen cap or toque on his head. The winters were long, but his steep-roofed, thick-walled house was warm, with ample supplies of wood roaring in the wide hearth. And winter was almost the best time of year. There were sleighing parties over the crisp snow, under an almost unbearably blue sky; there was horse-racing on the river ice. Far better off than the peasant of Old France, honouring his king, his curé and his seigneur, but sure of his own worth, the habitant was a sturdy and solid citizen. He was truly the backbone of New France, and of the province of Quebec in the era that followed.

5 *The Life of New France and Modern French Canada*

New France was authoritarian, hierarchical, firmly Catholic. The mass of its people were simple farmers, accepting their place in society and obeying those set over them. How does this influence modern French Canada? To-day the province of Quebec still has its quiet villages of whitewashed houses, the silver spires of Catholic churches soaring over them. Yet it is also a great industrial province, full of noisy cities and throngs of people whose life is far away from the farm. Nevertheless, many of the habits and ideas formed in an earlier age can still be seen.

French Canada is still broadly Catholic. There have been anti-clerical movements; but they, indeed, only reflected the very power of the Church and were largely made by Catholics who felt that their clergy had too much influence in matters apart from religion. In the Catholic religion, in fact, French Canada found a unifying force. Loyalty to Catholicism would become tied with the very idea of remaining French Canadian. The Church did much to shape French Canada. The descendants of New France sought to keep it strong by holding to the faith, which remains, despite modern secular trends.

The authoritarian and hierarchical sides of French Canadian society have declined far more. French Canadians took readily to the development of democracy and self-government in later periods, and social distinctions largely disappeared with the end of the seigneurial system. Yet still the background of New France comes out. French Canadians continue to show a greater respect for authority in government and thought, and still stress man's responsibilities rather than his freedoms. It is healthy, no doubt, for a country to have both sides stressed, and French Canada strengthens the Canadian nation to-day with its order and stability.

But finally, the period of New France really built up in Canada a people and a way of life that were distinctive in character. These people were not French any longer. They were North Americans, though not like the English Americans to the south. They were Canadians. More than distance by sea cut them off from France. They kept alive the old Catholic zeal when eighteenth-century France turned critical. Furthermore, after 1700 few immigrants came from the motherland and the French Canadians grew by themselves. By 1700 there were about 15,000 of them. By the conquest in 1760 there were over 60,000. The figure was small compared to the English colonies' million and a half; but a people that had grown like this on its own was never to be swallowed up.

Thus French Canada really developed its own traditions in the era of New France. The ideals of healthy farm life and the large family, strongly knit, working together, came from that time and lasted on. So did the ideals of Catholic and classical education and the belief in order and authority. At the same time the space and resources of a vast new continent had made these people freer and more self-reliant than those who had stayed in France. They were a proud and sturdy race. Besides the placid habitants, moreover, there were the daring fur traders, and explorers. And all had met and answered the challenge of the Canadian land. The result was a new people, born in New France, the seed of a nation in itself. They would not forget their heritage. 'Je me souviens' (I remember) is the official motto of the Province of Quebec today. The life of New France would continue to mould the French Canadians through later ages.

CHAPTER 6

THE STRUGGLE OF EMPIRES, 1702–60

1 *The Rivals for America*

At the opening of the eighteenth century, the French empire in America seemed secure. The War of the League of Augsburg, which closed in 1697, had indeed brought widespread conflict between French and English in America: in Hudson Bay, Acadia, Newfoundland, and along the border between New France and the northern English colonies. But by the end of the war an attack on Quebec had been beaten off, the French had gained ground in Hudson Bay, held their own in Newfoundland, and Acadia had been restored to them by the Treaty of Ryswick in 1697. Furthermore, in 1701 the Iroquois had at last been forced to make peace. While the fighting had not really altered the balance of French and English power in America, at least New France could be satisfied in 1702 to have come through the struggle so well.

But that year a new war broke out between France and England, the War of the Spanish Succession, and by its close in 1713 the French had suffered their first serious losses of territory in America. In the Treaty of Utrecht of 1713, France recognized British possession of Hudson Bay, Acadia, and Newfoundland. During this war, incidentally, the English empire became the British Empire, for in 1707 England and Scotland united to form the Kingdom of Great Britain.

The War of Spanish Succession was more than a partial British victory in America. It turned out to be the opening round in a conflict of empires that ended finally in the complete triumph of Britain and the fall of New France. The fighting before 1700 in America had been inconclusive. Thereafter a crucial struggle for a continent began to unfold, until by 1760 the British flag waved unchallenged over the main French possessions in America. The years between 1702 and 1760 had spelt disaster to New France.

That disaster could hardly have been avoided. The conflict of empires gradually grew into a fight for survival in America, and the stronger side finally won. The contest had really begun before 1700, but it had not reached fatal proportions then. As the French and British empires spread into America their main lines of expansion had begun to clash. Mounting conflict was the result, and it grew steadily more serious.

There were a number of more particular causes besides this general one. In the later seventeenth century, and through the eighteenth, France and Britain fought repeatedly in Europe and other parts of the world. The fighting in America thus formed part of these general wars, though it must be emphasized that the American warfare also had causes of its own. Besides the national hostility of France and Britain, affecting their possessions in America, religious antagonism between Catholic French Canada and the overwhelmingly Protestant English colonies added fuel to the fire. But more important than reasons of nationality or religion were reasons of trade.

In this connection, the fur trade was once more of prime significance. It was important to the English in America and it was the life-blood of New France. As the trade moved westward in its constant hunger for new supplies of fur, so the trading systems of English and French ran up against each other and were forced into a ceaseless contest for the fur supply. This, of course, had already led to war, as the English from Hudson Bay on the north or the Hudson valley on the south cut into the French lines of trade. In the later seventeenth century, the principal fighting—in the south—had been between the French and the Iroquois, the Indian allies of the English. First the Dutch, then the English, had backed the Five Nations from their main fur-trading base of Albany in the Hudson valley. But now the Iroquois had been vanquished, as once they had vanquished the Hurons, the allies of France. In the eighteenth century the main rivals in the fur trade stood nakedly opposed. French and English would have to take the chief parts in the clashes of fur empires.

Because, however, the English in America were not so dependent on the fur trade, they did not at first put forth a major effort against the French, not while furs were the main source of trouble. But in the course of the eighteenth century the spreading wave of English settlement began to flow towards the interior of the continent. And here the French had flung a line from the St Lawrence to the Gulf of Mexico, claiming the centre of America, seeking to hem the English in on the Atlantic coast.

At length the English became definitely aroused. With their far greater population they had to find new lands beyond the coastal plain, and English claims to the interior were at least as old as the French. On the other hand, the French had done far more to explore and occupy the vast regions beyond the Appalachians. And to preserve their vital fur trade they had to prevent English settlers from entering there. Settlement *versus* the fur trade brought on the final life-or-death battle.

Besides the central struggle for the heart of America, the battle of empires spread into outlying regions. The fight in the West Indies was a contest in itself for these rich tropical islands, although they were tied into the French and British empires in continental America. The fur trade of Hudson Bay and the fisheries of Newfoundland also involved the rivals, though these areas were fairly well settled in British hands after the War of the Spanish Succession. Acadia, however, remained an important zone of conflict throughout the period of wars. Its exposed position between the principal French and English possessions kept it in the forefront. As a French base to menace New England commerce or an English base for attacks up the St Lawrence, Acadia was concerned in many warlike operations.

In simplest terms, the mighty struggle of empires occurred in America in the eighteenth century because by that time both sides had developed sufficiently to let loose a continent-wide conflict. It was bound to come. There was no effective line of separation between the two empires. The French did hope to make the Appalachians the dividing line but were not strong enough to hold it. In any case the English fur trade had already found gaps in that barrier and had filtered beyond. Behind the English fur traders the resistless flood of settlement was rising. Both empires dreamed of final victory in America; neither really sought to head off conflict. Their rivalry had gone too far.

2   The British Empire in America

To understand the course of the imperial struggle it is necessary to know something of the British as well as the French possessions in North America. Besides the British islands in the West Indies, highly valued in the eighteenth century, thirteen mainland colonies or provinces had come into being, ranging down the Atlantic coast from Acadia to Spanish Florida. By the middle of the century they contained a population about one-third the size of England's. Although the British empire in America included other outlying areas—the Hudson Bay territory, Newfoundland, and Acadia after 1713—the thirteen colonies, rich, populous and powerful, were the stronghold of British power on the continent. Not long after 1760 they were to leave the empire, but in the struggle with the French the thirteen were all-important to Britain.

They varied considerably from north to south in their ways of life and their forms of society. The northern provinces of New England, led by Massachusetts, were largely concerned with fishing, shipping and ship-building, though small-scale farming was also general and there was some fur trade in the backwoods. The middle colonies, such as New York or Pennsylvania, also engaged in shipping on the coast and fur trading in the interior, but farming was their main preoccupation. They raised horses, cattle and plentiful food crops on good land. Sizable cities and some industries were beginning to appear here, and also in New England.

The warmer southern colonies, like Virginia and the Carolinas, concentrated on agriculture, and especially on large-scale farming by the plantation system. They produced a few basic or staple crops for sale abroad: for example, tobacco, rice or indigo.

Colonial society varied as did these business activities. In the more commercial north, rich merchants were at the fore, though the mass of the people were small farm-owners. In the plantation south, great planters dominated, but there were numerous small, independent farmers, as well as the large number of negro slaves who worked the plantations. On the whole, despite the existence of influential upper groups, the lack of long-established class barriers and the stress laid on freedom and equality already made this colonial society democratic in nature.

The forms of government fitted the society. The large degree of self-government in every colony was exercised by an elected assembly, on the British model, with considerable power over the public funds, without which government could not function. The general pattern of government in each province comprised a governor appointed in Britain, a council, also appointed, and an assembly elected by the colonists on a wider voting basis than in Britain at the time. The colonies originally had been controlled by chartered companies, or by a single proprietor or group of proprietors. But, as in New France, the crown had tended to take them over from private hands, and during the eighteenth century there was a steady trend towards establishing direct royal government in all the provinces.

This royal government, however, was very different from that of New France, because under it the colonies continued generally to manage their local affairs with little supervision from Britain. The royal governors, moreover, had always to contend with strong representative assemblies expressing the popular will. In two New England colonies, indeed—Rhode Island and Connecticut— the governor himself was locally elected.

Nevertheless, British imperial power attempted to supervise

carefully the economic life of the American colonies by means of regulating their trade. This was in accordance with the theory of mercantilism, which ruled the British empire as the French, and its purpose again was to make the empire a strong and self-sufficient unit. The colonies were to minister to the needs of the motherland by absorbing its manufactures and supplying it with raw materials. Imperial laws sought to prevent the colonies from engaging in much manufacturing on their own and at the same time to give their raw or staple products a preferred position in the British market. The British Navigation Acts, however, were the heart of the colonial system thus built up. They limited empire trade to British and colonial shipping, and ensured that colonies must buy their imports from Britain and send their chief exports there. The laws of trade were for some time only partly enforced, and it is not untrue to say that English America benefited from them where they served its interests and evaded them where they did not. Yet in the long run the attempts of Britain to enforce these restrictive mercantilist laws did much to lead the American colonies to revolution.

The way in which these first American colonies developed within the British empire was of much significance for the future history of Canada under British rule. Broadly speaking, the same colonial system was applied by Britain to the northern lands after 1760, while the structure and life of the original provinces had considerable influence on the later growth of an English-speaking Canada. Also important, however, for Canadian history were the other British American possessions beyond the thirteen colonies, the Hudson Bay territory, known as Rupert's Land, Newfoundland, and Acadia or Nova Scotia. They might have been of far less weight in the old eighteenth-century empire; but as provinces which were to continue under British rule, and become parts of Canada, they deserve special attention. In short, while Canada is often thought of as coming into British hands only in 1760, large tracts of the present country were under the British flag during the lifetime of New France. The beginnings of English-speaking Canada in the maritime, northern, and western regions run far back into the French period.

3 'English Canada' in the Day of New France

In the north and west of what is now Canada, British rule dated back to 1670, when Rupert's Land was established by the charter of the Hudson's Bay Company. That charter granted the Company control over all the lands draining into Hudson Bay, a vast shadowy domain whose limits were unknown. Thanks to this title, however, Rupert's Land actually included the larger part of the present prairie provinces as well as much of the sub-Arctic regions. But in the day of New France, and for long afterward, Rupert's Land remained a colony in a state of arrested development. No attempt was made to settle the barren lands about Hudson Bay, and the 'colony' did not progress beyond the stage of company rule under an absentee governor and board of directors in far-distant London. Still, Rupert's Land had been granted for its fur trade, not for settlement, and the fur monopoly remained the be-all and end-all of the Hudson's Bay Company. The monopoly was quite typical of the Canadian fur trade, except that, unlike the monopolists of New France, the Bay Company managed it most successfully. In part, being relieved of the burden of planting settlers made the difference, but also important were efficient organization, advantages of geography, and superior trade goods.

Private traders did not threaten this monopoly as they did those in New France, for only a big company could afford to equip large ships to trade by way of perilous Hudson Bay. The distant Bay was not plagued by unlicensed adventurers seeking furs as was the St Lawrence fur-trade empire. As for French competition from the south, the Bay traders had cheaper and better quality English goods that were sought after by the Indians. The Company could afford to sit down in trading posts by the shore and let the Indians come to them. From there the sea voyage to England was comparatively cheap and short: that is, in comparison with the trade route of the French, for they had to go to the western Indians themselves in order to divert furs from the Bay, and then make the long, costly journey back to Montreal and Quebec before their furs could be shipped to market.

The very success of the Bay Company led to vigorous French assaults on the English posts around the shore. These attacks had hardly been overcome by the end of the War of Spanish Succession when the English title to Hudson Bay was recognized. Then it was that the French sought to get behind the Bay by reaching into the western plains overland from the Great Lakes. The expeditions of La Vérendrye and his sons in the seventeen-thirties and forties took them to the Saskatchewan River. French attempts to control this prairie country, however, were soon cut short by the growing demands of the imperial struggle in other regions.

Meanwhile the English on the Bay had also reached the plains. Henry Kelsey had been the first white man to see the broad Canadian prairies in 1691. Anthony Henday reached the foothills in Alberta in 1754. But these journeys did not yet bring the Hudson's Bay Company to leave its profitable position beside the Bay. Rupert's Land remained largely unexplored and unoccupied up to the end of the French period, and beyond. Nevertheless, it was a valuable part of the British empire in America.

Newfoundland really began as an English colony in 1610, when an English company was chartered to found a settlement on the island, as a resident fishery. That is to say, the fishing industry would be carried on by residents on the island, instead of from the ships that made the long voyage from England each summer. This would permit a longer fishing season and lower costs. For these very reasons the visiting fishermen bitterly opposed the colony that was begun on Conception Bay in 1611, as they did all succeeding attempts to settle the island. In particular they feared that each year the residents would be able to occupy the best beaches for drying the catch. Because of this firm opposition, and its own internal troubles, the Newfoundland Company soon collapsed. So did several other attempts at settlement, although small groups of settlers were brought out. Then in 1637 Sir David Kirke, the captor of Quebec, secured a new grant for the colonization of Newfoundland. He established a successful colony and resident fishery, and from this time on, while beset with many troubles, English settlement slowly grew in Newfoundland. Harbours along the eastern coast gradually became permanent fishing ports, though life there was hard and the inhabitants poor. The chief settlement was at St John's. It became an important naval base, thanks to its fine harbour and location at the tip of the eastern Avalon peninsula, guarding the North Atlantic approaches to the American continent. Here there was some commercial life and farming as well as fishing. In the long run St John's naturally became the chief town and capital of Newfoundland.

Yet this required a very long run. Settlement in the island was consistently held back by the powerful visiting fishing interest. In the seventeenth century the summer fishermen were many, the residents few. Moreover, the visitors had great influence with the English government. They came mainly from West of England ports, and this 'West of England fishery' was looked on favourably by the imperial authorities of the time, because it fitted the prevailing doctrines of mercantilism.

One of the main aims of mercantilism was national strength, and the Newfoundland fishery was held in England to be a vital source of national power at sea. The fishery was 'a nursery of seamen'. It provided trained sailors and a reserve of ships in time of war, while in peace the large sale of dried fish to southern European countries brought in gold for the national coffers. Newfoundland was thus highly regarded by the imperial government; but as an overseas fishing station, not a colony.

Accordingly, settlement in Newfoundland had to struggle against official English policy as well as stern natural difficulties; in 1675, it was even briefly planned to remove the colonists. Furthermore, Newfoundland was not granted any regular colonial government. The summer fishermen had established the practice of accepting the captain of the first ship to reach a harbour in the island each year as 'admiral' in control of that area. The English government had officially recognized this system in the Fishing Charter of 1634. By it the fishery was really given authority over Newfoundland.

Somewhat later, convoys were established to escort the fishing fleet to the island, and the naval officer in charge of the convoy was placed in control. Finally, in 1728, he was named governor. Newfoundland at last had an official ruler—in the summer at least. Resident justices of the peace substituted for him in the winter. But this system of naval governorship again demonstrated the fact that Newfoundland was still regarded as a great fishing ship moored off North America. The naval regime lasted into the nineteenth century.

It was largely mounting danger from the French which brought the establishment of even the naval governorship, and caused Britain to give up any idea of removing the settlers, and, indeed, to recognize the necessity of a colony to hold the island. The French had long been fishing on the northern and southern shores, and, with the rising French interest in empire under Louis XIV and Colbert, they themselves planned a colony in Newfoundland. In 1663 settlers were sent out to Placentia on the south coast. By 1689 a vigorous French resident fishery and strong naval base had been established there.

During the War of the League of Augsburg there was much fighting back and forth in Newfoundland; raids by land or sea on Placentia and St John's, and the outlying harbours on either side. The inconclusive fighting began again in the War of the Spanish Succession. The French had the better of it, but British successes elsewhere, especially Marlborough's victories in Europe, decided the issue. In the Peace of Utrecht, British sovereignty over the whole island was recognized, except for French rights to fish and

MARTYRDOM OF THE JESUITS, 1649

THE CHARTER OF THE HUDSON'S BAY COMPANY, 1670

Frontenac treats with the Iroquois at Cataraqui (Kingston), 1673

COUNTRY DANCE OF THE CANADIENS

dry the catch on the unoccupied northern and western coasts. This 'French shore' would cause much trouble in later times.

But after 1713, Newfoundland's most stormy period of history was over. The old West-of-England interests were declining; the resident fishermen were steadily advancing. The French danger seemed ended. St John's, indeed, was attacked and captured by French forces in the final stage of the struggle of empires, but it was soon regained. The peace of 1763 that closed the conflict left Newfoundland still British, though the French fishing rights were renewed. By this time Newfoundland had well over 10,000 inhabitants. It was secure as a British colony.

Nova Scotia may be more briefly disposed of, seeing that it only entered the British empire during the War of the Spanish Succession. In 1710 Port Royal, the centre of French Acadian settlement, was taken once more by a British and New England force, though a greater joint attack on Quebec in 1711 failed even to reach that city. Port Royal was renamed Annapolis Royal in honour of Britain's reigning monarch, Queen Anne. This time Acadia remained British at the peace settlement, and the old name of Nova Scotia was revived for the new province. The French, however, kept Cape Breton Island and Ile Saint Jean, the present Prince Edward Island. Furthermore, they continued to occupy posts in northern Acadia (now New Brunswick) and claimed that only the Nova Scotian peninsula had been ceded. The British contended that the whole maritime region had been included in Acadia, and now formed part of Nova Scotia. Here lay more trouble for the future.

Until the founding of Halifax in 1749 as a naval base and provincial capital, there was little British settlement in Nova Scotia, although a large fishery developed, centred on Canso. A few British officials at Annapolis Royal uneasily governed a French-speaking Acadian people, which they could not wholly trust. Accordingly, the original plan to set up the regular type of British colonial government, of royal governor and elected assembly, was for many years not carried out in Nova Scotia. An assembly was only added to the governor and council in 1758, by which date the rising English-speaking population made it safe, and indeed necessary, to establish representative government. Thus by the time of the fall of New France Nova Scotia was becoming a fairly typical British province in America, one much like the New England colonies. New Englanders controlled its fisheries and were beginning to take up farms. Nova Scotia could now be rightly called 'New England's outpost'.

4 The Mounting Conflict

There was peace between Britain and France from 1713 to 1744, but in America the causes that were bringing the two empires into conflict went on working in growing intensity. Trouble was looming on every frontier between them. In the event of war, how would the power of the two American empires compare? Even a rapid glance makes it clear that if the French was much larger it was also much weaker.

While the principal British colonies still clung to the edge of the continent, behind the Appalachians the French ruled the vast domain of the Mississippi valley, as well as the realm of the St Lawrence. In this Mississippi empire, known as Louisiana, they had built New Orleans in 1718, as their main base at the entrance to the great river. From the Mississippi valley other posts formed a chain to the Great Lakes, whence Forts Niagara and Frontenac continued it to Montreal and the St Lawrence. Throughout this enormous area the French ranged free, filled with the vision of holding the continental interior for ever against the unenterprising English. To this end they had on their side a superior knowledge of the wilderness, the friendship of most of the western Indians, and a bold unity of purpose.

The British in America had anything but bold unity. They were thirteen separate colonies, sometimes as suspicious of each other as they were of the French. They had no very clear vision of empire—and thought more about the cost than the vision. Colonial governors often had great difficulty in gaining the assemblies' support for any imperial effort. In New France, on the other hand, imperial policy could be ordered in Versailles for execution in America, and there was no assembly to hamper the use of the colony's militia or to refuse the necessary funds.

But in the long run every advantage lay with the British. The French empire was far too big to hold on so small a basis as the population of New France. Stretched out too thin, with the fur trade its only real resource, French Canada gradually exhausted itself. The British colonies, occupying a relatively small area, had been able to build up a thickly populated community with many and varied resources. They were capable of far greater effort. There were, after all, more than twenty British colonists for every French Canadian. And if many of the thirteen colonies would not effectively support the struggle with the French, Massachusetts, which was active, alone had a larger population than all New France.

As for systems of government, that of New France only operated successfully as long as proper orders were received. The colony was not used to making its own decisions, often so necessary in time of war. It leaned on the homeland, while the British colonies looked to themselves. Once they had been brought to act, they would move with energy and initiative. Furthermore, the almost complete dependence of New France on fur-trading made it rely on the homeland for much more besides instructions. Only in years of good harvest could the colony even feed itself. In Canada prolonged fighting, with the militia away from home, might mean a ruined harvest and near-starvation. There was no such danger in the well-stocked thirteen colonies.

Finally, in regard to support from the motherlands, the British in America again had the advantage. It was true that France could send excellent troops to the American conflict. But first they had to cross the ocean. During the long imperial struggle the British navy gradually secured an ascendancy over the French, first gained during the War of the League of Augsburg. Thus, though both France and Britain sent regular forces across the Atlantic, in the long run the British fleet reduced the flow of French reinforcements to a mere trickle, while Britain freely built up armies in America. Sea power, which had already influenced the outcome of the War of the Spanish Succession, played a vital part in eventually deciding the struggle in America in favour of the British empire. The fate of the French inland kingdom of the Mississippi was in one sense settled by British naval victories in the North Atlantic.

That the peace after the War of the Spanish Succession was largely only an armed truce was shown by the French construction of Louisbourg in 1720. There on Cape Breton island they began a massive stone fortress and naval base to replace Port Royal, revealing that they had not altogether given up thoughts of regaining Acadia. Six years later the British on their side expressed their thoughts when they reached north to plant Fort Oswego on Lake Ontario, across from Fort Frontenac. Here was a British post right beside the vital French highway of empire, at the point where it entered the St Lawrence; and it was built on lands which the French had always regarded as their own. In their turn the French built Crown Point, to block attacks from the south by way of Lake Champlain, and placed it within boundaries claimed by the province of New York. The signs of conflict were growing.

Thus, in 1744, the clash of Britain and France in Europe in the War of the Austrian Succession unleashed new fighting in America. Nova Scotia and Louisbourg were the principal scenes of battle. New England was especially concerned over the new French fortress because of the likelihood of raids from there on New England shipping. In 1745 a force of New Englanders and a British fleet took the works of Louisbourg. Yet the peace of Aix-la-Chapelle, in 1748, handed Louisbourg back to France, much to New England's disgust, chiefly because the fortunes of war elsewhere

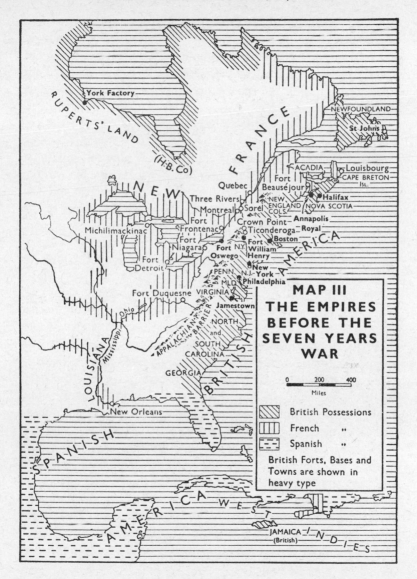

York Factory

RUPERTS' LAND

(H.B. Co)

FRANCE

NEWFOUNDLAND

St Johns

NEW

ACADIA · Louisbourg
CAPE BRETON Isl.

Quebec
Fort Beauséjour

Three Rivers
Montreal Sorel
NEW ENGLAND COLS.
NOVA SCOTIA
Halifax

Michilimackinac
Fort Frontenac
Crown Point
Ticonderoga
Annapolis Royal

AMERICA

Fort Niagara
Fort N.Y.
Oswego
Fort William Henry
Boston

Fort Detroit
PENN
New York
N.J.
Philadelphia
MD

Fort Duquesne VIRGINIA
Jamestown

Ohio
APPALACHIAN BARRIER
NORTH and SOUTH CAROLINA

LOUISIANA
Mississippi
GEORGIA

BRITISH

New Orleans

SPANISH

AMERICA WEST

JAMAICA
(British)
INDIES

MAP III
THE EMPIRES BEFORE THE SEVEN YEARS WAR

0   200   400
Miles

▨ British Possessions
▥ French   „
┅ Spanish   „

British Forts, Bases and Towns are shown in heavy type

had been too evenly divided to permit anything but a restoration of conquests on both sides. With this, America was nominally at peace once more. But the years that followed until war broke out again, in 1754, were hardly even a truce. From 1748 on, both sides were heading for renewed conflict in America; and this would be the final round.

5 *The Final Struggle*

The main contest between the empires was now shifting into a new area where there had not been fighting before. This was the Ohio country, which lay between the Appalachians and the Mississippi and was drained into that river by the waters of the Ohio. Hitherto the French had not occupied the Ohio region, and had generally used the upper Mississippi as their route to the Great Lakes and Canada. The route by way of the Ohio to Lake Erie was a shorter one, however.

Yet the French moved into the Ohio area chiefly to protect their hold on the Mississippi-St Lawrence chain of empire that ran farther west. The English colonies were beginning to advance over the Appalachians into the Ohio country. They had to be stopped at the mountain rim before they moved farther, for once past the Appalachians there was no other natural barrier between English settlement and the whole flat, continental interior. The French fur-trade empire was in deadly danger. The Ohio country had to be made its protecting bastion.

In 1748 an influential group in Virginia, a colony which claimed much of the west, had formed the Ohio Company, and had been granted lands in the Ohio valley to sell to settlers. The French acted accordingly. In 1749 they sent an expedition to take formal possession of the Ohio, which had previously been a no-man's land, and drove out English fur traders found there. This was partly a defensive act by the French empire. Equally it was an aggressive step, a move to advance right up to the Appalachians and pin the English colonies at that line. Given the mounting pressure of English settlement seeking to expand west, such a step could only bring an explosion.

It was not long in coming. New France backed the claim to the Ohio valley by building a series of forts through it, the chief one at the forks of the Ohio, Fort Duquesne. These activities had meanwhile roused some of the English colonies, and in 1754 the governor of Virginia sent a young major of militia, a certain George Washington, with a few troops to expel the French. He failed: but his little skirmish at Great Meadows, deep in the Ohio forests, was the explosion that set off the last great imperial conflict. When this war was over New France had fallen and the French empire in America was at an end.

While the Ohio clash began the conflict, it was also about to break in Nova Scotia. After the restoration of Louisbourg in 1748, France had sought to weaken the hold of the British on Nova Scotia by turning their French Acadian subjects against them. Ever since the Treaty of Utrecht Britain had not been able to bring the Acadians to take an oath of allegiance to the British King, largely because they feared that this oath might some day commit them to fight against France. The Acadians were not rebellious but sought to be neutral in any war. For more than forty years they managed to persist in this state, peacefully farming their lands, increasing to 10,000 in number by 1750—until they were caught up in the violence between empires and scattered to the winds.

If France now had not sought to incite the Acadians against Britain the British authorities in Nova Scotia might still have accepted this long established situation. But French agents began to urge the Acadians to reject the oath and to stir up the Indians. There were Micmac Indian raids and massacres at new British settlements. Then, in 1750, the French built Fort Beauséjour at the end of the isthmus connecting Nova Scotia with what is now New Brunswick. There they were joined by some of the Acadians. The British built Fort Lawrence on the Nova Scotian side. While disputes ensued as to the proper boundaries of Nova Scotia, tension mounted steadily. The British officials feared for a province largely populated by French Acadians who had taken no oath of allegiance and were being stirred into unrest from Louisbourg and Beauséjour.

In 1755, after fighting had begun in America, the British took Beauséjour and found Acadians in the garrison. The British governor at last decided that for the safety of Nova Scotia, Acadians must take the oath or be deported. He expected only to have to deport a few, but the Acadians, not believing after many years that the threat was real, still refused the oath. Most of them had not been involved with the French agents in their midst, but all suffered in the emergency. Hasty and ill-managed preparations added to their suffering. From August, 1755 onward, this quiet people was uprooted from the Annapolis valley and scattered through the English colonies. Some of them eventually made their way back to their Acadia, but most never returned. Displaced persons they were, tragic victims of a great war.

The fighting was well under way in America in 1755, although it did not break out in Europe until the next year, when France and Britain officially entered on the Seven Years' War. But in 1755 both countries sent large expeditions to America. The British force under General Braddock was chiefly designed to help the colonists drive the French out of the Ohio valley. The attempt resulted in disastrous defeat and Braddock's death; and of three other British attacks on French strong points only that on Fort Beauséjour succeeded.

By the next year an able general had taken command of newly strengthened French forces, the gallant but ill-starred Marquis de Montcalm. If bold leadership alone could have saved New France his might have done so. Yet, as well as facing the British with limited resources, Montcalm had to contend with a meddlesome, over-bearing governor, Vaudreuil, and a clever but corrupt intendant, Bigot, who made his fortune at the expense of the French war effort and the last defence of New France.

Because of the dangerous weaknesses of Canada, its long, thinly held defences, its short supplies, and the need of using its inhabitants both as militia and as farmers, Montcalm could not afford long campaigns. He struck rapidly with his few battalions of well-trained regulars, his Indians and forest-wise Canadians, keeping the British off balance so that they could not gather their superior forces for a crushing blow. At first he was aided by poor British generalship, quarrelling colonies, and a weak government in Britain. Thus the French took the advanced British post of Fort Oswego in 1756 and the next year went further to capture and destroy Fort William Henry on Lake George.

But in 1758 strong British forces under better leaders began closing in on the French empire in America. In Britain the brilliant minister, William Pitt, had taken over the direction of the war. British naval might was cutting off any hope of reinforcements for Montcalm, while they flowed readily to his enemies. Though the French commander won a striking success at Ticonderoga, in throwing back a British advance up the Lake George-Lake Champlain invasion route to Canada, to the west the loss of Fort Frontenac snapped the French life-line to the Ohio valley. Fort Duquesne was abandoned, and the Ohio prize fell into British hands. And far to the east the thick walls of Louisbourg were battered and breached by an army and fleet under Generals Amherst and Wolfe. A strange, sickly young man, this General James Wolfe, but in him lay the doom of New France.

Doom came in 1759. That year a three-fold British attack was launched: at Fort Niagara, which quickly fell, towards Montreal by way of Lake Champlain—and this attack was checked—and at Quebec itself. The fall of Louisbourg, guardian of the sea-gate to New France, had opened the way to the capital of Canada. Once again, as in 1629, 1690 and 1711, a British fleet sailed into the wide St Lawrence. Sea power reached up the river and placed Wolfe's army on its southern shore, across from the city of Quebec. For three months, however, he was held here, unable to reach the

French stronghold on the other bank; for on the northern shore Quebec was protected on one side by a line of steep cliffs and on the other by Montcalm's well planned defences that blocked every attack. And so the siege dragged on, until the night of 12 September.

On that night Wolfe boldly chose to try the cliffs above Quebec. Silently, under cover of darkness, he moved some of his troops in small boats to a narrow, rocky cove not far above the city. Here he had observed a path leading up the steep cliff-side to the heights. The heights above this difficult pathway were only lightly guarded, thanks to the interfering Vaudreuil, who had ordered one of Montcalm's regiments away for more useful service elsewhere. By dawn the British had struggled up the path to the Plains of Abraham. They stood at last on the weakly defended landward side of Quebec, their red coats shimmering like danger beacons through the morning mists that hung on the open plain.

As soon as he learned of Wolfe's successful approach, Montcalm resolved on an immediate counter-attack, to drive the British from the heights before they could bring up all their forces. Hastily his troops streamed forth from Quebec, the white-coated French regulars, the grey-clad Canadian militia. But the surprised and partly disorganized French were soon thrown into confusion by heavy British volleys and a bayonet charge. Almost before it began the battle was decided, and the French were pouring back in disorder, their cause in ruin. The surrender of Quebec soon followed. Neither Wolfe nor Montcalm lived to see it. Both had been fatally wounded on the Plains of Abraham, where the fate of New France was sealed.

The fighting was not yet finished, however. The remaining French forces rallied at Montreal, while the British fleet departed from the St Lawrence to avoid being frozen in the winter, leaving a garrison in the bombarded and ruined city of Quebec. Early next spring the British garrison, ridden with sickness, was itself besieged in Quebec by the French from Montreal. As the ice broke in the St Lawrence all eyes watched anxiously for the first sails to come up the river. It was British ships that appeared: once more sea power had played its telling role. With little hope left, the French retired to Montreal. There, as British armies advanced from three sides, from Quebec, from the west and from Lake Champlain, they made their final surrender. By the Capitulations of Montreal, of September, 1760, they transferred Canada to Britain, and the fleur-de-lis of France at last came down from the headquarters of the great French fur trade, the mission station and frontier post of the early days of the colony.

The war did not officially end until the Peace of 1763, although New France had fallen three years earlier. The struggle of empires had closed by creating British Canada. Yet French Canada would not die. The sure strength of its people, rooted in the St Lawrence land, their long memories, their French language, their Catholic faith, would still preserve French Canada. Nevertheless an age had ended. The day of New France was over. A new age had begun in Canada's history, the age of British North America.

PART III
THE BRITISH NORTH AMERICAN COLONIES

CHAPTER 7

THE AGE OF THE AMERICAN REVOLUTION, 1760–91

1 *Canada in the First British Empire*

In 1763 the Peace of Paris brought the Seven Years' War to a close, ending the great duel of France and Britain in Europe and in the world overseas. French Canada, however, had already come under British rule in 1760. As far as North America was concerned, the Peace of Paris only recognized an established fact in declaring all New France ceded to Britain. At the same time France transferred its Mississippi domain, Louisiana, to Spain. Except for the continuance of fishing rights on the northern and western shores of Newfoundland, and possession of the little fishing islands of St Pierre and Miquelon in the Gulf of St Lawrence, French empire in America was at an end.

On the other hand, the British empire now stretched unbroken from Hudson Bay to the Gulf of Mexico. The St Lawrence colony of New France had become the British province of Quebec. French Acadia, of course, had been the British province of Nova Scotia since 1713, although its boundaries had been in dispute. In 1763 they were defined to include the whole Acadian coastal region. At the same time the coast of Labrador was placed under Newfoundland control, and the boundaries of Quebec were also reduced in the west, making it a province of the St Lawrence valley alone.

In any event, there were after 1760 four British possessions within the present bounds of Canada: Quebec, Nova Scotia, Newfoundland and Rupert's Land. The latter two were relatively undeveloped, and Quebec was larger and more important than Nova Scotia. These northern provinces were not thought of at the time as composing a 'Canadian' unit in themselves. Along with the thirteen colonies, they were simply regarded as parts of one British American empire. Canada, in short, had been fully brought into the First British Empire, the old empire before the American Revolution.

Of the two main northern provinces, Nova Scotia was looked upon almost as one of the New England colonies, while, on the signing of peace, policies were fashioned for Quebec that were intended to make it much the same as any other British province in America. There was to be no special treatment for the new province, despite its unique French background and its French-speaking population. The rulers of the triumphant First Empire set forth their policies for America as a whole. Lax imperial controls were to be tightened, and the empire made a much more efficient unit. A common land policy was laid down for the newly-won American West in the royal Proclamation of 1763. The same document also dealt with the new province of Quebec, defining its boundaries and promising regular British institutions, including representative government.

Nova Scotia, meanwhile, had been given representative government in 1758. Equipped with a royal governor and an elected assembly, it was developing along the typical lines of the British American provinces. Following the expulsion of the Acadians, New Englanders had begun to take over their vacant farms around the Bay of Fundy. Settlement was spreading northward along the Atlantic coastal plain, and there was a steady flow of New England immigrants into Nova Scotia during the 1760's. The New Englanders brought their town meetings and Congregational churches with them. They built up the Nova Scotian fisheries. They sat in the provincial assembly. Nova Scotia was apparently becoming a new Massachusetts.

Nevertheless there were significant differences. In many ways Nova Scotia was not a northward extension of the New England mainland, but almost an island with its back to America, looking out to sea. This island was a British naval stronghold. In 1749

Halifax had been founded as a British answer to Louisbourg, and it was rapidly rising as an imperial citadel. In the American Revolution it would become the key British naval base in America. Furthermore, with the founding of Halifax, over two thousand settlers had been sent out from Britain, and Germans had been settled at Lunenburg further down the Atlantic shore. Yorkshire-men, Highland Scots, Irishmen, Germans, and remnants of the Acadians, varied the New England character of thinly-populated Nova Scotia.

In the garrison capital of Halifax, cut off as it was by rough country from the main areas of settlement in the province, government officials, rich merchants, and contractors to the armed forces could exercise a great deal of influence over the government of Nova Scotia. The power of this Halifax oligarchy, centred around the governor, rendered the provincial assembly rather weak and ineffective. Here again was an important difference from the New England colonies.

These differences would show more clearly once the American Revolution had broken out. But at least Nova Scotia was being mainly peopled by English-speaking settlers, used to British institutions. Quebec, on the other hand, remained a French community in a British-American empire. Few English-speaking settlers came to it after 1760.

At first it was expected that they would come. The Proclamation of 1763 invited migration to Quebec at the same time as it closed the western lands beyond the Appalachians to settlement. The door to the West had been shut because, at the end of the Seven Years' War, the western Indians had risen under the chieftain Pontiac to drive the white men back over the mountains. Closing the Appalachian frontier would give time for pacifying the Indians and for making treaties regarding their lands. And, also, the tide of American settlement might be deflected northward, as in Nova Scotia's case, until the French in Quebec were submerged in an English-speaking population.

In this way the unusual new province would indeed be absorbed in the British American empire. To begin the process of assimilation, and to invite settlers from the thirteen colonies, the Proclamation of 1763 promised English law and representative government in Quebec. But settlers still did not come. Quebec seemed too far, too cold, too alien; not at all like the tempting lands in the Ohio valley, just across the mountains. Thus the Proclamation failed in its aim of absorbing Canada completely in the First British Empire. Instead, by blocking the demand of American colonists for western lands, it became an important step on the way to revolution and the destruction of that empire.

2 *The Problem of Quebec*

New France had changed very little with the coming of British rule in 1760. The French officials and merchants, and religious orders like the Jesuits, had been withdrawn from the colony, and some seigneurs had also returned to France. Yet the mass of the population, Canadian-born as it was—seigneurs, habitants, and ordinary clergy—had remained in Canada. The Catholic farming colony of the St Lawrence was not greatly altered in character. The moderate British military government, that ruled from 1760 until after the peace settlement of 1763, had done much to establish good relations between the new authorities and the inhabitants. The Catholic Church, which was then outlawed in Britain, had been virtually left alone, and the temporary military regime had generally accepted the French colony as it was.

It might still be wondered whether 65,000 French Canadians could survive as a people in an English-speaking American empire of two-and-a-half million inhabitants. But after 1760 the only British immigrants to Quebec were a small number of merchants, who came originally as contractors and suppliers to the British army of occupation. They settled mainly in Montreal and Quebec city, filling the gap left by the removal of the French merchants. They began taking over the colony's fur trade, and other merchants joined them from American fur-trading centres like Albany. A new St Lawrence fur empire was in the making.

Combining the advantages of the St Lawrence route, the key to the interior, with the backing of powerful London commercial interests, allying British and Yankee business ability with French Canadian forest lore, these new St Lawrence merchants rose rapidly to a position of wealth and power in the province. Although a small minority in this thoroughly French colony, they came to control its economic life. At the same time French and English came together in a vital partnership in the fur trade. Money and leadership in Montreal and London combined with the skill and endurance of the Canadian *voyageur*, who worked deep in the western wilderness.

Nevertheless, trouble was being stored up for the future. Outside of the fur trade, all-important as it still was, and within the colony itself the two peoples were travelling separate paths. The French majority were engaged mainly in agriculture, the English minority in trade. Both sides were acquiring different interests; each began looking down on the other's way of life. The seeds of racial strife were being sown.

In 1764, after peace was signed, permanent civil government replaced military rule in Quebec, and the Proclamation indicated the lines it would follow. While the merchants disliked the restricting of Quebec's boundaries, which raised the problem of their access to the west, they were heartily pleased by the promise of British institutions. They wanted the English common law they had always known, and the representative government which they regarded as a basic right of British citizenship. But now there entered the new governor of the province, James Murray, to oppose the establishment of a representative assembly.

Murray had succeeded Wolfe in command of the army at Quebec, and thereafter had been military governor. On his new appointment as civil governor of the province he had been instructed to establish English law, appoint a temporary council, and arrange for the electing of an assembly. He appointed a small council, and worked slowly towards establishing a system of English law, but steadily postponed calling an assembly. In part his objections were practical enough. Bringing the unknown English law wholesale into the French colony would create widespread confusion. And as for an assembly, existing British enactments barring Catholics from political rights would put Quebec in the hands of a tiny Protestant minority.

Yet Murray was also much influenced by the prejudices of a soldier and official against noisy civilians and quarrelsome tradesmen. He preferred the placid French Canadian habitants and their authoritarian feudal system to the merchants and their dangerous democratic notions about self-government. As quarrels between merchants and governor grew, Murray made himself the champion of French Canadian rights. His position did him much credit. Still he blocked the introduction of British institutions in Quebec at a time when the French were not really aroused to seek special treatment. This led to further difficulties in later years. It was shortly made clear that British restrictions on Catholics did not extend to Canada. But by then the hope of an assembly, and of fitting Quebec into British political forms, was fast disappearing.

Strife between governor and merchants grew so bitter that in 1765 Murray was recalled. His successor, Guy Carleton (later Sir Guy), at first worked with the merchants. But he too was a soldier with a distaste for trade, and an Anglo-Irish aristocrat as well. He soon came to admire the orderly French Canadian society, with its aristocratic and military-looking seigneurial system, especially when His Majesty's subjects in the thirteen colonies grew increasingly radical and disorderly in their politics. As the discontent that led to revolution mounted in the south, Carleton began to regard Quebec as a valuable stronghold against disloyalty and violence in America.

In 1769 the British Board of Trade, the expert body advising on imperial policy, urged again that an assembly be called in

Quebec as promised, one now representing both French and English. Carleton argued against the Board's report. Canada, he insisted, was French and would always remain so. What was needed was not British institutions, but a full recognition of existing French institutions to bind Canadian loyalty tightly to the empire. In particular, the natural leaders of the Canadians, their seigneurs and clergy, had to be won over. Then, in the event of trouble in America, a French Canadian army could be raised, and Quebec would serve as a powerful British military base. These arguments told in Britain, where the government was growing increasingly uneasy over the discord in the America colonies.

Accordingly, the programme of the Proclamation, that aimed at the absorption of Quebec, was set aside. Why, in truth, absorb the French province into a rebellious empire? The Quebec merchants still sought the long-pledged assembly, but their efforts were doomed to failure. At length, in 1774, as American unrest moved towards open revolution, the Quebec Act was passed in Britain. It fitted Carleton's views, and represented the final abandonment of the policy of assimilation.

Under this measure Quebec received distinctive treatment, indeed. There was a complete acceptance of authoritarian rule. Government was to be by governor and an appointed council of both French and English, with no provision for an assembly. The English criminal law providing trial by jury was established, but French civil law was maintained. The seigneurial system was guaranteed, as was the freedom of Roman Catholic worship. The Church had already been allowed to hold its worship freely, and even to name a new bishop and to gather tithes; but now tithes were recognized and enforced by law. The Catholic Church in Quebec became a body backed by the state. The result was undoubtedly a generous grant of French Canadian rights and privileges, but at first the Act did more apparent harm than good.

In the first place, a further provision of the Quebec Act annexed the western lands between the Ohio and upper Mississippi rivers to Quebec. The extension of the boundaries was meant both to console the fur-trade merchants of Quebec and to tie the Ohio country to a 'safe' province. Yet this provision was a last straw to the discontented American colonies. The West they considered as theirs, that they had fought for during the Seven Years' War, was being given to their defeated foe, French Catholic Canada. In American eyes, the Quebec Act became one of the final 'Intolerable Acts' of Britain that put the spark to revolution. The colonists were also afraid that the privileges granted to the Catholic church and the return to authoritarian rule in Quebec showed that Britain intended to make Canada the check on the colonies' freedom which it had been in the days of New France. They were not entirely wrong.

But in the second place, and more important for Canadian history, the Quebec Act meant that the province of Quebec had been put on a special basis by an imperial act of parliament. This would complicate the future development of Canadian government. The chance to fit Quebec from the beginning into the ordinary pattern of British institutions had been lost. No doubt there was never any likelihood of completely assimilating (which after all, meant swallowing) the French Canadians in an English-speaking Canada. But in some ways the future co-operation between the two language groups in Canada was made more difficult by this measure which increased the French feeling of separateness. At any rate, the Quebec Act had not solved the problem of Quebec. Nor did it fully achieve Carleton's purpose of making the province a strong British base in the American Revolution: a revolution which it helped to bring on.

3 *The Impact of the Revolution*

The roots of the American Revolution, of course, ran far behind the Quebec Act, and at least to the end of the struggle with France. The very upsurge of British interest in empire, aroused by the victorious course of the Seven Years' War, came at the wrong time as far as the thirteen colonies were concerned. These fast-growing communities were already feeling restrained by British imperial controls, especially those on trade. The defeat of the French empire seemed to remove much of the necessity of accepting British authority. Hence Britain's attempt to tighten and strengthen the bonds of empire after the war ran counter to a rising spirit of American nationalism, though the colonists did not yet call it by that name. The clashes over the enforcement of British laws of trade in the colonies, the closing of the western lands, the rising argument over the right of Britain to tax in America, all aroused this American national spirit. The colonists claimed at first only to seek the full rights of Englishmen; but finally they demanded liberty and independence—that is, the right to establish a nation of their own.

The Revolutionary War broke out in 1775; and the thirteen colonies meeting in the Continental Congress hoped that Quebec and Nova Scotia would join in the fight for freedom. Yet the northern provinces did not join in. Why did they not enter the Revolution? Why had they remained British at its end? Was it merely chance, or the fortunes of war? To some extent it was both. But it was also the fact that, although parts of a single American empire, these provinces had viewpoints and interests different from those of the thirteen colonies. Quebec was plainly different in character; Nova Scotia less clearly so. The question of revolution did not arise in the outlying dependencies of Newfoundland and Rupert's Land. But in the two main northern possessions, while there were grievances against the British authorities, the forces working against revolution were far stronger.

In Nova Scotia there was naturally much sympathy for the American revolutionaries among the New Englanders who formed the bulk of the population; and there was a brief attempt in Cumberland County, in 1776, to bring about a rising. In general, however, the Nova Scotian Yankees sought to remain neutral in the conflict. They would not fight against their American kinsmen, but since geography kept Nova Scotia apart in a lonely corner of the continent they felt equally unwilling to fight for an American cause that seemed remote and far-off. Nor was theirs a strange stand, when a majority of the Americans still regarded themselves as subjects of King George III, though much aggrieved, and when about one-third of the people in the thirteen colonies were largely neutral during the Revolution.

Furthermore, few of the American grievances applied to Nova Scotia. The closing of western lands did not affect this colony, which had enough empty acres of its own. Government policies were fairly moderate and any quarrels were largely local. Above all, the British mercantile system seemed less a hindrance than a help. Weak Nova Scotia was not a Massachusetts, ready to stand on its own feet in world trade. It needed protected British imperial markets and had no desire to throw off the British trading system.

Even beyond this, as a British naval base, Nova Scotia thrived during the war on supplying the imperial forces. And with the Royal Navy ranging the seas about Nova Scotia and dominating this near-island, there was little chance of any successful rising, as George Washington himself stiffly admitted. Finally, there was the ascendancy of loyal Halifax over Nova Scotia; the power of the Halifax oligarchy, and the weakness of the assembly where a radical movement might otherwise have centred. It was by no means mere chance that this maritime colony remained in the British empire during the great Revolution.

At first glance, the case of Quebec might seem even clearer, since the overwhelmingly Catholic French population had little love for the Protestant Americans, their old foes, nor for their democratic ideas. But, on the other hand, they might seek this opportunity to throw off their British masters. And the Quebec Act, far from cementing French loyalty, had weakened it. The powerful merchant group was also angered by the Act. Thus the case of Quebec is not as simple as at first it seems to be.

The merchants' dislike of the Quebec Act arose naturally from its rejection of British institutions. But why the French discontent? The seigneurs and clergy were undoubtedly satisfied with the measure, but the mass of the people were not pleased by the legal enforcement of tithes and the renewing of their seigneurial bonds. Both tithes and seigneurial duties had been somewhat relaxed since the British regime began, so that the habitant had begun to think of escaping them. Now, therefore, a few habitants even listened to American democratic ideas and later joined the revolutionary cause. The bulk of them did not. They remained quiet under British rule, but they would not actively support it, though their clergy urged them to do so. Alas, for Carleton's hopes of a devoted French Canadian army! As the aristocrat he was, he had over-estimated the power of the seigneurs to command, and had ignored the feelings of the ordinary people in his plans.

The merchants of the province, however, whom he distrusted, turned out instead to be strangely loyal. True, there were many of them from the American colonies, some of whom at first openly sympathized with the colonial grievances. Yet life on the St Lawrence seemed to work some spell that turned even these against the American side. The truth was, that as the inheritors of the French St Lawrence fur empire these merchants were now in competition with the American traders to the south. Men from Albany were now firmly opposed to the Albany trade of the Hudson valley. The great St Lawrence trading system, the core of the Quebec colony, inevitably turned its masters against union with the American provinces, and directed Canada, French or British, to seek a separate destiny in North America. Then again, the commerce of Quebec fitted as closely as Nova Scotia's within the empire. The market for Quebec's vital fur trade, the source of its trade goods, lay in Britain, to which the St Lawrence route had now been tied. There was certainly no reason in this province to seek to escape the imperial trading system.

The thirteen colonies nevertheless hoped to gain Quebec; by force, if not by persuasion. Nova Scotia might be out of the grasp of the continental colonies, but Quebec was, as always, open to attack by land. In 1775 an American army moved north from New York along the historic Richelieu-River invasion route, to add a fourteenth colony to the provinces in revolt. As in 1690, 1711, and 1759, Canada was once more under attack from the south, though now the British flag flew over the northern colony and a new flag in the old English provinces. Yet the key point is this: that geography and history had again determined that, whatever the flags might be, there should be two different banners waving above Quebec and New York.

Weakly defended Montreal fell quickly to the American invaders, and Carleton, failing to gather his hoped-for grand Canadian army, was besieged in Quebec during the winter of 1775–6. The American forces from Montreal were joined by others which had grimly struggled through the Maine wilderness to Quebec. But their strength was still insufficient to reduce the city's fortifications, vigorously defended by Carleton. In the spring, as once before, sea-power turned the tables. A British fleet came up the river with ten thousand men and the Americans retreated. They did not return again. Sea power had shown too plainly that it could function in Quebec as well as Nova Scotia, and so keep Canada under British control.

Meanwhile the experience of living under an invading army, and having to accept an almost valueless American paper money, had revived the habitant's anti-American memories. After the invasion, he was more determined not to go over to the American side, and his clergy and seigneurs, thankful for the Quebec Act, worked to strengthen that feeling. Hence arose the paradox that in some degree Quebec stayed British because it was French; that is, because French Canada did not want to become American. This feeling among French Canadians continued as the Revolution went on, and endured long after the fighting ceased. When peace returned in 1783, although the British empire had lost the thirteen colonies, it kept sure possession of Quebec and Nova Scotia, and in them, as well as in Newfoundland and Rupert's Land, it held the basis for a new empire in North America.

4 The Coming of the Loyalists

The peace made in 1783, the Treaty of Versailles, not only had to recognize the establishment of the United States; it had to wind up the affairs of the old united British American empire. These involved questions of boundaries, fishing rights, and the fate of the large faction in the thirteen colonies who had supported the British side—the 'Tories' of American history, the 'Loyalists' of Canadian.

Now that the continent was to be divided between the new American republic and the remaining colonies of British North America, the peace treaty had to fix a final line of separation. By the close of the war, the British had gained ground down the Atlantic coast, and still dominated the Ohio country that had been attached to Quebec by the Quebec Act. But in part a shaken faith in the value of American possessions, in part a desire for a lasting settlement, led Britain to accept the boundary line of the St Croix river on the Atlantic coast; and, in the west, to give up title to the lands south of the Great Lakes. Nevertheless this border would cause difficulties in future. In the east, it would do so because the line above the St Croix, along the Appalachian ridges between Quebec and New England, was vaguely drawn through unknown country. In the west, trouble would arise because the lands that had been yielded cut in half the fur-trade kingdom of the St Lawrence, which still controlled the Ohio wilderness.

With regard to fisheries, the Americans in their colonial days had been used to fishing in the waters of the Gulf of St Lawrence and to drying their catch on shore. The New Englanders had built up a powerful interest in these northern inshore fisheries. It would have been hard now to keep them out. On the insistence

of the United States, Britain granted in the peace treaty the right
of Americans to continue to fish inshore within British North
American waters, and to dry their catch on unsettled mainland
coasts. This arrangement, whether necessary or not, represented
a continual invasion of the Canadian Atlantic fisheries, and was
also to breed future difficulties between the United States and the
British North American colonies.

Most significant for Canada, however, was the question of the
Loyalists in the Treaty of Versailles. It had been asserted by
John Adams, American revolutionary leader and later President,
that as much as one-third of the population of the thirteen colonies
had favoured the British cause; perhaps another third had actively
supported the Revolution. At any rate, over fifty Loyalist American units had fought on the British side, and at least a hundred
thousand Loyalists were finding life in the United States so unbearable at the close of the conflict that they were ready to
emigrate.

These British sympathizers found life unbearable in America
because the bitter feelings roused by the war had brought them
under repeated persecutions. No doubt the persecutions would
have been reversed, had they won; but those on the losing side,
which was quite heavily weighted with the upper classes and
richer members of society, had their homes pillaged, their property confiscated and their persons attacked. Mobs cried after them
and laws gave them very little protection.

Britain tried to secure protection for the Loyalists in the terms
of the peace treaty, but because the American Congress had not
yet much power over the states composing the young republic,
all the United States could agree to do was to recommend to the
state governments that a good deal of Loyalist property be restored and further seizures be halted. In the angry mood of the
time, this recommendation was almost completely ignored by the
citizens of the republic. Then it was that Loyalists began to leave
the country in large numbers, and Britain recognized that the least

that could be done was to give aid to these people who had fought to preserve a united empire.

Of the Loyalist emigrants, about a third returned to Britain and others went to the West Indies or Spanish Florida. Yet up to forty thousand of them turned north to Quebec and Nova Scotia. The main movement to Nova Scotia went by sea from the city of New York, which was held by the British until the end of the war. There in the closing stages of the conflict Loyalist refugees and soldiers gathered, well aware that their days in the former thirteen colonies were numbered. In the spring of 1783 the British authorities at New York, then commanded by Sir Guy Carleton, arranged a mass migration to Nova Scotia. During that year, whole fleets of ships carried nearly thirty thousand Loyalists to the province, in vessels crammed with men, women and children, and their chests of clothes and furnishings, their damask table-cloths and china tea-cups, treasured reminders of a life that had gone forever.

These Nova Scotia Loyalists came generally from the long-settled coastal areas of the American provinces. There was a large element of educated and formerly wealthy people among them. Now they were suddenly flung into a raw frontier colony, and many of them into the empty forests. No wonder that, despite government aid in land grants, provisions, and tools, harsh suffering and bleak despair were often in their midst. Some gave up, and drifted back to the United States or moved on to Britain. Some sought to be government hangers-on, and maintained a threadbare, unreal snobbery in minor official posts. Others collapsed frankly into ruin. But despite all the detractions from the Loyalist story, which are often too easily made to-day, this firm core of fact remains: that the mass of them fought through the bitter times and met the stern challenge of the hard northern land. They built a new age for Nova Scotia.

The population of the province during the Revolution had been only about 17,000. Almost double that number were added to it, swallowing the older 'neutral Yankee' elements in an ardently

Loyalist mass. The influx of professional men and cultivated people meant that this strengthened colony also advanced unusually rapidly from an unlettered frontier state to one of comparatively high standards of learning and culture. At the same time a new province, wholly Loyalist in character, came into being. So many Loyalists had settled on the northern shore of the Bay of Fundy, remote from the centre of government at Halifax, that this area was marked off from the peninsula of Nova Scotia and set up in 1784 as the separate province of New Brunswick. Saint John became its main port, Fredericton, up the Saint John river, its capital.

The Loyalist movement to Quebec was smaller and of a different kind than that into Nova Scotia, yet it was quite as significant. Only about ten thousand came, some by water from Nova Scotia. Yet many others moved overland, trudging on foot, their few possessions, saved from angry mobs, piled in rough carts. In winter they travelled by snow-shoe, dragging sleighs through the deep drifts. And so the determined little army came, north by Lake Champlain and the Richelieu river, or through the dark Iroquois country to the upper St Lawrence and the Canadian shores of Lake Ontario. Some journeyed to the far end of Lake Ontario, crossing at Niagara below the mighty Falls. Most of the Iroquois themselves, who had fought for the British during the Revolution, removed to Canada and were settled west of Lake Ontario on large reservations. The white settlers were placed in three main areas, all of them well to the west of the old St Lawrence farmlands of New France: in the Niagara peninsula, around the Bay of Quinte on Lake Ontario, and along the upper St Lawrence between that lake and Montreal.

The Loyalists who entered the province of Quebec (which then, of course, included the region of the Great Lakes) were largely drawn from loyal American regiments, together with their families, or they were often frontier farmers from the backcountry regions of the American colonies. They were better fitted than Loyalist town-dwellers who went to Nova Scotia for life in the wilderness, although at the same time they brought less learning and leadership with them. Quebec's Governor, Haldimand, set up a base camp at Sorel, between Montreal and Quebec, and from here transported many Loyalist parties to settle in groups along the upper St Lawrence, granting them land and supplies as in Nova Scotia. Yet this Quebec migration had much in common with the normal advance of the frontier in North America into new lands. It began while the Revolution was still in progress and did not really stop thereafter. The earlier parties of Loyalists came to Quebec because of their British sympathies and to avoid persecution; but the later groups increasingly came in order to obtain land. After the war Loyalists in Canada might write to friends in the United States who had not yet broken away, telling them of the free grants of good land given to the supporters of King George. In time, those who came to Canada might not be 'Late' Loyalists at all, but typical land-hungry American frontiersmen, part of the westward-moving flood of settlement, which here had overflowed the bounds of the United States.

Though the original Loyalists in western Quebec were at length outnumbered by the later American settlers, they still remained of crucial importance. These Loyalists would form the backbone of western resistance in a second war with the United States, the War of 1812. They were the original founders of the present province of Ontario, and did much to mould its character. On one hand they brought to Canada a conservative outlook, a quick distrust of any new idea that might be called republican, and a readiness to make loyalty the test for almost everything. On the other, they themselves represented a declaration of independence against the United States, a determination to live apart from that country in North America. As a result, they helped to create not only a new province, but a new nation.

The western Loyalists, despite their better preparation, had to face the hardships of wilderness life as did those of Nova Scotia.

There were times of near-starvation, times of grim fortitude, as they planted between the stumps of forest clearings and struggled to raise the first crops. But after the 'hungry year' of 1789, the western settlements took firm root and began to flourish. In consequence the same question was raised here as in Nova Scotia. Should this newly settled area, remote from the Quebec capital, be erected into a new province? In the case of Quebec, moreover, there were greater problems than distance to consider. Few Loyalists had settled in the French-speaking regions of Quebec; in particular, because they did not like the seigneurial system of land holding. In the western country they held their farms as they had in the old colonies. Besides, the language, customs, and religion of Quebec were not theirs; and under the Quebec Act they did not find the representative system of government which they had always known.

Accordingly, in 1791, the old province of Quebec was divided in half to meet the changed conditions; for despite Carleton's earlier arguments, Canada was no longer wholly French. The Constitutional Act of 1791 replaced Quebec by two provinces of Upper and Lower Canada. The western province of Upper Canada was English-speaking and received English law and institutions. It would become the modern province of Ontario. The eastern and mainly French-speaking province of Lower Canada (the present Quebec), kept seigneurial tenure, French law, and the privileges of the Catholic church granted by the Quebec Act. Representative government, however, was now established in both the Canadas.

The Constitutional Act signalized a new beginning for Canada. The British North American colonies were starting to take definite form; the age of the Revolution was drawing to a close. Yet the American Revolution had been almost as important for Canada as it had for the United States. In fact, by dividing the continent, it created modern Canada no less than it created the American republic. Furthermore, the Loyalists of the Revolution brought

The Taking of Quebec, 1759

A view of the Town & Harbour of Halifax from Dartmouth Shore

EIGHTEENTH-CENTURY HALIFAX—THE RISING NAVAL BASE

CAPTAIN COOK ON VANCOUVER ISLAND, 1778

LOYALISTS AT SAINT JOHN, NEW BRUNSWICK, 1784

CORDUROY ROAD IN EARLY UPPER CANADA

TRAVEL BY DOG CARIOLE IN HUDSON'S BAY TERRITORY

to those colonies that had remained British a population that wanted whole-heartedly to stay British. The Loyalists began to build a Canada that was not predominantly French. Modern English-speaking Canada really goes back to them, and to the Revolution that drove them out. In a sense the American Revolution itself really answered that old problem of 1763—of how to make Canada thoroughly a part of the British empire.

CHAPTER 8

THE SHAPING OF BRITISH
NORTH AMERICA, 1791–1821

1 *Constitutional Changes and the Second Empire*

By 1791 the reorganization of the British possessions in America made necessary by the shattering blow of the American Revolution, was fairly well complete. The colonies of the northern half of the continent were being refitted into a Second British Empire; British North America was settling into shape. While Newfoundland and Rupert's Land continued much as they had been from the old empire, the newly populated provinces of Quebec and Nova Scotia had been carved into several units. The former had been divided into Upper and Lower Canada, and from the latter four provinces had been created. Besides New Brunswick and a smaller Nova Scotia, these included the colonies of Prince Edward Island and Cape Breton. Cape Breton was reattached to Nova Scotia in 1820. The three other maritime provinces remained in existence, as they do to-day.

This division of the old northern provinces reflected a new imperial policy, one that was not only due to the desires of the Loyalists, but arose as well from the whole reaction of the British authorities to the American Revolution. The new governments constructed, the provisions of the Constitutional Act of 1791, were largely shaped by what Britain thought were the lessons of the American Revolution. As Canada had been brought into the First Empire under a general plan of unifying the American possessions, so it entered the Second under a rather disillusioned policy of keeping colonies small and dependent. 'Divide and rule' was the principle.

The general British view of empire had not really changed following the American Revolution. In time, it is true, developments largely within Britain made political leaders there doubt the value of a dependent empire. Then, indeed, the American Revolution was pointed to as proving that colonies were bound to grow towards independence, and that control of their trade was unwise and unnecessary. But for some time after the Revolution British authorities still accepted the old mercantilist ideas of empire, under which colonial government had to be subjected to imperial authority and colonial trade had to be made to flow in certain fixed channels. The 'Old Colonial System' of subject colonies regulated by imperial laws of trade by no means disappeared from the Second Empire after 1783.

As far as official policy was concerned, therefore, the lesson of the American Revolution was not that mercantilist restraints and imperial control over colonial governments had led to clashes and finally to disaster. It was instead that the Revolution had arisen from too much strength in the American colonies and too much self-government there. Colonies should be kept small, and hence dependent on Britain. The power of their representative assemblies should be limited, so that noisy democracy and dangerous radicalism could not grow too strong. If anything, colonies had to be more fully subjected to control from the motherland.

This was the policy applied in British North America after the Revolution. But there were redeeming features. There was much good will on both sides. Britain was not seeking to punish or keep down rebellious provinces but to preserve loyal and orderly communities in that contented state. The troublemakers, so to speak, had left the empire. The British North American provinces, and especially the Loyalists within them, also tended to agree that democracy and too much self-government were dangerous. For the Loyalists, democracy raised memories of armed rebellion and mob-violence. The provinces looked to Britain for guidance, and in their weakness readily accepted a state of dependence. Furthermore, far from quarrelling with imperial control of trade, they relied on the British trading system for protected markets for their products and for aid in developing their commercial life. The colonists of British North America themselves represented a rejection of the ideas behind the American Revolution. They stressed loyalty, not liberty, traditional ties, not a break with the past. They feared the power of the new United States and trusted Britain. Thus they were easier to deal with than the old American colonists, who had been only too conscious of their own strength and put no special weight on the imperial bond. Accordingly, the constitutional changes carried out after the Revolution met little opposition in the British provinces and for a generation at least gave reasonably satisfactory government to British North America.

The division of old Nova Scotia was in line with the British policy of forming small colonies. Prince Edward Island, in fact, had been set up by itself even as early as 1769. Representative government was applied in each of the new Maritime provinces, except for under-populated Cape Breton, where a governor and council ruled alone. In Nova Scotia proper, the old assembly was simply continued. New Brunswick and Prince Edward Island received a similar system of governor, council, and assembly. But in all three the assembly remained weak. This was particularly so in Prince Edward Island, which was gradually peopled by Loyalists and pre-Loyalists from the mainland, because the island was really controlled by a few absentee landlords who rented their wide acres to settlers but stayed in Britain. In New Brunswick the overwhelmingly Loyalist population founded a tradition of loyalty and obedience to authority at the start; so that the elected assembly was a docile body, content to leave real power in the hands of the governor and his appointed council.

Still, the fact that there were assemblies in these Maritime provinces showed that Britain did not mean to withhold the representative form of government. In part also, the presence of assemblies indicated that the Loyalists, however loyal, expected to have the same kind of constitution as they had been accustomed to in the old colonies. Those who came to Quebec had similar expectations. There was also the problem of taxation to be dealt with. Britain had indeed learned during the Revolution not to try to tax colonies against their will. Assemblies would be needed to grant taxes, in order that colonies might meet the costs of their own government.

For these reasons the Constitutional Act of 1791, while carrying out the policy of divide and rule, provided for elected assemblies in both Canadas. This provision, to some extent, also brought final success to the merchants of Quebec in their long agitation for representative government, though they did not want the colony divided. They had pressed their case vigorously, once the Revolution had showed the failure of the Quebec Act policy; and Carleton, now Lord Dorchester, who had returned to Quebec as governor, no longer had the same faith in his old ideas. Accordingly the unrepresentative government of the Quebec Act was readily brought to an end, although the special rights it had granted remained to give French Canada its separate character. The French could sit in the new Lower Canadian assembly; and this they speedily came to control, since the main body of English settlers now fell within the borders of Upper Canada—something the merchants had not at all intended.

The Constitutional Act also applied the British policy that aimed at restraining the representative or popular element in government. The same form of government was provided for both the Canadas. There was to be a governor-general over both of them, with nominal authority, rarely exercised, over all British North America. Upper and Lower Canada were each to have a lieutenant-governor, an executive council, a legislative council and a legislative assembly. The assembly's control of the purse was to be more limited than in the old colonies, so that it could not restrain the governor in the same way. Hence the assembly had far less power.

But the chief limitation on the assembly's power was meant to lie in the two appointed councils set over it. The executive council was not new. It was simply the old council, the group of the governor's advisors chosen by him to carry on the chief tasks of government. But now there was a legislative council as well, an upper house in the colonial parliament, whose members were appointed for life and were beyond the control of the assembly or the people. Without the consent of this legislative council no laws could pass. It was meant to be a colonial House of Lords, to check democratic or radical tendencies in the assembly. The legislative and executive councils gradually came to contain many of the same men, often early Loyalist leaders who had received large land grants. They formed a closed and compact official body, or oligarchy, about the governor who controlled the province, leaving the assembly to be little more than a debating club.

In further attempts to strengthen authority and to weaken the 'popular' element, the Constitutional Act also envisaged setting up a colonial aristocracy and an established church. The former scheme was never carried out—the thought of backwoods dukes pitching hay was too much—but the latter was effected in the provision for clergy reserves. In either province, so the Act ran, an amount equal to one-seventh of the public, or crown, lands granted, should be reserved in order to create a fund for the support of 'a Protestant clergy'. This for some years was taken to mean the clergy of the state Church of England. Through this clause, and later additions, the Anglican Church became a powerful state-endowed body in Canada, where it worked on the side of the governors and the conservative ruling groups against any radical tendencies among the mass of the colonists.

The clergy reserves and the restrictions on the power of the assembly were to spell much trouble in future, but a few good words may be said on leaving the Constitutional Act and the policy it expressed. 'Divide and rule,' had at any rate more reason in the Canadas than in the Maritimes. In the Canadas two very different communities had developed. The French in the east would not willingly have yielded their law and their special rights by the Quebec Act. The Loyalists of the west above all wanted to establish English forms of law and to escape the seigneurial system. Indeed, the line drawn between Upper and Lower Canada, when they were created, ran along the boundary of the farthest western seigneury. It would at least have been hard to have kept these two Canadas together, however beneficial it might have proved in the long run.

As for the 'anti-democratic' tendencies of the Constitutional Act, the inhabitants of the Canadas were, up to the War of 1812, on the whole content to leave most of the powers of government in the hands of a small group of leading men in church and state. The French authoritarian tradition in Lower Canada, Loyalism in Upper Canada, helped to make the colonists accept this state of affairs. Upper Canada, moreover, was still too backward and thinly populated to be much interested in governing itself or to question the rule of an oligarchy. Furthermore, the ruling oligarchy might represent the educated and public-spirited few as well as the office-seekers and parasites. Given goodwill, and the weak state of the Canadas in the first period after the American Revolution, the Constitutional Act could function without grave difficulty. For the same reasons, the somewhat restrictive policy of the Second Empire did not really create trouble for British North America during this early period.

2 The Rising Colonies of British North America

By 1791 the British North American colonies were beginning to advance within the framework of the Second Empire and to work out patterns of life which would remain much the same till the coming of railways, steamships and the factory age. In the western half of the continent, beyond the Canadas, a new kingdom of the fur trade was arising; a world in itself, it will be left for later discussion. In the east, Newfoundland was still under naval governorship, without representative institutions, but the resident fishery was steadily growing. The island held about 15,000 people by the closing years of the eighteenth century. Seal hunting began to emerge as a supplement to the cod fishery.

The Maritime provinces were slowly emerging as prosperous communities dependent on the sea: on its fisheries and on its commerce. There was not much immigration to this region after the Loyalist wave had swept over it, although some Highland Scots did come to Nova Scotia, Cape Breton, and Prince Edward Island thereafter. There were probably about 80,000 inhabitants in the Maritime provinces by the end of the century, and the very lack of a constant stream of new immigrants allowed these English-speaking communities to become more closely knit and relatively more mature than Upper Canada in the same period.

The comparative lack of immigrants arose from the fact that the Maritimes had less space and less fertile land to offer to settlers than Upper Canada. In this realm of the sea and the forest, farming was not as important as fishing, shipping, and lumbering, except in little Prince Edward Island. But on sea and forest the Maritimes successfully founded their way of life. Shipbuilding developed to complement the rapidly rising fishing industry of Nova Scotia. Lumbering, especially in the upland forests of New Brunswick, supplied the timbers for ship building. Nova Scotian vessels entered the British West Indies trade, carrying dried cod-fish and lumber to the sugar islands.

It seemed that the Maritime provinces would come to fill the role in the Second Empire that New England had played in the First; that is, of furnishing the British West Indies with necessary supplies while the islands concentrated on sugar production. The Maritimes, however, proved a weak replacement for New England. They could not supply sufficient foodstuffs, apart from fish. Nevertheless, because they were parts of the British empire they were in a privileged trading position. The mercantilist British Navigation Acts decreed that empire commerce should be kept for empire ships. Therefore the Maritimes were protected from a good deal of American competition in the British West Indies.

Thanks to the laws of the Old Colonial System, Nova Scotia in particular built up a thriving trade by sea, especially after 1806, when bad relations between Britain and the United States further cut down American competition in the protected imperial markets.

New Brunswick was more concerned with lumbering and ship-building than fishing and seafaring, though each province shared some of the other's main interests. When the imperial government gave a preference to British North American timber in the British market after 1794, New Brunswick lumbering was encouraged. During the Napoleonic Wars, moreover, the preferential rate for colonial timber was greatly increased, because Britain wanted a sure supply of ship timber for the Royal Navy that would be far from embattled Europe. As a result, New Brunswick embarked on a lumber boom. Each winter armies of lumbermen, who were often farmers in the summer, invaded the forests and set up camps. They cut out the straight, lofty tree trunks that were floated down the St John and Miramichi rivers in the spring in broad rafts of giant, square-hewed beams. On reaching the coast the big 'sticks' were loaded through large ports at the stern of specially built lumber ships, to lie the full length of the vessel in the voyage across the Atlantic.

Clearly, these Maritime provinces of British North America were flourishing within the Second Empire, and largely because of the trade preferences and protection supplied by the Old Colonial System. The Canadas were similarly advancing within the imperial framework. The timber trade with Britain developed in the St Lawrence valley as well as in the Maritimes, and lumbering cleared the land for settlers as well as providing a valuable cash crop. Square-timber rafts were floated downstream from Lake Ontario to Montreal and Quebec. The fine stands of trees in the Ottawa valley became a leading source of forest wealth. By 1800 lumbering had joined the fur trade as one of the main or staple activities of the Canadas. Moreover, as the land was cleared in Upper Canada a new staple, wheat, began to develop. The French Canadian farms of Lower Canada generally grew crops for home use only, but the rich new lands of Upper Canada early began to produce a supply of grain for sale in Britain. Again, the Napoleonic Wars, having largely cut Britain off from European grain fields, created a market for this British North American product. For some years after 1800, however, the market was very uncertain, and so was the crop. Still the foundations of the future Canadian granary had been laid. And as the three main exports of the Canadas, furs, lumber and grain, were tied to the British market, so these colonies, like the Maritimes, depended on the imperial trading system for their well-being.

Settlement continued to flow into the Canadas from the United States after 1791. In that year the two provinces contained approximately 180,000 inhabitants, of whom only about 14,000 lived in Upper Canada. By the time of the war of 1812 there were over 90,000 people in Upper Canada and more than 330,000 in Lower Canada. In the latter case, however, the growth was mostly due to the natural increase of the French-speaking population. Only about 9,000 Americans had come there, settling chiefly in the Eastern Townships south of the St Lawrence and mingling with earlier Loyalist elements.

While some settlers, principally Highland Scots, had come to Upper Canada from Britain, the great British immigration did not begin until after 1820. Thus during this first period of British North America, when the American frontier movement was spilling over the border into Canada, Upper Canada became almost an American community, only about a quarter of which was Loyalist in origin. Yet far from fearing this situation, John Graves Simcoe, the first lieutenant-governor of the province, busily encouraged American immigration. Simcoe, leader of the famed Queen's Rangers in the Revolution, himself looked down on American republicanism and revered the British constitution, whose 'image and transcript', he said, had been granted Upper

Canada in the Constitutional Act. Yet he had great faith in the power of an oath of allegiance and a generous land grant to convert Americans; or perhaps he was carried away by his eagerness to see Upper Canada populated. Still, it was not too difficult for men who had earlier in their lives been subjects of King George III to come back to that allegiance. The sense of nationality had not yet hardened in the United States, especially in the backwoods from which these 'new subjects' came.

Under Simcoe's energetic guidance roads were begun in Upper Canada, and a provincial capital founded: York, the future Toronto. The roads were little more than forest trails; traffic continued to go mostly by water. York, established in 1793, though graced with little brick parliament buildings, was still only a village in 1812. It was not yet a leading commercial centre and was noted chiefly for its mud. Nevertheless this new western province of Upper Canada had made the most rapid progress of any in British North America.

Lower Canada had also advanced. Montreal was now the chief city of British North America, with a population of some 30,000 by the War of 1812. Here the wealthy rulers of the fur trade dwelt in their stone mansions, while lumber merchants tended to gather in Quebec. In these cities, as in St John and Halifax, powerful groups of merchants had arisen, men who carried on business on a large scale. There was nothing small about their business activities, although they were in young colonies, because the staple trades of British North America demanded large-scale organization to bear the high cost of carrying goods to the far-off markets. As well as the merchants, the leading towns held the governing officials and the officers of the garrison. Altogether they formed a little upper-class society which copied the ceremony, dress, and customs of the courtly British aristocracy. In sharp contrast to this society was the rude frontier world of the Upper Canada clearings, the unchanging country existence of the Lower Canadian habitants, the rough life of New Brunswick lumber

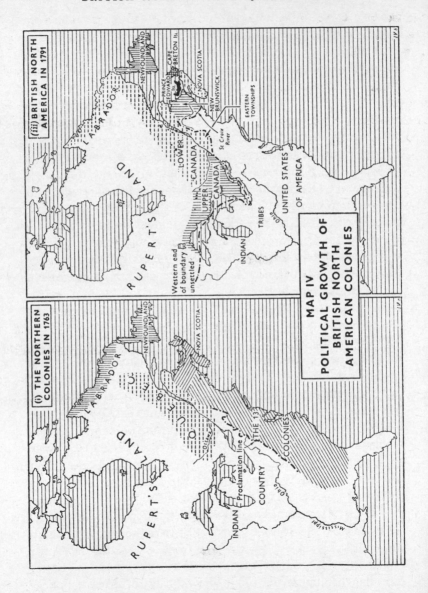

(iii) BRITISH NORTH AMERICA IN 1791

NEWFOUNDLAND

CAPE BRETON Is.

PRINCE EDWARD Is.

NOVA SCOTIA

LABRADOR

NEW BRUNSWICK

EASTERN TOWNSHIPS

St. Croix River

LOWER CANADA

UPPER CANADA

RUPERT'S LAND

Western end of boundary unsettled

INDIAN TRIBES

UNITED STATES OF AMERICA

MAP IV
POLITICAL GROWTH OF
BRITISH NORTH
AMERICAN COLONIES

(i) THE NORTHERN COLONIES IN 1763

NEWFOUNDLAND

NOVA SCOTIA

LABRADOR

RUPERT'S LAND

INDIAN COUNTRY

Proclamation line

THE 13 COLONIES

OHIO

MISSISSIPPI

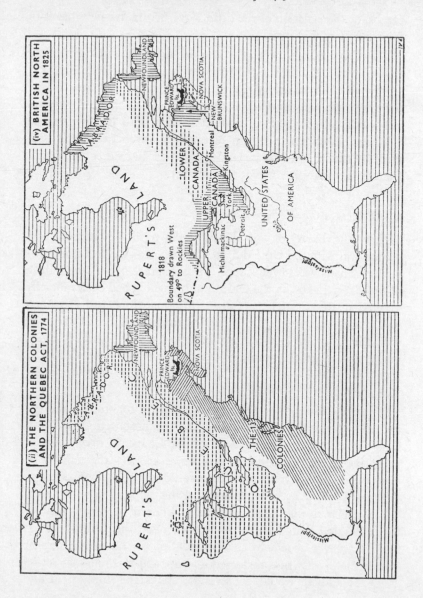

camps, or the isolation of the little Nova Scotia fishing villages in their lonely rocky coves.

The differences between the lives of the town and the country would be reflected in the politics later of British North America. In any case, however, by the time that the colonies had to face their next great test in the War of 1812, they had emerged as small but solidly established communities, each with its own special character, although the main distinctions lay between the provinces of the sea, the French lands of the St Lawrence, and the new frontier farming province of the interior.

3 Danger on the Western Border

From the Treaty of Versailles in 1783 until the outbreak of a second war with the United States in 1812, the western border of young Canada was never secure. Trouble arose in the lands south of the Great Lakes; in the Ohio country which had been officially granted to the United States in 1783, but which had remained tied to the St Lawrence fur trade. The final consequence was open war. The trouble began almost with the signing of peace in 1783, when Britain quickly came to regret the ready surrender of so much of the West, and sought at least to delay its transfer to the United States.

The chief reasons for delay arose from the fur traders and the Indians who were still the masters of the unsettled Ohio West. The Canadian fur merchants of the St Lawrence drew most of their trade from that country, and they asked that the transfer be postponed for two years until they could adjust their business to this heavy loss. The Indians supplied the major reason, however. They declared that they had been ignored in the Treaty of Versailles and that Britain had handed over their lands, which they had never ceded, to the United States. There was danger that if the West was transferred and opened to American settlement the Indians would, in revenge, attack the thinly held and almost unprotected British settlements in Upper Canada.

Taking advantage of vague wording in the peace treaty, there-fore, the British held on to the military and trading posts in the West below the Lakes, giving as their reason the failure of the Americans to carry out the term of the treaty that called for the restoration of Loyalist property. It was a sound reason, but not the chief one for failing to transfer the West.

This situation dragged on into the 1790's, while the Americans feared that the British were arousing the Indians against them, and the British feared that the Indians would become aroused. Dorchester, as governor, darkly expected a new war with the United States, and had some hope of building an Indian state in the Ohio country that would stand between the Americans and the Upper Canadian frontier and help to protect the latter. The Americans, meanwhile, were pressing forward from the region south of the Ohio, and sending forces against the Indians in order to break their hold on the western country. In 1794 one of these expeditions completely defeated the tribes at the battle of Fallen Timbers, and hope of an Indian 'buffer state' collapsed. The tribes ceded their lands to the United States.

In 1794 as well, Britain and the United States at last reached a settlement by Jay's Treaty. Britain agreed to surrender the western posts by 1796, while the United States agreed to allow British traders still to enter the West, and promised to handle the Loyalist claims more effectively. Yet the western troubles were not ended. Though the posts were transferred, the Indians con-tinued to come to posts on the Canadian side to trade. The British gave them supplies, still in an effort to keep their friend-ship and to prevent their attacking Upper Canada in the event of a war with the United States. Americans believed, as a result, that the British were forming an armed alliance with the Indians against the republic. At the same time American fur traders, who earlier had not been able to compete effectively against the Canadians in the Ohio, had managed to have the British right of free entrance for trading restricted until it was almost meaningless. The strain was increasing.

Other disputes added to it. At sea, Britain's life-and-death struggle with Napoleon after 1802 had led to decrees of blockade and counter-blockade. In an effort to prevent war supplies reaching French-controlled Europe, Britain was stopping and searching neutral vessels at sea, including American ships. British warships were also seizing suspected deserters from the Royal Navy aboard American craft, often on uncertain evidence and in high-handed fashion. The Americans protested against the right of search, and finally tried to cut off all their trade with the warring countries in Europe in order to force a settlement. The attempt did not succeed. Instead the quarrel over the right of search embittered feelings between the United States and Britain. It even led to a battle between the British ship *Leopard* and the American *Chesapeake* in 1807, and made the two nations look towards war.

The rapidly advancing western states of the American union made good use of the growing warlike spirit in the republic. They held that the place to punish Britain was in Canada. Filled with the forceful confidence and expansive drive of the frontier they wanted to add Canada to the American union: a Canada which American frontier settlement had already invaded. Was not Upper Canada by now practically an American state? The 'war hawks' of the American West clamoured for an easy conquest. Their chance seemed to arrive in 1811.

In that year the western Indians, being steadily pushed back by advancing American settlement, attempted a last stand. Led by the chief Tecumseh, they formed a league to resist further inroads. The Americans saw this as the threat of a new Pontiac uprising, of savage Indian raids on the frontier. They attacked the Indians, and by their victory at the battle of Tippecanoe, destroyed Tecumseh's league. Yet the American West was not satisfied. It was fully convinced that the British had been behind the Indians, although the Canadian government had actually sought to keep the Indian league at peace. It seemed that the West would only be safe when the British had been driven out of Canada. The war hawks cried for blood, the American frontier wanted new lands to conquer, and the American East was newly aroused by fresh skirmishes over the right of search. The United States declared war in June, 1812, and set out to capture Canada.

4 The Second Struggle with the Americans

The War of 1812 in British history is only a side-show, not altogether successful, during the huge and victorious contest with Napoleon. In United States history it is a second war of independence, chiefly against the weight of British sea-power. In Canadian history it is above all a land war, a second struggle against American invasion. All these pictures are partly true; and in studying the Canadian version one must bear in mind that it portrays only the War of 1812 as it affected Canada. Yet for Canada the war was vitally important; far more important than it was for Britain, and much more dangerous than it was for the United States.

British North America faced a foe that outnumbered it ten to one and was much further advanced in civilization. Nor did British support level the scales, for there were less than 5,000 British troops in Canada at the start of the war and no reinforcements could be spared from the greater conflict in Europe until close to the end of the fighting. Fortunately for the British colonies, the United States never gathered its full strength against them, since the republic was much divided over the war and by no means solidly behind it. Furthermore bad planning and unwise use of the American forces helped to balance the sides. Even so, it was a heavy task for the few regulars and the limited militia to defend the thinly-settled, spread-out northern colonies.

The war was fought chiefly in the Canadas. On the Atlantic coast British sea power kept the Maritime provinces secure. In any case their New England neighbours were not disposed to attack, for New England did not support a war that cut off most of its overseas trade. In the Maritimes, therefore, the War of 1812 meant chiefly profitable privateering ventures against American ships, which added to the legends and traditions of a seafaring people; though a New Brunswick Loyalist regiment did make a notable winter march overland through the wilderness to fight in Canada, arriving without losing a man.

The Americans attempted to carry the war into Lower Canada. They made efforts against Montreal in 1813 and 1814, but these expeditions were not powerful enough, nor well led, and they were thrown back at Chateauguay and Lacolle. Instead of concentrating on capturing Montreal, which would have cut Canada in two and certainly have doomed Upper Canada, the United States wasted its forces in invading the outflung western province, slashing away at the branch instead of cutting through the trunk.

Yet the reasons for this concentration on Upper Canada, if not militarily sound, were plain enough. This weakly-held province was closest to the warlike American West. It lay in the path of the American frontier and seemed fated to join the Union. And, particularly in the western half, Upper Canada was full of American sympathizers or, at least, recent American immigrants who were indifferent to British rule. In these dangerous circumstances, Upper Canada largely survived because of undecided American leadership and strong and successful British command at the outset of the war.

Though the American forces ranged against Upper Canada were large in comparison with those of its defenders, the quarrels among the attacking troops and their incompetent generals (until late in the war) were worth at least several regiments of British regulars to Canada. And, on the other hand, in General Isaac Brock the British troops had a commander worth several more regiments. The keen-minded Brock knew well the wavering sympathies of a large part of the people of Upper Canada, and saw that only rapid and resolute action could fix them on the British side.

Working with the fur traders, he struck quickly at the key western post of Michilimackinac and took it by surprise. The American fur-trade West again fell into British hands, the Indians came in on the British side, and the whole American frontier was in danger of Indian attack. The British held Michilimackinac throughout the war, giving the Canadian fur trade a last brief reign over much of the American West that had been lost to it.

Meanwhile the Indian peril raised by the British western victory, and Brock's own bold advance on Detroit, brought the American commander there to surrender his much larger army, with which he had been about to invade Canada. Brock then turned to repel another American invasion at Niagara, and fell in the battle of Queenston Heights which drove off this assault. He had commanded only from June to October of 1812, yet he did much to decide the war. There were no Americans in Canada at the end of the year; the American dream of easy conquest had been shattered.

But far more than that, the British successes under Brock, especially the surrender at Detroit, had really ended the danger of Upper Canada going over to the Americans. The Loyalists, of course, the backbone of the militia, were as always sternly determined not to fall again under American control. Now, however, the open supporters of the United States had been driven out and the indifferent majority in Upper Canada had swung away from the American side because they realized that Upper Canada was not going to fall as easily as had been forecast. Later experiences with American armies on Upper Canadian soil made these people view the United States forces as invaders, not liberators. By the end of the war it would have been hard to tell that the emphatically 'loyal' inhabitants of Upper Canada had not all been so emphatic in the past.

Of course, the war was not over because Upper Canada had become definitely anti-American. Two more years of changing tides of battle followed, years of invasions and repulses. The little capital of York was captured and its parliament buildings burnt in an American raid; but each time the main attacks were halted and the invaders flung back by regulars, militia, and Indians. Late in 1814, reinforced at last, the British began their first major offensives, attacking by sea on the Atlantic coast, south from Montreal and Lake Champlain, and finally at New Orleans. The raids from the sea were successful, and the capitol at Washington was burnt as York's had been; but the attacks on New Orleans and Lake Champlain failed. Apparently the British forces could do no better in someone else's country than the Americans could. Thus the war ended late in 1814 in a stalemate, which was probably a good thing for future peace.

It was not completely a stalemate. Britain still held the West and some of the Maine coast, and the British naval blockade was strangling American commerce. But in the peace negotiations the Americans made clear their readiness to go on fighting rather than yield territory. Faced with a revival of Napoleon's power in Europe at that very moment, Britain did not press the point. As a result the Treaty of Ghent of 1814 simply stopped the fighting, restored the pre-war boundaries, and said little about the problems that had caused the conflict.

Nevertheless in the next few years many of these problems disappeared. The question of the right of search ended with the Napoleonic Wars, and vanished in the long years of peace after 1815. The Indian problem declined as American settlement filled in the old West; the tribes had been too weakened by the war to offer any further resistance. The American war-hawks had found Canada no willing mouthful, and the United States was turning away to expand in a new direction, towards the south.

Moreover, the Rush-Bagot Convention of 1817 and the Convention of 1818 further made for peace on the border between British North America and the United States. The former declared that no more large war vessels should sail the Great Lakes. This agreement was reached mainly to forestall a naval building race. In later years it helped lead to an unfortified frontier, since, without warships, naval bases and forts to defend them could also be dispensed with on the Lakes. But the era of peaceful relations between the United States and Canada is often too readily dated back to this bare beginning. In the twenty years following the Rush-Bagot Convention, Upper Canada's greatest border fortress was built: Fort Henry, at Kingston, preserved to-day with all its heavy masonry and old-fashioned cannon as a memory of the bad old days along the boundary.

The Convention of 1818 sought to settle other outstanding difficulties between the United States and British North America. First, it defined the boundary line more fully, extending it from the Lake of the Woods, beyond the Great Lakes, to the Rocky Mountains along the forty-ninth parallel. From there to the Pacific, the empty land, the so-called 'Oregon country,' was left jointly in the hands of Britain and the United States for a term of years. The border in the far West would thus have to be settled in future; and in the east the Convention did not redefine the old vague line of the St Croix and Appalachians, leaving another problem for later settlement. The Convention, however, did somewhat limit the fishing rights of Americans in British North American waters under the Treaty of 1783.

Thanks to these Conventions, and to the passage of time, British North America by 1820 was on far more solid footing on the continent than it had been before the War of 1812. It had come through the perilous second struggle with the Americans successfully; and had even advanced towards settled, if not yet friendly, relations with the United States. Meanwhile the war had not interrupted the steady growth of the British colonies. The war, indeed, had meant a trade boom in the Maritimes and prosperity for the St Lawrence fur trade. Nor had it done any great damage in Upper Canada. One advantage of a pioneer community is that there is not as much to destroy or to rebuild.

Yet the war had left lasting marks. Pride in the successful

defence against invasion had planted the roots of Canadian national feeling. Both British and French Canada had shared fully in that defence. The French-Canadian militia had turned back the Americans at Chateauguay and Lacolle, as the English-Canadians had at Crysler's Farm and Queenston Heights. French Canada had been active in this war, as it had not been in the American Revolution, largely because the benefits of the Quebec Act, combined with representative government, were now much appreciated. The French realized that they would not enjoy their special rights of law and religion in the American republic. Besides, the French Revolution had destroyed the old Catholic feudal France from which Quebec had sprung. French Canada, as a result, had even favoured Britain in its wars with the revolutionary and irreligious French republic.

The War of 1812 thus tended to bring British North America together and strengthened the bond with Britain. Any common feelings among the colonists, however, were largely directed against the United States. This anti-American spirit was still a narrow basis on which to build a Canadian nationalism. Anti-Americanism was particularly evident in Upper Canada. Further American settlement was largely prevented there, and American settlers already in the province were in danger of persecution—the Loyalists' case in reverse—if their declarations of British sentiments were not loud enough. Nevertheless, on the whole these reactions to the strain of the War of 1812 were understandable; and not an extreme price to pay for the survival of British North America.

5   The Kingdom of the Fur Trade

While the settlements of British North America were slowly forging ahead, and struggling through the War of 1812, far to the west the Canadian fur trade was winning a vast, wild kingdom that stretched to the Arctic and Pacific oceans. This was a realm much larger than the old territory of Rupert's Land around Hudson Bay; it covered the prairies of the north-west, and crossed the Rockies to the Pacific slopes. And the whole domain was subject to the St Lawrence fur trade, ruled from Montreal by the North West Company, the powerful new rival of the Hudson's Bay traders.

The story of this empire of the north-west begins with the arrival of the English-speaking merchants in the old province of Quebec after 1760. These merchants, it will be recalled, had taken over the St Lawrence fur-trading system of New France and made it much stronger, thanks to their higher efficiency and greater resources. To the south-west, they controlled the trade of the region below the Great Lakes, the Ohio and Mississippi country. To the north-west, beyond the Lakes, they reached into the prairies, expanding the trade which the French had begun to develop under La Vérendrye.

In the north-west, of course, the St Lawrence traders came into competition with the Hudson's Bay Company, as the French had before them. But now the men from the St Lawrence could also offer the cheaper and better quality English trade goods, which had been such an advantage of the Bay Company in times past. Because the traders from Canada went directly to the Indians as the French had done, they could cut off much of the fur traffic before it reached the posts on the Bay. Hence the north-west Canadian fur trade flourished, threatening the masters of Rupert's Land as never before.

Yet for some time after 1760 the south-west fur trade, which the French had developed more fully, remained the mainstay of the St Lawrence merchants. When in 1783, however, the Treaty of Versailles ceded the lands south of the Great Lakes to the new American republic, the south-west trade was thrown on the defensive. It was only a matter of time till the United States took effective control of the Ohio and Mississippi and drove the Canadian traders out. Their position was still fairly secure until the British finally gave up the posts south of the Lakes in 1796, in accordance with Jay's Treaty. Even afterwards the St Lawrence interests managed to keep a large part of the south-west trade, and during the war of 1812 largely regained control of their old realm, thanks to the capture of Michilimackinac. Then the Peace of Ghent, destroying the last hopes of the St Lawrence traders, returned this western region to the United States. But the Canadian south-west trade was doomed in any case by the steady advance of American settlement. Settlers always spelt the end of forests and furs.

As the south-west fell away, more and more energy was turned to developing the fur trade of the north-west, where opportunity for expansion seemed almost unlimited. Even before the Treaty of 1783 forecast the end of the south-west trade, English-speaking adventurers from the St Lawrence had passed far beyond the limits reached by the French in the north and west. The French had known Lake Winnipeg, and had found the great Saskatchewan river that flows across the prairies into that lake. But in 1778 Peter Pond, a Yankee merchant come to Canada, had crossed from the Saskatchewan to the Athabaska river, reaching waters than ran northward to the Arctic. Soon Canadian traders were eagerly tapping the trade of the fur-rich Athabaska country.

A young Scotsman, Alexander Mackenzie, took up Pond's work at Lake Athabaska. In 1789 he journeyed 'down north' from there, down the long waterway that now bears his name to its mouth on the Arctic ocean. 'River Disappointment' he called it, because he had hoped that this broad stream would lead through the western mountains to the Pacific, and not to an ice-filled sea. Yet the Mackenzie river to-day is the vital trade route through what may be the last great Canadian frontier.

Mackenzie still hoped to find a way to the Pacific, that would open up the rest of the north-west of the continent to the Canadian fur trade, and would perhaps allow the far-flung western posts to be supplied more easily by sea, by way of the Pacific ocean. In 1793 he turned westward from Lake Athabaska, along the Peace river into the heart of the Rockies, and made his way to the dangerous Fraser that flowed out on the other side. Finding that roaring river too difficult, he left it and went on overland, to reach the Pacific at Bella Coola inlet, only a month before Captain George Vancouver arrived there by sea in the course of charting the north-west coast for the British navy. On a rock beside the ocean Mackenzie painted a sign in vermilion and grease: 'Alexander Mackenzie, from Canada by land, July 22, 1793'. The continent had at last been spanned.

Other Canadian explorers and traders followed. Simon Fraser in 1808 traced the river that Mackenzie had left down to the sea, and gave his name to it. The Fraser valley would be the route of Canadian transcontinental railways in a later age. David Thompson, in 1811, followed another great western river, the Columbia, through the ranges to the ocean further south. He uncovered the whole Columbia water system, and down its length the St Lawrence traders built a chain of posts that brought bountiful returns from this farthest mountain province of the fur trade kingdom. The Canadian traders obtained such a hold on the Columbia, indeed, that when Americans also entered the Columbia region, they could not compete successfully. Thus in 1813 John Jacob Astor, leader of the American Fur Company, sold his post, 'Astoria,' at the mouth of the Columbia to the Canadians, and left the north-west Pacific region, 'the Oregon country,' as part of the great British North American fur preserve.

This rapid conquest of the western half of the continent, this speedy realization of the hope of three centuries, to find the way to the Pacific, was a monument to the daring, skill, and fortitude of the Canadian fur-traders; both the English-speaking leaders and the French-speaking *voyageurs* who manned their canoes. Yet it was also a sign of the constant need of the fur trade to expand in the face of competition; to get behind rivals, and find rich new fur resources that would bear the mounting costs of the ever-lengthening line of transportation back to Montreal. The high cost of

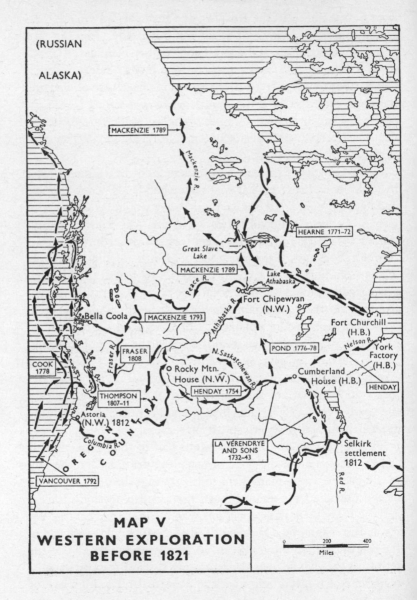

(RUSSIAN

ALASKA)

MACKENZIE 1789

Mackenzie R.

HEARNE 1771–72

Great Slave Lake

MACKENZIE 1789

Peace R.

Lake Athabaska

Fort Chipewyan (N.W.)

Bella Coola

MACKENZIE 1793

Athabaska R.

Fort Churchill (H.B.)

Nelson R.

POND 1776–78

York Factory (H.B.)

Fraser R.

FRASER 1808

N. Saskatchewan R.

Rocky Mtn. House (N.W.)

COOK 1778

HENDAY 1754

Cumberland House (H.B.)

HENDAY

THOMPSON 1807–11

Astoria (N.W.) 1812

Columbia R.

OREGON COUNTRY

LA VÉRENDRYE AND SONS 1732–43

Selkirk settlement 1812

Red R.

VANCOUVER 1792

MAP V
WESTERN EXPLORATION
BEFORE 1821

0   200   400
Miles

transportation had early led the St Lawrence traders to combine in their ventures to the far north-west. In 1787 the various temporary partnerships in Montreal were merged in one large, loose —but permanent—organization, the North West Company. The North West Company took over and controlled the building of the St Lawrence fur-trade kingdom from that time on. Mackenzie, Fraser, Thompson and many other bold adventurers were its agents. The Company constructed a great transport system across the continent, based on the waterways. Heavy supply canoes travelled regularly from Montreal to Fort William at the head of the Great Lakes, where, every summer, the 'wintering partners,' the men who stayed at the western posts, came in their lighter craft to meet the Montreal partners, to bring their furs and receive their supplies for the new season.

The enterprise and efficiency of the Nor' Westers soon aroused the Hudson's Bay Company. As early as 1774, the threat of the traders from Canada reaching behind them to the west led the men of the old Company to break with the long successful policy of staying on the Bay. The first inland Hudson's Bay post, Cumberland House, was founded to turn the trade of the Saskatchewan to the Bay. But then the Nor' Westers jumped beyond, into the Athabaska country. Here a steady struggle for furs went on, as North West and Bay posts were built almost side by side. The Bay still had the advantage of a shorter supply route to salt water. Thus Mackenzie sought the Pacific, to open a sea-supply route for the North West traders. When the Nor' Westers invaded the Peace Country the servants of the Bay again followed, and so the competition went on.

For a time, however, the most violent struggle was that between the North West Company and the 'New North West', or XY Company. This was another Montreal organization, largely made up of traders who had turned from the declining south-west trade. After much ruinous competition, and actual bloodshed, the XY was merged into the North West Company in 1804.

Nor' Westers and Hudson's Bay Company were again the chief foes. It was a contest between the trading systems of the Bay and the River.

The St Lawrence traders had the advantage in timing and enterprise. They moved first, on almost every occasion, getting behind the men of the Bay. Their western agents showed more enterprise, because they were profit-sharing partners, and not company servants on fixed wages. On the other hand, the Bay had the long-run advantage of geography that had defeated the French on the St Lawrence in days before. They could ship their goods from Britain to York Factory on Hudson Bay for the same cost as for goods sent to Quebec. But then the Bay supplies were half-way across the continent, while the Nor' Westers still faced the long canoe haul from Montreal. Indeed, the Nor' Westers had been forced to move first each time, to press on westward, in order to overcome the Bay Company's constant advantage of position. When there was no more west to advance into, when that forward movement meant only ever-rising costs, then the Nor' Westers faced inevitable defeat.

It came finally in 1821. But first there was a brief episode of open war that led quickly to the final collapse of the Canadian fur-trade kingdom. Lord Selkirk, a rich and philanthropic Scottish nobleman, had sought to relieve the suffering of dispossessed Scottish farmers by settling them in British North America. When his efforts to place them in Prince Edward Island and Upper Canada had only limited success, he boldly planned to start a further settlement on the distant north-western prairies, on the Red river that flows into Lake Winnipeg. The Red river country, however, lay within the bounds of Rupert's Land, and so the Hudson's Bay Company held formal title to the land. Of course, this title had not at all stopped the Nor' Westers from building posts there and elsewhere throughout the Rupert's Land claim, as well as far beyond it.

In order to found his colony, Selkirk secured a controlling

interest in the Hudson's Bay Company. He bought it with little trouble, for the Bay Company was also hard hit by the ruinous fur competition and only too glad to sell stock. In 1811 the first Selkirk settlers came out to York Factory. The next year on the fertile prairies they began the little colony of Red river, the ancestor of the present province of Manitoba. At once, however, they had to face the bitter hostility of the Nor' Westers. The Red-river colony lay across the main North West trade routes to the west, and in the heart of the buffalo country where the Company secured the pemmican supplies that were essential for feeding its western posts.

The Nor' Westers could only view the little settlement as a Hudson's Bay attack designed to destroy their transport and provision system; and they knew only too well that settlers were natural enemies of the fur trade. Hence they stirred up the French-speaking half-breeds of the Red river, the Métis, buffalo hunters who supplied the Nor' Westers with pemmican. Métis threats, thefts, and acts of violence against the settlers that were sharply returned, led at last to open battle. In 1816 occurred the so-called massacre of Seven Oaks, on the outskirts of the modern city of Winnipeg, where twenty-one colonists were killed, including their governor, Semple.

Selkirk took strong action to defend his little colony, bringing in some disbanded Swiss soldiers to seize Fort William, the main interior post of the Nor' Westers, from which the attacks on Red river had been directed. His action was too strong in fact. Since it was quite unauthorized, it led to a series of law suits in Canadian and British courts, where each side charged the other with unlawful activities. Meanwhile Selkirk had restored the Red river settlement. Henceforth it grew safely, although slowly, until, long after the fur trade had passed away, a new age of railways and wheat-farming found it lying across the gateway to the prairies. Out of the Red river farms the great city of Winnipeg at last emerged.

Selkirk had lost his health and his fortune in law suits between the North West and Hudson's Bay Companies. He died soon after, while in 1821 the heavy costs to both companies forced them to combine. It was a merger and not a complete victory for the Bay, since North West men and money went into the new combined company. Yet its name was still the Hudson's Bay Company, and, above all, it operated mainly from the Bay and not the river. The Montreal merchants had to find new trades to develop. The fur trade which had done so much to raise the largest city in British North America had left it, and returned to the masters of Rupert's Land. The brilliant but short-lived St Lawrence fur kingdom was no more.

Yet it too had left a lasting mark on British North America. Montreal and the St Lawrence merchants would not decline, but would turn to richer uses the wealth and the trading organization they they had built up under the fur trade. A new colony had meanwhile been born in the prairies, and British rule had been extended to the Pacific, to provide for western colonies of the future. The years of the fur-trade kingdom, in fact, had completed the shaping of British North America from sea to sea.

CHAPTER 9

IMMIGRATION, DEVELOPMENT
AND THE PIONEER AGE, 1815–50

1   *The Migration from Britain*

Following the War of 1812, an age in the movement of people
into British North America came to an end. Since the fall of New
France the main flow of immigrants to Canada had been from the
old thirteen colonies. Whether ardent Loyalists or indifferent republicans, most of the English-speaking settlers in this period had
been North Americans long established on the continent. But
now the American immigration by land largely ceased, and was
replaced by a movement by sea, from Britain, of people new to
North America. They not only greatly increased the population
and speeded the development of British North America; they
added new elements to its society and did much to mark it off
further from the American republic.

The flow of American settlement died away after 1815 for
various reasons. In the Maritimes, of course, American immigration had really ended with the Loyalist influx, and it had never
reached Newfoundland. Nor had it been large in French-speaking
Lower Canada, whether Loyalist or not. But in Upper Canada,
which had received the greatest number of settlers from the
United States, the anti-American spirit after the War of 1812, and
new enactments preventing Americans obtaining land until they
had been residents for seven years, discouraged further migration.
More than this, however, the westward movement of the American
frontier by now had carried it past Upper Canada. The frontiersmen of the United States saw broader fields to conquer in the
opening American Middle West.

Meanwhile new conditions had arisen across the Atlantic that
would provide a stream of immigration far greater than British

145

North America had yet known. Up to 1815, long years of war had kept most of the people of Britain at home. The dangers of war-time emigration and the constant need for man-power during the French Revolutionary and Napoleonic Wars had reduced the movement of British people overseas to a low level. Earlier, the American Revolutionary War, which had also involved fighting between France and Britain, had had the same effect. But after 1815 an era of peace followed in Europe, and a great tide of British emigration set in, to fall away only after 1850.

Hard times as well as peace were responsible for sending people from crowded Britain to empty, fertile fields overseas. The end of the Napoleonic struggle caused sudden depression and serious un-employment. Although times gradually improved, the very speed of industrial change in Britain continued to bring strain and suffer-ing to the poorer classes, and many among them turned their eyes abroad to look for a new life. Others besides the poor also looked to the colonies, attracted by stories of the great opportunities to be found in young lands crying to be developed. Accordingly, between 1815 and 1850, though mainly from 1820 on, British North America received a stream of settlers from Britain that ebbed and flowed but never really stopped. After 1850 the gold rush to Australia did much to turn the ebbing tide to the Pacific colonies, while the onset of mid-Victorian prosperity in Britain about the same time finally brought this first great age of British emigration to Canada to a close. There was far less desire to leave a more contented Victorian Britain, despite the so-called 'Great Depression' of the later nineteenth century.

Changed world conditions by 1900 led to a new flow of British settlers into Canada, but this second British migration was accom-panied by other streams from the United States and continental Europe. Hence it was not so striking nor so all-important as the first British migration of the earlier nineteenth century. During that time, of course, British migrants went to other British colo-nies besides those in America, and, indeed, went to the United

GOVERNOR SIMCOE OPENS UPPER CANADA'S FIRST PARLIAMENT, 1792

THE BATTLE OF CHATEAUGUAY, 1813 — FRENCH-CANADIAN MILITIA AND BRITISH
REGULARS IN ACTION TOGETHER

States in greater numbers than they came to Canada. Yet in the United States they were absorbed into a population that was already large. In Canada they almost swamped the small existing English-speaking communities, especially in Upper Canada. They made the North American colonies more British than they had ever been before. As a result, the significance of this first British migration can hardly be stressed too much in Canadian history.

Between 1815 and 1850 more people came to the British North American colonies from Britain than there had been in all these provinces at the earlier date. Their total population rose from under half a million in 1815 to nearly three million in 1850. In all, nearly 800,000 immigrants came; discharged soldiers and half-pay officers from Wellington's armies, Irish weavers and paupers, Scottish artisans and dispossessed crofters, English country labourers and factory workers. There were numbers of middle- and upper-class emigrants, who often failed in their hopes of becoming gentlemen-farmers in the wilderness, but the urge, indeed, the need, to emigrate was strongest in the lower ranks of society. On the whole those who came proved themselves hardy and self-reliant. Many, however, had scraped together their last funds for passage-money for themselves and family. They arrived almost penniless, to tax the limited resources of the colonies. The Irish famine-immigrants of the late 1840's were perhaps the worst case of this sort. Starvation and disease carried them off in hundreds in the 'emigrant sheds' on their arrival. Yet, if a man were strong, the constant need for labour in a new land gave even the penniless arrival a chance to earn a living, to learn the ways of the country, and to save enough to buy a farm of his own.

Although some of the emigrants received aid from the British government or private charitable societies, most came at their own expense. The more well-to-do travelled in the cabins of regular packet ships, but the poor made the long voyage under sail in the steerage of crowded emigrant vessels. Often they were crammed into the dark holds of timber ships, which thus picked up a cargo of living ballast for the trip back to British North America after having discharged their lumber in Britain. Even the cabin passengers had to carry their own supplies, and, despite regulations against overcrowding, the problem of cooking and eating, sleeping and living, in an airless confined space below decks, with seasick or possibly diseased neighbours close by, sometimes made the voyage in the steerage a nightmare. At least the coming of the steamship shortened the length of the nightmare, but undoubtedly the Atlantic passage helped the British settlement of Canada in a ruthless way by getting rid of the more unfit on the journey.

Of the new arrivals, about 40,000 went to Nova Scotia between the years 1815 and 1838. After this time the last frontiers in the province had been fairly well occupied, and immigration declined. More than half of the immigrants were Scots, who came to form the third group in Nova Scotia, following the Loyalists and the pre-Loyalist New Englanders. Scots went also to Prince Edward Island in considerable numbers. New Brunswick secured well over 60,000 settlers, two-thirds of them Irish, and filled up the fertile St John valley and the Gulf of St Lawrence shore. The crest of the movement to New Brunswick came later, particularly in the 1840's, when the 'famine Irish' arrived. The result was to lessen the staid Loyalist character of this province, as was the case in Nova Scotia, though in both provinces Loyalist groups continued to dominate society. Newfoundland did not share particularly in the great British Atlantic migration, though a trickle of settlers continued to go there. The island was being chiefly populated from Ireland and the west of England.

As for the Canadas, few of the British immigrants settled in Lower Canada except in the Eastern Townships or in Montreal and Quebec, but many passed through on their way to Upper Canada. The broad confines of Upper Canada received the largest flow of settlers. This province grew very rapidly. Rising only after 1820, the flood of British immigrants to Upper Canada reached 12,000 in the year of 1828, 30,000 in 1830, and 66,000 two years later. Outbreaks of cholera, the dreaded scourge of the immigrant, and troubled times in Upper Canada, sent more British settlers elsewhere in the later thirties, but a new peak of immigration was reached in the 1840's. English, Welsh, Lowland and Highland Scots and Catholic and Ulster Irish all shared in the immigration. The English, indeed, had entered into all the provinces, but since they did not settle in blocks as the Scots and Irish did, or retain their national characteristics as long, they are less easy to trace.

In Upper Canada several large group settlements were made. In the western part of the province, above Lake Erie, the Talbot Settlement considerably lessened the American character of the region. Colonel Thomas Talbot, an English backwoods despot, gathered in 30,000 settlers, founded the town of St Thomas, his namesake, and scattered British names in the forest, from the British edge of Lake Erie to the new village of London. On the shores of Lake Huron the Canada Land Company, formed in 1823 with John Galt, the novelist, as its first secretary, sought to settle a million acres. The towns of Guelph and Goderich were founded by the Company and this western Huron Tract began to flourish. Meanwhile the whole shore of Lake Ontario had been filled in and settlement was pushing inland. Settlers were also following in the wake of lumbermen up the Ottawa valley. The population of Upper Canada reached almost 400,000 by 1838 and nearly a million by 1850.

This expansion was not always achieved easily. The immigrant's troubles were by no means over with the trying Atlantic passage, even if he arrived with money enough to buy a farm. Confused policies of granting land in Upper Canada, favouritism among officials, the holding back of crown and clergy reserves from sale, combined with much land speculation, too often made farms either expensive to buy or hard to reach. The hard and lonely life of pioneering placed a heavy burden on people from an old and well-populated land, even if they had not been town-dwellers there. And finally, if their health and spirit were not broken in the dark forest clearings, they might find that the lack of roads and uncertain markets in Britain limited the sale of the grain crops they had raised with so much toil. It is every honour to these immigrants that so many of them survived the grave difficulties and won through to success, developing Upper Canada in the process, and helping to shape its society as they did so.

The influence of the British immigrants could be seen everywhere throughout the society of British North America. The Scottish imprint remained on Nova Scotia, and is still clear to-day, especially on the Gaelic-speaking Highlanders of Cape Breton. The Catholic Irish communities in New Brunswick and in the cities of Quebec and Montreal formed distinct and important elements in the population. In Upper Canada, Protestant Irish outnumbered Catholic Irish nearly three to one, and the Ulster influence in this community was visible in the wide growth of the Ulstermen's Orange Society. Unfortunately it was also seen in mounting religious friction between Catholic and Protestant settlers. The strongly pro-British and anti-American leanings of the Loyalists in Upper Canada were strengthened by the Orangemen's devotion to the British tie; while the anti-Catholic outlook of Ulster came to affect the Upper Canadian view of the French Canadians. In general, the powerful Ulster Irish influence increased the conservative tendencies in Upper Canada that had been brought into being by the Loyalists and by the reaction to the War of 1812. The English influence also tended to work in this direction. English gentlemen who entered the government service or the dominant Church of England brought a decided belief in class distinctions with them and a dislike of 'levelling' democracy. At the same time, the English half-pay officers or small gentry who settled on farms tended to supply what education there was in the backwoods, though a number of doctors, ministers and teachers continued to come to Upper Canada from the United States.

Not all British immigrants in Upper Canada, however, joined conservative ranks. Some brought new liberal or Reform ideas from Britain, or developed democratic feelings in North America. Some were roused by the land muddle to question the ruling powers in the colony. In any case, the entrance of immigrants in large numbers all over British North America nearly everywhere disordered society and raised pressing problems of government. Hence a new age of political change began, a time of growing pains for the expanding colonies. This age of change led finally to self-government for British North America, which, thanks to immigration, was becoming strong enough to manage its own affairs. And during the years up to 1850, while self-government was being achieved, immigration also went hand in hand with general economic development, another important aspect of the new age.

2 *Advances in Transportation*

The commercial development of the British North American colonies after 1815 generally followed lines laid down before the war of 1812. Lumbering and grain-growing remained the chief concerns of the Canadas; lumbering and shipbuilding, shipping and fishing, the principal employments of the Maritimes. The period up to 1850, however, saw great progress made in all these activities. This economic advance resulted both from immigration and from improvements in the means of transport. At the same time commercial prosperity invited more immigration, while improved transportation brought in settlers more easily and carried their goods more readily to market.

One of the greatest improvements in transportation came with the introduction of the steamship. In the long run this triumph of the Industrial Revolution affected the British North American colonies, as it did all the overseas possessions of Britain, by bringing them closer to the centre of empire. The bonds of the sea were knit tighter. The products of rising British industrialism were poured more freely into British North America. In return, the growing factory towns of Britain demanded more lumber for building and more grain for bread from the lands across the ocean. This was indeed a long-run development. The day of the sailing vessel did not finally pass away until the later nineteenth century. Yet the coming of the steamship and the whole age of steam pointed in the direction of continually increasing trade with Britain.

Steamships also came into use on the waterways of British North America. As early as 1809 the steamer *Accommodation* had been launched at Montreal and had successfully plied the St Lawrence between Montreal and Quebec, though sometimes she required the help of oxen pulling on shore to move her upstream against the strong current. By 1816 the first Canadian steamship on the Great Lakes, the *Frontenac*, had made her appearance. By the 1830's steamboats were found on even the smaller lakes and rivers. They were ungainly creatures that belched clouds of black wood smoke through tall thin funnels, and were often built like wooden boxes on rafts. Yet they supplied easy, and sometimes very comfortable transportation by water while much of the land was still almost impassable by road.

Especially in Upper Canada, the roads, to dignify them by that name, were often impassable for anything but a mounted rider or a pedlar's pack horse. Military roads like the Dundas highway west of Toronto, Yonge Street to the north, and the Danforth road to Kingston and Montreal in the east, were at least well surveyed and sometimes roughly bridged. But even they descended at times to deeply rutted paths cut through the all-embracing forest. The practice of building 'corduroy' roads, particularly in swampy sections—formed of logs laid side by side across the track —improved travel while the road was new; but sinking and rotting logs added a new hazard and made for a bumpy journey at best.

Travel by springless stage coaches was, therefore, none too pleasant. It was best in winter, when runners replaced wheels, and the stage glided over a frozen track. The mud of the spring thaw, however, closed down the roads for a considerable length of time. Of course, highways were gradually improved as the years went by, and the worst of the conditions described were found before 1830. Yet, until the building of railways, travel by land remained difficult in British North America. The first railways appeared well before 1850, but they were few, short, and relatively unimportant. The railway era did not begin for Canada until after 1850. It was only then that great interior areas could be opened up.

The period under discussion was thus the age of the waterways. In Upper Canada, the Great Lakes and the river systems draining into them, in Lower Canada, the St Lawrence, still supplied the means of communication, though sailing schooners and steamships had now replaced canoes. Even in the Maritimes, where distances were less and roads often better (though not in rugged Newfoundland) most traffic went by water. The coasting trade around the Gulf of St Lawrence and down the Atlantic shores handled most of the needs of the Maritimes and Newfoundland. A large local merchant marine developed in this region, as it did on the inland waters of British North America.

Because of the importance of water transport, steps were soon taken to improve it. Better types of vessel were developed in the Canadas long before the coming of steam. Bateaux, large open boats, usually driven by poles or sweeps, replaced canoes; Durham boats, still bigger craft that often carried sails, replaced the bateaux. On the open Great Lakes, in particular, quite large sailing vessels appeared. As a military example, the noble line-of-battle ship *St Lawrence*, built at the Royal Naval dockyards at Kingston on Lake Ontario in 1814, was larger than the *Victory*, in which Nelson had died at Trafalgar nine years earlier.

The most important improvement in transport affected the water routes themselves. After 1815 British North America embarked with great enthusiasm on canal-building. Canals had proved highly successful in Britain, where they preceded the railway-building age. They seemed to be having equal success in developing the inland waterways of the United States to their fullest use. In 1825 the most outstanding American canal was completed, the Erie Canal between Lake Erie and the Hudson River, which linked the Great Lakes by water with the Atlantic port of New York. The Erie entered on an enormously profitable career, since it carried much of the traffic of the American West to the ocean at New York City.

In British North America there were canal projects in the Maritimes, but the main efforts were made in the Canadas in an attempt to improve the St Lawrence-Great Lakes system as a great water highway between the West and the sea. The steady flow of traffic along this St Lawrence waterway was broken by the thundering cascade of Niagara Falls, by long stretches of foaming rapids in the upper St Lawrence, and by shallows between Quebec and Montreal which stopped the largest ocean-going craft at the former port. Canal-builders attacked these breaks in easy water communication. In 1825 the first canal was completed around the Lachine rapids, one of several of the 'white water' barriers in the upper St Lawrence. In 1829 the first of eight Welland canals was built to join Lakes Erie and Ontario and avoid Niagara Falls. Three years later the Rideau canal was opened, linking Lake Ontario at Kingston with the Ottawa river. It completely avoided the rapids of the upper St Lawrence, since small vessels could now sail to Lake Ontario from Montreal by going up the Ottawa to the entrance of the Rideau canal.

This, however, was a rather roundabout route. The Rideau canal had really been built by the British government for military purposes, to provide a pathway between Montreal and Upper Canada that would be distant from the United States border. Then in wartime the Americans would not be able to cut off communications along the upper St Lawrence as they had threatened to do in the War of 1812. Yet a better commercial route was necessary if the St Lawrence was to succeed as a great highway between the

West and the sea. High costs and political difficulties held this project back, but at last, by 1848, a chain of canals had been constructed around the St Lawrence rapids. A larger Welland canal had also been completed and the shallows below Montreal deepened.

Before 1850, therefore, ships could sail by the St Lawrence from the sea to the Upper Lakes along channels nine feet in minimum depth. The canals did not achieve all that their creators had hoped for the St Lawrence, and they were not deep enough for later ocean-going vessels. But they did provide a basic line of water transport, which steadily improved and is still vital to modern Canada, even though the age of the all-important waterways has passed away.

3   The Maritime and St Lawrence Trading Systems

While the population of British North America was rising and its means of transport steadily improving, far-reaching empires of trade were being constructed, based on the waterways and the advancing wealth and progress of the provinces. The day of the fur kingdom was over in the eastern half of the continent, but powerful business interests were thriving on exporting the staples of lumber, fish, and grain. In the Maritimes the commercial interests were built on trade by the Atlantic, in the Canadas, on the St Lawrence trade. They came to wield much power even in the political life of the colonies.

Maritime commercial life was not as tightly organized nor as closely focused on one city as that of the Canadas, which largely revolved about Montreal. Nevertheless the shipping interests of Saint John and the lumber kings of the Miramichi were powerful in New Brunswick, as the West Indies merchants of Halifax were in Nova Scotia; while the big commercial houses of St John's in Newfoundland came to dominate the island's fisheries. Most of the goods required by the fishing outports of Newfoundland came by way of St John's, which also gathered in their catch for marketing abroad. The island's fishermen, however, utterly dependent on their one 'crop' of fish, were often desperately poor.

This was the day of 'wood, wind and water' in the Maritimes, and it was close to being their golden age. Until the iron and steel steamship finally drove sail from the oceans of the world, the Maritimes were well equipped by position and resources to prosper in the age of wooden wind-ships. Trade still went by water, not by rail, along the coasts of the continent. Maritime coasters built of the plentiful Maritime timber, were busily occupied. Hundreds of fishing schooners sailed to the banks and carried their catch to the West Indies. New Brunswick shipyards turned out great wooden vessels for the open sea as well; and Nova Scotian 'Bluenose' seamen, sailing far over the globe, developed one of the world's leading merchant fleets. Saint John and Halifax harbours were crowded with ships from the seven seas. The clipper ship, the last and most splendid achievement of the age of sail, was so well fashioned in the Maritimes that some of the noblest American clippers were designed by Bluenose ship-builders who had gone to the United States.

Nor was the steamship ignored by Maritime sea-enterprise. In 1833, the *Royal William*, built at Quebec, had already been the first vessel to cross the Atlantic under steam the entire way, though she had also used sails to assist her. Soon afterwards the British government was considering the possibility of establishing a regular Atlantic steamship service for mails. Sailing ships might take from six to sixteen weeks in passage, if the winds so decreed, but letters could travel quickly and on schedule by steamship. Few men, however, in Europe or America would then risk establishing a steam mail line. Yet the leading business figure in Nova Scotia, a shareholder in the *Royal William*, was prepared to do so. In 1839 Samuel Cunard of Halifax secured a British government mail contract, and the next year the first Cunarder 'steamship on schedule' crossed the Atlantic. The huge Cunard Queen ships of to-day can trace their ancestry back to Maritime provinces of British North America.

In the interior provinces the one great trade route of the St Lawrence gave a single direction to commercial enterprise that was lacking in the Maritimes. As it had done since the time of the French fur trade, the St Lawrence route opened the way to the centre of the continent and carried inland commerce to the sea. Though furs had departed from it, the St Lawrence system flourished on forwarding grain and lumber to Europe and transporting British manufactures to the spreading farms of Upper Canada. Yet the powerful mercantile interests of Montreal, that had grown up with the fur trade, felt that handling the commerce of the Canadas was not enough. Once the St Lawrence traders had commanded most of the traffic of the American West besides, directing the flow of furs towards Montreal from south of the Great Lakes as well as from the north-west. Now that American settlements were reaching into the prairies, why should the St Lawrence not control their trade, carrying their farm products to European markets and supplying their wants?

The St Lawrence route still had its natural advantages, on which the Montreal merchants counted heavily. It supplied a direct water route behind the Appalachians from the Atlantic to the prairies. From points on the Great Lakes the rich American carrying-trade could be linked to Montreal and Quebec, which lay closer to Europe than the seaports of the United States. There were only a few breaks in the system of easy water communication. Thus it was that canal-building was so important to those merchants who shared the vision of a St Lawrence commercial empire ruling the whole interior of North America, Canadian and American alike.

Yet the grand St Lawrence dream achieved only partial success. American trade routes penetrated the Appalachian barrier and offered increasing competition. They tied much of the western carrying-trade to Atlantic ports in the United States. In particular, the Erie canal, that led to New York City, diverted a great deal of the traffic from the St Lawrence river outlets. Here once again was the old rivalry of the St Lawrence and Hudson valleys for the western trade, a rivalry that had begun with Champlain at Quebec and the Dutch at Albany. The 'Erie ditch', completed in the same year as the first St Lawrence canal, the Lachine, tapped the Great Lakes and carried traffic in a southerly direction to a port larger than Montreal and one that was ice-free all the year round. New York defeated the Canadian city. The difference in the present size of the populations of these two chief metropolitan centres of the United States and Canada seems to suggest the margin of victory: New York, eight million, Montreal, one million.

Nevertheless, the St Lawrence trading system still controlled the lands north of the Great Lakes and did not yield the commerce of the American West without a struggle. The final outcome was not clear in the years before 1850. After the building of the Erie canal the men of the St Lawrence countered with their thorough-going canal improvements, only completed in 1848. The construction of railways in the United States, however, overcame these canals; whereupon, after 1850, the main St Lawrence trading interests increasingly turned from waterways to railways, in an attempt to win the American western carrying trade through this new means of transport.

Hence the St Lawrence trading system did not abandon its vision of empire, although as well as American competition it had to face problems within its 'home' provinces of the Canadas. The farmers of Upper Canada were not always ready to pay tribute to a St Lawrence empire if they could import goods at a lower cost via New York and the Erie canal, or send crops to market more cheaply that way. The division of Upper and Lower Canada put the St Lawrence route under two governments and sometimes disputes over commercial policies and customs duties hampered the flow of trade. The St Lawrence was one economic unit, but politically it was cut in two. Finally, quarrels arose within Lower Canada between the English-speaking merchant group and the French Canadian majority, which opposed the great power of the trading interests and objected to their expensive plans for developing the St Lawrence.

All in all, however, the St Lawrence system proved that it did have strength by continuing to grow in the face of these disadvantages. It served still to bind Upper and Lower Canada together in mutual dependence. It brought wealth and development beyond what the Maritimes knew. New York may have defeated Montreal; but Montreal and its trading network remain to-day one of the largest commercial systems in the world. The traffic of the American West was not held in the long run, but the Canadas continued to pour their rising wealth into the St Lawrence. And, in a later day, that vast north-west that had been lost to the Hudson Bay fur traders would return to the St Lawrence commercial system, once railways, settlement, and grain-farming had opened it to civilization.

4   *The Pioneer Age*

Up to 1850, this growing, changing British North America was still in the pioneer age. Though conditions of life naturally varied a good deal between the sea coasts and the Great Lakes, the colonies at this time were, on the whole, in the stage of pioneer development, the first carving of civilized communities out of the raw North American forests. Lower Canada, where the French-speaking community had gone through its pioneering stage in the days of New France, seems the obvious exception to this statement. Since the end of the French regime there had been little change in the placid farming existence of the habitants in Lower Canada. Even here, however, English-speaking immigrants in the Eastern Townships and French Canadian farmers advancing inland from the long-cultivated banks of the St Lawrence provided a pioneer fringe. And in the Maritimes, though the areas of frontier settlement were smaller, there was still much pioneering to be done up to 1850. As for Newfoundland, in the lonely out-posts scattered along the coasts the inhabitants lived constantly under stern frontier conditions.

Yet Upper Canada was the chief centre of pioneer life, and the home of the largest farming frontier. It was only after 1850 that the last good wild lands were taken up in the fertile Upper Cana-dian peninsula between the Great Lakes. Until then, though towns on the Lakes were growing into busy commercial centres, and the farmlands of the 'Front' were taking on an old settled look, there was always a broad belt of back-country, a region of bush farms and lonely log cabins, where the frontiersmen were steadily cutting back the margin of the forests.

The life of the pioneer farm was hard and even brutal. There was no time for learning or social graces; the refinements that settlers might bring with them from a more civilized background soon tended to drop away. It is unwise to be too romantic about the simple charms of the crude shanties and the ignorant, hard-drinking and over-worked population who lived in them. But such a life had its merits as well. If it was lonely, then neighbours some miles apart by forest trail were the more valuable to one another. They combined against the weight of the wilderness in 'bees' to clear each other's land, or to raise the barns and hewn-log cabins that replaced the first rough shanties. If there was ignorance, there was also a desire to bring schooling to all, and not to a privileged few. If pioneer life could mean drab monotony and a bitter struggle to succeed, it also brought freedom, a sense of self-sufficient strength and the constant hope of a steadily im-proving future. Year after year, as the fields spread out, as frame or brick houses replaced cabins, and the forest gave way to a bountiful countryside, that hope seemed to be justified.

Apart from the mass of the pioneer population, the pedlar, the teacher, and the preacher were the notable figures of the frontier. The first brought the scant luxuries to be purchased in the backwoods or the few necessities not provided by the pioneer farm, whether clocks or shawls, salt or tea, or knives and iron pots. The second was usually a frontier-dweller too infirm or incapable to farm for himself: perhaps a disabled soldier, or an old seaman in the Maritimes. Men like these, who turned their little cabin into a school and often taught in return for food and firewood, obviously made poor teachers. They knew little more than their pupils and sought to fill in the gaps with frequent use of the rod. Yet from this small beginning popular education was born on the Canadian frontier, and from it rose a demand for a general system of public schooling.

The preacher was a most important figure on the frontier. His regular visits supplied almost the only release from the monotonous toiling round of daily life, and so it is small wonder that religious services among the pioneers were emotional in the extreme. The services held in the little log churches built for travelling ministers, or in great 'camp meetings' under the trees were religious revivals, popular holidays, and exciting public festivals all rolled in one. As a result, the more formal and restrained Church of England, which claimed religious control in the principal English-speaking colonies, was not widely popular on the frontier. Indeed, its clergy tended to stay among the officials and well-to-do merchants in the towns and left the back-country to Presbyterian, Methodist and Baptist ministers. The Methodist 'circuit-riders', in particular, who were often from the United States, built up the power of Methodism among the pioneers of British North America.

The widespread growth of churches in the colonies was also a sign of the beginnings of culture. Catholicism, of course, was firmly based in Lower Canada, but it came with the Irish and Highland Scots to Upper Canada and the Maritimes as well. In Nova Scotia, Presbyterianism early established a strong foothold, and rose with the growing Scottish population in that province. In Upper Canada the narrow but powerful mind of Archdeacon

John Strachan did much to advance the Church of England and to found higher education in the colony. Higher education, in fact, was closely connected with the churches. Thus in Nova Scotia in 1802, the Church of England foundation of King's College (now part of Dalhousie University) became the first university to be chartered in British North America. In 1827 the earnest Strachan secured a charter for a King's College in Upper Canada, which later grew into the University of Toronto. The University of New Brunswick came into being in 1829, and McGill University in Montreal, Lower Canada, arose out of the bequest of a rich North West Company trader, James McGill in 1821. Other institutions founded by religious bodies before 1850 included Queen's University (Presbyterian) and Victoria University (Methodist) in Upper Canada, and Acadia University (Baptist) in Nova Scotia.

Meanwhile education was advancing on lower levels. In the 1840's a province-wide system of government-controlled primary education was set in operation in Upper Canada, and the first public secondary schools were similarly established in the 1850's. Egerton Ryerson, Methodist minister, newspaper editor, political reformer and superintendent of education, was the true founder of this school system. In the other provinces as well, the state provided for public primary education. These 'common' schools were not generally under the control of the churches, except among the French-speaking people of Lower Canada, where the Catholic Church continued to manage the many tasks of education as it had in the time of New France. In Newfoundland, however, control of the school system was divided between the leading churches, Anglican, Methodist, and Catholic.

With increasing education went also an increasing interest in books and newspapers. As well, no doubt, the gradually passing of the hardest stages of pioneering produced a people with more time to read and to discuss public questions. British North America was becoming strongly politically minded. Hence little newspapers sprang up on every hand to recount the doings of the colonies' governments; some to cry out against abuses and to urge reforms. These journals were symbols of growing cultural maturity, though for a long time to come they were almost the only literature produced in the British North American provinces. Only in Nova Scotia, where traditions of culture had deeper roots, thanks to the educated Loyalists who had gone to that colony, were there the beginnings of a real native literature before 1850. Here Judge Thomas Haliburton, son of a Loyalist, produced his humorous chronicle of *Sam Slick the Clockmaker*, which won much fame in Britain and the United States as well as in Canada.

Before 1850, therefore, while the frontier stage was at its height in eastern Canada, not only were the colonies being solidly populated and their commercial life developed, but these pioneer communities were also laying the foundations for a culture of their own. Out of the pioneer age there came a growing self-conscious spirit, impatient of outside direction, that turned itself towards the goal of self-government for British North America.

CHAPTER 10

THE DEMAND FOR REFORM, 1815-37

1 *The Problem of Colonial Government*

By the 1830's the expanding colonies of British North America were outgrowing the forms of government laid down for them at the close of the American Revolution. Their inhabitants were less content to be ruled from above by small minority groups, backed by the imperial government in London. Grievances grew, reform movements developed. In the two Canadas, indeed, reform moved on into armed rebellion. Yet this too was a sign of advancing maturity, for it expressed the impatient desire of some of the colonists to gain control of their own affairs. The provinces were growing up.

In this somewhat painful process, the colonists were chiefly concerned with the local provincial authorities. There was not the same clash of interests of colony and mother-country that had marked the American Revolution. The old opposition to imperial controls over trade did not appear again; the northern provinces were flourishing within the British colonial system, thanks to the Navigation Acts that fostered their shipping, and the imperial preferences on their grain and timber. The comparative weakness of these colonies, their Loyalism and anti-Americanism, and the powerful influence of recent British immigrants in their midst, also kept them turned towards Britain. Hence the unrest in British North America did not really produce a movement to break from the empire. This was by no means a second American Revolution.

Nevertheless the imperial government was linked with the mounting discontent in the provinces, less because of what it did, than what it did not do. To be sure, the British government did not seek to rule these colonies with a strong hand or even to interfere actively in their affairs. Indeed, it often neglected them and paid only passing attention to their grievances. Their problems were tucked away in the Colonial Office, which, though it contained able and devoted civil servants, was a small and secondary department of the British government, and was given scant attention by the leading political figures of the time.

This lack of interest in colonial affairs was largely a result of Britain's rise to the industrial leadership of the world during the first half of the nineteenth century. Now that every country was eager to buy the products of British factories, the small protected colonial markets seemed of little value. When the whole world could serve as Britain's trading empire, colonies appeared to be only unnecessary burdens, costly to manage and defend. In any case, it was argued, they would separate from Britain when they grew up, just as the former American provinces had done.

This dark view of empire was of sufficient influence in British political circles to create an attitude of indifference to colonies. The Old Colonial System continued to operate, almost as a matter of habit, but its mercantilist restrictions were gradually cut down after 1820. At the same time, while the imperial government did not actually seek to set the colonies free ('adrift' would be a better word), it practically assumed that separation would come in time. As a result, small attempt was made to frame new constructive colonial policies, and Britain was largely content to keep things as they were in the realms of colonial government.

Keeping things as they were, however, meant supporting a political system in British North America which was becoming increasingly unpopular. Under that system, which was generally the same in all the colonies except Newfoundland, a British governor responsible to the Colonial Office ruled over each province with the assistance of an appointed council, or councils, while an assembly elected by the inhabitants passed laws and levied taxes. In the Maritime provinces the same body of officials sat either as the executive council, which advised the governor and carried on the daily work of government, or as the legislative council, which discussed and revised laws passed by the legislative assembly. In Upper and Lower Canada, of course, the Constitutional Act of 1791 had created separate executive and legislative councils, but here too their membership largely overlapped.

The assemblies that represented the people of the colonies did not fully control either law-making or public finances. Some of the main sources of government revenue, for example, were not under their control. Their laws could be revised in council, vetoed by the governor, or set aside by him for the consideration of the imperial authorities. Government was not at all responsible to the assemblies that voiced the opinions of the colonists. The real power lay in the hands of the council members and their connections, a small minority in each province.

True, the governor was the head of the government, but he was a visitor for a short term of years, while many of the officials were appointed for life and were leading colonial citizens who knew their country well. The governor usually saw his province through their eyes—they were the truly loyal and British element, they assured him—and their 'advice' generally settled the policies of government. Hence the principal officials formed powerful ruling groups or oligarchies, managing affairs, filling offices, and overriding the wishes of the popular assemblies as they saw fit. The chief business men and the higher clergy of the Church of England, which held a commanding position in most of the colonies, were allied with the oligarchies. The principal judges and the appointed justices of the peace in the countryside were also closely connected. The members of the oligarchies usually came from a fairly small number of well-to-do and long established families, often of Loyalist origin. Hence the use of the term 'family compact' to describe them.

The compacts were not necessarily corrupt or incapable in the government that they gave the British North American colonies. Many of their members were able, cultured, public-spirited citizens, who believed sincerely in the duty of the upper classes to rule, and distrusted the wisdom of the 'mob', as they would call the people. Yet the people of the advancing colonies, becoming conscious of their own power, and generally living a life of equality in the wide, free countryside, objected more and more to this rule by their 'betters'. Influenced by American democracy and by the rising British reform movement, they began to seek a larger share for themselves in the affairs of government.

In each province there were particular grievances felt by the colonists which were expressed in their elected assemblies. But, thanks to the British policy after the American Revolution that had feared too much popular power, these assemblies were weak in the face of the solidly planted oligarchies. Little could be achieved in the way of reform until the oligarchies had been dislodged. The various grievances all came back to the problem of government.

Consequently, the Reform movements that arose in the different provinces began to demand changes in the political system. Reformers were elected to the assemblies to make the most of the limited powers of those bodies, or to arouse such public feeling that the imperial authorities would be moved to step in and make changes. A large part of the population, however, sided with the oligarchies, fearing that the Reform challenges to established authority would lead to disloyalty, and were dangerously radical and 'republican' in their aims. And the sweeping language of some earnest radicals in Reform ranks lent at least a little colour to this view. Accordingly, since those supporting the compacts could appeal to the powerful British and Loyalist sentiments among the colonists, strong Tory parties, as well as vigorous Reform movements, sprang up. The two sides fought strenuously in the provincial assemblies and at the elections.

Despite the weighty local questions in each province, the core of the problem was still the power of oligarchy in government. But if that power were broken, and government were tied instead to the will of the colonists, what then? Each province would become master of its own internal affairs, the British governor would become largely a figurehead, no longer the effective instrument of the Colonial Office. The imperial government, in short, would lose much of its final control over the colonies. This was the rub; and here the problem of colonial government brought Britain in again, and led the authorities in London to oppose the reform of the political system in British America.

British statesmen believed that colonies could not be colonies and govern themselves; that is, manage their own internal affairs. And while Britain granted minor concessions in all goodwill, they could not really touch the heart of the matter, the need to do away with oligarchic government. Moreover, British leaders were often still inclined to distrust popular power in the colonies as unruly and disloyal. It was unruly; but it was not disloyal. What most Reformers wanted were British forms of parliamentary government under British rule.

In the last resort, the imperial government usually tended to decide in favour of existing authority when pleas were carried to it from both sides in the colonies. Hence oligarchy was supported and unrest continued to grow unchecked in British North America, although British officials sought honestly and sincerely to rule in the provinces' interests. At last the shock of actual rebellions jarred Britain out of indifference and led to a full investigation of the troubles in the colonies. Imperial policies were finally revised, and a large measure of self-government was granted to the British American provinces: a landmark in the development of the British empire and the modern Commonwealth. But for many years there was no solution to the basic problem of colonial government that lay beneath the troubles in British North America.

2 Reform and Rebellion in Upper Canada

Nowhere was the problem of oligarchic government more apparent than in Upper Canada. There the power of the group with the definite title of the 'Family Compact' had created numerous

causes of discontent. And if the Compact was not always responsible for grievances that were really beyond its control, its commanding position made it easy to blame. One good example in
this regard is the land question. During the eighteen-twenties
and -thirties, although settlement rapidly advanced in Upper
Canada because of British immigration, it still did not reach the
rate of progress attained across the border in the mid-western
United States, nor did Upper Canada enjoy the same soaring
heights of prosperity during good times. Some of the immigrants
to Canada, in fact, kept moving on and went out of Upper
Canada into the western states. Upper Canadians bewailed this
drain, and contrasted the 'stagnation' of the colony with the
bustle across the border. In reality, stagnation was not at all a
true description, and the greater advance in the United States
could be explained by the ever-constant fact that the American
community was far larger and much richer, and that there were
almost endless areas of fertile soil to be brought under the plough
in the American prairies.

Yet it was easier to blame land policy in Upper Canada for lag-
ging development and emigration to the United States, and to
seize on the harmful power of the Compact and its allies as the
cause of the trouble. Undoubtedly, land policy under the Compact did make for trouble. Crown or public lands were readily
granted to wealthy speculators but went far less easily to actual
farmers. Friends of the Compact held vast areas of empty land,
keeping the prices up and blocking regular and easy settlement.
Roads that opened the settlers' way to markets were slow to be
built, though the Compact officials were ready enough to spend
public money on canals that aided their merchant allies in the
towns. And there was evidence of extravagance and corruption as
well as favouritism in land-granting and canal-building. But the
core of the land question lay in the clergy reserves.

The clergy reserves, large tracts of wilderness, were the product
of the Constitutional Act which had resulted in one-seventh of the

lands in Upper Canada being set aside for the support of a Protestant clergy. The Anglican church, as the established church in England, had claimed that it was also the official church in Canada, and its ministers the Protestant clergy named in the Act. Thanks largely to its alliance with the Compact, this claim had been made good, so that the Church of England received the income from the rent or sale of the clergy reserves. Other Protestant churches contested this position; and the established Presbyterian Church of Scotland in time was also granted a lesser share of the reserves endowment. But meanwhile the clergy reserves stood as two-hundred acre lots of waste land scattered over the province, breaking the front of advancing settlement, cutting farmers off from their neighbours and blocking the building of roads. Gradually they were sold, but at high prices. The reserves were really a nuisance more than a serious burden; yet they added fuel to the grievances over the difficulties of getting farms, the privileges of the Church of England, and the power of the oligarchy that lay behind the whole land question.

The discontent over the clergy reserves was, of course, closely related to religious unrest over the favoured role of the Anglican church, which again was maintained by the oligarchy. While there was freedom of worship in all the colonies, and while the Anglicans were a large group in Upper Canada, they were nevertheless outnumbered by other Protestant sects which had no special privileges. It was far easier, for example, to maintain a state church in England where the large majority were Anglicans than in Upper Canada, where the Methodists were the largest sect. Archdeacon Strachan, however, the leader of the Church of England in the colony and a member of the Compact, insisted on Anglican dominance, and sought to extend it also over education. As president of the provincial Board of Education he tried to keep the school system an Anglican preserve and in securing the charter for a provincial university, King's College, in 1827, intended to make this an Anglican foundation.

The Methodists, accordingly, began a campaign against religious privilege led by one of their ablest ministers, Egerton Ryerson. In 1829 he became editor of the *Christian Guardian*, the voice of the new movement. The Methodists founded a college of their own, which grew into Victoria University, while Ryerson carried his campaign to the Colonial Office. He was able to see the right to celebrate marriage extended to the Methodists. Meanwhile other sects, and even some Low Church Anglicans, rallied to the cause of religious equality. They and the Methodists naturally joined with the rising forces of Reform in politics. By 1826 the Reformers were urging the secularization of the clergy reserves, that is, that they be sold and the proceeds be devoted to public education.

Other factors were also increasing dissatisfaction with Compact rule. The frontier farmers, often in debt, mistrusted the banks and businessmen of the towns. They blamed some of their woes on too close a connection between the merchants and bankers and the Compact. When the Bank of Upper Canada was founded in 1821 with the government holding a quarter interest, the farmers were sure that this was only creating a powerful machine that would plunge them deeper into debt. Bad times, in particular, increased this grievance. The western farming frontier, always a restless area, tended to support the Reform movement against the Tories centred in the towns and the older settled regions.

Furthermore, when serious criticism began after the War of 1812—by which time the province had advanced too far to accept rule from above without question—the oligarchy showed that it meant to repress popular protests sternly, and even harshly. A Scotsman, Robert Gourlay, was arrested and expelled from Upper Canada in 1819 because he began to arouse the pioneer farmers against the Compact's land policy. Soon afterwards, Marshall Spring Bidwell, who tried to carry criticism to the floor of the assembly, was expelled from that body on the grounds that he was the son of an American, an alien, and not eligible to sit there.

This assertion affected the rights of a large body of settlers of American origin, and as a result a movement began in the assembly to pass a law protecting these settlers. The Compact delayed its passage until 1828, but meanwhile a Reform party had begun to take shape in the assembly in 1824.

In that same year, however, William Lyon Mackenzie, a fiery little Scottish immigrant, had founded a newspaper to support the Reform cause. Thanks to his ability as a journalist, he quickly became the chief public figure on that side. Mackenzie was none too sure of what he wanted to put in the Compact's place, but he showed skill and courage in exposing its abuses. His telling but violent attacks, indeed, so angered the friends of the oligarchy that in 1826 a mob of Tories, led by sons of prominent Compact members, threw the presses of his *Colonial Advocate* into the waters of Toronto Bay. But this only made Mackenzie a Reform hero. In 1828 he was elected to the assembly which for the first time had a Reform majority.

The next few years saw a ding-dong battle between the fairly well balanced forces of Reform and Toryism. Yet the power of the councils and the weakness of the assembly kept the Reformers from achieving very much; while their failure to do so, and the widespread Loyalist and Orange feelings in the province, strengthened the Tories anew after every defeat. Violence flared at elections. Mackenzie was elected and expelled four times in a row from the assembly, and he grew increasingly extreme in his views. His growing radicalism was surely understandable, but it divided him from the more moderate sort of Reformers led by Bidwell and a quiet young man, Robert Baldwin. In 1833, moreover, Egerton Ryerson broke with Mackenzie and soon carried the strong Methodist wing over to the Tory camp.

Ryerson, the son of a Loyalist, had never been at all radical in politics, and the Methodists had been chiefly concerned with religious problems, not with the basic political changes that Mackenzie was starting to advocate. Mackenzie was now urging an elective legislative council, somewhat after the American republican model; that is, he wanted membership in this body, which was the chief check on the popular assembly, to be made subject to election. Thus an irresponsible oligarchy could not control the council, for it would be chosen by the votes of the people. Yet many other Reformers besides the Methodists did not want to go as far as adopting an American form of elective government. Men like Robert Baldwin, for instance, preferred the British plan of responsible government. That is to say, government would be made responsible to the assembly, and would stand or fall by the votes of this body. The calm, shrewd leader of the moderate Reformers and his practical plan would be heard of again.

Mackenzie and the radical Reformers moved on into strong language and sweeping remedies. In 1835 they issued the resounding 'Seventh Report on Grievances' in the assembly; but they were still blocked by the councils from achieving any of their cures. The following year a new and inept lieutenant-governor, Sir Francis Bond Head, was appointed to Upper Canada—by mistake, it is said. In the stormy elections of that year Head virtually made himself a candidate and loudly proclaimed that the issue was one of loyalty or republicanism. This appeal to the British tie, and against American influences, resulted in a Tory election triumph. Head had won his victory; but he had practically driven Mackenzie and the radicals to rebellion. They saw that reforms, apparently, could not be achieved by peaceful processes, and they knew now that the Colonial Office had declared itself against self-government in the colonies. And, exasperated by Head, they were ready to take up the role of disloyalty that he had cast them for.

The next year was one of severe hard times, and in the late autumn of 1837 rebellion broke out in Lower Canada. With unrest at its peak, the time seemed ripe for the Upper Canadian radicals to act together with those in Lower Canada. Early in December, Mackenzie and his followers gathered at Montgomery's Tavern, a few miles north of Toronto, planning to seize the capital and overthrow the government, for Head had sent his regular troops to aid in Lower Canada. But the whole plan was badly conceived and feebly carried out. Mackenzie was not a military leader. The date of the attack was changed; risings planned in the west of the province had not begun when the Toronto affair was over. Several hundred ill-armed rebels milled in confusion about Montgomery's, while alarm bells rang in the city and loyal volunteers gathered there. On a brisk December day in a field near Montgomery's, now a busy street-corner in the city of Toronto, the loyal militia scattered the rebel farmers in a twenty-minute skirmish. Mackenzie fled to the United States. The Upper Canada rebellion of 1837 had failed.

There were still border raids to contend with, for in the United States Mackenzie raised American sympathizers to fight for his cause. These raids went on during 1838, and at times, indeed, it seemed that Upper Canada was engaged in another War of 1812, since the American attacks cost far more fighting than had the rebellion at home. Yet the United States government did not favour these raiding ventures, and by 1839 the border had been restored to order. The rebel cause had been hopelessly lost. In truth, it had been hopeless from beginning to end. The rebellion had no definite purpose. Rebels sought variously to win terms from Britain, to gain independence, or to join the United States. The rebellion had been weakly supported. Only the radical wing of the Reformers had approved of it, and few of these radicals had actually been willing to fight.

In fact, the most obvious fact about the rebellion is how strong and immediate the resistance to it was. Loyal militia kept pouring into Toronto from outlying farming regions long after the fighting was over, or scoured the countryside trying to find any trace of rebels. The eastern and more populous half of the province was firmly loyal, and the western proved not as restive as expected. In general, the Upper Canadian colonists, and most Reformers, made clear they had no desire to take to violence or to break the British tie in seeking any changes. Yet the rising did much to awaken Britain to the necessity of change. In this way, then, the hopeless rebellion of the muddled, embittered, yet somehow heroic Mackenzie won success out of its very failure.

3 Racial Strife and Rebellion in Lower Canada

In Lower Canada the unrest over oligarchic government was greatly complicated by quarrels between the French- and English-speaking inhabitants of the province. In many ways, in fact, oligarchy was only the problem on the surface. Behind it lay the deeper and more lasting problem of the relations of the two peoples of different language, viewpoints, and interests. In general, the governing compact in Lower Canada was tied to the English-speaking minority, while the large French Canadian majority, thanks to their numbers, easily controlled the elected assembly. In this colony, therefore, the political conflict between the privileged oligarchy and the popular assembly reflected a racial conflict between English and French.

Nevertheless, as in Upper Canada, the grievances of the assembly and of the mass of the people centred about the power of the oligarchy. Grievances could only be remedied if that power were weakened. Thus the existing system of government, the same as in Upper Canada, came under fire, and a Reform movement developed. The causes of battle might have been different, but the battle-ground was the same. Here again, in short, the problem of government was all-important. The French-speaking majority necessarily came up against it in opposing the policies of the English-speaking elements who had the ruling compact on their side.

The racial split between the defenders of oligarchy and the champions of the assembly and reform was not complete. On the side of the compact, known as the Château Clique in Lower Canada (the governor's residence was the Château St Louis), were some French Canadians who held official posts or looked for government favour. On the side of the assembly, a group of English-speaking Reformers made common cause against compact rule with the main French-Canadian body. Still, the dividing line put most of the English-speaking community, and, above all, the commercial interests of the St Lawrence, on the Tory or government side, while the French-Canadian habitants, parish clergy, and professional men favoured the Reform ranks. The Tories in Lower Canada, indeed, referred to themselves as the 'British' party.

This racial division ran back to the Constitutional Act of 1791, and beyond. When that Act granted representative government to the two new provinces of Upper and Lower Canada, the French Canadians were quick to realize the value of an assembly, although they had not known one earlier in their history. In the overwhelmingly French province of Lower Canada they forged the assembly into an instrument for defending or advancing the special interests of French Canada. The people of the St Lawrence had not forgotten their heritage from New France. The Quebec Act, indeed, had already safeguarded much of that heritage, and by its special treatment had made the French more conscious of their separate position. The Constitutional Act enabled the French Canadians to make that position still stronger. Using the assembly, they set out to gain a secure place for themselves as a distinct community with its own language, laws, religion and customs. There was little desire to break with the British empire. Indeed, it was the British grants of privileges for their laws, church and seigneurial system in the Quebec Act, and the British grant of representative government in the Act of 1791 which made this whole campaign possible. Nevertheless, French-Canadian nationalism was being born in British North America.

As a result, after 1791 the English-speaking merchants of Lower Canada and the British governors found themselves brought together in the fact of rising French-Canadian nationalism. The governor could no longer work easily with the not-so-'docile'

French; the English commercial class found that they could only protect their interests against a hostile French majority by entrenching themselves in the oligarchy. They heartily protested their British loyalty, and the governors forgot their earlier suspicions of these once-democratic tradesmen, who at least were not foreign in their views and aims. The democratic tradesmen, in fact, rising in the world, had grown with the St Lawrence commerce to be merchant princes and true-blue Tories. Along with some of the Loyalists in Lower Canada, the leading merchants— the old foes of Sir Guy Carleton—filled the councils and the official positions in the province, forming the Château Clique.

Trouble between the French and English groups in Lower Canada might have arisen in any case because they lived largely different lives, each with its own outlook and aims that clashed one with the other. The French were still a farming people, dwelling in a stable society built on the firm authority of the Catholic Church and the seigneurial system. The English moved in the restless world of commerce, always ready to challenge and change. With the fall of the St Lawrence fur empire in 1821 the partnership of the two peoples in the fur trade, never an equal one, came to an end. As the English began building a greater commercial empire of the St Lawrence, the French held aloof. Even before, they had distrusted the English money-mindedness and desire for change, and had resented being made almost the lower class of Lower Canada. They were naturally suspicious, as well, of any threat to French culture or the use of the French language; that is, of any attempt to anglicize their people. At the same time they feared for their cherished peaceful rural society, should the unsettling power of commerce become too great: a fear still felt in French Canada to-day.

The English, on the other hand, deemed the French backward and hostile to progress largely because their standards of life were different. They could not see why the French opposed their plans for developing the St Lawrence trading system, although the French argued that its development benefited only the English merchants. On the whole, however, the French disliked being kept from the rewards of business although they condemned the business way of life. They set out in the assembly to tax and control commerce. They objected to granting public money for canal-building, so necessary to improve the St Lawrence. One of the great hindrances to the St Lawrence interests, therefore, in their competition with American routes for the western trade lay in the Lower Canadian assembly. It is understandable that the English business elements should thus rely on the overriding powers of the oligarchy in order to gain their ends.

In consequence, the political quarrels grew as the assembly sought both to advance French power in government and to defend French society by restraining English commercial development. Although the French Canadians in politics called themselves Reformers it should be remembered that in many ways they were very conservative. In commercial matters, at any rate, the 'British party' stood for change and growth. The French certainly wanted political reform, but they wanted it in order to break the hold of the English-speaking minority, so that their old way of life could be maintained. The French Reformers really sought self-government in order to preserve the old world of New France in a fast-altering British North America.

The racial division brought political clashes in Lower Canada long before they became significant in Upper Canada. Before the War of 1812 the assembly had launched attempts to fix the costs of government on commerce, while the merchants wanted them met through a tax on land. Sir James Craig, governor from 1807 to 1811, sided with the merchants and took strong steps to bring the assembly to order. The war, however, brought English and French together against a common American enemy. But afterwards the conflict began again, and on a growing scale.

The same factors of racial antagonism, concern for special

FUR-TRADE TRAFFIC AT FORT EDMONTON ON THE
SASKATCHEWAN, 1825

THE OPENING OF THE FIRST WELLAND CANAL, 1829

French rights, and quarrels over the St Lawrence commerce continued to bring clashes and discontent in Lower Canada. The disputes, however, turned increasingly on the question of the assembly's right to control public finances. As has been noted, the colonies of the Second Empire in America did not have command of a large part of their government revenues. But after the Napoleonic Wars the imperial authorities, really in the interest of simplifying and decreasing their colonial burdens, sought to transfer to the provincial assemblies the full control of local revenues in return for a fixed civil list, or a permanent sum set aside to pay the salaries of government officials. This bargain was made fairly easily in the Maritime provinces and was finally concluded after considerable dispute in Upper Canada in 1831. In Lower Canada it was warmly opposed by the assembly because a permanent civil list would make the English-speaking officials in the oligarchy even more independent of French control.

Instead, under the leadership of its new Speaker, Louis Joseph Papineau, the Lower Canadian assembly sought to take over all public revenue without conditions. The purpose, of course, was to make the government wholly dependent on the assembly for funds and to gain a complete control of commercial policy. The tall, courtly Papineau, elected Speaker in 1815, was an effective leader in this effort. He well understood the practices of English parliamentary government and he was a powerful parliamentary orator. He was also affected by the democratic and anti-clerical ideas of the French Revolution. Yet he was the champion of an old seigneurial and Catholic French-Canadian society. Papineau became a seigneur himself. He used his liberal and even radical political ideas to serve a conservative French nationalism.

In its budget of 1819 the assembly led by Papineau went so far as to reduce the salaries of some unpopular officials in an attempt to assert authority over the government. Thereupon the legislative council threw out the whole budget. The financial quarrels dragged on; and in 1827, when the assembly refused to vote a budget, the governor dissolved it. The British parliament now moved to investigate the political troubles of Lower Canada, and its Canada Committee recommended some limited concessions. When these were refused by the assembly, the imperial government in 1831 even handed over most of the revenues without conditions. But by this time the long dispute, with harsh language and strong actions on both sides, together with other clashes on racial issues, had raised tempers too high to permit an easy settlement. Papineau had now gone beyond demanding financial powers equal to the British House of Commons. He was seeking an elected legislative council on American lines, just as the radicals under Mackenzie were urging in Upper Canada.

In fact, in 1834, the Lower Canadian assembly produced a document, rather like Mackenzie's Seventh Report, that rang with admiration for American forms of government and with veiled threats on the possibility of repeating the American Revolution in Lower Canada. This document, the Ninety-Two Resolutions of Grievances, marked the turning towards revolt for Papineau and his more extreme followers. They really had no close affection for American ways, but they, too, intended somehow to throw off the English yoke.

The result, as in Upper Canada, was that the moderate Reformers took alarm. Although some English-speaking radicals led by Wolfred Nelson stayed with Papineau, the main body under John Neilson, who wanted change only on British parliamentary lines, broke with the French leader. So did the French-speaking moderates, who feared that the growing Americanism of the extreme group would end in French Canada being swallowed up in the United States. Finally, the Catholic Church, aroused by the anti-clerical utterances of Papineau and the radicals, made clear its opposition to any use of force. This was a telling blow to the radical cause in Catholic French Canada.

In consequence, the rebellion in Lower Canada, when it came, was almost as feeble as in Upper Canada. From 1832 to 1836 the eastern assembly and council had continued in a stalemate over finances. Then in 1837 the British parliament issued its Ten Resolutions, declaring that the colonies could have neither self-government nor an elective legislative council, and permitting the government in Lower Canada to use local revenues without the assembly's authority. The Reformers were outraged. Papineau talked of revolution.

He had even fewer plans for it than Mackenzie in Upper Canada, but his violent words inflamed his radical supporters. They organized the Sons of Liberty, in imitation of the earlier American revolutionaries. In reaction, English-speaking Lower Canadians organized semi-military bodies. In the tension of the times, and with racial suspicion and anger at their height, a riot soon broke out between the two organizations in Montreal, a largely French-Canadian city but also the capital of the English commercial interests and one-third English-speaking in population. To avoid more trouble Papineau and his chief lieutenants left the city; but nervous officials, fearing they had gone to raise a rebellion in the French-Canadian countryside, ordered their arrest. This order became a signal for actual rebellion.

Papineau fled to the United States, while a leaderless resistance broke out in several villages. On 23 November 1837, the *Patriotes* of St Denis, plain farmers like the rebels of Upper Canada, repelled a detachment of troops who were seeking Papineau and other leaders. More troops, however, defeated a rebel group at St Charles two days later. Another gathering of 500 *Patriotes* at St Eustache was shattered in December, and the rebellion was really over. It had occurred only in the district around Montreal, where racial antagonisms were most in evidence. Even here, lack of leadership, weak support, the presence of regular troops, and, above all, the opposition of the Church, had made the rebellion hopeless. No doubt far more habitants sympathized with the rebel cause in Lower Canada than had settlers in Upper Canada; but long habits of obedience to authority in church and state, and doubts about Papineau's American and anti-religious leanings, made their weight felt.

Thus the reform movement in Lower Canada had also apparently ended only in bloodshed and defeat. Yet this rising, too, affected Britain. In fact, by its greater bloodshed it aroused Britain more than that in Upper Canada. In consequence, a new era of reform and self-government was shortly ushered in. And this finally gave French Canada the broad political liberty and the national security that it had vainly sought in racial strife and rebellion.

4 Peaceful Reform in the Maritimes

During the period up to 1837 reform movements were both less active and less violent in the sea-coast colonies than in the Canadas. The high tide of reform in the Maritimes came later. When it came, however, it was far more orderly than in the Canadas, and in the beginnings of reform the eastern movements were similarly peaceful. Therefore, while it is of some interest to observe reform progress up to 1837 in the Atlantic provinces, it is more important to explain the absence of violence and rebellion there, in both these years and the years that followed, even though the Maritimes faced the same basic problem of oligarchic government.

Two great sources of angry feelings in the Canadas were lacking in the Maritime provinces. There was neither the racial division of French and English nor the heated appeal to Loyalism as found in Upper Canada. The first point is clear, but the second needs expanding. In Upper Canada there was still the half-healed scar left by the War of 1812. It could easily be inflamed by raising an anti-American cry and damning Reformers as Yankee republicans. In this province, moreover, the Loyalists had at first been a small group in a largely American settlement. They cherished their Loyalism fiercely and became a privileged element glorying in their devotion to the British tie.

Yet while the Maritimes were no less loyal, loyalty was not

really an issue there. The War of 1812 had been felt far less, and though there was little love for the United States there was not the same suspicion of American influence. Moreover, since the Loyalists had largely swamped the original New England character of the Maritimes, a Loyalist background on the Atlantic coast was not the special mark of a privileged Tory governing class but was found as fully among the Reformers. The red herring, as it largely was, of loyalty could not be drawn as readily across political conflicts in the Atlantic provinces, to rouse Tories to patriotic passion or to embitter Reformers and finally drive some of them to actual disloyalty.

Other factors also made for more peaceful political changes in the Maritimes than in the Canadas. They were smaller, more closely knit and more mature communities, in which popular movements could be effectively organized and directed into parliamentary activities. There were not the same local cross-currents, nor was the yeasty ferment of the frontier as strong within them. In general, too, Maritime Reformers had more success in gaining the ear of the Colonial Office: precisely because they could not be so readily condemned by their foes as disloyal French or 'Yankeeloving' republicans. Finally, many of the worst grievances of the Canadas were absent in the Maritime provinces. There was no great struggle over canals and commerce, over clergy reserves and Anglican dominance, nor were the oligarchies as high-handed in governing. Although the Anglican Church stood in a close relation to these oligarchies, its privileges weighed less heavily. In Nova Scotia it voluntarily gave up the possibility of clergy reserves in order to avoid breeding discontent.

Because of this general state of affairs there was less unrest in the Maritimes. Hence the Reform movements developed later and did not go to extremes. In Prince Edward Island, the chief grievance was the land question. The ownership of the land of the province by landlords living in England seemed especially grievous when it kept wild lands out of settlement. The provincial assembly sought to have these lands revert to the Crown. The assembly's case, however, was the weaker because its purpose was largely to gain the lands for local speculators, and some of the government officials joined it in this effort. The local oligarchy, in fact, was not really the foe of the assembly on the land question: the absentee landlords were. The council and assembly joined in a long memorial to Britain in 1838. Hence, despite constant agitation, the land problem of Prince Edward Island was not closely related to the problem of oligarchy, and rather distracted the reform movement there from an attempt to seek more self-government.

Land, apparently, was a major issue also in New Brunswick, but here the land in question was crown lands, and these were under heavy forest. In short, crown lands in New Brunswick chiefly meant timber preserves in that lumbering and ship-building province. The assembly sought to gain control of the crown lands and in so doing clashed with the governing oligarchy. This, however, was largely a clash of rival timber interests: the favoured friends of officialdom *versus* the powerful timber barons who dominated the house of assembly. In 'the Loyalist province' there were as yet few ideas separating the official, or Tory, party from the opposition in the assembly.

The New Brunswick political contest took shape as in Lower Canada over the question of the assembly's right to control public revenues, but with very different results. The income from timber duties on crown lands, or from their sale, was the chief revenue that the New Brunswick assembly sought to control. And what it wanted, in essence, was control over the thickly-wooded crown lands themselves. There were several delegations to the Colonial Office from the assembly. Seven of the list of eight grievances which the mission of 1833 took with them concerned crown lands and timber. Receiving a ready hearing, the delegations were able to win concessions. Finally, in 1837, after some opposition from the governor and officials, that arose despite the expressed will of the Colonial Office, control of the crown lands and public revenues generally were transferred to the assembly in return for a permanent civil list. Some members of the 'popular party' were also appointed to the executive council. With this New Brunswick was satisfied. It was, indeed, the most tranquil province in British North America in the year of revolt, 1837. Its reform goal had been largely a practical one, the imperial authorities had listened sympathetically, and with the rich plum of the crown lands in its hands there seemed no need for any further change in the existing political system.

There was no one outstanding grievance in Nova Scotia such as this crown-lands question; but on the other hand the reform movement attacked the general problem of oligarchic control, and sought to make government responsible to the assembly. This province, in fact, supplied the best example of a straightforward political contest to establish the colonists' will in public affairs, without major complications of a racial, religious, or economic kind. Led by the bluff but brilliant Joseph Howe, Reform in Nova Scotia by 1837 had set out on a clear-cut and orderly advance towards self-government: and this while the Canadas floundered in misdirected rebellion, and the New Brunswick assembly rejected the very thought of a government responsible to the representatives of the people.

The compact that ruled Nova Scotia dominated its economic as well as its political life, containing as it did the leading provincial bankers and merchants as well as the chief judges and the Anglican bishop, who virtually controlled education. Yet it was more able and more liberal in outlook than the oligarchies in the Canadas. This again made political life less bitter in Nova Scotia. Men like Joseph Howe, however, the editor of the *Novascotian* since 1828, opposed the compact's thorough-going, if gentlemanly control. The son of a Loyalist, Howe had a constant vision of a united British empire—but an empire united through freedom. He attacked government imposed from above on Nova Scotia, and distrusted 'the caprice of men in office'. The oligarchy thereupon tried to crush him and his newspaper by taking him to court for libel in 1835. Howe's skilful and courageous speeches in his own defence instead won him the suit, made him a popular figure, and carried him to the assembly in 1836. He soon rose there to be the leader of the gathering forces of reform.

Under his leadership Reformers turned from planning an elective legislative council to overcome the compact, and concentrated on a demand for the separation of the executive and legislative councils in Nova Scotia. Already achieved in New Brunswick, this would divide and considerably weaken the oligarchy. Furthermore, Howe and the Reformers also sought to tie the executive council to the assembly. Their efforts bore fruit, for in 1837 the Colonial Office ordered the separation of the two councils and also instructed that four members of the executive council should henceforth be chosen from the assembly. The rebellions in the Canadas for the moment checked the hope of any further advance towards self-government, but the path for Howe and Nova Scotia was clearly marked ahead.

Newfoundland, during much of this period, was really at an earlier stage of development. The rule of the island by naval admirals only ended in 1825, when the first civil governor was appointed. But this very act showed that at last Newfoundland had been recognized in Britain as a true colony, not a fishing base. It would not be long before representative government would also be established, placing the island under much the same political system as the rest of the British North American colonies.

Although the new civil governor, Sir Thomas Cochrane, a hard-driving, constructive ruler, well pleased the islanders, they began to demand regular British institutions for their rising population. Accordingly, in 1832 an assembly was granted. It was to share the work of law-making with a small legislative council. The first assembly met in 1833, but almost immediately there began the typical quarrels between council and assembly over the control of finances. They led, indeed, to violence at elections and appeals to the Colonial Office in 1837. Yet despite further years of political storms, Newfoundland gradually learned to make its new system work, and went on to seek more self-government. Even in this colony, therefore, both the oldest as a British possession and the youngest in political development, the problems of government in British North America led to a demand for responsible control of its own affairs.

CHAPTER II

SELF-GOVERNMENT WITHIN THE EMPIRE, 1837–50

1 *The Meaning of Responsible Government*

Reform movements and rebellions in British North America had made clear the necessity for solving the problem of government in the colonies. The bold and successful solution that began to emerge was responsible government. Through it the grievances of oligarchic rule were overcome, yet the British empire remained intact. The Canadian provinces were set on the path to nationhood; the Second Empire began its transformation into the modern Commonwealth: all thanks to the application of the principle of responsible government.

What was this principle that was first applied to the Canadian colonies of Britain and to a large extent took shape there? It was nothing more than the extension of the British cabinet system to the realm of colonial government. Under that system, the ministry or cabinet which governed the country was responsible as a body to parliament. It could rule only as long as it had the support of a majority in the House of Commons. Failure to keep that support—'loss of confidence'—required the cabinet to resign so that a new government could be formed with sufficient parliamentary backing. In practice, of course, this meant that the party which won a majority of parliamentary seats at elections formed the government. The party's leaders in parliament became the cabinet ministers, and the chief among them the prime minister.

Applied in the colonies, this system would make the colonial executive council a true cabinet, responsible as a unit to the representatives of the people. The oligarchic legislative council would be by-passed; the governor would become simply a constitutional ruler, like the king in Britain, taking as his ministers only those with the confidence of the elected assembly and accepting their policies of government. The leaders of the majority in the assembly would actually rule. In sum, under the responsible or cabinet system the colonies would govern themselves.

THE MEANING OF RESPONSIBLE GOVERNMENT

I. THE OLD COLONIAL SYSTEM

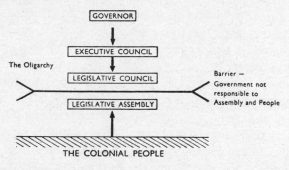

II. THE RESPONSIBLE SYSTEM

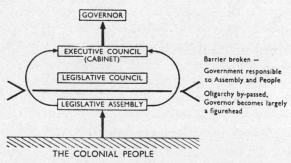

All this could be achieved without revolution, without changes in the existing structure of government, without introducing an elective system or destroying the governor's position as the link with imperial Britain. The colonists could obtain self-government without breaking with the empire, as the American provinces had had to do in an age before the responsible system had been clearly developed in Britain itself. And, in a later age, the colonies of the Second Empire in America could gain the benefit of a more advanced kind of government. For, despite many qualifications, the fact remains that the cabinet system has some advantage over the American congressional type of government. By linking the legislature (the law-making body) and the executive (the governing authority) together, the cabinet system permits greater flexibility and prevents friction between the two. At the least, the cabinet ministers under the responsible system sit as members of the legislature, where they are constantly available to supply information and enter debate, while under the congressional system the ministers (department heads) are appointed separately by the president and seem on occasion to be regarded as suspect outsiders by a congress with whom they are not as closely connected.

The realization that responsible government would meet the needs of the colonies, yet preserve the empire, came only slowly in Britain. For one thing, the workings of cabinet government were not fully recognized in that country in the late eighteen-twenties, at which time an Upper Canadian colonist, Robert Baldwin, saw that the extension of the responsible system might be the answer to the political problems of British North America. Baldwin was no radical. He wanted only the full British constitutional practice, and his very aim was to preserve the imperial bond. In 1828 his father, Dr William Baldwin, had sent a letter to the existing British government on this subject, but it received little attention at that early stage. Robert Baldwin tried again, in 1836. He visited the Colonial Office personally to propose responsible government as a means of removing the threat of radicalism in Upper Canada. He still had no success. Meanwhile Joseph Howe in Nova Scotia, another deep admirer of the British constitution, was also developing the principle of cabinet rule as the goal of his reform activities.

Yet in Britain as well there was, by this time, a rising group of men interested in the colonial problem. A prominent statesman and an ally of this group of Colonial Reformers, John Lambton, Earl of Durham, would himself propose responsible government as a broad, constructive imperial policy. Responsible government might not have been won in British America without the work of Baldwin and Howe, and it is probable that they had a clearer understanding of its operation there than Durham or his friends. Yet it is equally true that without the mighty voice of Durham and the efforts of the Colonial Reformers at the heart of the empire, Baldwin's ideals might never have been embodied in a grand new imperial design: one that produced an empire held together by freedom not force, bound by 'ties though light as air, as strong as links of iron'.

The Colonial Reformers somewhat tempered the prevailing British indifference to empire. Though few in numbers they were able and vigorous in proclaiming the value of colonies and the need for a systematic reform of the whole colonial system. They were chiefly active in politics in the eighteen-thirties and -forties, in the same period when Reform parties in British America were striving towards self-government. Here was a happy coincidence, indeed.

Colonies were particularly valuable, the Colonial Reformers declared, as spacious homes for the overcrowded British people. They encouraged organized emigration movements. They sought to develop new Britains overseas, under free British institutions, to grow as partners of the parent land. Granting the colonies self-government, they said, would not mean their incvitable separation from the empire but would bind them with ties of gratitude and interest. On the other hand, witholding the full rights of British subjects abroad would drive them to separate. Because of these views the Colonial Reformers attacked the irresponsible regime in the colonies. They blamed the overriding authority of the Colonial Office for much of the discontent in America. If the empire were to be held, it could only be held through generosity and a free spirit, not through a tight and interfering control. It was in this very spirit that Lord Durham came to British North America, after the rebellions of 1837, to inquire into the troubles there.

2 The Durham Report

When the news of the outbreaks in the Canadas reached Britain the weak government of the day, that of Lord Melbourne, had been dangerously shaken. The Colonial Secretary, Glenelg, had undoubtedly done his best to settle the colonial discontents; but given the existing system and view of empire, it had not been enough. Accordingly, in order to stave off some of the certain criticism, Melbourne appointed the Earl of Durham as governor-general of all British North America, charged with both calming the provinces and reporting the causes of their grievances. It was a clever move. 'Radical Jack' Durham was one of the most advanced liberals of the time and the idol of the Colonial Reformers. His appointment early in 1838 also took out of the kingdom a sharp-tongued critic of the government and a statesman, it was said, who might some day replace Melbourne as prime minister.

Durham was a strange mixture of ardent democratic ideals and proud aristocratic behaviour. A believer in freedom who ruled with absolute authority, he had inevitably a short and stormy career as governor-general. He was only in British North America for five months, and resigned his post in hot anger because the home government declared that he had exceeded his already sweeping powers. He stayed long enough, however, to gather with his capable assistants a mass of valuable information on the Canadian problem. This he issued in his famous Report of 1839, produced on his return to England. The Report set forth his recommendations for solving the problem in such a clear, constructive, and compelling way, with meaning for the whole empire, that this great document may well be regarded as the foundation-stone of the modern Commonwealth of Nations.

Durham died not long after, a victim of tuberculosis. Yet, though he never became prime minister, who should say that his short and feverishly active life had not reached fulfilment?

Durham brought with him to Canada the leading Colonial Reformers, Edward Gibbon Wakefield and Charles Buller, both of whom left their stamp on the structure of the empire around the globe. Without doubt, they did much to shape the Report. Yet it was the powerful figure of Durham behind the Report which gave it the weight and influence that otherwise it might not have had. He put the seal of a first-ranking imperial statesman upon it.

On arriving in Canada Durham found the real danger of rebellion past. There was a brief new skirmish in Lower Canada later in 1838, and during that year groups of 'Patriots', mainly American volunteers, raided the borders of Upper Canada. The Lower Canadian rising, another small, ill-conceived local outburst, was quickly suppressed, while Upper Canadian militia repulsed the American attacks; though one of them, indeed, at the 'Battle of the Windmill' on the upper St Lawrence, resulted in as many British casualties as the battle of Queenston Heights in the War of 1812. In Lower Canada representative government had been suspended, and Durham was authorized to rule there through a special council, which thus, in drastic fashion, removed the voice of the French majority in the assembly from politics. In Upper Canada the existing constitution was not suspended, but the Tory party was in the saddle, hunting hard for treason, and crying 'rebel' after even moderate Reformers. Nevertheless, on comparing the limited extent of the punishments meted out in Upper Canada under the Tories to the suppression of many another rebellion, and considering the actual warlike threat on the borders, some of the legend of Tory violence at this time seems rather overdone.

In any case Durham moved quickly to establish an imperial policy of generosity. Charges were dropped against all those accused of rebellion except for Papineau, Mackenzie and a few leaders who had fled the country, who could not return except on pain of death. Eight convicted rebels were exiled to Bermuda. Because that colony was not under Durham's control it was this act which exceeded his authority and caused his early resignation. But even after resigning he stayed on in British America to complete his tasks. Hence he saw that order within the Canadas was effectively restored, although French Canada, while not rebellious, was silenced rather than satisfied under government by a special council.

Order on the frontiers between Canada and the United States was also gradually re-established, to some extent because of Durham's wise dealings with Americans on the border. He had none of the then widespread British scorn for United States democracy. He was almost the first British statesman to win a good opinion from the Americans. The United States government and its military commanders on the border also worked to prevent American Patriot invasions and to put down the secret 'Hunters' Lodges' whose activities came close to banditry. It took several years, however, to solve various frontier problems. For instance, there was also a disturbance at this time on the border to the east, where New Brunswick and Maine lumbermen disputed the boundary line between them in a private struggle sometimes called the 'Pork and Beans War'. The eastern boundary between the United States and British America had been only vaguely drawn north of the St Croix river at the end of the American Revolution. At length in 1842, the Webster-Ashburton Treaty fixed the line, while each side claimed that its agents had given away too much— which was probably a sign of a moderate compromise. The Treaty also disposed of other points at issue, and closed the period of strain between British America and the United States that had begun in 1837. New border problems were soon to arise in the far west of the continent, to be dealt with in the Oregon Treaty of 1846, but its discussion properly belongs in another place.

Meanwhile, besides settling the immediate trouble in the Canadas, Durham had been investigating its roots, hearing complaints and suggestions from all sides, including a memorandum from Robert Baldwin on responsible government, soon to be reflected in the Report. When the Report was issued in 1839 it proved full of keen insight into the grievances of the Canadas, which was amazing, considering Durham's short stay. It also touched on the Maritimes, Durham having received delegates from there while at Quebec.

The Report condemned in ringing words the evils of oligarchic rule, the abuses in land-granting, and the narrow privileges of Anglicanism. It saw clearly what few British authorities then realized, that the struggle in Lower Canada turned on the racial conflict of French and English. It dealt with immigration, public lands, education, canal-building, local government, justice, finance —an astounding range. It offered a mine of information and a wealth of suggestions on material improvements in British America. But the main recommendations of the Report, those of greatest consequence, were three: the granting of responsible government, the division of imperial and local affairs, and the uniting of the two provinces of Upper and Lower Canada.

In advocating responsible government the Report did not make clear whether Durham meant the complete cabinet system as Baldwin understood it; that is, with the governor merely accepting policies of government put forward by a set of ministers who were backed by a majority in the assembly. Instead the Report rather suggests that the governor should still frame the government policies, although he should choose only men with majority support in the assembly as ministers to carry them out. But in any case Durham's main purpose was to do away with irresponsible government, and to tie it to the assembly where sat the representatives of the colonists. The colonies were indeed to be granted control of their own affairs. He stressed that the Canadians could be trusted with this grant. Giving them their freedom would only strengthen their loyalty. It was in sounding this note of bold confidence that the Report was at its best.

On the question of how imperial unity could be maintained in the face of colonial self-government, the Report noted that there were actually few imperial interests involved in the ordinary day-to-day governing of colonial affairs. Instead, imperial interference in matters of local concern had really threatened the unity of the empire far more by making the British government a party in every local squabble. Consequently local and imperial affairs could well be separated. The former could be left to colonial self-government, and the latter, covering only a few subjects, reserved for British control. The reserved subjects were: changes in the constitutions of the colonies, regulation of trade and foreign relations and the management of their public lands. In actual fact these imperial reserved powers were in time gradually taken over by the colonies, as they expanded their field of self-government from the purely local concerns that Durham had meant for them. Control of public lands was in Canadian hands from the first. Yet the Report's very division of imperial and local powers made it seem possible to grant colonies responsible government without endangering the empire. On this basis, and in its own day, this recommendation of Durham was very important, indeed.

The union of the Canadas was not as fortunate a suggestion, though Durham meant it to go hand-in-hand with the grant of responsible government in the two provinces. Union, in fact, was to be the answer to racial conflict in Lower Canada. It was to swamp the French, to make it safe to grant self-government without its falling under the control of French Canadian nationalism. Durham approved of the French demand to govern themselves, but did not approve of the desire to maintain a distinctive French Canadian community which lay behind their demand. While he liked the rural French Canadians, this son of progressive, industrial Britain considered them uneducated and backward in their thinking, a people doomed to fall by the wayside in the march of progress. Hence their out-of-date nationalism had to be overcome. Responsible government had to be granted in a way that would absorb the French, not strengthen them in their separateness. The old policy of assimilation was to be tried again.

A union of the Canadas, combining the English-speaking fraction in Lower Canada with the wholly English-speaking population of Upper Canada would leave the French in a minority in the united province. In this way responsible government would lie in English hands and would be operated on English terms, which the French would have to accept. Durham in no way considered this an unjust arrangement. Believing in the power and superiority of British civilization and government, he thought that the French in this union would be led gradually and naturally to give up their separate ways, until, without their religious faith at all being threatened, they could be peacefully absorbed into a wholly British Canada. This process, moreover, would not only end the racial conflict in politics but would permit necessary economic progress. In an English-dominated union the French could no longer hold up the development of the St Lawrence route and the rise of Canadian commerce. The unity of the great river valley would be restored.

It was a well-meaning and rosy dream, but it is understandable that French Canada did not view Durham's Report with a friendly eye, despite his support for self-government. In fact, on the whole, the Report at first made far more enemies than friends. Besides the French Canadians, the English-speaking Tories of Upper and Lower Canada were angered by Durham's onslaught on 'loyal' Compact rule; and while those of Lower Canada liked the idea of union, they objected to its price, responsible government, which would destroy the power of the English Tory minority. Only the Upper Canadian Reformers, now led by Baldwin, welcomed the Report.

In Britain the prevalent belief that, Durham or no, imperial unity could not be maintained along with colonial self-government led to a cool reception for the Report. Yet it was too great to be put by. Reformers in the colonies made Durham's recommendation of responsible government their goal. His impressive outline of a new imperial system began to work on the mind of Britain. Within ten years much of what Lord Durham had recommended had been accomplished in British North America, and a new age was beginning for the whole British empire.

3   The Union of the Canadas

One main point which the British Government did accept from Durham's Report was the project of Canadian union. In a desire to settle the racial problem by swamping the French, an imperial Act of Union was passed in 1840. In 1841, therefore, the United Province of Canada came into being. It had the same structure of government as the two Canadas: a governor and executive council, an appointed legislative council, and an elected assembly. But the union was not really complete because both old provinces were given equal numbers of representatives in the new united assembly. This was done because at the time the population of the mainly French-speaking Lower Canada was still considerably larger than that of Upper Canada. Giving Upper Canada as many representatives as Lower was an attempt to ensure a definite English-speaking majority in parliament from the start. Yet such a plan destroyed Durham's very idea of a complete blending of the two peoples. It kept alive two distinct sections in the politics of the union: Canada West and Canada East, which were often popularly called by their old names of Upper and Lower Canada. Equal representation only fastened sectional division on the new union and fostered the French feeling of separateness in Canada East. In consequence, if the project of union had ever had any chance of absorbing the French Canadians, as it was applied, it had none.

Nevertheless, the union of the Canadas did allow French and English-speaking Reformers to form a common political front to

seek the responsible government that Durham had dangled before
their eyes. This alliance grew only slowly. But in Canada West
the lively mind of Francis Hincks, Baldwin's chief lieutenant, soon
realized how powerful a united Reform front might be. In Canada
East, Louis Lafontaine, the new moderate leader of the French
Reformers, came to see that if the French Canadians were already
in the union they might at least make the best of it and seek
responsible government there, for this could still give them a share
in controlling their destinies. In fact, to the French responsible
government came largely to mean overthrowing English Tory control in Canada East. Clearly, in the French section the small
English-speaking Tory group could not reign supreme if responsible government were once established. French-Canadian nationalism, newly aroused by Durham's very scorn for it, began gradually to concentrate on gaining responsible government. Yet this
nationalism was more moderate in its aim and methods than in the
hot radical days of Papineau. It could work very well with the
Baldwin Reformers of English-speaking Canada West.

Before the vital Reform alliance developed, however, a new and
capable governor-general had come to Canada. This was Charles
Poulett Thompson, soon named Lord Sydenham. Sydenham had
come out in 1839, even before the union, with his first task to win
acceptance for that scheme from the two Canadas. A first-rate
administrator and a skilled diplomat, he quickly won over the
Upper Canadian assembly. Lower Canada, still under the special
council, could raise no objection in any case. The plan of union
went through, and Sydenham became first governor-general of
the united province. Thereupon he undertook two other tasks: to
develop the prosperity of the province and to make Canada content with less than responsible government. In both he largely
succeeded.

The fact was that the British Government with the best will in
the world, still could not swallow Durham's first great recommendation. Colonies simply could not rule themselves and be

colonies. The government sought earnestly to content Canada without yielding on this apparently basic point. A large loan for public works, practical reforms under Sydenham, the notable Lord John Russell in the Colonial Office, all this showed Britain's desire to please. Russell even sent instructions in 1839 which allowed colonial governors to change the members of their executive council as they saw fit. This was to overcome the tendency to make ministers life appointees, to free the governor's hands, and to break up the unpopular oligarchies in the council. As a result the old compacts at last lost most of their power, and Sydenham proceeded to change his ministers fairly readily, even bringing in Baldwin for a time, in an attempt to keep good relations between the governor and the elected assembly. And his strong and constructive policies of developing the country did win the warm support of a fair-sized middle group, a group that might better be called Conservative than Tory, the older, narrow term.

Now this was still not responsible government as Baldwin saw it; but nevertheless it was a long step forward. That is to say, the governor was at least trying to choose ministers acceptable to the assembly. He was doing so at his own will. He was still shaping government policy. In his very efforts, however to prevent an outburst over responsible government he was increasingly tying the ministry to the assembly. In his own opinion, Sydenham was succeeding very well in staving off responsible government, when a riding accident in 1841 caused his sudden death. But he had really been acting as his own prime minister in order to keep control over the assembly. A less skilful politician, with less money to spend for practical improvements, might find that Sydenham had simply built up an impossible position for the governor from which retreat was the only way out.

4 *Achieving Responsible Government in Canada*

The next governor of the United Province, Sir Charles Bagot, had to face the true difficulty: how to maintain a steady majority behind the governor in the assembly, to which government had now been closely tied. The growth of formal party lines meant that Sydenham's tactful ability to attach assembly leaders to himself would no longer have worked so successfully. The Tories, who, of course, had opposed responsible government, would readily back the governor; but they were a minority in the whole union. Baldwin's Reformers were declaring that responsible government was already half granted and should be completed, and the French under Lafontaine had formed a large block that was the real balance weight in politics. Bagot saw that to carry on government he must have French support. Accordingly, he took French leaders into his executive council, which rather upset both the Tories and the British government. But by now the Reform alliance had begun to work. The French leader, Lafontaine, successfully insisted on Baldwin's also entering the ministry. Thus a Reform group came to sit in the government, although this was not yet a solid one-party cabinet and the governor still dominated it.

In 1843, however, Bagot retired because of illness. His successor, Sir Charles Metcalfe, a strong-minded veteran of thirty-seven years' government service in India, was determined to yield no further. When Baldwin and Hincks sought the right of a responsible ministry to approve all official appointments, Metcalfe refused. The ministry resigned. An election followed in which the governor's supporters accused Baldwin and his friends of a greedy and disloyal desire for every last trace of power. Though the charge of disloyalty was unfounded, especially against Baldwin, a moderate but sincere imperialist, popular feeling was sufficiently affected by what seemed the excessive Reform demands to return a bare majority favourable to Metcalfe. Excited Reformers did not help their cause, moreover, by railing against the governor as 'Charles the Simple', or 'Old Square Toes'. At any rate a new government, that might loosely be called Conservative, was formed, and it held office for the next three years, facing increasing difficulties, while popular sentiment began to swing back to the Reformers.

But in the meantime a revolution in Britain sharply altered the whole confused political situation. This was the peaceful but profound revolution that brought free trade to Britain and her empire. Beginning in 1846 with the repeal of the Corn Laws, it finished by removing all the old mercantilist restrictions on the freedom of trade in the British empire. By 1849, the Old Colonial System had been ended. The colonies were free to trade as they wished. This was a vitally important step; important because in time past it had been argued that colonies could not be given self-government since the imperial authorities had to be able to control them in the interests of the colonial trading system. But now that the Old Colonial System was being abandoned, now that trade was freed and the colonies' economic life was not to be controlled, there seemed little reason to control their political life either. The colonies could have self-government. Moreover, in the free trade ministry that came to power in Britain, Lord Grey was the new Colonial Secretary, and he shared some of the ideas of the Colonial Reformers on the virtues of freedom as an imperial bond.

Grey was prepared to grant responsible government to the colonies. The ideals of Durham and free trade in Britain had now joined together to transform imperial policy. No longer was it argued that a colony could not govern itself and remain a colony. Instead Grey asserted (as early as 1846 in a dispatch to the governor of Nova Scotia) that the government of the British American colonies could only be carried on in accordance with the wishes of their inhabitants. This meant that governors were henceforth to take their ministers from whatever group held a majority in the colonial assembly, and to change them whenever the confidence of the assembly changed. This meant, in sum, the full responsible system for the internal affairs of the colony, with a party cabinet and a party prime minister, and the governor withdrawn from politics.

In 1847 Lord Elgin, an imperial statesman who was a worthy son-in-law of Durham, was sent out to replace Metcalfe in Canada and to carry out Grey's new policy, by which the Colonial Office frankly and freely granted what before it had yielded only reluctantly and piecemeal. Elgin's chance to apply the generous new imperial policy came with the elections of 1848. When the Reformers won a large majority in the assembly that year, the governor-general simply called on their leaders, Baldwin and Lafontaine, to form a government. In this quiet way the struggle over responsible government was settled at last, as a one-party cabinet, a solid Reform ministry, took office in the province of Canada.

Responsible government had still to face a less quiet test in Canada. In 1849 a bill was introduced in the assembly to pay persons in Lower Canada for losses suffered during the rebellion of 1837. A similar measure had been passed for Upper Canada during the Metcalfe regime, but the Lower Canadian bill was so broad in its terms that the Tories called it a payment for rebellion. They urged Elgin not to sign it. The Rebellion Losses Bill nevertheless passed the assembly and had the support of the Baldwin-Lafontaine ministry. Whatever his own private feelings, under responsible government Elgin had no course but to sign the measure.

He did so, for the sake of that system, in spite of a violent Tory outcry against the government and the governor-general. Not yet accepting the conditions of responsible government, the worst elements of Toryism broke into rioting in Montreal, attacking the homes of the Reform ministers and stoning Elgin's carriage, while he bore their anger with calm courage. The riot grew. A shouting mob invaded the parliament building in Montreal, ransacked it, set it on fire, and left it a glowing ruin. Yet the violence was over almost as the ashes cooled. It was clear the mass of the people, French or English, were not in sympathy with it. Despite the flames of the night of 7 April, self-government was secure in the province of Canada. This was only a last outburst in a troubled but tremendously important period in the colonies along the St Lawrence.

5 Achieving Responsible Government in the Maritimes

While Nova Scotia, like Canada, passed through a struggle for responsible government—and, indeed, achieved that principle shortly before Canada—the other Maritime provinces were given self-government later, once the system had been established by the Nova Scotian and Canadian contests. There was little that could be called a political struggle after 1837 in New Brunswick, which had been the most contented province in that year of crisis. The Reformers, led by Wilmot, were generally satisfied with the successful settlement of the crown lands and civil list question during 1837. A number of mixed governments of Tories and Reformers followed until 1854, although in 1846 the Assembly did carry a resolution approving the principle of responsible, one-party government. In any case Grey, as Colonel Secretary, intended that the new principle should be established in New Brunswick as elsewhere; and when in 1854 the Reformers won a sweeping majority at the elections they formed the first one-party, responsible ministry in the province.

In Prince Edward Island, the old struggle over the land question and a long personal feud between the governor and the speaker of the assembly did much to prevent concentration on the principle of responsible government; until in 1851, in line with Grey's established policy, the first responsible ministry was formed under George Coles. Newfoundland was granted responsible government similarly in 1855. Leaders of the provincial assembly had been appealing to the British government to introduce the system since 1848. Though the imperial authorities at first held back because of Newfoundland's undeveloped state, the wide concessions of self-government to the Cape of Good Hope and the Australian colonies, as well as to British America, by 1854 made it impossible to withhold the grant from the great Atlantic island. Nova Scotia, however, saw a long contest for responsible government, but without the violence of Canada's. This orderly development was, of course, the result of different conditions in the politics of Nova Scotia that have already been discussed. But much of the credit, as well, must go to the political genius of Joseph Howe. Here was a man who was as thoroughly loyal in temper as Robert Baldwin, who saw the meaning of responsible government quite as clearly, and yet had also the skill of Francis Hincks at party management and parliamentary tactics. Nova Scotia was really too small a stage for one of the ablest statesmen of the Second Empire.

Howe had already begun the campaign for responsible government before Lord Durham's Report; in fact, before the rebellions in the Canadas. The Report, however, gave a powerful British endorsement to the Nova Scotian Reformers. They hailed it with gleeful excitement as proof that a leading British figure also believed that imperial unity and colonial self-government could go hand-in-hand. Accordingly, when Lord John Russell spoke in the imperial parliament in 1839 on the Report, to deny that self-government could be combined with unity, Howe composed four public Letters to answer Russell, then the Colonial Secretary. In these he set forth the doctrine of responsible government with great vigour and clarity, founding it, as ever, on a desire to strengthen the bonds of empire.

In October, 1839, Russell issued his instructions allowing colonial governors to change their executive councils freely to suit 'public policy'. Howe seized on this as a chance to advance responsible government. Although the instructions were really meant to give the governor a free hand in shaping his ministry, Howe, like Baldwin in Canada, insisted that changing ministers to suit 'public policy' required the governor to choose his government according to the majority in the assembly; in other words, to establish the responsible system. On this point he moved a vote of want of confidence in the existing ministry and actually brought about the governor's recall over it.

This first blow at Russell's plan for 'everything but responsible government' (as it might be termed) was struck in 1840. However, that year Governor-General Sydenham briefly visited Nova Scotia and exposed Howe to his political charm. Howe agreed not to force the pace while Sydenham still faced so many problems in Canada. In return he entered a non-party coalition government in Nova Scotia—a typical Sydenham suggestion. But after Sydenham's death, the failure of Nova Scotia to advance further towards responsible government caused the Reform leader to break with the Tories in the coalition ministry. He and his friends withdrew in 1843, to begin the fight in the assembly again for the full responsible system.

The victory of free trade in Britain in 1846, the coming of a new imperial government with Lord Grey at the Colonial Office, spelt success for Howe and his close ally, J. B. Uniacke. In that year Grey issued the new instructions to the governor of Nova Scotia that ordered him to establish a responsible ministry. The elections of 1847 were a Reform triumph. Thus when the new assembly met early in 1848 and passed a vote of no confidence in the existing ministry, a new Reform government, a true party cabinet, was automatically put in its place. Nova Scotia, a small province, had won responsible government two months before Canada. By its own energy, moderation, and unquestioned loyalty Nova Scotia had done much to pave the way to self-government within the empire for the rest of British America—and, indeed, for the other British colonies around the world.

CHAPTER 12

THE QUESTION OF UNION, 1846–60

1 *The Canadian Commercial Revolution*

By 1850 a new question was beginning to emerge for the colonies of British North America. By that date, or shortly after, the principal provinces had achieved a large amount of self-government. Now that they had won the right to manage their own affairs, the first stage on the road to nationhood, could they go on to build a single nation-state in British America? Would union be added to self-government? Indeed, could British America survive, divided into a set of small colonies, however free, or must it be welded into a broad national unit in order to hold the northern half of the continent? The next twenty years decided the question of union. The rapid progress made in this era, the problems that arose, laid the basis for uniting the provinces. And the dangers that also developed, in truth, demanded a union, forcing it sooner than it might otherwise have come.

First, however, there were years of economic change, after 1850, that thrust the colonies forward and made union seem both possible and valuable for almost the first time. True, men had often dreamed of uniting the weak and scattered provinces. Durham had briefly toyed with the idea. But the Canadas and the Maritimes were separated by miles of wilderness. They had little contact and almost no trade with one another. The great West was an empty realm of the fur trade. It was only after 1850, then, that sweeping economic changes in the colonies began to bring union within the bounds of possibility.

These sweeping changes are sometimes described as the Canadian Commercial Revolution. To explain them, one must go back into the 1840's, and especially to the advent of free trade in

Britain. Until the day of free trade, while the old British colonial system was still in being, the North American provinces had continued to benefit from the imperial preferences for their timber and grain. In fact, in 1843 the Canada Corn Act, passed by the imperial parliament, had given a larger British preference to flour from Canada. As a result, the St Lawrence commercial interests had thrived as never before, shipping grain and flour from Canada and even bringing in wheat from the American West to be milled into flour in Canada for shipment to Britain. The vision of the St Lawrence empire, directing the whole flow of western commerce, seemed almost realized. The new canals were being finished, great business expansion was under way. Three years later the blow fell.

The repeal of the British Corn Laws in 1846 destroyed the privileged market in Britain for Canadian flour and grain. Other free trade measures also wiped out the timber preference. The St Lawrence interests found themselves over-expanded, and at the same time world trade depression closed in. There were stirrings of discontent in British America, not, as in the case of the former thirteen colonies, because of the weight of the British mercantile system, but for the very opposite reason: because it had been removed. The dependent British American colonies found themselves flung suddenly out of the old sheltered system of empire trade into the cold, hard realm of world trade, where they were ill-equipped to compete. Truly, the coming of free trade had struck them with all the shock of a revolution.

It seemed to some of the leading St Lawrence merchants, supporters, of course, of the Tory party in Canada East, that Britain was abandoning them, the steadfast British garrison in a mass of rebellious French. At the same time responsible government was transferring power in Canada East from the English-speaking Tory minority to the 'disloyal' French-speaking majority. In their shock at defeat and abandonment, especially after the passage of the Rebellion Losses Bill, some Montreal merchants and Tories signed the Annexation Manifesto of 1849. This document called for the province of Canada to be joined to the United States, proclaiming that without the old British trading system Canada was ruined and could only find new markets and new prosperity within the American republic. Britain herself had made clear that she wanted to free herself from the weight of colonies. She was adopting a purely self-interested free trade policy to suit Manchester manufacturers, who saw the empire as only a drain on their profits. Or so the Montreal Tories said, and they were not completely wrong.

The Annexation Manifesto, however, was overwhelmingly rejected by popular opinion in all parts of the province of Canada. The Maritimes were not concerned in the matter. Tories in Canada West called for a general British American union, instead of annexation, as the best means of making the colonies strong enough to overcome the loss of the protected imperial trade. Those Tories in Canada East who had signed the Manifesto soon regretted that they had done so in a fit of gloom; and after 1850 annexationist feelings all but disappeared in Canada. Yet there had been one important truth in the Manifesto: to make up for loss of markets in Britain, Canadian trade had to gain entrance into the rich American market. Some way had to be found through the high tariff wall that kept so many foreign products out of the United States.

Reciprocity was the answer. That is to say, the British American provinces and the United States should lower the trade barriers between them by a mutual, or reciprocal, removal of customs duties on a wide range of goods. The coming of free trade had ended imperial restrictions on the flow of Canadian commerce, as well as making a new trade policy necessary for British North America. Accordingly, discussions concerning reciprocity could be undertaken with the United States. The governor-general, Lord Elgin, was especially interested in obtaining some agreement for reciprocal trade. He believed, indeed, that only reciprocity could prevent annexation, by filling the colonies' need for new trade outlets.

As it turned out, this dark view was not wholly justified. Before reciprocity with the United States was finally secured in 1854, Canadian commerce had managed to recover from the worst strains caused by the end of the old colonial system. World prosperity had begun to revive in 1850. Canada found that it still could hold some of the British grain market, and a wave of British investment in the province brought rapid development. The Crimean War with Russia (1854–6) also increased the demand in Britain for Canadian grain by cutting off much of the eastern European supply. Thus when reciprocity was achieved it was not just a means of preventing annexation. Instead it was a constructive measure that aided an economic recovery in Canada which was already well under way. Nevertheless reciprocity proved enormously valuable to the colony.

The successful arranging of a Reciprocity Treaty, however, largely depended on another issue than trade: on the fisheries question which affected the Maritimes more than the inland province of Canada. Ever since the Convention of 1818 had set limits to the right of Americans to fish inshore in British North American waters there had been disputes with the United States over the extent of this right. The fishermen of New England, as of old, were busily engaged in getting all that they could of the rich fishing harvest of the cold northern waters. There were sharp new clashes with them in 1852–3. Thus when free entrance to British American fisheries was offered to the United States as one term of a reciprocity treaty, that country soon became interested.

At length the Reciprocity Treaty was signed in Washington in 1854, its way eased by Lord Elgin's genial diplomacy and large quantities of champagne. It provided for a free exchange of natural (not manufactured) products between the United States and British America, free navigation of the American-controlled Lake Michigan and the Canadian-controlled St Lawrence, and free ac-

THE CLASH AT ST EUSTACHE — REBELLION OF 1837

THE BURNING OF THE PARLIAMENT HOUSE, MONTREAL, 1849

THE RAILWAY ENTERS LONDON, CANADA WEST, 1858

VICTORIA, VANCOUVER ISLAND, IN 1860

cess to each other's fisheries. The points which mattered most in practice were that the Americans could now share freely in the northern fisheries, while the Canadians could send grain and timber to the United States, and the Maritimes their fish and timber.

Because of this Reciprocity Treaty, and later the wartime boom of the American Civil War (1861–65), British North American trade with the United States rose rapidly. It grew with the ever-increasing American market, as the republic spread across the continent. The Maritimes found another important outlet for their goods besides the British West Indies, which were declining with the failing prosperity of their overworked sugar plantations. Furthermore, although the colonies' trade in massive ship timbers would soon be threatened by the passing of the wooden ship, the rapidly growing towns of the United States produced a steady demand for building planks and sawn lumber from the Canadian and Maritime forests. Saw-mills and lumber towns sprang up in Canada West, in particular, and a busy north-south lumber trade began to replace the old east-west one across the ocean.

Thanks, therefore, both to reciprocity and to the changing economic patterns of the age, the Commercial Revolution began transforming British North America. Half Canada's trade and two-thirds of the Maritimes' was still with Britain, but now as well there was an expanding commerce on the North American continent. Canada was shaping a long-lasting system of trade, whereby she stood with one foot in the British market and the other in the American. She would shift her weight more to one foot or the other with the passage of time, but the position itself was the outcome of the Canadian Commercial Revolution. The British North American colonies had adjusted themselves to the coming of free trade, and had changed total economic dependence on Britain for partial dependence on both Britain and the United States.

But the Commercial Revolution meant still more. It led, for instance, to another step towards nationhood: the right of the colonies to direct their own trade policies even, if necessary, in opposition to Britain. Thus in 1859 the province of Canada imposed a tariff of its own which burdened manufactured goods from abroad, including British, with heavier duties. This caused an outcry among some manufacturers in Britain as it denied the now-accepted British principle of free trade. However, the Canadians declared that when Britain had dropped the direction of colonial commerce she had also thrown on the colonies the responsibility of making their own trade policy; and while free trade might be best for Britain, it might not be for the colonies. Besides, responsible government was meaningless if a colony could not control its own economic life. As a result, it was recognized that free trade for Britain also involved freedom for the colonies to settle their own trade and tariff policies.

Finally, the Commercial Revolution leading as it did to new British American prosperity, pointed a finger towards union. The very growth of the colonies laid a much sounder basis for uniting them. They were more now than backwoods settlements. They were increasingly wealthy and enterprising communities, and might think with new confidence of joining together to control half a continent. And the very fact that reciprocity might not last for ever made them consider the prospects of developing more trade relations among themselves, in case the American market might some day be cut down as the British had been. Before reciprocity had been won, a British American union had been proposed as a means of building up a vigorous commercial exchange between the provinces. When reciprocity did come to an end in 1865, the colonies turned back upon themselves in an attempt to keep, through union, some of the prosperity they had gained out of the changes of the Commercial Revolution.

2   The Coming of Railways

Mounting British American prosperity in the 1850's was not only due to reciprocity. It was due also to the coming of the railways. The building of railways produced a great boom, and even though the boom burst in 1857, the new lines further developed the colonies and provided more solid groundwork for union. Railways, in short, made it possible to link the far-spread provinces together, while their high costs finally required a union, because only a union could afford to meet them. The first railway lines in British North America had been built in the 1830's. But they were only a few miles long, and although longer lines were planned in the next ten years, it was only in the fifties that the railway age really began. By then there was an ample supply of British money and railway-building skill looking for new worlds to conquer. And the now flourishing American provinces were eager to acquire that latest instrument of progress, the railway.

Lines were built in the Maritimes linking Halifax and Truro in Nova Scotia, and Saint John and Shediac in New Brunswick. But the principal railway building went on in the larger province of Canada. Here the first lines constructed were attempts to improve the existing water transport system. Though the St Lawrence canals had been built, most of the traffic of the American West still flowed through American channels. Railways, in the right places, it was hoped, would turn the flow into the St Lawrence. Thus a line was planned from Montreal to the ocean at Portland, Maine, to overcome the closing of the St Lawrence by ice for half the year. This winter route to the sea, the St Lawrence and Atlantic, was opened in 1851. Then the Northern Railway was built from Toronto to Georgian Bay on Lake Huron, to bring traffic down from the Upper Lakes and the West beyond. The Great Western similarly shortened the distance to the West by reaching across the Ontario peninsula from Hamilton, on Lake Ontario, to Detroit, opposite the western tip of the province.

All these lines had some success in tapping the trade of the American West for Canada, but the greatest project of them all was the Grand Trunk Railway. The original plan for a through route called for a line from the western end of Canada to the ocean at Halifax, to be built by all the provinces. The eastern link, however, the Quebec to Halifax, or Intercolonial railway, could not be agreed upon, and the province of Canada went on alone with its own Grand Trunk. It was to cross the whole province from the western end to the lower reaches of the St Lawrence. This Grand Trunk, therefore, represented a new stage in the dream of the commercial empire of the St Lawrence. If canals and river could not gain mastery of the western trade for the Canadian route, especially now that the preferences in the British market had gone, then perhaps a new St Lawrence route of steel could win the day for what was still the most direct path between the sea and the heart of the continent.

Accordingly, contracts for building the railway were let to a British engineering firm, and British money, backed by the great British financial name of Baring, was freely invested in the new Grand Trunk. The Canadian government poured in money too, by borrowing large sums to put towards the cost of the line. The weight of these debts came to be a steadily growing burden on the Canadian taxpayer. As construction advanced, the railway company had to appeal repeatedly for more aid from the provincial government, which meant more public debts. But by 1859 the tracks had been laid from Quebec to the western end of the province, and the St Lawrence and Atlantic had been taken into the Grand Trunk. The result was the longest railway in the world in that day, 1,100 miles in length. Yet from the first it did not pay. By 1861 the Grand Trunk was bankrupt and owed thirteen million dollars.

Again the best hopes of the St Lawrence interests had failed. It was the old story: New York and the Hudson valley had once more defeated Montreal and the St Lawrence in a commercial contest that began with the fur trade. When canal barges had replaced fur-canoes, the Erie canal had conquered for New York City. When the St Lawrence had built canals, New York had built railways. When the St Lawrence built its Grand Trunk it came too late and it was too expensive to win the American western trade away. The much bigger American population again meant greater traffic and lower rates for the railways in the United States. New York's port facilities were larger and cheaper than Montreal's and on the open sea all the year around.

Yet though the Grand Trunk failed in its main purpose, the railway-building era was by no means a failure for British North America. Perhaps the American western trade was not gained, but there was a growing traffic within Canada itself. Though this could not make the Grand Trunk a paying proposition it had important results for the province as a whole. Its districts were joined together, towns rose rapidly as trading centres. The colony grew busier and richer. Montreal and Toronto forged ahead as the capitals of a thriving Canadian business world. The railways, besides, really brought the Industrial Revolution to British North America. Iron foundries, locomotive shops, rolling mills, appeared. Factories sprang up in the larger towns to produce for all the regions joined by railway lines.

Railways also brought large public debts, made higher tariffs necessary to raise the money to pay them, tied the government to the fate of railway companies, and caused extravagance and corruption in politics. Yet it would be hard to say that they were not worth the price. With the scream of the locomotive whistle through the dark Canadian forests, the pounding of the wide-stacked engines and swaying cars through the backwoods, pioneer loneliness and hardships fell away. In the mid-nineteenth century railway-building carried British North America out of the pioneer age. The Railway Revolution went hand-in-hand with the Commercial Revolution.

But more than this, railways led toward union. If their tracks had linked up the province of Canada, they could join Canada and the Maritimes—or Canada and the Pacific. New interprovincial contacts and trade could come with them. Moreover, the very problems raised by railways suggested British American union as an answer. If separate provinces could not agree on constructing a line from Quebec to Halifax, could not one country build it? And if the Grand Trunk could not pay within Canada, could it not pay if it were extended across the whole continent, and one large country shouldered the cost?

The point was that the Grand Trunk had failed because it reached only the American West, and insufficient American traffic had come to it. But to the north west, beyond the province of Canada, lay great tracts of land under the British flag that stretched to the Pacific. If these could be opened up by railway lines, and a union, the Grand Trunk might yet succeed. In time this thought took hold. Gradually attention began to turn from the American West to the North West of British America, where the dream of a trading empire tied to Montreal and the St Lawrence might once again come true, just as it had in fur-trade days.

3 *The Question of the West*

In 1850 all the British lands beyond the province of Canada, from the Upper Lakes to the Arctic and Pacific Oceans, were still under the Hudson's Bay Company, as they had been since 1821. In that year the amalgamation of the North West Company with the older company of the Bay had left the latter in undisputed mastery of the vast West. In Rupert's Land proper, that broad indefinite region that drained into Hudson Bay, the Company ruled in any case by right of charter. In the lands beyond it henceforth had a monopoly of trade, and carried on whatever government there was.

Under a vigorous governor, Sir George Simpson, who ruled like a king over the great western domain during most of this period, Hudson's Bay government was orderly and efficient. The tireless, demanding Simpson kept his widely scattered posts under almost military discipline. The Bay Company brought law to the West at the same time as it enjoyed its golden years of fur-trade monopoly. Simpson kept up efficiency by constant tours through his fur-trade kingdom, and insisted on being treated with the proper ceremony due his authority. When his brigade of canoes would sweep up to a fort deep in the wilderness, flying the Company's own red ensign, the fort guns would boom out an official salute to the formal little top-hatted figure seated stiffly behind his hard-paddling *voyageurs*.

But although Hudson's Bay Company government might mean order and efficiency in the fur trade, it did not bring settlement to the North West. As always, fur trade and settlement were enemies. In any case few settlers would yet have gone to the distant West while much more easily available land could be found in the American prairies or, under the British flag, in the Canadas to the east. Yet the weakness of Company rule when faced with an on-rushing tide of settlement was made very clear in the case of the Oregon country.

The Oregon country lay on the Pacific coast between California and Alaska. Fur traders from Canada, men of the old North West Company, had first opened it up by land. During the war of 1812 they had driven out American traders. On the union of the Hudson's Bay and North West Companies, accordingly, the Bay Company had gained effective control of most of the Oregon trade. The Convention of 1818, however, had extended the boundary line between the United States and British North America westward along the forty-ninth parallel from the Lake of the Woods to the Rockies, and had agreed that beyond the Rockies, for the time being, Oregon would be under joint British and American occupation.

This uncertain state of affairs still existed in the 1840's when American settlers began to cross the continent and enter the fertile Pacific slopes of the southern half of the Oregon country. They formed their own government and demanded entrance into the American union. The weak Hudson's Bay posts in the region could do nothing about this move. In the United States a cry went up for 'fifty-four forty or fight': that is, for a boundary line up to Alaska, then held by Russia. Preparations for war were begun. But Britain had no desire to fight, and endanger Canada, and the United States was on the verge of war with Mexico. A treaty was signed in 1846, dividing Oregon by extending the line of the forty-ninth parallel to the Pacific, but leaving all Vancouver Island in British hands.

The Oregon Treaty had all but finished the division of the continent between British America and the United States. It had also shown the danger of leaving a fur-trade company to hold a region when a settlement invaded it. Consequently, the imperial government took some action to try to strengthen the British position in the far West. In 1849 they set up Vancouver Island as a Crown colony and sought to found a settlement there. The Hudson's Bay Company, however, was granted the island on condition of establishing settlers. As usual, a fur-trade company put very little effort into this task, and the colony grew very slowly; though Victoria did emerge as a minor port-of-call and a miniature capital.

Then in 1856 a new threat loomed. Gold was discovered on the empty mainland opposite Vancouver Island, on the Fraser river. American miners rushed up the coast into the gold reefs in the canyons of the Fraser. A wild new frontier developed overnight, and there was the danger of another Oregon. In this crisis, the bold James Douglas, governor of Vancouver Island and chief Hudson's Bay official there, moved rapidly. He proclaimed his authority over the mainland and at once enforced order. Courts were set up; Royal Engineers acted as police. The miners found this a very different frontier under British law, but they accepted and obeyed it.

In 1858 a separate colony of British Columbia was created on the mainland with Douglas also as its governor. It was ruled by governor and council; Vancouver Island by now had also a little 'assembly' of seven elected members. As gold discoveries spread, the Royal Engineers carved a soaring, winding roadway along the mountain sides to the Cariboo gold fields, and over this 'Cariboo Road' came men on foot and riding, pack mules, ox wagons, stage coaches, and even camel trains. In 1862 the 'overlanders', men from Canada, reached the Cariboo fields. They crossed bush, swamp, plain, and mountain to become the first settlers from eastern Canada in what would some day be the Pacific province of a transcontinental dominion. The gold rushes died away; most of the American miners left. Nevertheless the foundations of the modern province of British Columbia had been laid, and the rest of the British Pacific Coast had been saved, thanks largely to Douglas. But it was not yet secure. Only union with the rest of British North America could promise any permanent sort of answer to the danger of an 'Oregon' settlement.

Such an answer, however, seemed absurdly remote while the whole huge territory between the Rockies and the Great Lakes was a wilderness dividing the eastern colonies from the tiny provinces of the Pacific. In all this lonely land only at the Red river was there any settlement. Here Selkirk's few Scots farmers had hung on and built a little colony around Fort Garry (now Winnipeg), the chief Hudson's Bay post in the plains. By 1850 there were about 5,000 settlers in the Red River Colony, the original group having been increased by retiring Hudson's Bay servants and their descendants, often French or Scottish half-breeds. Here also the Company showed no wish to see the settlement spread, though at its existing size it was useful as a supply base for the posts further west.

The Red river inhabitants accepted this state of affairs. They felt no particular desire to see their colony grow through contact with Canada to the east. They had no real ties with that province and the few Canadian settlers who made their way to the Red river in the 1850's were frequently unpopular. This was largely because they wanted, and expected, to see the colony joined to the province of Canada, which had a somewhat thin claim to the western plains running back to the French period. But while the people of Red river hoped some day to escape the absolute Hudson's Bay Company control, they thought of separate existence as a Crown colony, not of union with a far-off and unknown province of Canada.

Yet there were forces making for union. These again were bound up with the danger of approaching American settlement. The westward movement of the frontier in the United States was raising a whole row of new states across the plains and American railways were creeping steadily west and northward. American expansion would not be stopped on the open plains by a fur trade company, any more than in Oregon. Already in the 1850's the Red river was being tied into trade with the American state of Minnesota, and a small American element was appearing in the colony, and there urging annexation. The Canadians in the Red river in alarm called on Canada, in 1857, to annex the colony first, in order to head off the growing danger from the south.

Meanwhile in Canada there was increasing support for such a step, and in Canada West in particular. Here most of the good farm land had been taken up by the early 1850's. The rest of the province fell within the rugged Shield. The next good land lay far beyond the Shield in the western plains. Thus the 'land hunger' of Canada West farmers was reflected in a demand for Canada to take over the North West and the Red River Colony from the Hudson's Bay Company.

The demand was most strongly voiced by the so-called 'Clear Grit' Reformers of Canada West, who particularly represented the farming element. George Brown, their powerful leader, also had allies in the Toronto business world, which had schemes of its own for opening the North West and gaining its trade. Brown owned the Toronto *Globe*, the most influential newspaper in Canada. The *Globe* began a steady campaign for acquiring the West, and in 1857 the Clear Grits adopted this demand as a leading party aim. In the same year the British government, also worried about the future of the North West in the hands of the fur trade, opened a parliamentary inquiry into the position of the Hudson's Bay Company. The Canadian government sent representatives to London to press its claims to the West. The inquiry, however, decided that the Hudson's Bay charter of 1670 was still valid, although the Company's monopoly in the regions beyond Rupert's Land was to end in 1859. As for the Red river, it might be ceded to Canada on terms reached with the Company.

Such a decision left things as they were, since Canada would not yet agree to pay for territory which she had claimed as her own, and which she could not yet settle in the absence of any system of communications. And as Canada did not assume control, the Hudson's Bay Company was left in actual possession of all the West. Yet the threat from American settlement was still present, and growing. Union remained the only possible answer, and the very threat would one day make it necessary.

4 Sectionalism and the Canadian Union

The question of union really came to a head in the province of Canada. Oddly enough, it was a breakdown of union, within Canada itself, which finally forced the issue, since the Canadian troubles led to a discussion of new forms of union which might include all the provinces of British North America. The breakdown was due to the violence of sectional conflicts in Canada, and these in turn arose from the unfortunate terms by which the two old Canadas had been tied together in the Act of 1840.

It will be remembered that, despite Durham's recommendation, Upper and Lower Canada had been given equal numbers of seats in the parliament of the united province. Thus a clear-cut division was made between two evenly balanced sections in the new province. Far from French-speaking Canada East being absorbed in an English-speaking majority, it preserved a special character. It kept its own system of laws, land-holding, and Church authority that dated back to the Quebec Act. Its racial feelings had been newly aroused by Durham's hopes of assimilation. Hence the French Canadians drew together to control Canada East, and to make it a solid block in the politics of the united province. Having equal power, this block could not be overcome.

In fact, since the great majority of the French in the assembly combined into one group, while English Canadians were divided into various groups of Tories and Reformers, the English-speaking majority could not assert its total strength. Under responsible government as a result, any cabinet had to be a loose alliance of French and English, representing equally the English-controlled Canada West and the French-controlled Canada East. There was really a double premiership, such as that of Baldwin and Lafontaine, with a leader for each of the two racial and sectional divisions. The very capital had to be moved every four years from Toronto to Quebec, because Montreal had disgraced itself in 1849, and East and West could not agree on any other city.

French and English also tended to have different political ideas and aims. In consequence, any government was bound to be a shaky alliance, and a solid, province-wide party system cutting across sectional lines was impossible. Under these conditions party politics tended to collapse into sectional disputes and angry prejudices. And there was little hope of any remedy as long as the unsound union endured.

Yet the union did have great value in overcoming old trade barriers between the two Canadas. Geography had declared that the St Lawrence lands were one. The union recognized that fact. Commercial advance and growing wealth went with it, even while, politically, the united province was falling apart. Thus it was that any return to two separate provinces seemed a backward step, and in the long run the principal desire was to recast rather than to destroy the union. And the powerful St Lawrence interests, who for reasons of trade had always sought to keep the St Lawrence lands united, were determined to avoid a separation.

After 1850 the demand to alter the form of union came mainly from Canada West. Chiefly because of continued British immigration, its population had climbed level with Canada East's, and now was steadily moving ahead. Year by year, therefore, the scheme of equal representation was becoming more and more unreal. Though Canada West had more inhabitants it still had no more seats in parliament than Canada East: it was said that four voters in the eastern section had as much power as five voters in the western. But, of course, most of the French Canadians had little wish to change a scheme of union that gave them, a minority group, a position of practical equality and provided good protection for their special interests.

Canada West complained, however, that while it paid much the greater share of taxes most of the public money was spent for Canada East. It charged that government was under 'French domination', and with some truth, for any government had to depend on keeping the support of the key French block in the assembly. Accordingly, a rising cry went up in the western section for 'representation according to population', which indeed would alter the union by giving Canada West a majority of seats in parliament. French Canada resisted this demand, for while 'rep by pop' would create a true union, it would also swamp the French vote and destroy the special sectional position of Canada East.

Given the problem of sectionalism in the union, it was not surprising that the old party lines began to break down once the question of responsible government had been settled. After the rights of self-government had been won there was little to keep the French and English Reformers together. The Baldwin-Lafontaine alliance, that had formed a strong majority and carried through responsible government, rapidly crumbled away. In 1851 its two leaders retired from parliament. They had had enough of the bewildering new state of politics. Many English-speaking Reformers in Canada West wanted to press on with a reform programme, in which the responsible system had been only the necessary first step. But the French Reformers of Canada East drew back, revealing their basically conservative outlook. Indeed, they now wished above all to conserve the favourable position that they had won in the union.

In Canada West, however, a new radical movement arose that

was impatient with even the main body of English-speaking Reformers. This was the 'Clear Grit' movement, so called because it wanted only pure-hearted radicals, men who were 'clear grit' all through. The Clear Grits were largely a revival of the old radical group that had followed William Lyon Mackenzie and which had been submerged after his defeat and during the leadership of the moderate Robert Baldwin. Like Mackenzie, the Grits wanted an elective system of government on American lines rather than the British cabinet system, and they began to seek complete democracy as well—a very radical idea in Canada of that day. The Clear Grits began, moreover, to take the lead in the demand for secularizing the clergy reserves, that old sore-spot of Upper Canadian politics. The money derived from the sales of reserves had been divided in Sydenham's time among the leading churches, with the Anglican church still receiving the lion's share. But secularization called for a final settlement of the reserves, and for turning the funds over to public education.

With these policies the Clear Grits made a rapid advance in Canada West. Meanwhile a somewhat similar radical movement was emerging among the French in Canada East. This, the *Parti Rouge*, was partly a revival of Papineau radicalism, and it too believed in American-style government and complete democracy. Yet the Rouges were strong French nationalists besides, and attacked the British connection. They also attacked what they considered to be the excessive power of the Catholic clergy in French Canada, and this anti-clericalism only weakened their chances among a people devoted to its church. Hence, unlike the Grits in Canada West, the Rouges soon ceased to make headway. If anything, they confirmed the mass of the French Canadians in their conservatism.

This very conservatism made possible a strange new political partnership. The main French group, known as the Bleus, came to ally with English-speaking Tories—with the party that had formerly condemned the French Canadians as disloyal and had tried to keep them from political power. But the Tories, after 1850, especially as influenced by bright young men like John A. Macdonald, were growing ready to accept responsible government and French political power as accomplished facts. They saw that by joining forces with French power they could gain a majority and govern once more, even under the responsible system. The Tory merchants of Montreal, the centre of the great St Lawrence business interests, soon realized that with French support such a government could carry through their railway schemes for the St Lawrence route. The French in their turn, eager to protect their Catholic conservatism, were ready to make terms with Toryism in order to gain a political majority, even at the price of dropping their old dislike of commercial expansion.

Therefore the St Lawrence commercial Tories lay down with their old French enemies in a common conservatism. They agreed jointly to protect French rights in the existing union and to develop English business interests. With them were allied a moderate group of Canada West Tories—or Conservatives— under John A. Macdonald and those Canada West Reformers, led by Francis Hincks, who opposed the Clear Grit radical demands. These 'Hincksite' Reformers were also interested in business development and railway-building; whereas the Grits, being largely western farmers, tended to be suspicious of the cost and corruption involved in these policies.

In consequence, in 1854, the Tory-French-Hincksite combination came to power under the inspired name of the Liberal-Conservative party. The party was to have a long record in Canadian history, especially under the gifted master politician who did much to shape it, John A. Macdonald. It was to be distinguished for both nation-building and expensive, or even corrupt, politics. But perhaps it was most distinguished for having successfully combined French and English in a political partnership which, though loose, was lasting, and fulfilled Macdonald's deep-felt desire to maintain unity in Canada. With Macdonald went his close and constant ally as French-Canadian leader, the lively and determined Georges Cartier. It was a notable sign of the French-English alliance that Cartier had been solicitor for the new Grand Trunk, which the Liberal-Conservative party vigorously pressed forward, despite debts, scandal, and blistering criticism.

This criticism was forcefully directed by the earnest George Brown, a first-rate journalist who began to rally the shattered forces of Reform in Canada West. An ardent admirer of the British constitution and friend of the British tie, Brown had at first sharply opposed the 'bunkum-talking cormorants', the Clear Grits, in his Toronto *Globe*. But in 1851 he entered politics to battle for the separation of church and state; that is, to prevent any church being supported or recognized by the government: a popular cause in Protestant Canada West, especially among Clear Grits. Brown pressed for the secularization of the reserves, to end Anglican privileges. He also opposed bills for establishing state-supported Catholic schools in Canada West, which, he said, would undermine the existing system of general public education. He claimed that the bills to found 'separate' schools in the largely Protestant West were the result of French-Catholic domination of the government. This separate school question would long continue to trouble Canadian politics.

The Liberal-Conservative Coalition of 1854, however, at least agreed to secularize the clergy reserves; and also to do away with the seigneurial system in Lower Canada, which had now been outgrown, and was unpopular among the French Canadians. Meanwhile Brown and the Grits came together to oppose the Coalition and 'French-Catholic domination'. They demanded representation by population. With this cry, and attacks on the costly failure of the government's Grand Trunk policies, Brown increasingly swung Canada West behind the Clear Grits. At the same time his strong-minded leadership brought them to drop their early support of American democratic ideas. George Brown made the Grits much more a regular (and respectable) British Liberal party, believing in free trade, parliamentary government, and the British empire.

Yet as Brown and the Grits swept ahead in Canada West, the Rouges, led by A. A. Dorion, fell behind in Canada East. They were Brown's natural Liberal allies, but his attacks on French power and their dislike of the bond with Britain made any working agreements between them far less successful than those between Macdonald and the main French group. As a result, a Brown-Dorion government formed in 1858 lasted only two days.

But the very fact that one came to be formed at all, showed how sectionalism was undermining the Conservative strength. The Macdonald-Cartier government had fallen, indeed, because a number of its French supporters had left it temporarily when Ottawa had been chosen as the new capital of Canada. They did not like the capital going to English-speaking Canada West, even if the choice was not Toronto, and although Ottawa lay in the middle, on the river separating the two sections of the province. Cartier and Macdonald returned to power after this brief French protest. But the strange shifts and devices which they had to adopt to form a government—known as the Double Shuffle—showed that they too were in a weak position.

In short, government was failing. Canada West was becoming increasingly Clear-Grit Liberal, insisting on 'rep by pop'; Canada East increasingly French Conservative, or Bleu, determined to resist the demand. The Canadian union was splitting into two hopelessly opposed and equally balanced halves. Final deadlock did not come until the 1860's. Yet its shadow was already there. Thus it was that from both Liberal and Conservative sides plans for new kinds of union were now put forward. They led to the great plan of Confederation, the linking of all the provinces of British America. Thanks to the pressing problems of Canada, the largest province, the question of union took on new urgency. Out of the sectional struggles came a driving force that went on to mould a new nation in North America.

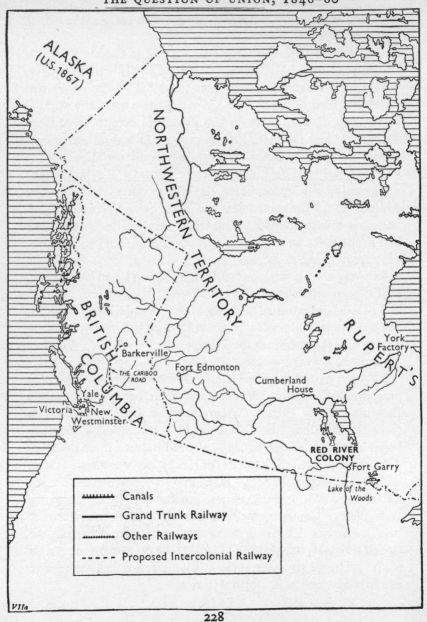

ALASKA
(U.S. 1867)

NORTHWESTERN TERRITORY

BRITISH COLUMBIA

RUPERT'S

York Factory

Barkerville

Fort Edmonton

THE CARIBOO ROAD

Cumberland House

Yale

Victoria   New. Westminster

RED RIVER COLONY

Fort Garry

Lake of the Woods

┈┉┈	Canals
──	Grand Trunk Railway
┉┉┉	Other Railways
-----	Proposed Intercolonial Railway

VIIa

MAP VII
BRITISH NORTH AMERICA
BEFORE CONFEDERATION

0   200   400
Miles

LABRADOR

LAND

St John's
NEWFOUNDLAND

Rivière du Loup

(LOWER
CANADA)
1791–1841

P.E.I. Charlottetown

PROVINCE
OF CANADA

NEW Shediac
BRUNSWICK

Truro

Fort
William

Quebec

Saint Johns

Halifax

(UPPER
CANADA)
1791–1841

Montreal
Ottawa

Richmond

NOVA SCOTIA

Kingston

RIDEAU
CANAL

LACHINE
CANAL

Portland

Toronto

Boston

Sarnia

Hamilton

ERIE CANAL

Albany

Detroit

Buffalo

Hudson
River

Windsor

WELLAND CANAL

VIIb

New York

CHAPTER 13

THE PATH TO CONFEDERATION, 1860-7

1   *The Movements Within*

On 1 July 1867, the separate colonies of British North America united in Confederation to become the Dominion of Canada. The seven years before were one of the most important periods in Canadian history. During those years, powerful movements within the colonies and strong pressures from outside carried British North America onward to Confederation. They answered the question of union. It took a few years more before the new Dominion stretched completely from the Atlantic to the Pacific, but the final stage, that of bringing in the Great West, was already decreed by the successful uniting of the main provinces in 1867. The advance to Confederation at that date was the all-important achievement. It is one of the most compelling stories in Canadian history.

Picture the colonies of British America in 1860, when the story begins. On the Pacific shores are two little outposts, Vancouver Island and British Columbia, linked only by sea with the outside world. Between them and Canada by land lie two thousand miles of silence, of mountains, endless plains, and the bush-country of the Shield. Only the cluster of farms at Red river breaks this empty expanse. But south of the forty-ninth parallel the restless, ever-spreading flood of American settlement is sweeping up over the prairies. Beyond the Great Lakes, in Canada, where some voices are raised in warning for the West, the St Lawrence province is racked with angry sectionalism, turned in upon itself. Yet while parties wrangle and French and English accuse each other of wrecking the union, the hum of mills and factories begins to rise, railway lines creep east and west. And the feeling grows that

230

sectional troubles, trade development, railways, all point to a new and grander union.

On the Atlantic coast, meanwhile, the Maritime provinces are glorying in the height of the age of wood, wind and water. Water-driven local industries, easy water transport, wood for their tall wind-ships: the Maritimes are well provided with these. They have brought golden prosperity. But what of the future? How will the Maritimes fare in the approaching age of iron and coal, of large steam-driven factories, railways and steel steamships? The Atlantic provinces have far less resources for this new era. They must plan carefully for the future. One of their most cherished plans is for a railway to link their ocean ports with Canada and the West. Then in an age of steam and steel the Maritime ports, closer to Europe than those of the United States, may still flourish, pouring forth the rich trade of the continental interior. But the Martimes cannot build an Intercolonial Railway alone. They may be led to unite with Canada in order to arrange and pay for the expensive line.

Canada is still a far-away and strange place to the Maritimers, who look with doubt on the stormy Canadian record of rebellion and racial conflict, and pride themselves on their own loyal and orderly political development. Yet thoughts of a great British American union linking the Atlantic with the Pacific are not un-known in the eastern provinces. And was it not Nova Scotia's own Joseph Howe who predicted in 1851 that some of his audience would live to hear the whistle of the locomotive in the passes of the Rockies?

This, then, was British America in 1860, and some of the stir-rings in its mind. Proposals to investigate the prospects of union had already been heard in the Maritime parliaments. But the most definite proposals had been put forward in Canada, by far the biggest province. Here the idea of federal union had been taken up, and this was a most fruitful suggestion. The British American colonies were actually too divided by geography and distance, too different in their interests, to see themselves swallowed up in a complete, or legislative, union under one government. The smaller ones would find themselves powerless to protect their special interests because the bigger provinces, containing a majority of the population, would regularly be in control. French Canada, on the other hand, would be fearful for its particular rights in a largely English-speaking British American state.

A looser, federal form of union, however, would meet the difficulty. Under federalism the powers necessary to maintain a single large state would be given to a central government while those matters of regional or sectional importance would be kept for provincial governments. The United States supplied the obvious example of how a federation could overcome the problem of North American distances and regionalism. In the Canadian case the movement for federal union went under the name of Confederation, as if to distinguish it from the American example. But the essential plan and purpose were the same.

In 1858 Alexander Galt had proposed a British American confederation in the Canadian assembly. He suggested that the federal principle could be applied to a general union of Canada East, Canada West, and the Maritime provinces. Galt, a leader of the Montreal business world, shortly afterwards joined the Cartier-Macdonald government as Minister of Finance. Here he was responsible for the 'protective' tariff of 1859, which by raising the duties against British manufactured goods had protected Canadian manufacturers and caused an outcry in freer trade Britain. Galt had entered the Conservative government of Macdonald and Cartier on their promise to take up his project for general federation at the Colonial Office. Such a change in the constitutions of British America would, of course, still require action by the imperial parliament. But Britain showed that she was not yet interested in a general union, particularly because the other colonies had so far not pressed for it. Therefore the Cartier-Macdonald government let the matter drop, having fulfilled their promise; for aside from Galt they were not yet convinced of the need for such a federation.

Nevertheless the Liberal-Conservative side in politics had thus proposed federation. Next the Reformers, or Liberals, under George Brown, took it up, although they sought only a federal union of the two Canadas. In 1859 a crowded Clear Grit convention in Toronto endorsed a plan, backed by Brown, that would remove the sources of sectional conflict yet preserve the merits of the existing union. It aimed at setting up a general authority for both Canadas and two provincial governments to handle subjects of sectional or racial concern. And Brown in a mighty speech full of vision and persuasion made clear that this plan was to be the first step in building a great British American nation.

For several years after the Convention, however, the Clear Grits still hoped to gain representation by population, and concentrated on that rather than federation. But French Canada would not yield 'rep by pop' and be swamped by the English in parliament. Hence the sectional struggle dragged on. No government could last long. Neither Conservative or Liberal cabinets could find a secure province-wide majority when the West was falling ever more completely into the hands of the Grit Liberals, and the East to the French Conservatives. Macdonald, his own Conservative support sinking in Canada West, strove gamely and skilfully to build cabinets and to make the union work. But government was slowing to a halt. By June of 1864 there had been two elections and four governments in the previous three years. None had succeeded; little work could be done. Clearly the union could not continue on this basis.

2 The Great Coalition in Canada

As hopeless deadlock settled down on the province of Canada in 1864, George Brown carefully but firmly stepped forward. He proposed a parliamentary committee to discuss the problem on a non-party basis and suggest the best solution. Here was a statesman-like act, seemingly unlike Brown. It had often been charged, with some justice, that Brown's violent outbursts against French-Catholic power and Conservative corruption had done much to embitter provincial politics; though it might also be claimed that the roots of bitterness were there without George Brown. At any rate, the impatient and hot-tempered Scot, warm friend and grim enemy, had of late been showing surprising restraint. He had decided that the dangerous question of the union must now be settled, and could only be settled by moderation and a turning-away from sectional and party strife.

He soon made clear this decision of immense consequence. In June of 1864 Brown's committee reported to the assembly, recommending a federal union of all the colonies or at least of the two Canadas. On that very day yet one more cabinet fell, and Brown announced that he was willing to form any government with the Conservatives that would be devoted to solving the problem of union. Willing to join with his worst enemies—it was a brave and dramatic move. At once the political picture changed. Deadlock vanished. A strong government of both Liberals and Conservatives could readily be formed to end the sectional evils. No wonder the assembly burst into cheers when they heard the news. No wonder an excitable little French Canadian member dashed across the floor and flung his arms happily about the towering, and startled, Liberal leader.

The coalition government that was now formed, the 'Great Coalition' of 1864, agreed that it would first seek a general British American federation and, if that failed, would then bring in a federal union for the two Canadas with provisions for including the West. The first and larger scheme thus represented the original Conservative proposal made by Galt, the second, the plan of the Clear Grit Convention of 1859. Brown, who now entered the government with Macdonald, Galt, and Cartier, was quite satisfied if the first could be won, since in any case it included the smaller Liberal scheme of federating the union between the two

Canadas. And federation would mean that in the central government Canada West would receive the proper number of members that its population deserved; there would be representation by population. Canada West would also obtain its own provincial government, to look after the sectional interests that had been interfered with under the 'French domination' of the old union. In addition, Brown, as a British American nationalist (though none the less devoted to the imperial bond), could enter eagerly into the project for building a continent-wide union.

On the Conservative side there were also grounds for satisfaction. For Macdonald and his English-speaking followers, it meant a continued share of power when they had felt themselves slipping. The unity of the St Lawrence they had fought to save would not be lost. It would be built into a larger whole. Furthermore, Conservatives had been more interested than Liberals in the suggestion of union with the Maritimes and in building the necessary Intercolonial Railway to give that union meaning. Now the railway-building party could plan the eastward expansion, while the 'land-hungry' Clear Grits could look to bringing in the West. French Canada, too, could find its rights safeguarded under federalism, which would leave its language, laws and religion safe under a French-Canadian provincial government. Hence Cartier joined with Macdonald in accepting the offer of alliance that Brown had made. Cartier's acceptance was no less brave and statesmanlike than Brown's offer. It was brave to join with the man his French supporters hated most; and it was statesmanlike, despite their suspicions, to see that, while French Canada could not hold out for ever in the old union against the demands of the English majority, federation offered it every necessary protection.

Brown and Cartier were perhaps the vital figures at this critical stage in the movement for confederation since they controlled the largest blocks of votes in the Canadian parliament. Yet also important in the province of Canada were Galt, the far-seeing financier, who had first put forward the confederation plan, and

Thomas D'Arcy McGee, the brilliant Irish orator, whose national vision of a dominion from sea to sea put fire into the movement and aroused wide popular support. Above them all in the long run, however, rose the ambling, friendly figure of John A. Macdonald.

He had been lukewarm towards federation almost to the last. He had fought always to make the existing union work. But when the sweeping scheme of general confederation was adopted as the first aim of the Coalition of 1864, Macdonald came into his own. It caught his imagination. This was union in a larger realm, and it was the idea of a firm and powerful union that Macdonald stressed above all. His tactful diplomacy and ready good humour did much to carry it through in the discussions that followed with the other colonies. He left his mark on the strong structure of federal union that was finally adopted for the Dominion. And his long career of nation-building—that really began with the Coalition of 1864—deservedly makes John A. Macdonald appear as the greatest Father of a Confederation which other men set under way.

Yet the work of Confederation had only begun with the formation of the Great Coalition in Canada. While the largest province had definitely set the movement going, the other provinces, and Britain, had not yet spoken. It was largely Canada's own internal difficulties which had led it to act first. Perhaps the other provinces, not facing these problems, would not feel the same urge towards federation. Fortunately, however, there were other forces, from outside British America, which affected all the colonies and pressed them on towards union. These outside influences came from both Britain and the United States. But in particular, they stemmed from the American Civil War, and the grave problems it raised for British North America.

3   The Forces Without

In 1861 the great and terrible Civil War broke out in the United States. From the start the British American colonies were affected.

It was not merely that an earnest dislike of slavery bound their attention to the war so close at hand, and even led some Canadians to fight in the Northern armies against the slave-holding South. It was rather that bad feelings between Britain and the American North threatened to involve the British provinces in war themselves. For in the event of war between Britain and the United States the Americans would strike at the closest British territory. The colonies would be invaded, as in the war of 1812; but this time they would face a far stronger foe, who had one of the largest armies in the world.

The hard feelings between Britain and the United States were the results of faults on both sides. In Britain, old anti-American prejudices were expressed in a belief, or perhaps a hope, that the United States had finally failed. There was a tendency in some quarters to look on the South as a new and separate nation and to decry the Northern efforts to restore the American union. On the American side there was fire-eating talk of 'punishing' Britain for being too friendly to Southern rebels, and there were suggestions that the American armies could find better employment in the conquest of Canada. Nor was the feeling entirely absent that a war against the old British enemy of American Revolutionary days would close the breach in the republic and turn its warlike passions outward. However, despite the fire-eaters, cooler counsels in government circles on both sides of the Atlantic prevented such a tragic conflict. But the people of the time could hardly be sure that a war would not break out.

For British America, in particular, the first battlefield of such a war, there was a new period of strain in relations with the United States. Looking back on history, one can see that the general peace between Canada and the United States dates from 1815; but in the mid-nineteenth century there was no sense at all that permanent peace had yet been secured. There had long been boundary problems and mutual suspicion. There had been border fighting in 1838 and a war-scare over Oregon in 1846. Why should the Civil

War of the 1860's not release a new and desperate struggle? Through most of that decade the strain continued. It did not end when peace had been restored in the United States in 1865, for now there was a fear that the victorious Northern forces, freed from their tasks in the south, might be turned against Canada.

It was during these years of strain, of repeated crises, that Confederation was achieved. In part, Confederation was an attempt to band together the strength of British North America to resist any American threat. The United States, therefore, not only supplied an example for a new northern federation: it supplied an urgent reason for it. A union would at least be better equipped to meet the general problem of British American defence. As the Civil War progressed, and quarrels flared between the United States and Britain, the question of defence loomed ever greater in the northern provinces. A sense of urgency began to invade the discussions of union. As D'Arcy McGee put it, the opening guns of the Civil War had warned Canada that she might sleep no more, except in arms, in constant readiness to defend herself.

Now this awareness of a defence problem varied considerably throughout British North America. The colonies of Newfoundland, Prince Edward Island and Nova Scotia, for instance, felt secure enough under the protection of the Royal Navy. But New Brunswick, and Canada especially, had long land frontiers to guard. Canada West was the most exposed, the furthest from British aid. Even here, however, there were many, George Brown among them, who felt that certain angry-voiced American newspapers did not represent the good sense of the American people or government: that there was no reason to fear war. Still, there was always the possibility to be guarded against, and several alarming incidents sharply brought home the unprepared state of the British colonies.

The first of these incidents was the *Trent* affair of November, 1861. Two Southern envoys to Britain were seized in high-handed fashion from the British steamer *Trent* by a United States warship at sea. Restraint by both British and American governments avoided war, and the envoys were set free. But the problem of defending British territory in America became suddenly plain. Over ten thousand British reinforcements were hastily shipped to Canada while the danger of war was at its height. To reach the St Lawrence colony in winter they had to go overland in sleighs from New Brunswick by the Madawaska 'snow road'. If there had been war, much of Canada might already have been lost before their arrival. Accordingly the British government began an inquiry into the reorganization of Canadian defences, while the provincial government had to make plans for raising a larger and more effective militia force to aid the regular troops.

There were other incidents. In 1864, for example, a band of Southerners (many of whom had sought refuge in Canada) slipped over the provincial border to raid the town of St Albans in Vermont. The provincial government acted to seize the raiders on their return to Canada, but not firmly enough to suit Americans, who felt that, at the least, the Canadians were not patrolling their borders properly, and, at the most, were aiding the Southern rebels. The United States government put strong controls on border crossings to Canada and announced that it might have to rearm on the Great Lakes, left free of warships since 1817, in order to protect its boundary. American warships on the Lakes would require British warships there too: the thunder of naval guns, silent since 1815, might be heard again on these freshwater seas.

Fortunately, the Civil War in the republic came to an end in the spring of 1865, and the United States did not move to rearm on the Lakes. Yet a spirit of resentment was left on the American side of the line. When the following year saw raiding in the opposite direction the American authorities did little to check it. These new raids were the work of the Fenians, an Irish revolutionary group dedicated to ending British rule over Ireland. If they could not reach Ireland, at least their powerful Irish-American supporters—often discharged soldiers from the Northern armies—could do the next best thing and attack British lands in North America. Fenians massed at points along the border in 1866. They made only one actual invasion of Canada, near the village of Fort Erie in the Niagara peninsula, where local militia threw them back after three days of alarms and excitement. Yet the threat of Fenian raids was widespread. An attempt on New Brunswick helped to convince that province that strength lay in unity, and so inclined it more towards the plan of British American federation.

Militia marched and counter-marched in the colonies, and the same kind of enthusiasm and feelings of common loyalty were roused as in the days of 1812 or the American raids of 1838. It was clear to the colonists that Fenian attacks were an annoyance rather than a real menace to their safety. The Fenians were not the United States army. The American government made no move towards war, and finally checked Fenianism when that movement was dying of its own failure. Yet the raids did reveal American unfriendliness, and underlined the need to show that the colonies would stand together to ensure their own future in North America. Some Americans were talking again of annexing Canada. A proposal for its peaceful annexation was even briefly made in Congress. Perhaps more significant, however, was the ending of the Reciprocity Treaty by the United States, another sign of American unfriendliness, and a hard blow at all the northern colonies.

The United States announced early in 1865 that it meant to end, or abrogate, the Reciprocity Treaty. This was in accordance with the Treaty term that it was to run for ten years and then be renewed or cancelled by either party, with an extra year of grace if it should be cancelled. The Treaty would end, then, in 1866. A flourishing system of commerce would be cut off. Maritime fish, Canadian lumber, and many other colonial goods would no longer have free entry into the United States. The American abrogation of reciprocity was undoubtedly influenced by the thought that these losses would lead to the annexation of British

America, that the colonies could not survive without the American trade. While reciprocity was the happiest state for the provinces, however, they were not so utterly dependent on it as Americans believed; and in reaction to that belief British America only became more determined to shape a future of its own.

Thus was encouraged that general feeling of British American nationalism which had almost been forced upon the provinces by the strained relations with the United States during the Civil War and by the Fenian outrages afterwards. As a result the movement for union was strengthened, particularly in the Maritimes, where it had been weaker. A British American nation should be the answer to talks of annexation. A union would remove trade barriers between the colonies, encourage an interprovincial commerce to replace what had been lost. It would even build the railway over which the new trade would flow between the St Lawrence and the Atlantic centres. An Intercolonial Railway and general federation seemed even more tied together—and even more necessary.

Railway problems, as well as matters of trade and defence, were also influencing the colonies. The world-wide money power of the Barings' bank, which was behind the Grand Trunk of Canada, brought pressure to bear on the cause of union in an effort to save British investments in the railway. In 1861 Edward Watkin, a Baring financial expert, was sent to Canada to investigate the 'organized mess' of the Grand Trunk. He reported that the railway lacked traffic and could only be made to pay by extending eastward and westward, from the Atlantic to the Pacific, until it became a transcontinental line carrying a great trade from ocean to ocean. Thanks to this dazzling suggestion, British banking interests became concerned both with the projected Intercolonial Railway, the link with the Atlantic, and with opening the West, so that a line could be constructed to the Pacific. In 1863, indeed, Watkin and a financial group in London even bought a controlling interest in the Hudson's Bay Company, intending to open its western lands to Canada in order that a Pacific railway might be begun.

Old enemies, the Clear Grits and the Grand Trunk banking interests, were coming to share a common desire to unlock the West.

As yet, however, Canada was unwilling to pay the price asked for the West. Indeed, it looked as if a British American union would be needed to take over all the lands from the Atlantic to the Pacific. Only such a big union would have sufficient credit to undertake to acquire the West and construct the railways to the two sea-coasts. Accordingly, British bankers and the Grand Trunk joined in working for the Confederation movement, and they had much influence in official circles. They looked with approval on Maritime desires for an Intercolonial Railway. Renewed conferences to discuss the Intercolonial were held between Canadian and Maritime representatives even before the Canadian Coalition of 1864 took up the question of a general federation.

Watkin, moreover, had the ear of the Colonial Office. The British government was becoming increasingly interested in the ideas of opening the West and building new railways in British America—the ideas that led logically to union. Yet more important in the mind of the British government were considerations of defence. Opening the West to Canada was the only means of saving it, in the long run, from advancing American settlement; and a Pacific railway could carry British colonists there. An Intercolonial Railway would end the dangerous weakness displayed during the *Trent* Affair of 1861, the fact that British troops could not be rushed to the defence of Canada when the St Lawrence was frozen over in winter.

Indeed, the stress and dangers of the American Civil War aroused the British government on the question of defence even more than it did the colonists of British America. Britain faced the main task of defending the empire and bore most of its costs. And at this very time when North American defence seemed to raise so grave a problem, a large element of opinion in free-trade Britain was proclaiming that colonies were only a burden and

THE LONDON CONFERENCE COMPLETES THE PLAN OF UNION, 1886

Seated at the far end of the table, from left to right, are Galt and Tupper (under the Queen's portrait) and Macdonald and Cartier. Tilley sits in the left-hand corner, holding a book. Lord Monck, the Governor-General, is the bearded figure at the near end of the table.

WINNIPEG AND THE RED RIVER, 1873

North West Mounted Police at Dufferin, Manitoba, 1874

PARLIAMENT HILL, OTTAWA, 1880—THE OLD PARLIAMENT BUILDING

expense. Some free traders, like Cobden and Bright, even demanded that the British American provinces be let go—be 'allowed' to join the United States.

While this view was not general in Britain there was at any rate a widespread desire that the costs of colonial defence be reduced, and that the North American colonies assume more of the burden of defending themselves against the United States. Here again a union of the provinces promised to allow them to shoulder that burden more cheaply and effectively. In time Britain began to exert strong pressure to bring about Confederation, and chiefly because of the defence question. In this case, too, the emergency raised by the Civil War had made its influence felt. It had fused together the movements within and the forces without, into a great drive that achieved Confederation.

4   The Achievement of Confederation

In June of 1864 the Great Coalition had been formed in Canada to seek general federation. In September of that year the Maritimes were to hold a conference of their own to discuss a smaller project: a union of the Atlantic colonies. This plan was a result of the growing concern of the Maritimes for their future. 'Maritime union' would strengthen them both politically and economically. It was fairly popular in the coastal provinces and it had the blessing of the British government. But Maritime union was destined never to be achieved. It was swallowed up in the plan for a greater union. Representatives of the Canadian Coalition, seizing the moment when Maritime delegates were meeting to consider new ties, swept down on their conference at Charlottetown, Prince Edward Island, and captured it for the Canadian project of general federation.

The Canadians succeeded at Charlottetown because they came at a critical time. The Civil War was crashing to a bloody victory of North over South, and no one knew what might happen when the Northern armies were free to turn to other quarrels. The outside pressures of defence, of trade questions, were rising. So was British American nationalism. The Canadians drew splendid pictures at Charlottetown of a strong and secure new northern nation, linked by railways, in which Canadian wheat and industry would complement Maritime mines, fisheries, and ocean commerce. It was a noble prospect, and in it the Maritimes saw the question of their future answered. They agreed to send delegates to a further conference at Quebec to work out a scheme of British American union.

In the next few months the movement for Confederation was at its peak all over British North America. Party differences and party feelings were forgotten in the general enthusiasm. A Conservative government in Nova Scotia, for instance, under Charles Tupper, and a Liberal government in New Brunswick, under Leonard Tilley, worked with the Coalition in Canada. The great figure of Howe, then out of power in Nova Scotia, gave at least a first approval to the idea of general union. And the Grand Trunk railway, labouring hard in the cause, carried Canadians to the Maritimes and Maritime delegates on tours across the province of Canada. Furthermore, late in 1864 and early in 1865, the St Albans raid and the American announcement of the abrogation of reciprocity increased the sense of the urgent need for union.

In this time of strong feeling for Confederation the Quebec Conference of October, 1864, was able to draft plans for an enduring British North American federation. The conference, indeed, went through its business speedily and quietly, although in time to come it would be charged with showing too much haste. But in those burning, eager weeks there seemed no reason for delay. There was, besides, general agreement that the new federal union had to be a strong one. It was to provide wide powers for the central government in order to avoid those weaknesses of the American system, where the states had the wider powers, which had apparently produced the Civil War.

The Conference that met in a hall overlooking the broad sweep of the St Lawrence, as it curved beneath the heights of Quebec, was composed of some of the ablest men in British North America. Among them were Macdonald, Galt, Tilley and Tupper, Cartier, Brown and McGee. They were there from French and English Canada, from the three coastal provinces and Newfoundland too; for the great island was meant to become a partner in the general union. These Fathers of Confederation, in their dark Victorian clothes and stiff collars, might seem a less colourful assembly than the eighteenth-century group in wigs and bright waistcoats that met in Philadelphia in 1787 to frame the American constitution. But the Quebec Fathers also held in their hands the future of half a continent. And it was fitting that they should meet in the old capital of New France, beside Cartier's great river of Canada. For here in the seventy-two resolutions that the conference drew up a new Canadian nation was born.

The Quebec Resolutions, the plan of union, now had to be accepted by the provinces themselves, or rather by their parliaments, before Confederation could go forward. In the spring of 1865 they were adopted in the Canadian provincial assembly, after some of the fincst debates in the political history of Canada. The French and English Conservatives and the Canada West Liberals under Brown gave them a resounding majority. The only considerable group opposing were the Canada East Liberals or Rouges led by Dorion, who charged that Confederation was merely 'a Grand Trunk job', designed to get the railway out of bankruptcy. As usual with half-truths, this was a dangerous statement, because there was an element of fact in Dorion's charge which obscured the many other forces behind Confederation. But the weak Rouge opposition was not sufficient to turn the tide.

In the Maritimes, however, the Resolutions ran into difficulty. By now a natural reaction against the excitement of Confederation was under way in these provinces, which had not inspired the project of federation, as Canada had, but had rather been led into it. Once the federal terms were on the table all the forces of Maritime criticism could be turned upon them. The financial terms of the Quebec Resolution were attacked: it was said that the eastern provinces had not been provided with sufficient income under the new arrangements. The old suspicion of the unknown Canadians was revived: the Maritimes would be swamped in the federation, which was only a trick to get Canada out of her own problem of deadlock. These were negative influences; but on the positive side, the easterners' love for their own little self-governing provinces made them reluctant to see their identities lost in a large new state.

Accordingly, Prince Edward Island and Newfoundland rejected the Quebec resolutions outright. The former, a farming and fishing island in the Gulf of St Lawrence, shared little of the interest in a railway to Canada that Nova Scotia and New Brunswick felt; and, of course, the Royal Navy had sheltered the island colony from the alarms of the Civil War. Newfoundland had only been an observer at the Quebec Conference, and had even fewer ties with the continent of America than Prince Edward Island. Much of its trade was with Europe. In addition, having so recently achieved self-government, Newfoundland did not want to lose some of it in a union with far-off Canada. Government from Ottawa seemed as distant and uncontrollable as that from London. And Newfoundland in the 1850's had just won a fight to keep London from ignoring its interests by granting France too many fishing rights on that annoying 'French shore', which dated from the Treaty of 1713. Looking outward to sea, the island would have nothing to do with the 'desert sands' of Canada, as the Newfoundland foes of Confederation described them.

The fate of Confederation did not turn on these two relatively small eastern provinces but on Nova Scotia and New Brunswick. Anti-federation forces were strong there too. In Nova Scotia, Howe organized a powerful opposition to the Tupper government that supported the Resolutions. Howe had turned from his early approval of union; in part, perhaps, because he had not been able to attend the Quebec Conference and appreciate the problems of arranging the Resolutions; in part because he believed his beloved province was being sacrificed to Canada. At any rate, Tupper had to hold back and did not even dare to bring the Resolutions to a vote in the Nova Scotia assembly.

Nor would such a vote have mattered for the time being, since New Brunswick had meanwhile rejected the Quebec scheme. Confederation was impossible unless the middle province, New Brunswick, agreed. Its whole future hung here. In March, 1865, when Tilley decided to hold an election over the Quebec scheme, he and his government were thoroughly defeated. All the anti-federation forces in New Brunswick had come together, including powerful business interests that did not want the province's money spent on its share of a railway to Canada, but rather on a line to the American border to link up with the railways of Maine.

Gradually the balance began to turn, as the anti-federation reaction played itself out. The new government in New Brunswick proved unable to settle the railway issue or offer any alternative to federation. The abrogation of reciprocity, which came finally in March, 1866, made Nova Scotia and New Brunswick see more value in a union with Canada, and the Intercolonial supporters urgently demanded it. The Fenian attempt on New Brunswick further influenced public opinion. On one thing the Maritimes were determined: they would remain British in America, and if this required union, union there would be.

Yet the deciding factor was the influence of the British government. From an early indifference to general union and an approval of the limited Maritime union, Britain late in 1864 had come swiftly to favour the plan of Confederation. Defence was the great reason. After the *Trent* affair, she had been alarmed by Canada's apparent failure to raise sufficient militia to share effectively in her own defence, and there was always the demand at home to lower the cost of imperial burdens. If, as Canadian delegates to England now assured her, a general union would be able to deal fully with defence, as well as take over the exposed West, then Britain would support such a union.

Therefore in 1865 the British government closed its ears to anti-federation protests from the Maritimes and instructed the British governors in the two main eastern provinces to use their influence on behalf of Confederation. Their influence still was wide, even under responsible government. It came into play the next year, when the weak anti-federation government began to collapse in New Brunswick. At a new election in that province the governor's power and Grand Trunk money was thrown in on the side of Confederation, although the latter perhaps only cancelled out other money spent by those desiring the railway to Maine.

The result was a sweeping victory for Tilley and Confederation; and, in Nova Scotia, Tupper was now able to get support for sending delegates to a new conference on British American union. It met in London, late in 1866, under the encouraging eye of the British government, and included representatives from New Brunswick and Canada as well as from Nova Scotia. At last Confederation was on the high road to success.

The London, or Westminster Conference accepted the Quebec Resolutions as the basic plan of union and made only minor changes, including larger money grants to the Maritimes and a definite statement that the Intercolonial railway would be built. There would be four provinces in the new federation: Nova Scotia, New Brunswick, and Ontario and Quebec (the former Canada West and Canada East). Meanwhile talks were proceeding on the method of handing over the vast North West to the new federation. One notable result of the Conference was that the name Dominion of Canada was adopted for the British American union. Tilley, it is said, found the key word, 'Dominion' in Psalm lxxii. 8: 'He shall have dominion also from sea to sea, and from the river unto the ends of the earth . . .'

'From sea to sea' would be the well-chosen motto of the new Dominion. Soon it would stretch from the Atlantic to the Pacific, and from the St Lawrence to the end of land on the edge of the Arctic Ocean. But first the imperial act creating the new state in accordance with the resolutions of the Westminster Conference had to be put through the British parliament. Early in 1867 this measure, the British North America Act, embodying the new federal constitution of British America and the terms of its union, was passed by both houses of parliament. On 1 July the Act came into force. The Dominion of Canada began its career. By 1873 it had brought in the North West, British Columbia, and Prince Edward Island. Newfoundland remained outside until 1949. But the vital step had been taken in 1867, when the plan of Confederation triumphed, when the age of the British American colonies passed away, and that of the Dominion of Canada began.

PART IV
THE CANADIAN NATION

CHAPTER 14

THE NEW DOMINION, 1867–78

1 *The Structure of Government*

In the autumn of 1867, the first parliament of the Dominion of Canada met in the rising town of Ottawa. Ottawa, chosen a few years earlier as the capital of the province of Canada, had now been selected for the Dominion capital. There beside the Ottawa river, on steep cliffs that looked northward to the blue line of Laurentian mountains, fine new parliament buildings had already been erected. They were too fine, George Brown had declared, for a mere province; but they would suit the dignity of a young nation. At any rate, these expansive buildings with their Victorian Gothic spires (one of which reminded Macdonald of a cow-bell) well served the needs of the new federal government. But what was the form of government housed within their walls?

As set forth in the British North America Act of 1867, it was a combination of federalism and the British parliamentary system. There was a Governor-General at the head of the government, and two Houses of Parliament, the Senate and the House of Commons. Because, of course, responsible government continued in effect, a prime minister and cabinet actually governed Canada, dependent on the support of the House of Commons. The Governor-General largely played the formal part of the Crown in Britain; although for some time he continued to exercise more influence on the counsels of government than did Queen Victoria at Westminster. The Senate, the members of which were appointed for life, gave equal representation to the principal sections of the Dominion. The House of Commons was elected on a basis of representation by population and represented the people of Canada as a whole. The right to vote in electing this house was still restricted to men with property, but the amount required was low, the number of voters was large, and by the end of the century Canada was generally speaking a broad-based democracy, with manhood suffrage the rule in both provincial and Dominion elections.

The House of Commons was a much more powerful body than the Senate, since the cabinet rested solely on the Commons' vote of confidence, and not on that of the upper house. On this vital point Canada was following the established practice of the British parliamentary system. But federalism entered the Canadian constitution in the principle of representing sections equally in the Senate, and in the more important fact that certain powers of government did not belong to the Dominion parliament but lay with the provinces.

The provinces had much the same structure of government as the Dominion. There were provincial parliaments or legislatures and provincial prime ministers or premiers, who governed according to the cabinet system. Lieutenant-governors, appointed by the Dominion, served as the formal heads of the provincial governments. On entering Confederation New Brunswick and Nova Scotia had kept their old provincial legislatures which contained two houses, an appointed legislative council and an elected legislative assembly. Because, however, the province of Canada had now been divided into Quebec and Ontario (the former Canada East and Canada West) two new provincial constitutions had been required. They were set forth in the British North America Act. That of Quebec had two houses, as in the Maritimes, but Ontario adopted only a single elected chamber. To-day all the Canadian provinces except Quebec have adopted this simpler, single-chamber form of legislature.

The provincial governments had been given the necessary powers to look after affairs that were largely of local concern, including control over property and civil rights, civil law, municipal governments, licences, the chartering of companies within a province, and the right to raise money by direct taxation in order to meet government expenses. These powers—sixteen in all—were listed in Section 92 of the British North America Act. Education, especially, was a jealously guarded provincial power; and nowhere more than in Quebec, which thus sought to preserve the special ways of French Canada by keeping control of the teaching of its young. The division of federal and provincial powers, moreover, generally served to protect the French minority in Quebec. And as an extra safeguard, it was decreed that Quebec should always have sixty-five members in the federal House of Commons, in order to give the French Canadians a fairly large representation there. Other provinces would have more or fewer members, in so far as their population was greater or smaller than Quebec's. As population patterns altered, membership was to change accordingly, around this central pivot of Quebec.

The powers of the Dominion government were listed in Section 91 of the British North America Act under twenty-nine headings. They included control of the armed forces, postal service, coinage and banking, fisheries, criminal law, the regulation of trade and commerce, and the right to raise money by any mode of taxation, direct or indirect. Obviously the Dominion powers were wider and more numerous, as was fitting for the government of a large state. The Dominion was given a general authority over all matters affecting 'peace, order and good government', except when they fell within the fixed provincial fields. It was made clear that any remaining (or residuary) powers lay with the central government. The provinces had no more than the set of powers definitely listed for them.

This was done because the British North America Act was meant to create a strong union: to shape a federal government with wide authority and local governments with only limited powers. The explanation of this fact goes back to the Quebec Conference, which largely drafted the plan of union that was later embodied in the British North America Act. At Quebec in 1864, there was every desire for a strong union. The pressures from outside were high, driving the colonies together. There was a sense of urgency created by the growing troubles with the United States. At the same time Macdonald, who was becoming the leader of the Confederation movement, had still his old preference for complete union. If that were not possible, then the strongest possible federal union was the next best thing. The central government, therefore, was not only provided with wide powers; it was also given the right of naming the provincial governors, who were to be its local supervisors, and the right to review provincial laws and if necessary to reject or 'disallow' them. Clearly the central authority was the superior. Furthermore, the principle that residuary powers belonged to the Dominion was also meant to strengthen the union. It was intended to avoid the apparent flaw in the federal system of the United States, then in the throes of Civil War. In that country the reserve of power had remained with the states, and half the union had gone to war to assert the supremacy of 'states' rights'.

If the strength of the federation was one distinctive feature of the new system of Canadian government, another was the imprint of British influences upon it. It would be wrong to think that because this was a federal system that it was generally a copy of the American constitution. A 'British American' constitution, Canadians proudly called it; their own particular blend of British and American influences, as was their country itself. Though the designers at Quebec turned naturally to the United States to study federalism in North America, they did so largely to see what to modify or avoid. The Canadian Senate, for example, had only the same name as the powerful American chamber. As an upper house on the British parliamentary model it was not meant to be more than a revising body, or a brake on the House of Commons. Therefore it was deliberately made an appointed house, since an elected Senate might prove too popular and too powerful, and be able to block the will of the House of Commons. The Canadian Senate was really the old British colonial legislative council under a new name. Besides, it did not represent separate provinces or states, as in the American system, but sections; Ontario and Quebec each had twenty-four members, and Nova Scotia and New Brunswick twenty-four together. This 'section' principle was continued as new provinces were added to the Dominion.

The Canadian structure of government, moreover, wedded the British cabinet and the whole unwritten British constitution to a written plan of federalism. Although the written part of the constitution, the British North America Act, would hereafter be subject to the decisions of courts of law, which sometimes hampered it in adjusting easily to new needs, the unwritten part could go on developing in parliament, as in Britain, in order to meet the changing requirements of government. Finally, the whole manner in which this new structure of government was established in Canada showed its British background. It was not done by a compact between independent states, as in the American case. Although the colonies did plan the federal union, and agreed to adopt it, in legal fact the union was enacted by the authority of the imperial parliament. A British act created the Dominion of Canada. The right of framing colonial constitutions still lay with the British parliament. This power to alter the Canadian constitution long remained at Westminster, though it was used only at Canada's request. Nor did the Dominion make any attempt to change this situation for many years to come.

The British North America Act also dealt with other matters than forms of government, such as providing for the admission of new provinces to the east or west, agreeing to begin the Intercolonial within six months after union, and, most important, fixing the financial terms on which the Confederation should operate. The question of financial arrangements had been one of the hardest to deal with at the Quebec Conference. Dissatisfaction with the terms adopted had been a main factor in the anti-federation movements in the Maritimes afterwards. The problem was still in existence when the Dominion began its career. The great difficulty was that, in giving up to the new central government the right to collect indirect taxes, the right to fix a tariff and levy customs duties, the provinces were losing their main source of income. This hit the Maritimes particularly hard. Direct taxation had never been as fully developed in the Atlantic provinces as in Canada.

In consequence it was agreed at the Quebec Conference that all the provinces should receive certain yearly payments or subsidies from the Dominion, in accordance with the size of their population, because of the taxing powers which they had given up. These subsidies were later raised for the Maritimes, when they complained that their financial problems had not been met, and pressed for 'better terms'. All in all, the principle of subsidies was really a basic part of the new structure of government: a main factor in making it possible, and an important item as well in the dispute which in time would arise over the relations between the provinces and the government of the Dominion.

2 Rounding Out the Dominion

The first great task of the young Dominion was to extend its boundaries from sea to sea to bring in all the broad northern lands of the continent. This was done within six years of the founding of the new Canadian union and under the guiding genius of its first prime minister, Macdonald—now Sir John A. Macdonald. By 1873, only Newfoundland among the former British American colonies had failed to join Confederation. Supporters of union had carried on an active campaign in the island between 1865 and 1869. Though the colony had not shared in the London Conference of 1866–7 that had drawn up the final plans for the British North America Act, talks had been reopened in 1868 between Newfoundland and Canada. A delegation had visited Ottawa and returned to the island with the draft of an agreement for union. The next year, however, the Newfoundland government which backed the agreement was thoroughly defeated at an election. The people of the colony thought the financial arrangements were insufficient, and the general ignorance, and even suspicion, of Canada were successfully played upon by the enemies of federation. As a result, after 1869 Newfoundland dropped thoughts of union for some time to come, and determined to go forward on its own.

There were other questions as well as that of Newfoundland facing the Dominion in the east. For example, the promised Intercolonial railway had to be constructed. It was begun at once as a government project and finished in 1876. The line ran through New Brunswick as far from the American border as possible, for reasons of defence, and so was too remote from the settled areas to gain much traffic. Yet though it did not pay, this first railway link between the Maritimes and the interior was a necessary step in completing the Dominion. Railway lines at last had pierced the Appalachian barrier, through the deep, wooded trough of the Matapedia valley, to join the St Lawrence region with that of the Gulf and the Atlantic.

Another and more serious eastern problem was the renewed antifederation movement in Nova Scotia. In 1867, at the first Dominion elections, anti-unionists led by Joseph Howe had swept that province. Howe still had his fears for his native province, and managed to swing the closely balanced forces in Nova Scotia in his favour. It was here that Macdonald found a chance to display his talent for union-making. When Nova Scotia's anti-unionists failed to influence the British government and parliament, Sir John undermined their stand on separation by arranging better financial terms for their province and by persuading their leader, Howe, to accept a seat in his coalition government. Nova Scotia was fairly well settled in Confederation thereafter, though for Howe this was the last, and perhaps the least, period of his great career. But it would not be the last time that Macdonald's political skill and the Dominion treasury would work together to cement the new Canadian union.

The financial power of the Dominion also served largely to bring in another province in the east. Prince Edward Island was running into money problems, and looked on union with Canada with new favour. The island had built a railway for itself, but had gone heavily into debt. Funds were needed as well to end that age-old burden of the little province, the absentee ownership of land. Entrance into the Dominion would provide more money for the railway and help in buying out the absentee land-owners. By now the island province also wanted a good connection with the growing railway system on the Canadian mainland. The guarantee that a regular ferry service would be maintained formed one of its terms for union. In 1873, therefore, Prince Edward Island became the third Maritime province to join the Dominion of Canada.

But meanwhile the main expansion of the Dominion was proceeding westward. The transfer of the North West to Canada had been one of the prime aims of the Confederation movement. The new Dominion at once took up this question, which chiefly involved settling the price for which the Hudson's Bay Company would agree to give up its charter to Rupert's Land. In 1868 the British parliament passed the Rupert's Land Act, to ensure the transfer of the Hudson's Bay domain to Canada when terms had been reached, and in 1869 the Company accepted a Canadian offer of £300,000 and large western land grants. Rupert's Land and the North West Territory beyond, where the Company had held the trade monopoly, could now be transferred to Canada. The young Dominion would reach to the Rockies, and north to the Arctic Ocean. This tremendous addition it decided to rule as the North West Territories, under a lieutenant-governor and council appointed in Ottawa.

Yet the feelings of the little settlement at the Red river, in the heart of this great new empire, had not been consulted during the transfer. Under the absolute authority of the Hudson's Bay Company, the settlers had little voice in their own government. They began to wonder what their future might be. While, on the whole, they had come to accept the idea of union with Canada there were some who hoped to establish a separate colony under British rule. The rather noisy, overbearing handful of Canadians in their midst, who looked down on the other inhabitants, the unexpected appearance of Canadian land surveyors, who plotted out square land divisions as if the long, thin river-bank farms of the Red river did not exist, added to the uneasiness of the settlers.

The largest group at Red river were the English- and French-speaking half-breeds, who feared for their free life of the plains if Canadian settlement should begin in earnest. The more numerous French-speaking half-breeds, the Métis, were also worried over the fate of their Catholic religion and French culture when English Canadians poured in. Their hope of raising a new French Canada in the West, a hope shared by the Catholic Church and Quebec, seemed dangerously threatened. And now the danger was at hand. In the autumn of 1869 the new Canadian lieutenant-governor, William McDougall, who had worked with George Brown in seeking the West for Canada, reached the Red river to take over the colony.

At this point the Métis found a leader, the clever but unbalanced Louis Riel, a French-speaking inhabitant of Red river with a dash of Indian blood. Seizing on the fact that McDougall had arrived ahead of the date when his authority was to begin, while that of the Hudson's Bay Company had lapsed, Riel set up a 'provisional government' of his own. He took over Fort Garry, the chief Hudson's Bay post at the Red river, and stopped McDougall at the border of the settlement. Yet this was not quite a rebellion. There was no thought of rebelling against Britain; Canada had not yet actually taken over the West, and would not do so until she could obtain peaceful possession. Riel's government, moreover, established orderly rule and set up a representative assembly; it was accepted by most of the Red river colonists, the French and English half-breeds, the former Hudson's Bay men, and the descendants of Selkirk's settlers. Only the small Canadian group opposed it. And this led to the one act of violence that in the long run proved fatal: the execution of Thomas Scott, a young English-speaking Canadian who resisted Riel's authority. He brought down on himself the fury of the Métis leader, whose vanity could hardly bear opposition.

Riel's purpose in setting up his government was to win terms from Canada, so that the Red river could enter the Dominion as a separate province with guarantees for the Métis land and protection for French rights, as in Quebec. Accordingly Red river delegates travelled to Ottawa, while Macdonald sent a new representative to the West to replace the unsuccessful McDougall in treating with Riel. Terms were reached that gave the Red river almost everything it sought, and it was clear that the Riel government would peaceably disband. But in order, as well, to give the new Canadian authority proper force in the West it was agreed that a military expedition should go to the Red river. A few hundred British regulars and Canadian militia under Colonel Garnet Wolseley marched west through the wilderness beyond the head of the Great Lakes in the summer of 1870. And that year the Red river settlement was set up apart from the rest of the North West Territories as the new province of Manitoba. By the Riel rising, therefore, Manitoba had been forced into being as a full partner in the Dominion, although as yet its population was quite small. In the new province both the French and English languages were to be in official use, and Catholics and Protestants were to have their own school systems. Apparently the French Métis had succeeded in creating a little Quebec in the west.

But meanwhile feeling was rising in English-speaking Canada, especially in Ontario, over the execution of Scott. Ontario denounced Riel as a traitor and murderer and regarded the Wolseley expedition as an army sent to put down rebellion. Quebec naturally regarded Riel as a hero, and warmly defended him. Perhaps he was both hero and murderer, for despite the orderliness of his provisional government it did not have the power to put a man to death. Here Riel's lack of balance had carried him into needless violence. Accordingly, when the Wolseley expedition approached, fearing punishment, Riel fled the Red river. His government collapsed. Canada had gained the West and made a province; but the Riel rising, with the bad feelings it caused between French and English in Quebec and Ontario, was to cast its shadow over the Dominion in years to come.

The next step for Canada was expansion to the Pacific coast. There on the western slopes of the continent Vancouver Island had been joined to the province of British Columbia in 1866. But the province was still weak and backward, with only about ten thousand inhabitants, and representative, but not responsible, government. The gold rush was over by now; British Columbia not only did not grow but floundered in financial difficulties. The only way out seemed to be union with Canada or with the United States. When, however, a document calling for annexation to the republic was put forward in 1869 only one hundred and four persons signed it. The majority wanted 'British' Columbia, indeed.

On the other hand there was a growing desire for union with Canada. This became particularly strong when the Dominion took over the North-West and so moved next door to the Pacific province. The campaign for union with Canada gained force, pressed on by a colonist who had taken the splendid name of Amor de Cosmos (his real name was Smith). Led by de Cosmos and the imperial authorities, who still wielded much power in British Columbia, the unionist cause readily won its victory. In 1870 delegates from the province reached terms of union in Ottawa, including the promise that the Dominion would begin a railway to the Pacific in two years and finish it in ten. And in 1871 British Columbia joined Confederation, as another full partner, with its own responsible provincial government.

The Dominion stretched from sea to sea—*A mari usque ad mare*, as its motto declares. It had taken only four years to reach across the continent, while the United States had taken more than half a century. Yet this very difference in speed was a result of the presence of the United States. The constant threat of American expansion, that had made the question of union so pressing, had created a constant sense of urgency. Canada had grown so fast because the ceaseless advance of American settlement in the west and the aggressive mood of the United States after the Civil War had driven her on. These dangers had also made both the British colonists outside the borders of the Dominion and the government in Britain eager to support the cause of union. There were Fenian stirrings at the Red river, though the Métis rallied against them; the United States had bought Alaska from Russia in 1867 and was talking of taking over the entire Pacific coast. The Dominion had need to expand quickly. Of course, the fact that it brought in territories that were already British enabled Canada to grow as rapidly as it did.

At the same time this rapid expansion stretched Canada thin. Because of the need for haste, the Dominion did not grow as the United States had done, hand in hand with settlement and commerce, but far ahead of them. In rounding out the Dominion not much more had been accomplished than the staking of a claim across the continent. Now it had to be filled in, if it were to endure. Railways and settlements had to move west. The union had to be made real in men's interests, hearts, and minds. These were the next problems for Canada.

3 *Macdonald Conservatism and a Liberal Interlude*

During the dramatic first six years of the Dominion, when Canada gained far more land than she had held in 1867, Sir John A. Macdonald had governed the country. There followed five short years of Liberal rule, and then Macdonald returned to power, to hold it from 1878 until his death in 1891. Nor did the Liberal-Conservative party which he had moulded finally fall from office until 1896. Macdonald Conservatism, therefore, is vitally connected with the first thirty years of the Dominion's history. And it was during Macdonald's first Dominion government that the outlines and policies of Conservatism took shape.

Officially, his first cabinet was a coalition. Before the elections were held in the summer of 1867 to fill the new federal parliament, Macdonald and his allies had raised a cry for a no-party government to launch the Dominion in a spirit of unity and patriotism. It was a highly successful appeal. George Brown, once more Macdonald's chief foe now that Confederation had been carried, found himself and the Clear Grit Liberals put in a false position as unpatriotic 'anti-unionists'—which they were not—because they wanted to start the new governing system on the basis of party politics. And so, despite Brown's strong hold on the largest province, Ontario, Macdonald swept into power. Thanks largely to his no-party cry, he gained many Liberal votes in all the provinces; and these together with his Conservative support gave him a firm majority. The Ontario Grits retreated angrily to opposition. George Brown retired into private life, although as owner of the chief Liberal journal, the Toronto *Globe*, he continued to exercise much influence over his party until his death in 1880.

In office meanwhile, Macdonald brought into his cabinet some lesser Liberals from Ontario, as well as Tilley from New Brunswick, and soon Howe from Nova Scotia, in order to prove that this was indeed a coalition government. Yet the leading men in the cabinet, including Cartier and Tupper of Nova Scotia, were Conservatives. Under Macdonald's powerful leadership, moreover, the whole cabinet began to take on a one-party colour. It became a Conservative government, devoted to building up the Dominion and to preserving the federal union. To these ends it was ready to spend money freely, to make grand and costly plans for a big Canada, and to tie itself closely with wealthy business and railway interests. Such an attitude, of course, came down from the Liberal-Conservative party of the old province of Canada. And the vital partnership between the French Canadians and leading English-Canadian business men was also carried over into the Dominion Conservative party. It stood for a union of the two peoples and all the provinces. To maintain that uncertain union Macdonald used all his warm personal charm and sharp political craft—which once brought a prominent Liberal to exclaim, 'Ah, John A., John A., how I love you. How I wish I could trust you!'

On the other side Liberalism was also taking shape in the Dominion, building largely on the Clear Grits of the former Canada West. The Liberal party was at first much looser than the Conservative because it represented a jumble of discontented provincial groups rather than one general national alliance. The Liberals remained strong in the province of Ontario, however. Here Oliver Mowat, a former follower of George Brown and a Liberal Father of Confederation, ruled the provincial government for at least as long as Macdonald controlled the federal government at Ottawa. In Dominion circles, the Liberals gradually took on definite form as they steadily opposed the sweeping and expensive schemes of Conservative ministers. As the earlier Clear Grits had done, they attacked the dangerous influence of railways and business on the government, and stood by the farming interest. They called for a slower, more cautious development of Canada, in keeping, they said, with the true limits of the country's wealth. In particular, the Liberals came to stand for provincial rights, whereas Macdonald repeatedly stressed the superior power of the central government. Accordingly Liberalism gathered support in most of the provinces from those who felt that the Dominion was riding rough-shod over the just rights of the different sections that had entered Confederation.

The fall of the Macdonald government came in 1873 with a full-blown scandal that seemed to prove the Liberal arguments concerning the waste and corruption of Conservative rule. The scandal, moreover, was linked with the government's policy of rapid expansion and expensive railway building, and the promise to British Columbia to begin a Pacific railway within two years after that province's entry into Confederation. The Dominion government had offered a charter on very attractive terms to any company that would build the Canadian Pacific Railway. Two powerful financial groups, one centred in Toronto, one in Montreal, had been struggling to gain the Western railway contract. When in 1873 some of the Montreal interests were granted the charter, their enemies alleged that the award was the result of a corrupt bargain, whereby the favoured group had poured money into the Conservative party's election funds. Copies of letters and telegrams were produced as proof of the 'Pacific scandal', and the Liberals in parliament demanded that the government resign.

Now it is clear that Macdonald had not personally been bribed, and the system of 'friends' contributing to party funds in the hope of favours was an unfortunate but well-established practice in Canada and elsewhere. Besides, the company that had been given the charter was not wholly the same as the original group that had contributed funds. Nevertheless public opinion was thoroughly aroused, and the Liberal party swept a new election to form a government under Alexander Mackenzie. It seemed that the Pacific scandal had revealed the worst features of Conservatism, that arose from dealing too freely with great sums of money and having too close a connection with powerful business groups.

The new Mackenzie ministry looked very different. Mackenzie had been Brown's chief lieutenant and succeeded him as Dominion Liberal leader. Sharing Brown's dislike of extravagant government, Mackenzie was honest and hard-working; but he lacked the vision of either Brown or Macdonald. And while he determined to give Canada what it seemed to need—cheap, efficient government—his ministry turned away from the Macdonald programme of nation-building. With regard to the Pacific railway, Mackenzie found it impossible to attract capitalists and proceeded to build the line as a government project in sections between existing waterways. British Columbia became impatient with the slow progress of the railway, and angry arguments developed. It took the cool diplomacy of Lord Dufferin, the Governor-General, to smooth down the disputes, after a special trip to British Columbia. Nevertheless under Mackenzie some hundreds of miles of track were laid in British Columbia and between the Great Lakes and Manitoba. A survey was also carried out for the whole route, which selected passes through the lofty western ranges. During this time, moreover, new settlements were begun in Manitoba. The western wheat lands were opening.

Aside from this limited expansion westward, the chief achievement of the Mackenzie era lay in carrying Canada farther along the road from colony to nation. The Liberals were at their strongest in this kind of nation-building, in widening Canada's powers of self-government. Through Edward Blake, as Minister of Justice in the Mackenzie cabinet, a Canadian Supreme Court was set up, which reduced appeals from Canadian courts of law to the imperial Privy Council in London. Blake also managed to have the instructions of the Governor-General changed, in order to limit the power that he still had to act on his own, without the advice of the Dominion cabinet. From this time forward the Governor-Generals of Canada on the whole had much prestige but little power. All in all, however, any advances towards nationhood made during the Mackenzie period were overshadowed by the government's failure to make practical gains in unifying and strengthening Canada. By 1878, when the Liberals fell, their government faced a mass of discontents with little policy for the future.

The root of the problem was the great world trade depression that began in 1873 and lasted, with only a few short periods of recovery, until 1896. The Mackenzie government could hardly be blamed for the effects of depression on Canada—but, human nature being what it is, it was blamed. And undoubtedly, the Liberals' dislike of strong government action and their belief in keeping down expenses prevented them from taking any bold steps to meet the sharp decline in Canada's trade and the growing

discontent in the country. Their one hope had been a renewal of
the Reciprocity Treaty with the United States. Believing in free
trade, the Liberals looked back, as to a golden age, to the time when
the Treaty had removed trade barriers between Canada and the
United States and brought a high level of commercial prosperity.
George Brown had been sent to Washington in 1874 to obtain a
new reciprocity agreement. He had failed, since the United States
was following the opposite policy to free trade, of raising tariffs
ever higher and higher.

After this failure, the Mackenzie Liberals had really no programme, as financial difficulties mounted, except to try to cut
expenses. But they themselves were forced to increase the Canadian tariff slightly, in order to bring in sufficient revenue as trade
fell off. By now there was a powerful agitation in the Dominion,
especially among manufacturers, for a higher Canadian tariff.
Faced with heavy competition, the manufacturers wanted to keep
the Canadian market for Canadians by burdening goods imported
from abroad with heavy customs duties. The sharp-eyed Macdonald saw in this high-tariff or protectionist movement a means
of returning to power. He seized on the demand that, if there
could not be reciprocity of trade with the Americans, there should
be 'reciprocity of tariffs'; that is, Canada should impose her own
high tariff to strike back at the United States.

It was not a wholly sound idea, but it suited the mood of the
times. The Conservative leader, moreover, could claim that, since
the tariff would have to be increased in any case to meet the
government's need of revenue, the increased duties could be
arranged to the advantage of Canada: to protect the home market
for Canadians, to foster Canadian industry, and so to bring about
a national revival of trade. Under the persuasive name of the
'National Policy,' Macdonald put his plan before the country in
the election of 1878. The free-trade Liberals clung to a low tariff.
But having failed to halt the trade decline, failed to build the
Canadian Pacific, and roused discontent in most of the provinces,

they were readily defeated. Macdonald swept back to power, and the first uncertain age in the Dominion's history came to a close. The hard times of 1878 put a gloomy ending to the era. Yet Macdonald Conservatism was back in control, and hopes were high for the future.

4   *The Life of the Young Dominion*

When the Dominion of Canada came into being in 1867 it contained about 3,300,000 people, and the addition of new provinces in the next few years did not bring many thousands more. Ontario and Quebec together held about three-quarters of this population. While Ontario had the larger share and continued to grow fairly steadily, Quebec's population increased only slowly, thanks to the constant drain of large numbers of French Canadians into the factories of the north-eastern United States. The emigration to the United States from all parts of Canada was, in fact, the chief reason why the Dominion did not grow as fast as expected in the years that followed. The peak of immigration from Britain had passed before Confederation and a great new wave from the British Isles did not begin until the turn of the twentieth century. Consequently, by the time of Macdonald's death in 1891, the population of Canada had only risen to 4,800,000. But one result of the decline of immigration was that the people of English-speaking Canada grew increasingly 'Canadian' in their outlook. And though the Dominion rose rather slowly, foiling the brightest hopes of the nation-builders, it still gave a good life to the mass of its inhabitants, even in the long depression after 1873.

The main ways of life in the new Dominion had not changed greatly since the pioneer age. Lumbering was still of prime importance in 1867; wooden ship-building reached its highest peak in the years after the American Civil War. Fishing in the Maritimes, farming in central Canada, and mining and the fur trade in the West remained the other chief employments. Yet the comforts of life had improved considerably since pioneer days. Towns had grown, railways and manufacturing spread; and already by 1867 important changes were under way that would greatly alter Canada in the next thirty years.

These changes were for the most part the result of the rise of industry in central Canada. Compared with the industrialism that came in a later day, this was small-scale manufacturing, a matter of boots and shoes, woollens, furniture, and farm machinery. But compared with what had been, it was an important step forward for the Dominion. As the factories of central Canada grew, so its farmers turned increasingly from growing grain for export to mixed farming in order to supply the local manufacturing towns. Ontario's grain fields in any case were passing their prime. Thus by the 1890's, central Canada was becoming a region of mixed farming, dairying, and fruit growing; while, of course, broad new grainlands were being brought under the plough in the far western prairies. Various minerals, copper, lead and gypsum, for example, were being produced in central Canada, and other minerals, especially coal, in the Maritimes. Eastern Canada as a whole was broadening out into new activities, and its old basic occupations of lumbering and ship-building were less important than before. Central Canada in particular was becoming a well-rounded, thickly settled region of small farms and busy towns.

The Maritimes, however, were falling behind in the rising industrial age. Their coal went to central Canadian factories; industry did not come to the Maritimes. Nor did the great flow of trade that they had hoped for come to their ports over the new railways. Although the lines did bring some traffic, the plain fact was that, since water transport is cheaper than land, it paid to ship most inland goods through Montreal or American ports, and not to make the longer rail journey to the Maritimes' harbours on the eastern tip of the continent. And so the Atlantic provinces made far slower progress than the rest of Canada.

In Ontario and Quebec, meanwhile, the growing strength of industry showed itself in the mounting demand for a protective tariff that would preserve the home market for Canadian manufacturers. The growth of finance went with industrial advance. Toronto had now become a powerful rival of Montreal; its own great banks and financial companies competed with those of the older centre for control of Canadian business. By the 1890's Toronto had become the second metropolis of Canada. Two other leading Canadian cities really began in this era. With the completion of the Canadian Pacific in 1885, Vancouver came into existence as the western outlet of the transcontinental railway system, while Winnipeg soon rose out of Fort Garry as the chief prairie business centre, once western settlement was under way.

Although Canada was altering, in the first thirty years of the young Dominion, most of its people continued to live in the country, not in the towns. The life of the Quebec farm, or the Maritime fishing village had changed but little, even though the roar of trains and the humming of telegraph wires through the countryside told of a changing pace in Canada. In Ontario stone or brick farmhouses had replaced pioneer log cabins, orchards and pastures the dark bush, and trim buggies on springs the bone-bruising carts of early days. Yet still the people lived close to their own countryside and found their pleasures in the family circle, the church 'social' or perhaps the political picnic. Though communications had greatly improved there was not yet much travel from province to province, except for the 'drummer', or travelling salesman, from some city trading-house.

The principal towns showed signs of progress in the many new churches or the large public buildings raised—most of them, unfortunately, in the worst period of Victorian bad taste in architecture. Gas-lighting and horse-drawn tram cars made their appearance. Yet even the main streets were usually still unpaved, and 'sidewalks', where they were found, were frequently only of planks. In the towns, however, the level of culture was rising. Theatres were well attended, especially when European 'greats' from Jenny Lind to Madame Modjeska arrived on tour. Musical societies, public libraries, philosophical clubs, all sprang up. Painting and sculpture were slower to develop, though the first Canadian artists made a beginning at this time, and French Canada had long had a tradition of fine wood-carving.

A truly Canadian literature was also slow to appear. Quebec had laid foundations with F. X. Garneau, the first great historian of French Canada, who died in 1866, and with Octave Crémazie, the 'father of French-Canadian poetry', who lived till 1879. Worthy successors followed them in prose and poetry, but in English-speaking Canada there was less literary development. In 1877, however, William Kirby wrote *The Golden Dog*, a tale of Quebec City in the last days of New France, and this was probably the first important English-Canadian novel. In English Canada, moreover, some of its ablest journalists were at work in the period after Confederation. Out of this journalism gradually came monthly and weekly periodicals that showed promising ability and an earnest desire to be Canadian; in short, to give the new Dominion a character and viewpoint of its own.

Much of this development was related to the Canada First movement, which began in the early 1870's among a group of able young men in Toronto. Its aim was to build a new nationality; to shape a national spirit in Canada, and unite the parts of the Dominion in a common outlook that would, indeed, put Canada first. The movement largely expressed the bright confidence of the first few years after Confederation, and soon foundered in the Great Depression that followed. Yet before its death Canada First produced the writings of William Foster and Charles Mair, the poet, as well as a short-lived but brilliant journal, the *Nation*. The *Nation* (1874-6) was influenced and supported by Goldwin Smith, former Oxford professor of Modern History, who had settled in Toronto with high hopes for the future of Canada. Edward Blake, the prominent Liberal, at first also befriended Canada First, believing as he did in greater national freedom for Canada. But Canada First was not to capture the Liberal party. The older

Liberals feared that it meant the empire last or not at all, and George Brown's mighty *Globe* strongly attacked the *Nation*. Blake also abandoned the movement, although it was not really opposed to the British tie. And Goldwin Smith, who had certainly looked to national independence for Canada, became bitterly disillusioned. He spent the rest of his long life in the Dominion attacking the dreams of nationalism and suggesting annexation to the United States as the only way out.

Canada First and the *Nation*, however, left a heritage for the future. The *Canadian Monthly* (1872-82), both a political and a literary paper, carried on the effort to develop Canadian culture and sounded the national note of Canada First. *The Week* (1883-96) was less directly connected with the earlier movement, but its literary merit was even higher. In fact, it has been judged the best weekly journal that Canada has yet seen. Charles G. D. Roberts, a youthful poet from the Maritimes, edited it briefly. His writings and those of Archibald Lampman and many other new authors appeared in its pages. In 1880, Roberts had published his *Orion and Other Poems*; with this a Canadian school of poetry began. Lampman, then a university student in Toronto, found in *Orion* proof that Canadian literature no longer need lag behind, making colonial copies of the work of older lands. He was greatly stirred by it, and so were other young poets. By the 1890's, Lampman, Roberts, Bliss Carman, and Duncan Campbell Scott, were shaping the 'golden age of Canadian lyric poetry'. This far, at least, the young Dominion had come. Despite the discouragements of depression years, Canada was beginning to express her own spirit and feelings.

Education was also developing steadily in the new Dominion. The University of Toronto was already a large institution when the Dominion was born, and several other colleges came to unite with it on a federal basis, like that of Canada herself. The flourishing universities were founding a tradition of Canadian scholarship. Public education was general, and by now it was usually

CHIEF BIG BEAR TRADING AT FORT PITT, SHORTLY BEFORE
JOINING THE RISING OF 1885

VOLUNTEER TROOPS ON THE PRAIRIES IN THE NORTH WEST
REBELLION OF 1885

First C.P.R. Through Train reaches Port Moody, 1886

free and compulsory. On the whole the young Dominion had little to be ashamed of, either in the standards by which most of its people lived, or in the amount of learning that they could obtain. Granted that progress was faster and prosperity greater in the United States; granted that learning and the arts were more advanced there—and above all in Europe: Canada still offered ample opportunities for a healthy, diligent people. Its life might seem less spacious and comfortable than the American, its culture far behind Britain's. But the young Dominion that had so recently emerged from the pioneer age had reason only for self-criticism, not for disappointment.

CHAPTER 15

MACDONALD NATIONALISM AND
SECTIONAL DISCONTENT, 1878–96

1 *The Brave Days of the National Policy*

When Sir John Macdonald returned to power in September 1878, he laid down plans for one of the most daring periods of nation-building in Canada's history. For his ventures he had the eager support of the mass of the Canadian people, who felt that the Liberals had failed them in their time of need, leaving the Dominion divided, the western empire still empty and the Pacific railway unbuilt. In the next ten years Liberalism could make little headway against 'John A.' Mackenzie had been replaced as Liberal leader by Edward Blake, the ablest lawyer in Canada and a powerful parliamentary debater. But all the sharp thrusts of the keen, cold mind of Blake against the government's follies and waste could not convince the people that the Liberals' grey policy of caution was the right one for Canada. They believed in Macdonald's bold national plans, shared his breezy, dauntless confidence. And a brief recovery of trade, soon after the Conservatives were elected, seemed at first to justify that faith.

Macdonald had at once plunged ahead with his National Policy of tariff protection. The tariff of 1879 made the greatest change of any up to that time in Canadian commercial policy. It brought in a thorough-going scheme of protective customs duties, on farm products as well as on manufactures, and raised the duties on manufactured goods from $17\frac{1}{2}$ per cent to 25 per cent and over. This was still not as high as the American tariff; in general, Canadian protective tariffs would not rise as high as those of the United States. Yet it was a far cry from British free trade and even from past Canadian tariff policies before Confederation. After the removal of the old colonial system had permitted the colonies to control their own tariffs, Canada, and the Maritimes especially, had kept their customs duties fairly low. Because young countries have not much wealth to tax directly, it had been necessary for them to raise government revenue through duties on imported goods. Hence, although free trade was the ideal, low or 'revenue' tariffs had been the practice in British North America. True, the Canadian tariff of 1858–9, that had caused an outcry in free-trade Britain, had given a certain amount of protection to Canadian manufacturing. Its stated purpose, however, had been to raise more revenue to meet large public debts. The duties had been lowered again before Confederation, and from the birth of the Dominion to 1879 revenue tariffs had once more been the rule. But now the National Policy was bringing in protection. Could it be justified?

A protective tariff plainly meant that goods would cost more to buy in Canada, since purchasers would have to pay the extra cost of the customs duties, or their equivalent. This affected the farmers particularly. They sold a large part of their own products abroad, and thus could not reap the full advantage of higher prices in the Canadian market, although they still had to pay more for the goods they bought. In time, opposition to the protective tariff was to centre among the farmers of the Dominion. On the other hand, manufacturers, or any interest that sold mostly in the home market, would be helped by higher prices and the cutting down of competition from abroad. Given protection, it was argued, these interests would grow, and Canada's wealth and prosperity with them, until the demand for all sorts of goods at home became so large that every kind of producer, farmers included, would benefit from good times and ample markets in Canada.

The value of such an argument can hardly be settled here. Clearly the widespread adoption of protection harms world trade and has left nations to-day struggling against a world-wide tangle of extremely high tariffs. Just as clearly, no country has been able to afford free trade, except Great Britain at the height of her power. The answer, as usual, lies probably between the two extremes of trade policy. Yet as far as Canada is concerned, the protective tariff system that was adopted under Macdonald, and which still exists, with increases here, decreases there, did much in the long run to develop the wealth and encourage the industry of the Dominion. The system begun in 1879 has become woven into the history and life of the country, though no one can truly say what else 'might have been'.

Macdonald's National Policy, moreover, was adopted at a difficult moment, when other policies had failed. It was arranged to promise something to everyone, even the farmers, and it was coupled with two other great designs: the building of the Canadian Pacific and the settlement of the West. All three were meant to work together. The tariff would shape a national market, the railway would serve it from coast to coast. The railway, also, would carry settlers to the West and bring their farm products to eastern purchasers. And, thanks to the tariff, eastern industry would grow rapidly; both to supply manufacturers for the rising numbers of western farmers and to provide a large town population that would constantly need western foodstuffs. The National Policy, then, was really a three-cornered scheme of nation-building, dependent on railways and settlement as well as the tariff for its full success. Its aim was a well-balanced, prosperous nation.

The tariff had been easily adopted, but now railway-building and western settlement had to go forward. Settlement, obviously, could not come until the railway was built, for no great number of settlers could move to the vast and far-distant West except by railway; nor would they want to go until they could obtain supplies fairly easily and ship their products out to market. The Macdonald government accordingly turned to the question of the Canadian Pacific. They considered that only a private company could build the line quickly enough. Although their fingers had been burnt before, they again offered terms for a charter to build the C.P.R. The charter terms seemed sufficiently generous. The railway company was to receive the track mileage already completed, a money payment to aid in meeting construction costs of twenty-five million dollars, and a grant of twenty-five million acres of good land, consisting of every second 'section' (six hundred and forty acres) within a belt twenty-four miles wide on either side of the railway line across the prairies. The idea behind this railway land grant was that the company, by selling farms to incoming settlers, would earn back the tremendous costs of building the transcontinental, and, it was thought, make a good profit besides.

Besides all this, the Canadian Pacific company was to be for ever free of taxation on its railway property, and to have a monopoly of traffic for twenty years in western Canada. That is to say, no competing railway could be built to the border to link up with American systems until the east-west traffic of the C.P.R. had been established with a twenty years' head-start. In return for these terms the company had to build a railway from central Canada to the Pacific within ten years. Surely the Liberals were right in attacking the charter as a most extravagant kind of bargain.

And yet the task involved was so tremendous that before the railway was finished the charter terms had proved insufficient. The United States had been a powerful, wealthy nation of forty million people when it built its first Pacific railway in the 1860's. The young Dominion had only four million when it undertook a similar line in the 1880's. Moreover, while American lines could begin in the rich and well-populated Middle West, the Canadian railway had to cross nine hundred miles of the Shield, a barrier of bleak, difficult wilderness, offering small hope of traffic, before the great prairies were even reached. Then, too, the Pacific mountains were higher and harder to cross in the Canadian half of the continent. A pass suitable for a railway through the blank rampart of the Selkirks was only found in 1882, when the track was nearing the mountains. And in addition, the Canadian Pacific company found it hard to raise funds in the London money market, the financial centre of the world. British investors remembered the losses of the Grand Trunk, and would have little to do with this new Canadian railway—that would one day turn out to be a striking success.

Consequently, the company that secured the Pacific railway charter in October, 1880, was for the most part a Canadian group centred on Montreal. By constructing the Canadian Pacific, Montreal renewed its old commercial links with the far west, lost since fur trade days. A new commercial empire of the St Lawrence sprang up, based on railway lines, but far greater than that of the unsuccessful Grand Trunk. Once again an east-west trading system reached across the northern continent, linking it together, tying the Pacific slopes and the North-West prairies with the great river and the Atlantic. And the men who built the railway, who gave the vast and vague Dominion a backbone of steel, were no less daring and determined than Alexander Mackenzie and the fur lords of the old North West Company. Donald Smith and George Stephen, the railway financiers, William Van Horne, the construction manager: these were the new moulders of Montreal's destiny, and moulders, too, of a Canadian nation

While Smith handled affairs at headquarters in Montreal and Stephen toured New York and London money markets in search of funds, Van Horne pressed the building forward with all possible speed. The line crept along the edge of the Shield, beside the rugged shore of Lake Superior, around rocky bluffs and over bottomless muskeg swamp, until it came into the prairies, where it raced rapidly ahead, over the flat lands. But meanwhile the Company's financial problems had grown steadily more pressing, and time after time it had to seek more aid from the government. Finally even the confidence of Macdonald, under relentless Liberal attack, was shaken by the mounting cost and the prospect of pouring money into a C.P.R. pit as bottomless as the muskeg. It was then that a party follower reminded him that 'the day the

Canadian Pacific busts, the Conservative party busts the day after.' The two had become so thoroughly entwined. But at this critical moment, in 1885, a rebellion broke out in the prairies of the North West, and, strangely enough, saved the railway by proving its value to the public.

2 Problems of Opening the Prairies

The North West rebellion of 1885 had much in common with the earlier rising in the Red River. Most of the Métis had moved west to the empty banks of the North Saskatchewan river as settlement spread in Manitoba. They could not breathe easily in civilization. But now, as the railway approached, civilization was threatening them once more on the Saskatchewan. Surveyors appeared again, and again the Métis feared for the titles to their land. When petitions to Ottawa brought little response the Métis sent to their old leader, who was living in the United States, to ask his help. Louis Riel returned to his people. But this was an even more unbalanced Riel, who had spent two of the fifteen years since the Red River rising in mental hospitals. If Macdonald's government deserves blame for not meeting the Métis' grievances in time, Riel brought no benefit to his followers.

He soon launched the Métis' protests on a more violent course. This time there was the presence of Indian bands to add to the violence. The plains Indians, tied by blood to the Métis, shared their confusion and their fears. The buffalo herds that they lived by were fast disappearing from the prairies. The approach of the railway and settlement threatened to destroy their world of endless horizons and leave them only the limits of the Indian reservations. For them as for the Métis, therefore, the rebellion of 1885 was a last-ditch defence of the old life of the hunter and fur trader against the new age of the locomotive and the farmer. There were several sharp and bitter clashes—Duck Lake, Frog Lake, and in the gun-pits at Batoche. Indian war cries for the last time struck terror into white men in Canada, and Métis' hunting rifles made guerilla warfare effective and deadly.

Yet the rebellion, a hopeless effort, was quickly put down. Riel was filled with wild dreams of a new state and a new religion and gave no effective leadership, while the Catholic priests of the French Métis were thoroughly opposed to the rising. More than seven thousand troops were hurriedly raised in eastern Canada. Under General Middleton they moved west, crushed the rebellion, captured Riel, and made terms with the Métis and Indians. And the troops sent west moved swiftly over the Canadian Pacific to the 'end of steel' at Regina. They took days to reach the prairies, whereas the expedition to the Red River in 1870 had taken months. It was striking proof of what the railway could do.

After this there was little trouble in granting the Canadian Pacific sufficient aid to finish the job. It was very near completion now. On 7 November, 1885, at Craigellachie in a rocky pass high in the British Columbia mountains, the last spike was driven. East and West had been joined—in five years, not ten. Joseph Howe's prophecy had come true, as the whistle of the locomotive echoed through the lonely canyons of the Rockies. Macdonald was one of the early passengers to cross the continent on the new railway. As he stood by the Pacific shore on Burrard Inlet, where the new port city of Vancouver was rising, he might have reflected that this was the end of a journey that had begun at Charlottetown on the Atlantic twenty-two years before. Steel and steam, vision and daring, had met the challenge of a continent.

The C.P.R. was in being; now western settlement could proceed. Much had already been done under Macdonald towards opening the West. In 1873 the North West Mounted Police—later the Royal North West Mounted, now the Royal Canadian Mounted—had been formed to bring order to the great domain. In 1874 three hundred men had ridden west in the bright scarlet tunics that were meant to remind the Indians of the British redcoats, whom they had long ago learned to trust. By sheer will and

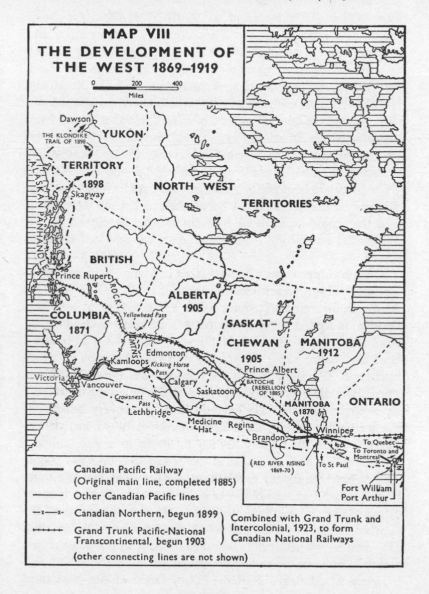

MAP VIII
THE DEVELOPMENT OF
THE WEST 1869–1919

0   200   400
Miles

Dawson
THE KLONDIKE
TRAIL OF 1898
YUKON

TERRITORY
1898
Skagway

NORTH WEST

TERRITORIES

ALASKAN PANHANDLE

BRITISH

Prince Rupert

ROCKY

ALBERTA
1905

COLUMBIA
1871

Yellowhead Pass

SASKAT-

CHEWAN

MANITOBA
1912

MTNS

Edmonton
1905

Kamloops

Kicking Horse
Pass

Prince Albert

Victoria

Calgary

Saskatoon

BATOCHE
(REBELLION
OF 1885)

MANITOBA
1870

ONTARIO

Vancouver

Crowsnest
Pass

Lethbridge

Medicine
Hat

Regina

Winnipeg

To Quebec

Brandon

To Toronto and
Montreal

(RED RIVER RISING
1869-70)

To St Paul

Fort William
Port Arthur

—————— Canadian Pacific Railway
(Original main line, completed 1885)

—————— Other Canadian Pacific lines

-x—x- Canadian Northern, begun 1899

++++++ Grand Trunk Pacific-National
Transcontinental, begun 1903

} Combined with Grand Trunk and
Intercolonial, 1923, to form
Canadian National Railways

(other connecting lines are not shown)

force of character the men of the North West Mounted earned respect and established law. They drove out American whisky traders who were ruining Indian health and morals. They successfully moved Indian tribes on to reservations in order to open lands for farming. In general, they prepared the West for settlement. Nor did the short outburst of 1885, which affected a limited area only, change the general picture of orderliness that marked this last great North American frontier. Meanwhile, in 1877 a separate government for the North West Territories had been set up at Battleford. The Dominion government had also established a general western land policy which offered land for sale at reasonable prices, but included a large amount of free or 'homestead' land that could be secured by farmers who developed it. Yet settlers did not come in the onrushing wave that had been expected.

There had been some new settlement in Manitoba in the seventies, part of it group settlement, such as that of the Icelanders, or the Mennonite religious communities. Pioneers came as well from Ontario; indeed, it is often said that Manitoba is the child of Ontario. In the early 1880's the building of the C.P.R. had caused a brief land boom along the railway route in Manitoba and Saskatchewan. Winnipeg had jumped ahead. But the bubble burst when it was discovered that settlers were not following the railway in, except by handfuls. The brief world trade recovery had ended; the flurry of activity in Canada, due to the railway construction, stopped when the railway needed no more men and building materials. The fact was, that in the renewed depression people did not have the money to strike out for the Canadian West and begin a new life there. In any case the American West was easier to reach and still had land available. Moreover, because of the depression, the world did not need—could not buy—the produce of a great new wheat-producing region. And so the West stayed empty. There was no reason to settle it yet.

Hence Macdonald's National Policy failed at the vital third

point, western settlement, and because of this, the whole design failed. The railway did not flourish; the tariff did not build national prosperity, but only rising discontent in those sections which felt especially burdened by the weight of customs duties. Though Macdonald's nation-building had accomplished an amazing amount in a few short years, it had not achieved its main objects. Now the brave days of the National Policy were to be succeeded by a long period of mounting protests against the ideals and policies of Macdonald nationalism.

3   The Rise of Sectional Discontents

Many of Canada's troubles in the later eighties and early nineties could be traced to the great depression that had gripped the world since 1873. As its shadow did not lift, but darkened, the early spirit of unity and confident nationalism that Macdonald had won for the Dominion was succeeded by reviving sectionalism. Perhaps the depressed times hit the Maritimes the hardest, for in the Atlantic provinces there was little industrial growth, as in central Canada, which the tariff at least might shelter from the worst effects of depression. Instead the Maritimes seemed to be going into a decline. The depression, indeed, had come at the worst possible time, when the old Atlantic trading system had fallen on evil days. The steady shrinking of the important West Indies trade as the sugar islands went downhill, the loss of Maritime shipping advantages in the new era of iron and steam, the comparative failure of Maritime ports to make railways pay—all these things spelt gloom and discontent in the three Atlantic provinces. They condemned Macdonald's protective tariff for adding to their burdens and doing them no good. They accused it, too, of raising industry in central Canada at the expense of the Maritimes, though it was natural that industry should concentrate itself in the much bigger central market. In addition, because Confederation had unluckily occurred when the Maritimes' golden age of 'wood, wind and water' was coming to an end, they tended to blame their changed condition on the federal union. Hence sectional unrest grew strong in the Acadian region. In 1886 a Liberal government in Nova Scotia even introduced a resolution for separation from the Dominion as the only possible answer to the problems of that province. The resolution was largely a talking point, however, and no steps towards separation were taken.

Sectionalism was growing in the West as well. British Columbia was fairly content, now that the Pacific railway had been built, but Manitoba was anything but pleased with the C.P.R. It did not like the term of the Canadian Pacific charter which gave the railway a monopoly of traffic for twenty years. This, in Manitoba's eyes, simply allowed the C.P.R. to charge high rates, since it had no competing railways to fear. The province therefore passed laws chartering lines to the border that would link up with American railroads. But the Dominion government was determined to protect the monopoly guaranteed to the Canadian Pacific and repeatedly used its power of disallowing provincial laws to cancel the Manitoba railway charters. Meanwhile the weak little province of Manitoba, struggling in the depression, felt that high railway rates were holding back its development. Besides, since the public lands of the province had been put under Dominion control for purposes of settlement, Manitoba had lost an important source of income, and its government was hard put to make ends meet. For these reasons feeling mounted in this prairie province over what seemed the Dominion's disregard for its just rights.

Ontario under the Liberal government of Oliver Mowat was even more outspoken in defending provincial rights against the Dominion. Mowat had early made himself the champion of the provinces in opposing the powerful central government that Macdonald believed in. The Ontario leader fought numerous battles in the law courts and on the election platform to preserve what he considered to be the rightful field of provincial authority, especially against the wide use of the Dominion's power of disallowance. Accordingly, as Macdonald's national policies failed to live up to their early prospects, and zeal for nationalism declined, Mowat led the attack on the 'over-mighty' rule of Ottawa. Probably Macdonald had pushed the Dominion's young national spirit too far and too fast. He had used the powers of the federal government vigorously, treating the provincial governments as little more than county councils. But loyalty to the Dominion was new, while loyalty to the provinces was old, and might well be put first in times of stress, when the federal union did not seem to be progressing too successfully.

The power of provincial loyalty was particularly evident in Quebec, always a special section of the Dominion. For some time after Confederation, however, Quebec had raised fewer problems for Macdonald than the other provinces, since the Conservatives had maintained their hold on French Canada. Cartier had died in 1873 but Macdonald had found new French-Canadian lieutenants in Langevin and Chapleau. The Quebec Liberals, or *Rouges*, moreover, continued in a state of weakness. Their previous history of opposition to the power of the Catholic clergy continued to brand them as anti-clericals, a damaging title in Quebec. And in the 1870's the sworn foes of anti-clericalism, the ultramontanes, who believed in broad powers for the church in this world, were advancing rapidly in French Catholic Canada. They linked the very idea of Liberalism with hostility to Catholicism. The Rouges were struggling hard just to keep alive in Quebec when, in 1877, an able young Liberal, Wilfrid Laurier, who had been reared in English as well as French thought, began a campaign, to align Quebec Liberalism with British Liberalism. He sought to show that his party in Canada was not in the anti-religious, revolutionary tradition of the Liberals of Europe, but in the Christian, tolerant and moderate tradition of British Liberalism. Laurier put his faith in British political ideas of freedom and justice. His ability to set them before his fellow French Canadians did much to save his party and to give it a new lease of life in Quebec.

This Liberal revival under Laurier took some time to affect

French Canada. Meanwhile Macdonald Conservatism, backed by the ultramontanes, seemed solid and secure in Quebec. But in 1885 came the North West Rebellion, and the reappearance of Louis Riel let loose a harsh new racial conflict. Conservative unity began to crumble. Indeed, French and English in Canada threatened to break apart as the old gulf between them that had apparently been closed by Confederation spread wide once more.

The problem really went back to the first Riel rising, and to the fact that Louis Riel was a hero to almost half the Canadian people and a rebel to the other half. Riel's escape from Red River to the United States had prevented the dispute over him from coming to a head in 1870; but in 1885 he had been captured. English Canada was determined that this time the dangerous 'fanatic' should pay the full price for two rebellions. French Canada was quite as convinced that Riel was a patriot who had fought unwisely but bravely for an ill-treated French-speaking people. The murder of Thomas Scott, committed in 1870, rose up again to embitter the issue. English Canada, Ontario especially, demanded that Riel be hanged for his crimes; Quebec spoke earnestly for mercy. Riel was tried in Regina, North West Territories (now Saskatchewan), in the summer of 1885. Though there seemed to be good reason to call him insane, he rejected such a defence and was sentenced to hang. Quebec at once called for the sentence to be altered. But Macdonald, who had been only too happy to see Riel escape in 1870 saw that the question could not be avoided this time. He made a firm decision to carry out the sentence, however bitterly Quebec protested. In November Riel was hanged, and probably did more by his death than by his life to affect Canada, and in no way for the good.

His hanging heightened the sectional passions. In Quebec Macdonald Conservatism steadily lost ground. The skill of Macdonald, backed by Langevin and Chapleau, held Quebec votes in the federal field for a few years more, but in the provincial election of 1887 the Conservatives were driven from power. A new French

Nationalist Liberal government, led by Honoré Mercier, took office. Mercier had all the resentment of French Canadian nationalism behind him, and he was no anti-clerical Rouge but a friend of the ultramontanes. In the federal sphere he allied with the Liberals, now led by Laurier, and in the provinces he made common cause with Mowat of Ontario against the power of Macdonald and the Dominion. Riding on the wave of protest against Macdonald and his policies, Mercier called a conference of the provinces at Quebec to reconsider the basis of Confederation, and see whether the federal union should not be changed—naturally in the direction of weakening it.

The Interprovincial Conference met at Quebec in October, 1887. This outburst of sectional discontents represented a powerful reaction against Macdonald nationalism, with its expensive, sweeping policies that had not succeeded, and its lordly domination over the provinces. Yet this second, and less constructive Quebec Conference achieved very little. Macdonald kept the Dominion out of it. British Columbia and Prince Edward Island also stayed away, and of the provinces represented at Quebec all but Manitoba were under Liberal governments. Macdonald could therefore shrug off the Conference as a Liberal party gathering. But more significantly, the provinces at Quebec were united only in attacking the Dominion government. They had little else to agree on. The Maritimes objected strongly to the tariff, Ontario and Quebec were not as concerned; Manitoba's railway problem did not interest the others. And while Ontario and Quebec were divided by racial feelings, they stood together as wealthy provinces in the suspicion that the smaller ones chiefly wanted more federal money grants, which, in the main, citizens of Ontario and Quebec would have to pay. The Conference resolutions therefore had to be vague. They did call for larger subsidies for the provinces, to please Manitoba and the Maritimes, and for a reduction of the Dominion's powers, mainly to please Ontario and Quebec. But on the whole the Conference achieved little except to blow off steam.

Yet it was important. In the first place, it was the beginning of a line of interprovincial conferences which, for better or worse, have greatly affected Canadian political development, and have set up almost a new organ of government in Canada. In the second place, despite the obvious strength of sectional feelings, the Conference revealed how the variety of these feelings prevented the development of a really united opposition to Dominion authority. This would work in the federal government's favour in conferences to come. But in the third place, and most important in the day of Sir John Macdonald, the Conference of 1887, whether the Conservative leader by-passed it or not, revealed how limited still was the nationalism that he had tried to develop. It showed the dangers of sectionalism that loomed ahead. The skill of 'Old Tomorrow' might yet steer a course through them but under any lesser captain they could wreck the Conservative ship.

4 The Fall of Macdonald Conservatism

In 1887, the year of the Interprovincial Conference, Macdonald managed to win yet another Dominion election. The magic of his presence had not vanished, and behind him rallied all the hope that remained in Confederation. Sectionalism had not completely conquered. The same forces which had always bound Canada together along the St Lawrence route, which had determined that British North America should build its own life, still expressed themselves in support for Macdonald and the Dominion, even in Quebec. For nationalism as well as sectionalism was present in every province, and Conservatism still had strength.

In fact, after the election of 1887 Edward Blake resigned from the leadership of the Liberal party, oppressed by his constant defeats at the hand of Macdonald. Laurier now became Liberal leader, and he and his chief followers brought forward a powerful new policy to pit against the National Policy of Conservatism. Instead of the old Liberal refrain, calling for a revenue tariff and rigid economy in government, a dull tune at best, the Liberals proposed complete or unrestricted reciprocity with the United States as the cure for Canada's woes. It was an attractive idea, the removal of all tariff barriers between the two countries— complete free trade. Surely this would bring prosperity to Canada, as reciprocity had done once before. Instead of costly half-successful schemes to build a national market in the Dominion by means of the National Policy, the rich American market would open again to Canadian trade. And there seemed to be reason to think that if Canada suggested complete reciprocity, not partial, as in times past, the United States might accept the offer. At the same time, however, unrestricted reciprocity meant a complete abandoning of Macdonald's hope for a well-rounded Canadian economic life to fill out the bonds of Confederation.

Accordingly, during the last four years of his life Macdonald was on the defensive, struggling to save all he could of his work of nation-building. The Conservative government gave ground, repealing the monopoly clause of the C.P.R. charter that had angered Manitoba, rearranging tariff duties to soothe Nova Scotia, giving up its free use of the power of disallowance that all the provinces had attacked. But Macdonald was determined not to yield on any main point. As the 1890's began the Dominion seemed to reach a low point in its career. Its population was almost at a standstill, since the number of people leaving the country for the United States nearly equalled the rate of births and the trickle of immigration put together. This 'drain to the States' of some of the oldest-established elements of the Canadian people was one of the Dominion's gravest problems. Together with the state of deep trade depression and the discontent aroused by the tariff, it gave new strength to the Liberal demand for unrestricted reciprocity. As the demand rose, in 1891, another election had to be faced. Macdonald was ready to make it the fight of his life.

He was convinced that the policy of unrestricted reciprocity meant not only the end of his cherished national plans but the end of the Dominion of Canada as well; since it would tie Canada into the United States so completely that annexation would become only a matter of time. And so Sir John at the age of seventy-six hurled himself into a campaign for 'the Old Man, the Old Flag, the Old Policy.' This was more than just an effective slogan, or a flag-waving appeal to Canadian loyalty. It covered what seemed to be the main question to Macdonald: whether Canada should continue as a united British dominion, following his designs for building a separate nation in America, or accept the total dependence of the various sections of Canada on the United States, with little real future for them but annexation.

Certainly Macdonald's appeal to old anti-American sentiments and British loyalties helped to win him the election. But he was also appealing to the struggling spirit of Canadian nationalism. And it is worth noting that the former Liberal leader, Edward Blake agreed with him, and opposed unrestricted reciprocity as dangerous to Canada. Many Liberals also agreed with Blake. This split in Liberal ranks, as well as the power of Macdonald's appeal, saved the election for the Conservative party, despite all the discontent in Canada. As a result, the Liberal party not long afterwards abandoned unrestricted reciprocity. Actually it had been an unreal policy, from the start. For all Liberal hopes, the United States had little intention of lowering its tariff wall to suit Canada. It would have done small good to establish the policy in the Dominion when the republic would then have rejected it.

Yet the victor of 1891 had exhausted himself. Worn out, he died shortly after this, his last battle. He died when the Dominion he had given his life to build was still in its darkest hours. For the last twenty years he had almost been Canada himself; and by sheer will as well as skill and confidence had held Confederation together. Yet though he died at a dark moment, and five more years of trouble lay ahead, a bright dawning would follow, when the dreams he had had for his country would come true, and his bold national policies would succeed at last. And so passed the greatest of the men who made modern Canada; a man accused of many faults, of political trickery and lack of principles; but a man as well of kindness, courage, and one all-embracing idea: the creation of a Canadian nation.

Macdonald was succeeded by four Conservative prime ministers in a short space of years. Some were leaders of ability, but all were lesser men who had to face the great problems that he had only just been able to deal with. Unrestricted reciprocity was dead, and the most angry attacks on Conservative national policies had been quieted. Sectionalism, however, was very much alive; and now there arose a burning sectional issue that wrenched Canada apart and ended in pulling the Conservative party from office. It was the Manitoba schools question, which awoke the whole provincial rights movement.

By the Manitoba Act, which had set up the first prairie province in 1870, French-speaking inhabitants of Manitoba were assured of their own Catholic schools, supported by the government. But since that date the original French community that had once been so important in the province had been almost swamped by incoming English-speaking settlers, mainly from Ontario. In 1890, therefore, the largely English-speaking and Protestant provincial legislature passed an act that established a single, state-supported, non-sectarian school system and abolished Catholic separate schools. The Catholics of Manitoba, English as well as French, now felt that rights guaranteed to them in the Manitoba Act had been ignored. French Catholic Quebec warmly agreed. Ontario, meanwhile, was being swept by an 'Equal Rights', ultra-Protestant movement, in reaction to Mercier's strongly pro-Catholic policies in Quebec. It readily supported the abolition of separate schools in Manitoba.

The terms of the Manitoba Act had provided that the Dominion government might step in and pass a Remedial Bill if the provincial legislature interfered with the rights of a religious group in the field of education. The Manitoba Roman Catholics now appealed to the federal government to pass such a measure, and the ultramontanes in Quebec fervently echoed their demand. It was a difficult situation for the Conservative government, and the wisdom of Macdonald was gone. Quebec insisted on a Remedial Bill; Ontario and the majority in Manitoba were opposed. French and English members of the Dominion cabinet themselves were divided. At length the Conservatives decided to bring in a Remedial Bill, although this was wielding the Dominion's sword of authority over a province when Macdonald himself might have let the weapon lie. Before the Bill could be passed in 1896 it was time for an election. The election naturally emphasized the Manitoba schools question.

While Sir Charles Tupper, the Conservative prime minister, fought the election on the grounds of the Dominion's right to interfere to protect a religious minority, Laurier, the Liberal leader, who had wisely kept silent as long as he could, came out unexpectedly in defence of the right of Manitoba to fix its own educational system, even if this involved doing away with Catholic separate schools. It was a daring step. Laurier, the French Canadian Catholic, was opposing the clearly expressed will of the ultramontane leaders of the Roman Catholic Church in Quebec, who had ordered their followers to support the Remedial Bill. But was it unwise? Laurier had taken his stand squarely on the well-established Liberal principle of provincial rights: the Dominion should not interfere in education, a field which by the British North America Act belonged to the provinces. Laurier had removed the issue from the hottest sectional grounds. He also made clear that, while a faithful Catholic, he was not ready to accept the Church's orders in political matters. On this stand he swept the election of 1896 for the Liberals.

Protestant Ontario, where the Liberal Mowat ruled, took to Laurier's doctrine of provincial rights. Provincial feelings across the Dominion supported the Liberals. Yet Laurier still needed seats in Quebec—which surely would reject him. But it did not: Quebec would not lose the opportunity to make a French Canadian prime minister, who might be better equipped to settle Catholic rights in Manitoba. In this French Canada undoubtedly went against the judgment of its Roman Catholic bishops, yet it did so in part from feelings of French Canadian nationalism. And Laurier, after all, was still a Catholic, who shortly afterwards secured the approval of the Papacy for his policy in Manitoba. He also managed to save some special school rights for Catholics there, by discussion, as he had hoped, and not by the forceful use of Dominion power.

In such a way the long rule of Macdonald Conservatism came to an end in Canada. It might seem that a very different era was about to begin under Liberals, stressing provincial rights. Yet Conservative nationalism was played out. It had ended in a new outburst of sectional strife, and in this outburst Macdonald's policy of making strong use of the Dominion's power would only have increased sectional unrest. Laurier's policy of protecting the provinces was necessary to calm angry feelings and reunite the Dominion. In his own way Laurier, too, was a nation-builder, one who had other tasks than Macdonald to accomplish for Canada. Above all, he had to bring the two peoples in the country together through policies of moderation, tolerance, and co-operation.

To a great extent, however, Liberal rule under Laurier did not begin a new era but maintained and built on the basic national policies of Macdonald: the protective tariff, the transcontinental railway, and the opening of the West. Macdonald nationalism had not failed. It was the age that had failed, the long lean years of depression. For the final summing up of Macdonald comes to this: he had shaped the new federal union, rounded out its borders, built its Pacific railway, planned its economic development. In the years of bitterness he had still held his Dominion together, and saved the main points of his programme. Whatever successes came after his death, it is certain that Macdonald had not failed during his own lifetime.

5 *Macdonald and the North Atlantic Triangle*

Macdonald nationalism was not taken up entirely with developing the Dominion at home. It was also concerned with advancing Canada's place in the world, to suit the new importance of the continent-wide union that had replaced the separate British American colonies. As Canada looked abroad, two countries engaged her attention above all: Britain, the centre of empire, and the United States, the great neighbour to the south. Indeed, all three countries were closely connected with each other, whether they liked it or not. They formed what has well been called the 'North Atlantic Triangle.' And Canada, the weakest point of the triangle, was the most open to the forces that flowed around it: for example, during the American Civil War, the clashes between Britain and the United States had only affected those nations briefly, yet they did much to shape an enduring Confederation for Canada.

Trouble between Britain and the United States would always spell grave danger for the Dominion, a British possession exposed to the full power of the republic. On the other hand, the might of Britain put weight and influence behind a thinly settled Dominion striving to hold vast stretches of territory next door to the thickly populated, fast-expanding American union. Without the British tie, Canada might never grow to be a nation. It might cease to exist, fall piecemeal into the republic. Macdonald saw these things very clearly and shaped his policies accordingly.

First and foremost he placed the necessity of maintaining the British tie, in order to preserve a separate life for Canada on the North American continent. If this was imperialism, it was nationalism as well. And as long as this first principle was safe, Macdonald was ready to seek changes in Canada's relation to Britain in order to make her less a colony and more a partner in the empire. To that end he decided to place a minister in London to represent the Dominion in the imperial capital in a way befitting its new size and dignity. This led to the appointment of the first Dominion High Commissioner in 1879, a post first held by

Sir Alexander Galt and later by Sir Charles Tupper. Although the Liberals under Blake and Mackenzie talked more of widening the scope of Canadian nationality, in actual practice Macdonald worked much as they did in this direction.

Accordingly he showed little interest in the idea of uniting the empire through an overall federal system of government, an idea which was much discussed in Britain and the colonies during the 1880's and '90's. There were ardent supporters of imperial federation in Canada, but the lead came mainly from the Mother Country. In Britain, at the time, interest in the colonies had revived considerably and there was an earnest desire to make the empire stronger and more effective by knitting it more closely together. Imperial federation was only one plan proposed for this purpose by the rising British imperialists of the late nineteenth century. The revival of British interest in empire had many causes. For example, the long trade depression after 1873 made colonial markets seem far more valuable than in the hopeful flush of free trade prosperity at the middle of the century. New dangers of war, linked chiefly with the rise of German power after 1870, had underlined the need for uniting the strength of the empire. And there had been a reaction in Britain against the old, cold policy of waiting for the colonies to leave home—particularly when it was realized that the colonies did not want to leave after all.

On this last fact, however, the new imperialists built too much. If the colonies did not want to break away from Britain, neither did they want to move in the other direction. As for Canada, on the whole she had no desire to turn back on the path towards full self-government within the empire, on which she had been moving since the time of Durham, Baldwin, and Elgin. Macdonald therefore took no step towards closer imperial unity, despite the flattering attentions showered on the colonies at the first Colonial Conference, held in London in 1887. But while the prime minister politely sidestepped all proposals to tighten the imperial bond, he equally rejected any policy which he thought would loosen it.

Thus he opposed the Liberals' plan of unrestricted reciprocity on the grounds that it would turn Canada from Britain to the United States, and fought his last election on a cry well designed to get votes and yet deeply meant: 'A British subject I was born, a British subject I will die.'

Perhaps the value of the British tie as a counterbalance to the United States was most evident in the early years of Macdonald's rule over the Dominion. Between Confederation and the Treaty of Washington, signed in 1871, Canada continued to watch her American neighbour in all uneasiness. The United States felt new yearnings for more territory, and after the purchase of Alaska from Russia, in 1867, Americans talked of rounding out their hold on the continent to the north. In addition, bad feelings between Britain and the United States still ran high in the years after the Civil War, and the republic laid heavy claims for damage done by Southern raiders, notably the *Alabama*, that had fitted out in British ports. These '*Alabama*' claims, the United States suggested, might be met if Britain withdrew from North America completely, leaving her northern colonies free to join the American union. And, in fact, it could be said that so far the republic had hardly recognized that there was a new Dominion of Canada occupying the northern half of the continent.

In these circumstances the value of the British tie as a security to Canada seemed only too plain to Macdonald. The United States, however, did not seek to press further for northern expansion once it realized that Britain would not yield, sell, or trade British North America. Accordingly it was finally agreed that British and American representatives should meet in Washington in 1871 to discuss all the questions that had arisen out of the Civil War. Sir John Macdonald was to attend as a member of the British delegation in order to represent Canada's interests.

The Treaty of Washington that emerged from the discussions to a great extent did settle the outstanding questions, and brought to an end the period of strain with the United States. Yet in many ways Canadian interests were set aside, thanks to the British desire to win good relations with the Americans and the American intention of making the wooing expensive. As a single member of the British delegation there was little Macdonald could do. Thus Canada's claims for damage due to the Fenian raids were not discussed. The Americans were granted free navigation of the St Lawrence and the Atlantic fisheries of each country were opened to the other for ten years. Canada had no opportunity to bargain again for reciprocity with her more valuable fishing grounds, although five and a half million dollars was later awarded to her for their use by the United States. Macdonald was attacked over the Treaty on his return to Ottawa; but he had simply had to pay the price for Canada's being a colony.

And yet this price was also connected with Canada's position as the weakest member of the North Atlantic triangle. If the good relations with the United States that Britain sought had not been won, Canada stood to suffer most of all. By herself, moreover, she would have had small chance, in 1871, of making a bargain with the republic. Again the security of the tie with Britain was the most important concern for Canada, and for this Macdonald accepted the losses involved. Besides, the Treaty of Washington really brought to a close the long-felt American pressure on the Canadian lands to the north, for by the Treaty the United States recognized that the Dominion had made good its claim to the northern half of the continent. Gradually thereafter the unfriendly feeling between the two neighbours disappeared. The term, 'the undefended boundary', came to have real meaning. The period of true peace between Canada and the United States properly goes back to the Treaty of Washington of 1871.

As a result, Macdonald's later years in office saw no major problems in relations with the United States, although the fishery question re-emerged. And while the unrestricted reciprocity campaign revived charges that the Americans looked to reciprocity to bring about the peaceful annexation of Canada, on the whole it seems that the United States at that time was not much interested in Canadian proposals for reciprocity or anything else. Consequently, when Macdonald Conservatism finished its course in 1896, it left Canada on good terms with the republic and on close terms with Britain: secure in her separate place within the North Atlantic triangle and still advancing towards nationhood.

Nationhood involves duties as well as privileges, responsibilities as well as rights. During this first age of the Dominion, that closed in 1896, Canada began to assume one of the basic duties of a nation: that of defending itself. In 1871 the last British troops were withdrawn from Canada, except for a garrison at Halifax, which was still the Royal Navy's main north-west Atlantic base. The Dominion took over the task of its defence by land, though naval defence was still an imperial responsibility. And so it was that while in 1870 British regulars as well as Canadian militia marched west to the first Riel rising, in 1885 Canadian troops alone put down the second rebellion. Only a few years after 1896, during the South African War, Canada would even send armed forces overseas. This was clearly a sign of the growing stature of the Dominion, the result in part, of long years under the sway of Macdonald nationalism.

CHAPTER 16

LAURIER AND CANADA'S CENTURY,
1896–1914

1 *Immigration and Western Settlement*

The year 1896 not only saw Laurier and the Liberals take office in Canada. It witnessed the revival of world trade and the return of prosperity to the Dominion. In fact, Canada embarked on the greatest boom it had yet known. A new tide of immigration set in, the West was rapidly occupied, and all parts of the country flourished. Laurier and the Liberals, who were fortunate to be in office during the boom, fell from power in 1911, yet the good times continued almost up to the outbreak of the First World War in 1914. By that date, the outlines of the Dominion had been filled in, and a prosperous Canada had developed a new, confident national spirit. It was a mark of the national confidence that Laurier could say, 'The nineteenth century was the century of the United States, the twentieth century will be the century of Canada.'

The basic achievement of the new era, on which the rest of the national advance depended, was the settlement of the West. And here the prime reason for the success of the Laurier government was the recovery of world trade. As the factories of Britain and western Europe throbbed in quickening pace, their crowded industrial towns demanded new supplies of foodstuffs from the soil of North America. The demand for food rose constantly, yet the good western lands of the United States had by now been occupied and what remained was of far less agricultural value. Only in the 'last, best West' of Canada was there a great reserve of fertile soil whose crops could feed the factory population of Europe. Now at last there was good reason to settle the Canadian West. Settlers flocked to the empty prairies, from Britain, from the

United States, from continental Europe. Year by year the rustling wheatfields reached further into the western grasslands, year by year the crops poured eastward through the narrow funnel of the Canadian Pacific, and yet the demand for grain continued to grow.

There were other developments which aided the settlement of the Canadian West. The filling up of the American plains before 1900 turned the whole western frontier movement northward into Canada. Once before, in the years between the conquest of 1760 and the War of 1812, the frontier in its march across the North American continent had swung into Canada. In that day, New Englanders, Loyalists, and American frontiersmen had done much to occupy the eastern lands of British America. In later years, although large numbers of settlers had come to the colonies from Britain, the main movement of the North American frontier had been westward across the United States. After 1850 there had been little frontier advance in Canada at all. But around the turn of the twentieth century, the Canadian frontier came into its own again, and by the time the movement had run its course the western half of the Dominion had been peopled.

Another factor in successful settlement was the improvement in farming methods and the development of new strains of wheat. The prairies were lands of fairly low rainfall. They required a system of 'dry' farming, and this by now had been worked out in the equally dry American plains. The system demanded farms of large size, but the development of agricultural machinery by this time made it possible to work large farms effectively. And if the problems of low rainfall and early frost could be overcome, no finer land for grain crops could be found anywhere than in the Canadian West. As for the question of frost, the answer lay in the new strains of wheat. High-yielding, quick-maturing varieties were developed. Once they were tested, it became possible to grow grain in a shorter season, with the result that the wheat lands could push further and further towards the north. The greatest triumph, Marquis wheat, came in 1908, when the western boom was at its height. Its development by Charles Saunders, a botanist in the service of the Canadian government, is one of the most fascinating and significant stories in Canadian history. Maturing in under a hundred days, bountiful Marquis added thousands of northern acres to Canada's wheat lands. In recent years still other kinds of wheat have advanced the western farming frontier far north to the Peace river country, where grain has been produced that has won the world wheat championship.

Government policies also had their share in the successful opening of the West. In many ways they merely continued on lines laid down under Macdonald, but they were ably administered by the Laurier government. Clifford Sifton, the Minister of the Interior in charge of western settlement, brought driving energy and enthusiasm to his task. He organized vigorous publicity campaigns in Britain, the United States and Europe to attract immigrants to the Canadian West and stationed immigration agents widely in all three. He arranged train tours of the prairies so that selected Canadian and American farmers and newspaper men could see for themselves the value of the soil. The Dominion's land policy, carried over from the previous period, made farms easily available. The prairies were surveyed in numbered square sections of 640 acres each. In the odd-numbered sections the Dominion sold the land at moderate prices to raise a revenue. These sections also contained the lands granted to the Canadian Pacific, and other types of grant, which were sold in the same way. In the even-numbered sections farms could be obtained free, as homesteads, if the homesteader fulfilled certain conditions of developing his 'quarter section' of 160 acres. So great was the demand for farms that both homestead and purchased land were readily taken up. And the Canadian Pacific, the Hudson's Bay Company, and other interests which held grants soon saw that it paid to sell their land cheaply in order to develop the West, increase its railway traffic, and gain from the general prosperity. In fact, the government at length decided that it was worth while to give the rest of its western lands away to keep up the flow of settlement. In 1908 it opened what was left of the odd-numbered sections to free homesteading.

Thanks to all these circumstances, Canada was swept by the greatest wave of immigration in her history. Between 1896 and the First World War, about two-and-a-half million people entered the Dominion. Well over half a million came from continental Europe, more than three-quarters of a million from the United States and close to a million from the British Isles. During the height of the movement, between 1901 and 1911, the population jumped from five to seven millions, an increase of over one-third. But the change in the size of the population was no more striking than the change in its composition. While the new immigrants were English-speaking in the great majority, a sizeable number were from Germany and Scandinavia, from Russia, Poland, and the Ukraine, from Austria and Italy. Canada for the first time became what the United States long had been, a melting pot of peoples. Canada was still much less a melting pot than the republic, and the British and French stocks continued to dominate. But whereas persons of other than British or French origin had formed only a tiny part of the Canadian population at Confederation, by the First World War they formed almost one-fifth of it.

On the whole these European immigrants were gradually absorbed into the two older Canadian peoples, though mostly into the English-speaking majority. Group settlements of foreign-born in the West, particularly if they were religious groups, proved the most difficult to absorb. The Doukhobors, a small but earnestly religious sect from Russia, provide an obvious example here, since an extremist minority among them, which has settled in British Columbia, has even found it hard to fit its religious ideas to the accepted laws and customs of the Canadian people. Yet the mass of the foreign-born came to think of themselves simply as Canadians, while they added colour and variety to the Canadian personality and new arts and crafts to Canada's culture.

At the same time, the largest group of immigrants gave Canada a new infusion of British stock, while the next largest set of arrivals, from the United States (about half of them returning Canadians), supplied farmers already trained in North American agriculture. These were of particular value in bringing the West under cultivation. Not all the immigrants went west by any means. Many of them settled in the now thriving eastern towns or entered into new northern mining and lumbering developments. Altogether, about a million new inhabitants went to the prairies and British Columbia in the peak period, 1901 to 1911. Probably the majority were Canadians and Americans, and the rest British and continental Europeans in about equal numbers. The Barr 'colony', for instance, at Lloydminster, Saskatchewan, was a strikingly successful example of a British community settlement.

With the inrush of settlement the West advanced rapidly. Railway lines branched out, roads were built, and towns sprang up. Regina and Saskatoon, Calgary and Edmonton mushroomed out of trading posts and board shanties. The first sod huts of settlers —the open prairies did not supply wood for log cabins—were soon replaced by frame dwellings, planks for which were shipped in by railway. The red-brown grain elevators began to dot the plains, and on every side there was a sea of grain, trembling in soft green shoots in the spring rains and tumbling in golden waves under the hot, blue summer sky. The plains turned almost overnight from the wilderness life of trapping and hunting to the complex business of raising a crop for the world market, with every aid of science and machinery. There was really no stage in between, of pioneer farming for bare existence, as in eastern Canada.

From the first the western settler was a business man, producing for a cash sale and buying his needs, even some of his food, from the world outside. He was supplied by the same railways that carried his product on its way to markets half-way around the globe. And although the size of western farms scattered settlers

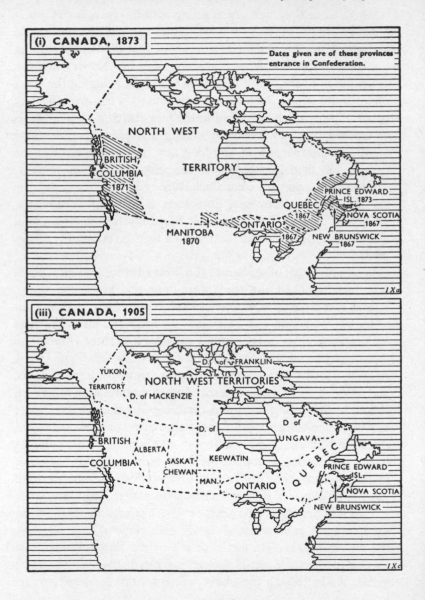

(i) CANADA, 1873

Dates given are of these provinces
entrance in Confederation.

NORTH WEST

BRITISH
COLUMBIA
1871

TERRITORY

PRINCE EDWARD
ISL. 1873

QUEBEC
1867

NOVA SCOTIA
1867

ONTARIO
1867

MANITOBA
1870

NEW BRUNSWICK
1867

IXa

(iii) CANADA, 1905

YUKON
TERRITORY

D. of FRANKLIN

NORTH WEST TERRITORIES

D. of MACKENZIE

BRITISH
COLUMBIA

ALBERTA

D. of

D. of
UNGAVA

SASKAT-
CHEWAN

KEEWATIN

QUEBEC

PRINCE EDWARD
ISL.

MAN.

ONTARIO

NOVA SCOTIA

NEW BRUNSWICK

IXc

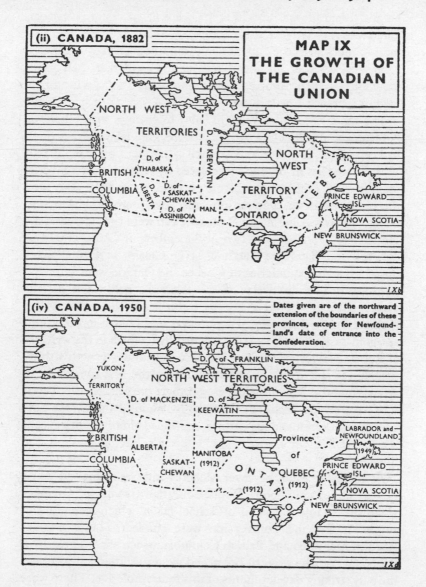

(ii) CANADA, 1882

MAP IX
THE GROWTH OF
THE CANADIAN
UNION

NORTH WEST

TERRITORIES

D. of KEEWATIN

NORTH
WEST

TERRITORY

D. of
ATHABASKA

BRITISH
COLUMBIA

D. of ALBERTA

D. of
SASKAT-
CHEWAN

D. of
ASSINIBOIA

MAN.

ONTARIO

QUEBEC

PRINCE EDWARD
ISL.

NOVA SCOTIA

NEW BRUNSWICK

IXb

(iv) CANADA, 1950

Dates given are of the northward
extension of the boundaries of these
provinces, except for Newfoundland's date of entrance into the
Confederation.

D. of FRANKLIN

YUKON
TERRITORY

NORTH WEST TERRITORIES

D. of MACKENZIE

D. of
KEEWATIN

BRITISH
COLUMBIA

ALBERTA

SASKAT-
CHEWAN

MANITOBA
(1912)

Province

of

ONTARIO
(1912)

QUEBEC
(1912)

LABRADOR and
NEWFOUNDLAND
(1949)

PRINCE EDWARD
ISL.

NOVA SCOTIA

NEW BRUNSWICK

IXd

far apart, their life was not the solitary one of the eastern pioneers. There was no barrier of thick forest; roads and railways kept farmers in touch with the outside; and from the start they organized in groups, whether for social reasons, or to market their grain more effectively, or to bring pressure to bear in politics for a new road or a branch-line railway.

The rapid rise of the West led also to changes in the field of government. Even before the great boom, gradual western growth had caused the governor-and-council system set up for the North West Territories in 1875 to be replaced by representative government in 1888, and by responsible government in 1897. But now the rapid rise in the population called two more provinces into being. In 1905 Alberta and Saskatchewan were carved out of the North West Territories as two new members of Confederation.

A few years later the North West Territories were further reduced when the boundaries of Quebec and Ontario were extended northward. The discovery of the Klondike gold-fields on the Yukon River in the far north-west also led to the creation of a separate Yukon Territory, when miners raced north in the dramatic gold-rush of 1898–1903, so colourfully set forth in the writings of Robert Service. Klondike gold also helped western growth by making the sub-Arctic west important for the first time. But in a few years the Yukon fields passed their prime, and the Territory's population declined. And the remaining North West Territories, still a tremendous empire, continued almost empty except for the Indian fur trapper, the Hudson's Bay factor and the missionary.

At the same time, however, Alberta and Saskatchewan came quickly out of childhood. Public education was made province-wide, thanks to the system of 'school lands' which were sold to support it. Provincial universities were founded. They also flourished in Manitoba and British Columbia, which shared greatly in the boom. Yet the western boom and western settlement were not the only striking developments of this remarkable age. There were others, all across Canada, all of them closely linked together, and tied as well to the triumph in the West.

2 The Success of the National Policy

The western growth was so sudden that it strained the existing Canadian railway system. The Canadian Pacific was jammed with traffic at its Winnipeg bottleneck each year as the crops moved out. A new transcontinental line seemed necessary. In 1903, when the Liberal government announced its whole-hearted readiness to support vigorous railway-building, two powerful railway groups were eager to go ahead. The Grand Trunk was prosperous at last and was dreaming again of extension to the Pacific. The western railway promoters, Mackenzie and Mann, who had strung a number of small lines together, were hoping to make theirs a transcontinental railway system. The obvious plan, since Mackenzie and Mann wanted to extend to the east and the Grand Trunk to the west, would have been for the two groups to join hands. But neither wanted to give up their own scheme for a transcontinental railway. And so strong was the confident mood of the time that they believed there was room for two new great railways in Canada. The government and the people believed it too.

Hence Mackenzie and Mann built their Canadian Northern into a transcontinental railway, while the Grand Trunk laid the Grand Trunk Pacific across the West. In addition, the government undertook to construct a new eastern route of its own, the National Transcontinental, which was to be leased to the Grand Trunk. This trunk line stretched east from Winnipeg, reaching high across Ontario and Quebec, to open up their northern regions and provide a main track direct to Quebec City. From here it ran down through the Maritimes by a shorter route than the old Intercolonial, yet stayed wholly in Canada, as the Canadian Pacific's 'Short Line' to Saint John did not.

The new age of railway-building bound all the regions of Canada together in a far stronger web of steel. It linked the Pacific coast, where the northern port of Prince Rupert was now opened, through several more mountain passes to the rest of Canada; it crossed the barrier of the Shield with two new trunk lines, and joined central Canada more effectively with ice-free Maritime harbours. Yet the happy belief that all these tracks would pay was only the over-confidence of boom times. Canada's railways were gravely overbuilt. Through the Shield in particular, competing lines often ran side by side for miles through a country that could not supply traffic enough for one. And because the new railways had been constructed in a flush of prosperity, when prices were high, they had to carry an extremely heavy burden of costs. Very early, therefore, they began to collapse under their load of debt, even before boom conditions had fully disappeared.

As a result, by the end of the First World War the Dominion government had been forced to take over the bankrupt Canadian Northern and Grand Trunk. They were combined with the government's Intercolonial and National Transcontinental to form the Canadian National Railways, a state-owned rival of the Canadian Pacific, which successfully survived as a private company, thanks to the much sounder state of its finances. The Canadian National continued to run into difficulties in later years, largely because of the heavy load of debt it had inherited from its bankrupt parents. Within the Laurier era, however, the building of railways added greatly to national prosperity. Their construction offered employment to many immigrants. It made mighty demands on Canadian industry and lumbering for materials, and the new lines across the Shield uncovered hidden mineral riches. In this northern realm a new Canada began to develop, once the railways had opened the door to its resources. In northern Ontario, in particular, a mining boom was under way, as gold, silver, copper, and nickel mines were brought into production. The softwood forests of the Shield started supplying wood-pulp for hungry mills that made the world's newspapers. And the Shield, that had been a dividing waste land but was now emerging as Canada's treasure-house, was promising to become a power-house as well. The new century had brought the age of electricity made from water-power; the many rivers of the Shield could readily be harnessed. Hydro-electric power was also being developed outside the Shield, at Niagara Falls, for instance. This new source of vital energy was of great significance to the booming factories of central Canada, which had been compelled to bring in coal to furnish them with steam power.

Despite these important developments, the most significant feature of the new age of prosperity was the growth of trade from east to west, carried across the continent by the railways. As western settlement advanced and western grain production mounted, the east-west trading system of Canada began to flourish as never before. While wheat moved east to Atlantic ports, farm machinery and manufactures went west from eastern factories. The St Lawrence interests of Montreal controlled a golden commercial empire beyond the dreams of the days of the fur canoe or the canal era. Winnipeg grew as Montreal's outpost, gathering in the western trade. Toronto competed with Montreal to some extent, but thrived on the east-west commerce as the heart of a large industrial region. The outlying sections and their cities also gained from the growth of east-west trade. Vancouver benefited as the Pacific outlet of the continent-wide system, and British Columbia supplied the prairies with fish, lumber, fruit, and minerals. The Maritimes advanced less, but were aided by the development of Saint John and Halifax as the winter ports of east-west commerce.

More than this, Canada's trade relations with Britain grew closer, for Britain became her best customer for western grain; the east-west system really ended on the other side of the Atlantic. As a result, an enduring pattern of trade developed, whereby Canada sold the bulk of her farm exports in the British market, and these soon included meat, dairy products, and fruit as well as wheat. Yet grain remained the staple export of the east-west trading system. Canada's old staple of fur had long since lost its importance and the cutting over of eastern forests had affected the export of lumber. Sawn lumber still went in great quantities to the United States, but the old square timber trade with Britain disappeared about 1900. And then came western grain to strengthen or rather transform, the trading ties with Britain. Although Canada continued to sell many products to the United States and to buy from there rather more than she sold, she balanced her books by the sales to Britain. A new period of heavy British investment in Canada during the Laurier boom also strengthened trans-Atlantic commercial ties.

The rise of east-west trade had another powerful consequence. It spelt success at long last for the National Policy of Macdonald, which the Liberals now took over as their own. The National Policy of protection was firmly fixed on Canada from then on, since both major parties had accepted it. The Liberals might still talk more of lower tariff rates and work to reduce some of them, but they had really dropped any intention of interfering with the basic policy of a protective tariff.

The Liberal conversion became clear almost at the start of the Laurier government's career. Its first tariff, that of 1897, did not really alter the protective system, and left out the offer of reciprocity with the United States which had long been included in the various Canadian tariffs. Laurier, indeed, announced that there would be 'no more pilgrimages to Washington' to seek reciprocity from the United States. This changed Liberal attitude was in part an expression of the new national confidence caused by the age of prosperity. Yet the Liberal conversion had deeper roots. The party had altered its character. No longer was it based chiefly on the farm vote and opposed to a Conservative party supported by big business. Though the Liberals had still kept most of their farm support, they had gradually built up a powerful backing of railway, banking, and industrial interests. As the party in power during the boom, they attracted an even larger business following, and served it well enough with their policies of railway-building, tariff protection and lavish government expenditure—shades of Macdonald Conservatism! In fact, there was not much difference now between the two great Canadian parties. In this era of boom, free trade and government economy were forgotten. The Liberals had simply adopted most of Macdonald's expensive nation-building policies, and had generally succeeded with them.

The reason why the Liberals succeeded where the Conservatives had failed, is not hard to see. Macdonald's national plans had required a Pacific railway and western settlement as well as the protective tariff. In the long depression, the failure of western settlement had meant that the railway had been half used and the tariff had but partly served its purpose. But now the life-blood of settlement and east-west trade coursed through the system Macdonald had moulded. The railways, vastly extended under the Liberals, carried both the settlers and their crops; the industries that had been built up behind the tariff found ample western markets: and the West fed the East and the world overseas. The purposes of the national policy had been achieved. Canada at last had a balanced economic system, a unity based on trade.

The balance was still far from perfect. The success of the system depended greatly on good times and a healthy world market. The west would soon complain that it carried the larger share of the tariff burden and railway charges for the benefit of eastern industry. In years to come there would be repeated protests against the tariff and railway costs in both the West and the Maritimes. Yet the uneven burden of the tariff could be offset by the practical, if not always admirable, policy of increasing subsidies for the provinces that complained. And the Dominion government could work to modify objectionable railway rates, as, for instance, in the Crowsnest Pass agreement of 1897, wherein the Dominion gave aid to the Canadian Pacific's new Crowsnest Pass line in return for a lowering of rates between the West and central Canada.

In general, complex, uneven and expensive as it might be, the national policy succeeded during Laurier's day in making Canada more than just a collection of governments or a name on the map. It was, in a sense, another response to the challenge of the land, to the forces that divided the country into separate regions. Though the policy of protection helped to build up powerful and privileged business interests, the majority of Canadians accepted its costs and its faults as part of the price of successfully maintaining their separate existence in North America: as part of the price they paid for their geography.

3 Nationalism and Imperialism

With the prosperity of the Laurier era and the success of the national policy, sectional strife dwindled away in Canada, and unity and nationalism again became the order of the day. The feeling of harmony was widespread, though not complete. There were still mutterings of the racial storm between Ontario and Quebec, and in the latter province the purely French-Canadian kind of nationalism was soon to rise in an angry new outburst. Yet for the time the dominant mood was one of national pride, a belief that Canada was at last coming into her own in the world, and that all Canadians could stand together to see their country receive the greater recognition which she now deserved. Laurier himself was a living symbol of this nationalism, stressing as he did that Canadians should think neither of English Canada nor of French, but of Canada as a whole.

The feeling of nationalism was clearly evident in literature; for example, in the writing of history; for during this period the first large-scale studies of the Canadian past were undertaken as group projects. It appeared in poetry, where the chief representatives of the golden age of the 'nineties—Roberts, Carman, Duncan Scott—were striving still in the new century to set forth the scenes and spirit of Canada, as were Wilfred Campbell and many others. And by 1914 young artists were emerging—later, notably, the Group of Seven—who viewed Canada through Canadian eyes, and no longer approached the rocks, sweeps, and storms of their northern landscape with the painting styles developed in the milder countrysides of Europe. In every way Canadians were growing more self-conscious, more eager to assert themselves.

In this new mood, under Laurier, Canada looked to the world outside. As yet she had little contact with countries other than the United States and Britain, but within the North Atlantic triangle she showed much more independence of mind. With regard to the United States, the turning away from reciprocity was a sign that Canada felt a new readiness to make her own way in North America. With regard to Britain, Canadians on the whole stood out against the tide of ardent imperialism which was still running high in the mother country. Imperial questions bulked large in this era, because of Britain's hopes of strengthening the empire's trade, government, and defence to meet the mounting rivalry of great powers in the darker world that loomed ahead. And yet, however understandable were Britain's intentions, and though she meant only to realize them through free agreement between motherland and colonies, the fact was that these imperialist aims ran up against the growing counter-force of nationalism in the principal colonies. Nationalism was not only appearing in Canada, although, as the eldest Dominion, it was more advanced there.

This nationalism, however, was of a fairly moderate sort. In opposing centralized imperial control it still believed that the empire might be strong through the free development of its parts, and generally thought that ties of friendship and common loyalties might prove more lasting than new imperial machinery. This was the viewpoint of Laurier nationalism in Canada, where there were keen imperialists as well, but moderate nationalism proved more powerful. There was in truth little basic disagreement among Canadians over relations with the empire. Few nationalists, even among the French Canadians, had any desire to break the British tie, and few imperialists meant to abandon Canada's national economic policies. The disagreements, which could be noisy, were on smaller, particular questions. Hence, while the Conservatives still talked more warmly of empire, they stood by the National Policy they had created in the face of British free trade. And while the Liberals wanted fuller national rights they continued to seek them inside the imperial framework.

To some extent both the so-called imperialists and nationalists in the Dominion expressed the same spirit of the new century: the desire to have Canada assert herself. The nationalists wanted her to do so by avoiding tighter imperial bonds and by gaining more freedom to deal with external affairs. The imperialists wanted her to play a greater part in the empire and to win some share in the framing of imperial policies. But both wanted Canada to make a larger mark in the world.

Imperial questions came to the fore almost as soon as the Liberals took office. In 1897 a Colonial Conference was held in London on a grand imperial occasion, the celebration of Queen Victoria's Diamond Jubilee. To London thronged representatives from the Queen's vast domains around the globe. From Canada came a tall, distinguished French Canadian with a courtly air and a cordial manner, equally at ease in French or English, in Windsor Castle or among his rural supporters of Arthabaska, Quebec. This was the Dominion's prime minister, Wilfrid Laurier. Laurier, to be knighted Sir Wilfrid in London, came to Britain when the strong-minded Joseph Chamberlain ruled the Colonial Office and there had made his goal the achievement of empire unity. If imperial federation or an imperial customs union could not be obtained, then some form of imperial council representing Britain and the chief colonies might be established. But Laurier said no, in the politest of terms, at the Conference; and apparently the other colonies largely felt as he did, since the meeting broke up expressing satisfaction with the existing ties of empire.

Laurier and Canada pointed instead to the principle of imperial preference, which the Liberals had introduced in their first tariff, that of 1897. The imperial preference was a lower rate of customs duty specially granted to British goods. Actually it was a compromise measure, which did not really affect the principle of tariff protection that had now been adopted by the Liberals, but which somewhat appeased both low-tariff and imperialist feelings in Canada by reducing the protective rates in Britain's favour. If, however, all the parts of the British empire could give each other similar favoured treatment, then a system of imperial preferences might increase the flow of trade within the empire and strengthen imperial bonds in quite a practical fashion. But while the centre of empire, Britain, maintained a policy of free trade and a market open to all the world she could not respond with special favours for her colonies. Canada's grant of an imperial preference, broadened in 1898, remained a one-way offer.

The next year a far more urgent question arose in imperial relations. The South African War broke out in 1899, and Canada had to decide what its policy would be towards this empire struggle. Chamberlain felt that imperial unity might be strengthened by the leading colonies sending troops to the war. Lord Minto, the Governor-General in Canada, and many Canadians also hoped to see a force dispatched. Laurier, however, was faced with a difficult problem of maintaining national unity. As British forces met defeats in South Africa in the early stages of the war, the demand swelled in English-speaking Canada for the sending of troops. But the French Canadians were uninterested or opposed; both because they felt the war was not Canada's concern and because they tended to compare the position of the Boers to their own in an English-speaking empire. A purely French-Canadian nationalism stirred again, condemning English Canadians as war-mad imperialists who put Britain ahead of their own country, Canada. The old racial division began to crack open: a challenge to Laurier who had dedicated his life to harmony between the two peoples of Canada.

In these circumstances the government took a middle course. Laurier, a French-Canadian, determined to raise and send a force to South Africa in response to the will of the English-speaking majority. On the other hand the force was made up of volunteers and was maintained in South Africa by Britain. The first contingent sailed from Quebec in October, 1899, and more followed. In all, more than seven thousand Canadians served in South Africa, through the bloodshed of Paardeburg, the relief of Ladysmith and the capture of Pretoria, until the war ended in 1902. Meanwhile at home Laurier's policy had avoided serious trouble between French and English, and between nationalists and imperialists as well. For once more, the sending of troops to South Africa had been almost as much nationalism as imperialism. Canada was asserting herself, and acting by her own decision.

After the war, Chamberlain in Britain hoped to build on the feelings created by a common imperial war effort. However, in the Colonial Conference of 1902 Laurier opposed plans for greater unity in defence or government, and again held to the idea of trade preference. Chamberlain himself came to support that plan, which would require Britain to drop free trade. But in a campaign to bring 'tariff reform' in Britain, Chamberlain succeeded only in splitting his own Conservative party, so that the Liberals came to power. Although the free-trade British Liberals could not consider imperial preference, they still thought that some other means of strengthening the empire might be found. Laurier agreed to their plan of making colonial conferences regular meetings held every four years, under the more imposing title of the Imperial Conference. He shared fully in the conferences that followed. But he still held back from any proposals for more centralized controls over the empire, fearing that Canada would find herself committed to policies which she had not been able to influence, since the British government maintained that relations with foreign countries had to be left in the hands of Britain. Then too, his particular problem of finding a middle ground between both French and English in Canada required him to be ever-cautious.

Defence, particularly naval defence, was now becoming the central problem in imperial affairs. As the dangers of war in

Europe mounted, Britain and Germany entered on a grim race to build the most modern type of battleship. The new German fleet was coming perilously close to the British in size. To Germany, a land-power, the building race was largely a matter of prestige; to Britain, living by the sea, it was a matter of life or death. The cost was enormous, and since the Royal Navy defended the whole empire, the British government sought to have the colonies share in its support by making definite contributions to the imperial fleet. Laurier again held back, on the same ground that, in contributing, Canada would be committed to aid where she could not influence. He stated clearly that, 'When Britain is at war, Canada is at war,' but felt that in the event of any war the Dominion, as a self-governing colony, had to decide on its own contribution. By keeping commitments beforehand as low as possible, Canada would be more able to decide freely.

In any case, the British Admiralty's belief that imperial naval forces would have to be under one command removed another possibility; that, instead of a direct contribution to the Royal Navy, a Dominion might raise its own naval forces as it already did its army. In 1909, however, the naval race with Germany was running so close that the Admiralty gave up its stand in order to obtain whatever aid it could. As a result, at the special Imperial Naval Conference of that year Australia and Canada agreed to begin their own fleets, though New Zealand would offer ships and men direct to the Royal Navy. Early in 1910 Laurier introduced a bill in the Dominion Parliament to create a Canadian navy, and this Naval Service Bill was passed.

The Canadian Prime Minister had carried his point on a major imperial question. To a great extent his policies of nationalism within the empire had so far been successful. At the least he had steered between imperialist and nationalist extremes, kept Canada reasonably united, and brought her wider national powers, of which the founding of a Canadian navy was only a part. At the most, he had largely prevented the rigid centralizing of the empire, leaving it free to develop into the Commonwealth. But his day was almost over, and the Naval Bill would help to cause his fall.

4   *American Problems and the Naval Question*

Laurier lost office in 1911, in an election in which the Naval Bill played a large part. Another main reason for his fall, however, concerns the United States rather than the British empire, and involves examining Canada's dealings with that country during the Laurier era. Relations with the United States had been disturbed around the turn of the century by the Alaska boundary dispute, and for a time tempers had been high in the Dominion, although the anger soon passed.

The question of the indefinite Alaskan boundary on the northern Pacific coast, where Yukon and British Columbia bordered the Alaskan 'panhandle', first became important with the Klondike gold-rush in 1898. Skagway in the panhandle, or coastal strip, was the chief harbour that gave entrance to the Yukon river and the Klondike. It lay up a long inlet; and if this inlet reached beyond the limits of the coastal strip that was part of Alaska, then Skagway was a Canadian port and goods from Vancouver could enter there duty free. If the American claim extended inland beyond Skagway, then American customs houses could enjoy the gold-rush traffic. This dispute over trade thus drew attention to the boundary line which had never been clearly drawn when the United States had purchased Alaska.

The United States probably had the better case for drawing the border further inland than Canada desired, but the manner in which the question was handled showed that the Americans did not mean to rest their case on arguments alone, and roused much resentment in the Dominion. The republic was now going through a period of imperial expansion of its own; its temper was firm and unyielding. Though the United States brought Britain to abandon treaty rights in Panama, where the great Panama Canal was to be built, it refused to make any returns in Alaska. It refused to refer the boundary to an outside decision, while President Theodore Roosevelt ordered troops to Alaska and announced that he was prepared, if necessary, to run the boundary without regard to Britain or Canada. And when a six-man 'impartial' commission was set up to decide the line, the three American representatives were selected because, in advance, they had already publicly accepted the claim of the United States.

As for the other side, two Canadians and the Lord Chief Justice of England were chosen to sit on the commission. The old difficulty of divided interests, as in the Washington Treaty, appeared once more, and it is not beyond understanding that Britain put the cause of Anglo-American friendship ahead of the Canadian claims. At any rate, Lord Alverstone, the Lord Chief Justice, under both British and American pressures, voted with the United States members of the commission. The boundary settlement, announced in 1903 in American favour, was not as important as the influence of the whole dispute: and that is why it deserves attention. Not only did it revive old Canadian suspicions of the United States; it made Canada feel that it was not wise to leave too much to imperial authorities, and so strengthened Laurier's hand in opposing the movement for closer imperial relations.

Gradually, however, Canadian anger cooled, and relations with the United States improved. Anglo-American friendship was now well established, and Canadians had forgotten their old fears of American attack. Although there would still be disagreements, the plain fact was that Canadians and Americans got on well together and the Canadian way of life was closely tied to the American. But in this era as well, the settlement of several outstanding arguments further helped the growth of good-will. For example, the age-old Atlantic fisheries question was settled by an award of the International Court in 1910, an award, incidentally, which favoured Canada. The previous year an International Joint Commission was set up by the two countries to deal with questions arising from their common water boundary of the Great

Lakes, or, indeed, with any border problems referred to it. This permanent body, working quietly with a mass of practical problems, was a landmark in the development of friendly co-operation between Canada and the United States. In fact the two countries were getting on together so successfully that in 1910 the question of reciprocity emerged once again—and this time it was raised by the United States.

It was not the state of trade but the fortunes of politics that suddenly revived reciprocity. In the United States rising prices had brought outcries against the lofty rates of the American tariff of 1909, and President Taft was anxious to head off the growing opposition by some new measure of tariff reduction. A reciprocity agreement with Canada seemed the answer. When Laurier heard of Taft's readiness to discuss reciprocity he was doubtful at first. But he faced his own mounting political difficulties. Besides problems raised by his Naval Service Bill, he was confronted by a vigorous western demand for a lowering of the Canadian tariff. In the summer of 1910 Laurier had made his first trip to the West, and there he had met powerful organizations of western farmers with long lists of grievances, chief among them the height of the tariff. Late that year, indeed, the new national farm organization, the Canadian Council of Agriculture sat down in Ottawa to press the western demands. It seemed that the reciprocity offer had come at the perfect moment, to charm all the Liberals' troubles away. Both parties were astounded by the golden gift that had fallen into Laurier's lap.

Agreements on reciprocity were speedily reached. Unlike the agreement of 1854 there was to be reciprocity in certain manufactured goods as well as in natural products, and it was not to be established by treaty but by laws passed in both the United States congress and the Canadian parliament. But while reciprocity passed through congress it was held up in parliament, both by the Conservatives and by a group of Liberals under Clifford Sifton who had left Laurier's side. And opposition grew outside parliament. It was another strange turn of events. After years of hoping for reciprocity, long denied by the Americans, it was now offered by them, and Canada held back. How could this be? In part it was plain enough. All the powerful interests in Canada entrenched behind the tariff, the Canadian Manufacturers' Association, the railway interests, the Conservative party, and the Liberals allied with business and banking, began a violent campaign against reciprocity. They largely appealed to the emotions, to loyalty and the British tie, and hailed reciprocity as the first step to annexation. And here prominent Americans helped by making unwise statements stressing that very point. The speaker of the United States House of Representatives supported reciprocity on the ground that it pointed towards the day when the American flag would float as far as the North Pole. Though the United States government quickly denied any such purpose behind reciprocity, the damage was done. Since some Americans insisted, as in former days, in coupling annexation with reciprocity, Canada, as in former days, was put on her guard.

But this is not sufficient explanation. More significant is the fact that by 1911 reciprocity had been a dead issue in Canada for almost twenty years, and she was prospering nicely without it. The sudden revival of the old theme did not rouse a very deep response. The east-west system seemed to be working effectively, and questions of north-south trade were not pressing. Furthermore the spirit of Canadian nationalism developed in the Laurier era worked against American reciprocity, just as it did against British imperialism. Canada was doing very well on her own— too well to seek entanglements with Americans who assumed that she could not stand on her own. Nor was American stiffness in Alaska wholly forgotten. Though such a reaction might have been mainly emotional, it was a root cause of the defeat of reciprocity. Laurier decided to hold an election on that issue in the autumn of 1911. When he went down to defeat, he was in part beaten by the very nationalism which he had helped to develop.

He was beaten as well by another sort of nationalism, the strong French Canadian variety that was revived in Quebec by his Naval Bill. The Bill that passed parliament in 1910 called for a Canadian navy of five cruisers and six destroyers. It was only to be a beginning, a unit for training and coastal defence, but the Conservatives attacked the 'tin-pot navy' as useless in the empire's time of danger, and called for direct contributions to help supply the battleships that Britain really needed to match the German fleet. The chief attack on Laurier's navy, however, came from the other side, from French nationalists led by Henri Bourassa. Bourassa was a grandson of Papineau, and like his grandfather had great powers of mind and oratory and a staunch patriotism for French Canada. Unlike Papineau, however, he was also a firm ultramontane and thus was well equipped to lead the clerical and racial extremists of Quebec. Although he professed to admire British Liberalism, as Laurier assuredly did, he had little of the tolerance that marked both Laurier and British Liberalism at its best.

The extreme nationalists of Quebec had been fairly quiet in the earlier years of Laurier's rule, especially after his notable victory over ultramontanism in that province in 1896. But gradually they began to revive, as Laurier's external policies, which were too lukewarm for the imperialists of Canada, seemed too friendly to English and imperial interests to suit many French Canadians. When the Naval Bill was passed, all the French hostility to imperialism and the dominance of English Canada burst forth, skilfully fanned by Bourassa. Quebec wanted no navy at all. A French Nationalist party took shape, denouncing Laurier as a traitor to his people, and the Bill as an imperialist trick to involve Canada in foreign wars. The result was to split the vote in Quebec in the critical election of 1911. The great influence of Laurier still carried the province for the Liberals, but with a much reduced majority; and they lost sufficient seats elsewhere, particularly in Ontario, to lose the whole election.

The Conservative victors of 1911 had little to be proud of. On the whole Laurier's defeat was due to the unpopularity of his own measures, the Naval Bill in Quebec, and reciprocity in most of the other provinces. Yet the way in which his opponents attacked these policies gave them a resounding but unlovely triumph. It was not merely that the Conservatives made frantic appeals to every imperial sentiment while battling reciprocity, but that at the same time they allied with the violent anti-imperialists of Quebec. In Ontario they attacked Laurier's navy because it was hopelessly insufficient, in Quebec because it was far too much. The two ends successfully combined against the middle.

Once in power, however, the Conservatives threw off the restraints of the Quebec Nationalists and produced a naval measure of their own. Their new leader, Robert Borden, a serious, rugged Nova Scotian, showed in office that he had views as definite as Laurier's on what Canadian external policy should be. Borden proposed that because of the continuing naval emergency the Liberals' navy measure should be dropped for the time being and a direct contribution be made to Britain to provide the Grand Fleet with three battleships at a cost of $35,000,000. This plan he introduced in a new Naval Bill in 1912. It was not, however, simply a matter of emergency aid. Borden believed that before any permanent defence measures were decided upon, Canada must secure from Britain some share in the making of imperial foreign policy. In short, he was ready to take on imperial defence burdens in exchange for a voice in the control of imperial policy. Laurier had sought to avoid commitments; Borden would accept them and make use of them. His was that sort of Canadian imperialism that wanted to see Canada gain more standing through the empire itself. And in this way he too was a nationalist, seeking to assert the new power of Canada.

As for the emergency contribution of three battleships, this Borden desired because he recognized the vital significance of British naval power in the world. Without the shield of the Royal

Navy the overseas empire lay open to German sea power, and the strength of that shield depended then on battleships above all. Germany's building programme was still pressing dangerously on Britain's lead, as the First Lord of the Admiralty, Winston Churchill, made plain to Borden. His Naval Bill for a contribution, however, was defeated in 1913 by a Senate full of Liberals appointed during Laurier's long reign. Liberalism still believed it was Canada's place to build her own navy and not turn over the task to Britain. But before another naval plan had been framed the state of emergency had ended in open war. In August 1914, the First World War began. There was no more question of giving battleships. They would have been built in British shipyards, and now Britain was building all she could. Canada's money could best go to her own war effort. Hence the naval question came to an end without Canada ever having settled it.

Yet in the few years before war burst upon it the Borden government worked at home to modernize the army and to establish the common standards for British and Dominions forces that had been recommended by the Imperial Conference of 1907 and the Imperial Defence Committee. Otherwise the Conservatives largely carried on the policies of the Laurier government, aiding railway building and promoting western settlement. The West, however, was almost filled, and in 1913 the long boom period was coming to a close. There were signs of depression when the outbreak of war caused a new flurry of activity and hid the fact that an era had ended for Canada. Though Laurier after 1911 was Leader of the Opposition and no longer Prime Minister, this whole period was truly the Laurier era. He had risen with it, helped to build its prosperity, its confidence and nationalism. The age that followed after 1914 would strain that nationalism severely, but would also see Canada advance to the full achievement of nationhood.

CHAPTER 17

THE ACHIEVEMENT OF NATIONHOOD, 1914–31

1 *Canada and the First World War*

In the golden summer of 1914 the muttering thunder clouds that had been gradually rising suddenly burst over Europe. War descended on a world long at peace, as Germany's swelling military might and restless plans of expansion finally overturned the uneasy balance of power. In the tremendous struggle that followed, Germany and Austria faced Russia in the east and Britain, France, and Italy in the west. Yet so powerful was the well-prepared German war machine that it took all the efforts of the European Allies, together with those of the United States and the British Dominions, to turn back the German invaders and bring their military empire down. Before the collapse came in 1918, Germany had forced Russia from the war in the throes of a communist revolution, had swept deep into eastern Europe, and in the west had made France the main battleground of the war with the western Allies. It was on this western front that Canada was chiefly to be engaged.

When on 4 August, 1914, the cables and the new wireless telegraph flashed the message 'War' across the Atlantic, Canada for the first time found herself flung into the midst of world affairs. Since the conquest of New France, great European conflicts had largely passed her by. Canada had been a remote colony, weak and dependent, with struggles of her own, but she had been kept securely distant from the quarrels of Europe by a wall of British sea power. Now the distant colony, no longer weak and struggling, entered a world of stern dangers and high responsibilities, the world she has been in ever since. This new stage brought sacrifice and heavy burdens for Canada. Yet with them came the rights of nationhood. Out of the vast world conflict Canada became a nation, a full partner in an empire that had been transformed into the British Commonwealth of Nations.

In the period before 1914, Canadians had not worried greatly about the prospect of a world war. Despite the naval building race, the growing strain in Europe, and the arguments over the naval question, they had in general been too busy with their own development at home. They had enough to think about in railway questions, the problems of western settlement, or the booming state of trade. Not only British sea power but the American Monroe Doctrine seemed to keep them safe. Since their only close neighbour, the United States, was no longer to be feared, the Monroe Doctrine, which declared that the republic would oppose any attack on the Americas from without, virtually presented the Canadians with the further protection of a nation of ninety million people. This, of course, had tended to make the Dominion feel less concerned over defence problems than Britain was herself. And how could anyone worry in the bright new twentieth century, where all was progress? Canada had yet to learn that this was the false brightness that comes before a storm.

When, however, the storm broke, Canada went wholeheartedly into the war. French and English Canadians alike supported it, and there was no question that Britain's declaration of war had bound Canada as a part of the empire. But what led Canadians to accept the conflict so readily? To some extent, no doubt, it was lack of awareness of what might be involved; there was still a colonial habit of mind in Canada which simply accepted decisions made outside. To a degree, also, it was the strong desire to help Britain felt among English-speaking Canadians, and an eagerness for adventure as well. Yet beyond these things, the national interests of Canadians were deeply concerned in the war: their trade, their security, the kind of world that they lived in, and for which Britain stood. Distant North America could not stand aloof; as even the much more self-contained United States decided in 1917.

As quickly as possible, in August of 1914, the Dominion parliament was called into special session, and the Canadian war effort began to take shape. The War Measures Act was passed, which gave the federal government extremely wide power to deal with the wartime emergency. The raising of 25,000 troops was ordered, and the army grew rapidly from its tiny pre-war size as volunteers flocked in. Within two months the first contingent had set sail for England in a swift convoy of liners, cruisers and destroyers, the largest troop movement that had yet been made across the Atlantic. The first Canadians crossed from England to France early in 1915, and by that autumn the two Canadian divisions that had now arrived on the western front were set up as a separate Canadian Corps. Before 1917 there were two more divisions in the Corps, as well as separate bodies of special troops. In all Canada raised over 600,000 men for the army, while others served in British or Canadian naval units and supplied a sizeable part of the Royal Flying Corps, later the Royal Air Force.

In the air, in those days of light aircraft and no parachutes, fighting was a matter of daring and personal skill, with little reliance on organized battle tactics. The Canadians took readily to the man-to-man air combats, and counted some of the leading Allied aces among their number, including 'Billy' Bishop, who had a record of seventy-two enemy aircraft destroyed. A group of seasoned Canadian pilots was developed, some of whom would use their skill and knowledge after the war to conquer Canada's vast northern distances by air.

At sea Canadians took a less spectacular part. The tiny Canadian navy was chiefly engaged in patrolling the coasts in two old cruisers lent by Britain, in motor launches and in armed yachts. But during the endless watch at sea, through Atlantic fog and blizzard, a group of trained men was built up which, in later years, would be able to expand the Royal Canadian Navy into the third largest convoy fleet in the world, in order to meet the needs of a second World War.

It was on land, however, that the Canadians played their largest role. In 1915 the First Division met the first German gas attacks at Ypres, and when French Colonial troops next to them fled before the murderous green clouds they blocked the hole in the line. They held on when the gas was turned against them, coughing and dying without gas masks. In 1916 the whole Canadian Corps entered the massive Somme attack, working with the new secret tanks, and henceforth, as Lloyd George said, the Corps was marked out as the spearhead of attack 'in one great battle after another'. Nineteen-seventeen saw the mud and bloodshed of Passchendaele and the perfectly executed capture of Vimy Ridge, the key to the whole Arras battlefront. Here a great Canadian war memorial now crowns the Ridge, raising its twin white shafts high above the Ypres flatlands. In 1918 came a long, unbroken string of Canadian victories in the final, successful Allied attack. Then in 'Canada's Hundred Days', from 4 August to 11 November, the Canadian Corps sliced through the deep defences of the formidable Hindenburg Line and driving ahead with the First British Army reached Mons on the last day of the fighting; the town where—so long ago it seemed—the little British army of 1914 had first met the advancing German legions. When the war ended Canada had lost as many men as the powerful United States, out of a population of less than a tenth the size. Sad and heavy as the cost was, it was an imposing effort for the young Dominion to make.

Home-front developments were no less remarkable in their own way. Since the war was cutting off or destroying much of Europe's farming production, Canada's wide farmlands became immensely important in feeding the western Allies. Almost as much prairie land was brought under the plough in the war years as had already been farmed in 1913. Wheat, flour, meat, and cattle exports soared. So did lumber, since Germany blocked the way to Baltic forest lands. The need for Canadian wood pulp also rose, because the Swedish supply was not available. Mining, in particular, jumped ahead in the Shield and the Rockies, as the roaring armament factories demanded more and more metals—copper, lead, zinc, and above all, nickel. Near Sudbury, Ontario, there lay one of the richest supplies of nickel ore in the world, and nickel was essential for hardening armour plate and making armour-piercing nickel-steel shells. Canada came to control over ninety per cent of the world's nickel production.

Thanks to all this activity, the east-west trading system was strained to the limit. The transcontinental railways throbbed with traffic, the Atlantic ports were crowded. Halifax came into its own again as a naval base, and its magnificent harbour saw many a long, grey convoy assemble in Bedford Basin; and saw too the terrible explosion of 1917, when a fire on board a French munitions ship ended by wiping out half the city. But Halifax recovered and worked on ceaselessly, as did all Canada in the feverish haste of wartime production and shipment.

Yet perhaps the most striking developments came in industry. Canada had already had numerous factories before the war; but except, perhaps, for railway shops and farm-machinery plants, there was a lack of heavy industry and large-scale machine production. Canadian mineral products, for example, were chiefly exported to industries in other lands, and there were few skilled machinists in the Dominion. It remains true today that because Canada produces such a great quantity of minerals and other raw materials, most of them still go abroad. But, under the pressure of war, heavy industry and machine skills began to spread in Canada as the need for the weapons of battle mounted constantly. Most of this war production was taken up with shells and guns, under the guidance of both the Canadian government and the Imperial Munitions Board. By 1917 close to a third of the shells fired by British forces in France had come from Canada. This was a bitter kind of industrialism, its products shattering themselves in spreading destruction, but it was a matter of stern necessity. And after the war the factories built and the skills learnt in machining shells, fuses, and guns could be turned to broader uses. Besides, by the war's end Canada was also turning out steel ships and aircraft frames, and had built up a large industrial labour force with a high standard of living.

The Borden government played a considerable part in shaping this war effort. Since Canada had never before sought to produce on such a scale it was not surprising that there were mistakes and blunders as well as notable successes in the government's wartime policies. One great problem was the financing of the war. Canada until now had been a debtor country, borrowing money for her development mainly from Britain. But Britain, pressed to the limit, had no more funds to spare; and as well as paying her own way, Canada found that she would have to lend to Britain to help pay for British war purchases in the Dominion. A drastic change was taking place in the financial relations of the two countries. Almost overnight the Canadian government found that it must stand on its own resources, though provinces and private industry resorted more and more to the American money market. In consequence, new taxes were laid on the Canadian people, including, in 1917, the first Dominion income tax. But the government's main resource was the Victory Loan. Victory Loans were repeatedly floated, until over $2,000,000,000 had thus been raised. Their success was a mark of the growing financial strength of Canada; but they also helped to stimulate greatly a runaway wartime boom that brought ever-mounting prices and serious difficulties for the ordinary mass of the people.

Attempts to control the rising prices and share out goods in short supply were none too successful. The Borden ministry clung to the long-accepted attitude in Canada, that government should interfere as little as possible in economic affairs. But the rising public demand for state action, forced them to set up partial and rather half-hearted controls: a Cost of Living Commissioner in 1916, a Food Controller in 1917, and a War Trade Board in 1918. The lack of connection between these offices only increased the demand for effective government control of wartime living problems. Unrest remained, labour and farm organizations grew, storing up grievances that would burst forth once the war was over. Perhaps the most successful government system of control was that established in 1917 to handle and market the whole Canadian wheat crop. This became the Canada Wheat Board in 1919. It too would have its consequences for the future.

The chief home-front problem, however, was that of manpower. It was a question of finding sufficient men in this nation of eight million people not only to carry on the strenuous work of production in farms and factories, but to maintain the armed forces that were meeting heavy losses on the western front, in a conflict that cost the Western Allies a far higher rate of casualties than the Second World War. To some extent the Borden government succeeded in meeting the manpower problem. The need for labour in the rising factories was met, partly by calling on the great reserve of woman-power. One well-deserved consequence of this was the extension of votes to women, by acts passed during and shortly after the war. The government also managed to keep the Canadian Corps up to strength. In all, it assembled a volunteer army of well over half a million men. Yet, as the blood-letting of war went on, the question of maintaining the flow of new recruits grew ever more pressing. And it was here, in meeting the manpower problem, that the Borden ministry encountered its gravest difficulties. Its policies produced a new division between French and English in Canada, and a racial crisis that left lasting scars.

2 Conscription and the Racial Crisis

When the war began there was no sign that it would endanger the national unity that had been built up in the Laurier era. Laurier himself, as leader of the Liberal opposition, pledged his full support to the war effort, and swung his wide influence in French Canada behind the war which, he declared, was a struggle both for world freedom and for very existence. Even Henri Bourassa approved Canada's entry into war, while the leaders of the Quebec clergy urged loyal support for Britain. French Canadian volunteers streamed in as readily as English-speaking Canadians. Never had Canada been more united than in preparing for the great conflict.

If only matters had been better handled, this mood of unity might almost have made the shock of war seem worth while. But very soon racial disputes began to arise again. The fact that at first they were not even connected with the war only made them more tragic. There was another schools quarrel, this time in Ontario, where the new Regulation 17 sought to limit teaching in French in a few 'border' areas of the province inhabited by French Canadians. This unwise effort to absorb French-speaking citizens was only the largest of a number of petty disputes on the home front: petty, that is, in comparison with the tremendous struggle that had to be faced overseas. Yet, to the French Canadians, whose gaze turned inward from living so long in their own world of the St Lawrence, such questions loomed larger than they did to the English Canadians, who had been led to look outwards by their much closer ties with Britain across the sea.

As French irritation grew, so did that of English Canada, because of reports that the French Canadians were falling behind in supplying men for the army. In some degree this was true. As calls went out for more and more volunteers, the rate of French enlistments declined. The French did not share the strong emotional drive to enlist that affected English-speaking Canadians. They viewed the war as a noble adventure, not as a life-or-death struggle. Their feelings for Britain were those of respect or thoughtful support, not of warm sentiment, and they had too long gone their separate way to feel deeply about Britain's ally, France. In addition, they were a farming people, and farmers traditionally are harder to enlist than the less firmly rooted population of the towns. It seems clear, as well, that French Canadians did not fully sense the meaning of the war: that their whole secure, isolated world would be in danger if the conflict were lost. Here English Canada showed more awareness. Yet at least the French attitude was understandable.

And it might have developed on other lines if the Borden government had not mismanaged French-Canadian recruiting. Little attempt was made to see the French point of view. There was not much understanding of the language problem in training French-Canadian volunteers, who sometimes knew no English, although the brilliant overseas record of a regiment such as the Royal Twenty-Second, the famed 'Vandoos', showed what a wholly French-Canadian unit could do. Yet few distinctly French-Canadian units were raised, despite the natural French desire for them. Nor did the direction of the Minister of Militia, the energetic but wayward Sir Sam Hughes, help matters. He shared the superior attitude and uninformed prejudice regarding French Canadians that are among the worst characteristics of some English Canadians (although the same thing might also be said on the other side). As if it were not enough to have an anti-Catholic Ulsterman as Minister of Militia, some Protestant clergymen were among the recruiting officers sent to Quebec: a measure not likely to soothe the feelings of that Roman Catholic province.

In these circumstances, it is not altogether surprising that French Canadian enlistments lagged. But, as casualties mounted, it was also natural that English Canada, suffering much heavier losses, should accuse the French of not doing their share. Harsh words were exchanged, and French Canada began to retreat more and more into its old narrow nationalism. The French Canadians could see in the English Canadian demand for an all-out war effort only that imperialism again, which put British interests ahead of Canada's. By 1916 there were riots against recruiting in Quebec towns and Bourassa was openly opposing the war.

At the same time the need for recruits was becoming serious. The already large number of men in the forces and the demands of farms and factories meant that it was increasingly difficult to keep up enlistment through the volunteer system. By the end of 1916 it was failing to meet requirements for recruits. The government had previously opposed the idea of conscribing men for military service, which was not then fully accepted in the Dominions. But early in 1917 Borden returned from a visit to England, where the critical need for every last man in arms had been pressed upon him. While realizing the bitter opposition it would arouse among the French, he was convinced that Canada must accept conscription.

Other countries faced their troubles in adopting conscription; but in Canada, with its two peoples, one of them feeling as the French did, it was either a very brave or very foolish thing to do —or both. A Military Service Bill for conscription was put before parliament. Borden hoped to avoid splitting the nation over the dangerous question by forming a union government; that is, by combining with the Liberals to carry conscription as the only patriotic policy. Many English-speaking Liberals were willing to support a union or coalition government, for they too were convinced that conscription was necessary. Laurier, however, refused Borden's offer of alliance. He knew that French Canada would not accept conscription, even from a party coalition, and he felt that such a measure could never pay for the destruction of national unity. Up to this point Laurier had fully supported the war effort. He continued to believe in Allied victory. But he could not believe that Canadian conscription would be vital to that victory, though he feared it would be ruinous to Canada. Indeed, he saw the whole work of his lifetime hanging in the balance.

But though Laurier felt thus, he could not prevent a split in his own party. Led by Sir Clifford Sifton, most of the English-speaking Liberals, especially from Ontario and the West, left Laurier for Borden. In October, 1917, a Union government was established, under Borden, containing ten Liberals and thirteen Conservatives. An angry, excited election followed, in which, as might be expected, the government carried every province but Quebec. Laurier, on the other hand, won all but three seats in Quebec, and only twenty in all Canada beyond. This result showed how dangerously far the racial division had gone. In effect English Canada was ranged against French Canada, and passions were high. Conscription was assured; but was it worth it?

One thing was certain. A new breach had opened in Canada which robbed the national successes of the war effort of much of their effect. The bitterness and suspicion produced on both sides would take a long time to live down. And politics and governments would long be affected by the memories of the conscription crisis. As for the conscripts, only about 60,000 of them had been raised by the time the war ended, and few of them ever reached France. The whole result, then, seems definitely not worth it. There are, however, a few things to be said by way of qualification.

In the first place, it is easy to judge by the wisdom that comes after the event, and say that 60,000 men who were hardly used were not worth all the trouble. Manpower policies had to be set ahead, and there was no way of knowing in the bleak days of 1917 that the next year would see the sudden collapse of Germany. In the second place, the division of races was not quite as sharp as it first appeared to be. In the total of the votes cast in Canada, in the election of 1917, Laurier was not too far behind Borden; it was the soldiers' ballots and the government's arrangement of special voting provisions to strengthen its hand, that gave it such a telling majority of seats in parliament. The point here is that others besides the French Canadians strongly opposed conscription, especially among the farmers and the trade unionists. And in the third place, Canada continued to hold together once conscription had been established. There was rioting in Quebec City and there were some attempts among French Canadians to avoid being conscribed as a matter of principle. But considering the heated feelings roused by the question of conscription, one might say that this new racial crisis had revealed that by now the bonds that knit the Dominion together had toughened considerably.

At any rate, Canada emerged from the conscription crisis as she did from the war, shaken and strained, but by no means exhausted or gloomy. And if Canadian nationalism had suffered a setback at home, abroad it was advancing steadily, rounding out the new position that Canada had earned by right of blood and effort.

3 Borden and the Commonwealth

During the war the Dominions of the British empire made heavy contributions to the Allied cause. Britain's contribution was on a greater scale than theirs, but the aid freely given by these young, self-governing countries was plainly important; so important that they began to occupy a larger place in the world. By the close of the war they were becoming nations in their own right, though they still kept the bond between them. Out of the empire, in fact, the British Commonwealth of Nations was now emerging as a group of free peoples sharing equal membership in a world-wide community, held together by freedom and common ideas, and not, as in times past, by the ultimate authority of Britain. Of course, the British empire was already far advanced in the development of freedom and self-government. Because of that fact it could move on still further to achieve the Commonwealth, a striking example of a working world-partnership in an age that sorely needs co-operation between its peoples.

The British empire had been changing before the First World War, but that mighty conflict much increased the rate of change. National sentiment in the Dominions was strengthened by their war efforts; they had been suddenly called on to undertake grave new responsibilities and had found themselves able to meet the challenge. There was a new awareness of nationality among the large bodies of Dominion troops overseas, while, at home, pride in the fighting record of these soldiers roused a keener spirit of

A SETTLER'S FIRST HOME IN MANITOBA

THE LAURIER SMILE — SIR WILFRID CAMPAIGNING IN 1908

SCOTTISH IMMIGRANTS AT QUEBEC, 1909

DUTCH IMMIGRANTS AT QUEBEC, 1909

nationalism. That spirit was reflected in a growing desire for a fuller recognition of Dominion rights in the empire. In the changes that followed, Canada played a leading part. Just as Sir Wilfrid Laurier had stood for wider Dominion powers before the war, so did Sir Robert Borden in the time of battle and in the peace settlement that followed.

One problem affecting the position of Canada within the empire during the war revolved about the control of Canadian troops overseas. While British military commanders at first planned to absorb the Canadians into British or imperial army formations, Borden, with Canada behind him, insisted that they be treated as one unit—as a Canadian army formation. This demand was met by the establishment of the Canadian Corps, into which most Canadian troops were fitted. The Corps served in various British armies but kept its own unity within them. After a successful career under a British general, moreover, General Byng, of Vimy fame, the Corps received an able Canadian commander in General Arthur Currie, who led it until the end of the fighting in the final 'Hundred Days'.

More significant than this question of purely military control was the wider one of the general management of empire war policy. This at first was wholly in the hands of the British government. Borden felt keenly that while Canada might put half a million men in the field she had no voice in shaping plans for waging a war in which she was vitally concerned. 'Is this war', he asked, 'being waged by the United Kingdom alone, or is it a war waged by the whole empire?' For some time his protests received sympathy but little more from the British government. The British authorities still held to the principle that the control of the empire's external policy could not be divided but must remain with Britain. At the Imperial Conference of 1911 it had been agreed that the Dominions would be kept informed on major foreign questions by Britain, but the mother country was still to have sole direction of imperial foreign policy.

By 1916, however, the Asquith government that had expressed these views had been replaced in Britain by a coalition under the energetic Lloyd George. Seeking in every way to strengthen and reorganize the British war effort, at a time when the fortunes of war were hanging in the balance, he sought as well to urge the Dominions to further activity. Therefore Lloyd George was willing to reconsider the problem of directing the war, and to meet the stronger national feelings of the Dominions by forming an Imperial War Cabinet in which they would be represented. Such a body was set up in 1917, and consisted of the Dominion prime ministers or their representatives sitting with the British war cabinet, the inner group of five ministers chosen to guide Britain's war programme. At the same time an Imperial War Conference was called to consider ways of permanently reorganizing the imperial structure in order to give the Dominions a share in its control.

The Imperial War Cabinet was a weighty step, and was received with much enthusiasm in Canada and in the other Dominions. The Dominions had at last been given a voice in shaping empire policies that greatly affected their interests. It was, besides, an answer to Borden's chief demand that if Canada took more responsibilities in the world she should in return have greater rights. It met his view of nationalism: that Canada should no longer have external policies made for her, but should enter into making them. Such a plan, he believed, would give the Dominions full power in world affairs and yet would preserve an undivided imperial foreign policy. The Imperial War Conference endorsed this view, declaring that the empire had become a Commonwealth of free and equal members, who should meet in 'continuous consultation' to lay down a common policy for their relations with the outside world.

During the rest of the war the Imperial War Cabinet carried out the plan of a common imperial policy and 'continuous consultation', although Dominion prime ministers could usually attend its meetings only for short periods at a time. When the war ended the same plan was adopted for making the Peace Treaty of 1919. Indeed, the Imperial War Cabinet virtually became the 'British Empire Delegation' that went to France to work as a unit at the Versailles peace conference. The aim, in short, was still to maintain a common imperial foreign policy, in peace as in war. Yet difficulties arose almost from the start, as Borden found on his return to England after the Canadian conscription crisis. Britain had begun talks with France and Italy, without informing the Dominions, and had hoped that Borden would serve on the single British Empire Delegation as representative of all the varied Dominion interests. Instead the Canadian leader made clear that Canada, at any rate, expected her full share of recognition at the peace conference in view of her notable rôle in the war, especially when small independent countries, which had taken much less part, would be separately represented. In consequence, all the Dominions were given the right of separate representation, although in practice they continued as well to sit on the British Empire Delegation, which carried on the real work of the conference.

This double role was really a sign in itself of the double position of the Dominions—still half colonies and half nations. Yet it also showed that the idea of a common imperial front was beginning to lose its force now that the urgent pressures of war were removed. Dominion nationalism was again making itself felt. This time it led further to the separate signature of the Peace Treaty by each Dominion, although there was also a general signature for the empire as a whole. Borden held out as well for the right of the Canadian parliament to approve the Treaty for his own country, and this too was accepted. Nor were these mere formalities. Borden was trying to gain recognition of Canada's right to decide for herself on vital questions of war and peace. These powers of the Dominion to act in matters of external policy were further increased when Borden won for Canada a seat of her own in the new League of Nations that was meant to prevent another world war. Separate seats were also given to the other Dominions.

Aside from these questions of national standing, which Borden pressed firmly, Canada was fairly quiet in the long debates over the terms of peace. She was a small power, with no desire to gain territory, and sought only to make a sound and lasting treaty. As a result, though she took only a minor part in the drafting of the Treaty of Versailles, her influence was a useful and moderating one, and Borden played an admirable and highly respected role on various committees. But from Canada's viewpoint, the important points to her were those principles of national recognition that she had secured through her prime minister: the right of signing and approving the Peace Treaty herself, the right to sit as a member nation in the League and the International Labour Organization, and the right to send her own diplomatic representatives to foreign countries. This last power Borden also obtained, although it was not exercised for several years.

In general, Borden had led the way in securing broader recognition for all the Dominions, but other Dominion leaders had shared largely in this effort, especially General Smuts of South Africa. By 1920, when ill-health forced Borden to retire from political life, it could almost be said that he himself had given Canada an established place in world affairs. And by helping to build up the national rights of all the Dominions he had sent the empire further on its way to becoming the Commonwealth.

Yet in all this development Sir Robert Borden had not forgotten the idea of a common imperial foreign policy based on continuous consultation. What he wanted, however, was to round out the rights of the Dominions as he saw them, so that they could then join in imperial counsels with Britain on an equal footing. He and Smuts both hoped to maintain a single imperial front in foreign affairs through the Dominions entering freely into discussions to fix policies, which would then be carried out by the

British Foreign Office. The failure of this common-policy idea, after Borden's retirement, led to the full development of the Commonwealth as it is today, and, in other hands, to the complete realization of Canadian nationhood.

4 Mackenzie King and Nationhood

On Sir Robert Borden's retirement, one of his ablest lieutenants, Arthur Meighen, became prime minister. Meighen was a man of undoubted talent but of firm and uncompromising character, and his imperialist leanings and strong conscriptionist stand during the wartime crisis had made him many enemies in French Canada. He and the Conservative government were swept from power in the first post-war election, in 1921. In part, the result was due to French Canadian dislike of the Conservative conscriptionists, a feeling which would long affect the party's fortunes. In part as well, it was the natural swing away from the wartime government when post-war problems and grievances emerged.

Meighen's successor in office was the new Liberal leader, William Lyon Mackenzie King. Laurier had died in 1919, his last years darkened by the racial strife he had always sought to avoid. The man who assumed his mantle was a devoted follower of the great French Canadian. King, an Ontario man, had been Canada's first Minister of Labour in Laurier's pre-war government, and had been out of politics studying labour problems in the United States during much of the war. He had supported Laurier but was not too involved in the conscription question: a very fortunate thing for the future of the Liberal party in Canada. King had little of Laurier's charm of manner nor his splendid powers of oratory. Yet he showed political skill matched only by Macdonald. This quiet, reserved, plump little man turned out to be the most successful party leader Canada has yet seen, and this in an era when sectional strains were often acute. As a result, he made a period of Canadian history as much his own as Macdonald or Laurier had ever done. He governed the Dominion from 1921 to 1948, with only one real break, the five years from 1930 to 1935 when the Conservatives returned to office.

Mackenzie King held office longer than any other Canadian prime minister had done: longer, even, than any British prime minister, for he passed the old eighteenth-century record of Sir Robert Walpole. And in this, Canada's Walpole era, King, like that famous English statesman, largely followed a passive policy of 'letting sleeping dogs lie'. It may be argued that Canada needed such a long period of comparative inaction in government to rebuild the national unity that had been seriously strained at home. But in external affairs, at least, King pursued a very definite policy. He worked to round out national rights, in order to give Canada the complete status of nationhood. As his name might suggest, William Lyon Mackenzie King was a descendant of the 'little rebel'. He was Mackenzie's grandson. And King seemed to feel a mission to carry on the work of his grandfather. Not that he was in any way a rebel, nor did he ever seek to break the tie with Britain; but he believed in freeing Canada from the last traces of colonial restraints, restraints that his ancestor had struggled against when they bore more heavily on the country.

King believed that full nationhood must come for the British Dominions. In this, time has apparently proved him right, though his work itself did much to make the Commonwealth a loose organization of separate nations. Yet it would be wrong to call it a 'mere' association of separate nations. If formal ties were reduced to a minimum, the ties of friendship remained strong; and King put his faith in these. In any case, he was determined that nationhood should be finally achieved for Canada.

Now nationhood is not inevitably a good thing in itself. There is no thought in these pages that its gradual achievement is the grand or final theme in Canada's story. In many ways, besides, Canadian nationhood is still weak, especially when it comes to trying to distinguish the Canadian 'national character' from the American. Furthermore, any blind worship of nationhood is unreal and unwise in an age where all parts of the world are closely tied to each other and no nation can afford to stand alone. Nevertheless, for better or worse, the rise of nationalism has seemed to play a prominent part in the history of peoples, and so it has been in Canada's case. If Canadian nationality still has limits, the growth of nationalism has formed an important theme in Canadian history, at least since Confederation. And because Canadian nationalism arose within the British empire, and grew gradually there, it has seldom gone to the extremes of the worship of independence for its own sake or a belief in complete isolation from the world. Nationalism did not destroy the British empire. It changed it to something new for a new age; the Commonwealth. Canada, therefore, rose to final nationhood under King without withdrawing from the great world association; and while this national advance is plainly significant, it should not be allowed to overshadow other aspects of Canadian development.

It might well be asked why Canada at this time pressed her advance to nationhood within the Commonwealth more, say, than Australia or New Zealand. The answer that Canadian national feeling was more fully developed itself needs explanation. Canada was older than the other Dominions; that was one factor. Beyond this, however, Canada contained a large and influential minority of a non-English-speaking people, the French Canadians, who were always much more advanced in thinking on national lines, and at the same time were suspicious of empire 'entanglements'. This naturally affected Canadian policy, as the presence of the Afrikaner majority in South Africa also shaped the nationalistic policy of that Dominion.

Furthermore, Australia and New Zealand developed apart by themselves, linked only to Britain. Canada grew up beside a large, free, English-speaking republic and had strong ties in this direction as well. In the beginning, the presence of the United States stimulated the early growth of Canadian nationalism because of the challenge it set before the weak northern colonies.

In later, more friendly days the powerful United States seemed to provide extra security for Canada, in addition to British sea power. While Australia and New Zealand, fearing rising new powers in the Pacific—first Germany, then Japan—drew closer to the empire and sought to find security there, Canada felt much more able to follow her own course. This had been true under Laurier. Now, under King, the only great sea menace to Canada, the German navy, was gone, and her only close neighbour remained the friendly United States. Canadian nationalism that had been so much aroused by the war thus continued to flourish in a state of security.

There was a feeling in post-war Canada that the problems of Europe and the rest of the world were remote, that even the problem of a common imperial foreign policy was no longer of concern, and that all that mattered for the Dominion was the achievement of complete freedom in international affairs. The Commonwealth should be maintained: few would still break the old links of tradition and sentiment. But there should be no involvement in quarrels that were not Canada's, and Canada should settle her own policies for herself. To some extent this was a narrow programme of isolation, and so it was not wholly realistic. Yet in the disillusion that followed the war, when it was seen that all the blood shed had in no way solved the troubles of Europe, it was a natural enough reaction. Besides, this truly 'Canada first' policy also expressed a resolve to let the Dominion stand on its own feet, to let the world know that Canada had come of age and was no longer a colony.

Canada, of course, had made many practical gains towards nationhood under Borden. Yet theory had now to catch up with practice. It had to be made clear what these gains implied, they had to be completed, and the whole Commonwealth had to be redefined to fit the new world standing of Canada and the other Dominions. King took up this project from the start, though he moved slowly and only as particular questions arose. The first thing to be altered was the common imperial foreign policy that Borden had believed in.

The system of continuous consultation and joint action had seemed much more possible during wartime, when close cooperation against a common foe was utterly necessary. But once that main purpose had been removed, the Dominions had varying interests in many different parts of the world. The difficulty of shaping one single imperial foreign policy was soon made apparent, despite some success in maintaining it at the Washington Conference of 1921 on disarmament. In 1922 Britain faced renewed trouble with Turkey, an enemy during the First World War. This was the so-called Chanak crisis. The British government had to take a stand before the Dominions could be consulted, but when it cabled Canada to ask for aid in event of a clash, the King ministry would not commit the Dominion over an issue that was outside its knowledge. The fact that the request for aid came without warning and was announced in the British press before it was officially received in Canada added to the feeling that Britain was forcing the pace on a question that was not really of Canadian interest. As a result, the King government's unwillingness to act caused a breach in the idea of a common imperial policy. The breach went further in the Treaty of Lausanne, shortly reached with Turkey. Canada declared that since she had not been a party to making this agreement she would not consider herself bound by it. The old unity of the empire in diplomatic affairs was coming to an end.

That fact was made even plainer in 1923, when Canada signed the Halibut Treaty with the United States in her own right, without the formal addition of the British minister's signature, which had previously been the rule. Then the Imperial Conference of that year, instead of working out a permanent basis for a common imperial policy, as had earlier been expected, affirmed the general right of Dominions to make treaties with foreign states. Canada had thus obtained a most necessary power for conducting her own foreign relations. At the same time the plan of the common imperial policy based on continuous consultation was finally abandoned. The nations of the Commonwealth, of course, might still co-operate and consult with one another as need arose, but the fact that these nations had varied interests was now definitely recognized. Each member of the Commonwealth would henceforth conduct its own foreign policy as far as it desired, a principle pressed by King and Herzog of South Africa.

By now it was plainly necessary to draw up a definition of the developing Commonwealth and to make whatever changes were required in the imperial system of government to suit the much-altered state of affairs. This important problem was dealt with in 1926 at the next Imperial Conference, which produced the Balfour Report. The Balfour Report, the foundation-stone of the modern Commonwealth, declared the members of that association to be 'equal in status, in no way subordinate one to another,' though united by a common allegiance to the Crown and working together in complete freedom. 'Every self-governing member of the Empire is now the master of its destiny.'

A number of recommendations were then made in the Report in order to make this new declaration of equal partnership a reality. Henceforth the Governor-General of a Dominion should clearly represent only the great unifying symbol of the crown, not the British government in any way. Any Dominion which did not enter in the making of a treaty would not be bound by it. And various legal problems which remained were set forth for reference to committees of Commonwealth lawyers and experts for study and settlement. In 1930 the experts' views on these questions were put before a further Imperial Conference, which adopted their proposals. The year after they were enacted into law by the British parliament in the Statute of Westminster. The Statute recognized rather than established the new Commonwealth, but in so doing made it a legal fact.

The Statute of Westminster of 1931, which has been termed the

Magna Carta of the Commonwealth, fulfilled the Balfour Report and made the legal changes necessary to effect the Dominions' new position of equality with the mother country. It repealed the Colonial Laws Validity Act of 1865 which had declared that in the event of any conflict, a British law was to override a colonial law, and henceforth Dominions might alter any imperial law in force within their borders; it granted the Dominions control over their own merchant shipping and in general gave them the full powers of nationhood in the field of law. There was still some imperial authority left. Only Britain still could pass laws for all the Commonwealth, though these would only apply to a Dominion with its consent. The British parliament was still entrusted with the power to amend the Canadian constitution, although the amending power remained because Canada had not yet decided how to use it herself. and it would only be exercised at Canada's request. The Judicial Committee of the imperial Privy Council was still generally maintained as a final court for deciding certain classes of legal cases, although again this arrangement rested on the consent of the Dominions. But on the whole the Statute of Westminster completed the development of Dominion nationhood, and, for Canada, filled out her national powers while keeping her within the free circle of the Commonwealth.

Canada's new world standing was meanwhile being rounded out in other directions as well as on legal lines. She began official diplomatic relations with other countries of the world. In 1926 the first Canadian minister was sent to the United States, and by 1930 Canadian diplomatic posts had been established in France and Japan, two world powers with which Canada had important connections. Canada had long had a High Commissioner in London, but in recognition of the new equal Commonwealth relationship a British High Commissioner was sent to Ottawa and later Canada exchanged High Commissioners with the other Dominions. Of course, it remained true that Britain and the Dominions were 'equal in status but not in stature'; that is, that Britain and Canada, for example, were equal in national standing but not in power and influence in the world.

There were still changes to come in the Commonwealth and in Canada's relation to it; but on all important points the development was complete. Nationhood at last had been achieved. It had been won not by revolution and separation but by a process of careful discussion and gradual growth. The benefits of friendship and trust, frequent consultation and free co-operation had not been lost. These invisible bonds of the Commonwealth would prove their value in the Second World War. In the evolution of the great world partnership Canada had taken a major part. Indeed, it had really begun when Canada first won responsible government on British lines. From the days of Robert Baldwin to those of Laurier, Borden, and King, Canadians had not only been shaping their own nationhood. They had been building the Commonwealth as well.

CHAPTER 18

CANADA BETWEEN TWO WORLD WARS, 1919–39

1 *Post-War Growth and Renewed Sectionalism*

After the First World War there was a short post-war boom followed by a three-year slump in trade. Then in 1923 began a bright flush of prosperity that lasted until late in 1929, when the 'great crash' occurred. A long and ruinous world depression followed in the 1930's, but during the booming 'twenties Canada seemed to have returned to the Laurier era of rapid advance. And many features of the development under Laurier continued into the post-war years. Immigration went on, reaching a peak of 165,000 in 1929. Still more western farms were taken up, and Alberta and Saskatchewan grew steadily. New strains of wheat pushed the grain frontier into the northern half of these provinces, while bumper wheat crops in the 'twenties kept the east-west trade system running busily. Canada, apparently, was launched again on the limitless Laurier boom.

Yet there were differences in the post-war scene. The Laurier period had really completed Canada's advance across the continent. She could not go on advancing for ever; western farmlands were not limitless. Already, under the encouragement of wartime demands, farms had spread too far into areas that were really grazing country, as in the dry 'Palliser's Triangle' of south-western Saskatchewan and south-eastern Alberta. Here a prolonged drought could spell disaster. It could turn the powdery soil, stripped of protecting grass roots, into whirling clouds of dust. Furthermore, the railways, whose building had played so large a part in pre-war prosperity, were in constant difficulties after the war. The Canadian Pacific was paying its way, but the government's Canadian National was in trouble even in boom times, both because of the debts it inherited and because of the expense of keeping up many miles of track that did not pay but were necessary to the people who settled along the line.

On the other hand, many features of the post-war growth were new, or had been much less important in the earlier period. The greatest developments were not in wheat farming but in manufactures, minerals, pulp-wood and newsprint. The most striking advance was not in the prairie West but in the North, especially in the semi-barren Shield. And the conquering gods of the new era were not the steam engine and the railway, but oil, electric power, the automobile and the aeroplane. Finally, the old Canada of farms and frontier settlement was passing away. To the north lay a broader frontier than there had ever been before, but it was being mastered by the aeroplane and it did not invite settlement. The majority of the Canadians were becoming a race of townsmen. In the 1920's the Dominion's urban population passed that of the countryside, and most of the city-dwellers were found in the two main industrial provinces of Ontario and Quebec.

But these post-war developments were of high importance. They gave Canada a more balanced, stable way of life, less dependent on the ups and downs of the world market. They gave her new staple exports besides wheat. The post-war period saw the steady rise of gold, copper, nickel, and other base metals, and of pulp wood and newsprint. These new staples, however, travelled more on north-south lines than along the east-west system. Their main markets were in the United States. Britain remained Canada's chief outlet for the older products of farming, but the high value of the new products meant that in 1921 the United States took a slight lead to become Canada's best customer once more, despite the high American tariff wall.

The rise of new staples brought developments all over Canada. Along the Appalachian ridges and across the Shield lumbering took a new lease on life, this time devoting itself to the thick softwood forests, to cut for wood-pulp. Large pulp-mills sprang up in the North, driven by the plentiful water-power of these hilly regions. Whole new towns appeared among the rocks and birches of northern New Brunswick or northern Ontario and Quebec. The gold of Noranda in northern Quebec, the asbestos carved from open pits in the Eastern Townships, the copper and nickel of Copper Cliff, Ontario, the oil of Turner Valley, Alberta, the lead, zinc, and copper of the Kootenay region in the mountains of British Columbia—all these brought tremendous advances in the realm of mining. The list seems endless: gold at Flin-Flon in northern Manitoba, in the Porcupine and Kirkland Lake regions of northern Ontario, radium and uranium mined at Great Bear Lake, high in the North West Territories, and shipped out by air; suffice it to say that the endless rock barrens of northern Canada had turned into a national treasure chest.

Another important advance came with the wide development of hydro-electric power, which in Ontario, under the province-owned Hydro-Electric Power Commission, gave the province one of the cheapest and most efficient supplies of electricity in the world. The building of automobile highways that linked up the settled parts of Canada far more effectively was another feature of this prosperous period. So was the amazing rise of 'bush flying', which carried even bulky machinery into the roadless North and brought Canada the world's heaviest air freight-traffic. And through the air the conquest of northern distances became possible. Hudson's Bay posts, missions to the Eskimos, and radio weather stations, that were now extended to the shores of the Arctic Ocean and the islands beyond, were linked by the aeroplane. Steamboats to the Arctic on the long Mackenzie river in the summer and tractor-driven sleigh-trains in the winter supplied heavier transportation for this new Far North. The Arctic really entered Canadian history for the first time, in terms of furs, oil, gold, and other minerals.

Yet much of this post-war growth tended to cut across the east-west unity of Canada and was felt unevenly in the different regions.

The northern development, for example, chiefly benefited the provinces of Ontario and Quebec and the powerful business interests concentrated there. Toronto built a great mining empire in northern Ontario, but its connections generally ran north and south, strengthening regionalism, not the east-west system of Canada. Vancouver and British Columbia flourished, especially after the opening of the Panama Canal in 1913 gave the Pacific port a good sea-way to the markets of Europe. But, as a result, Vancouver began to drain part of the western prairies' trade into this sea-way, competing with the railway links across the continent to the East. The Pacific coast and central Canada were thriving as separate regions. Other parts of the Dominion were not doing as well.

The prairies were still growing, but plainly not at the same rate as these other sections. Their own hope of a short sea-way to Europe, led to the building of a railway from the plains to Churchill on Hudson Bay. But this northern route, however, facing ice dangers, a short season, and high shipping charges, did not develop successfully. At the same time the Maritimes were again feeling themselves the step-children of Confederation. They were sharing little of the post-war development; in fact, they were close to depression. The division was sharpening between 'have' and 'have-not' sections of Canada.

The Maritimes were still facing their old problem, the fact that they had few resources left to develop after the age of wooden ships had passed away. Their area was small, good farmland was limited, and while Nova Scotia had excellent supplies of coal, that in itself was not sufficient to bring industry to this outlying region of the continent. The Atlantic provinces still relied heavily on the fisheries, but since the war fish prices had been low. The wartime boom at the ports of Halifax and Saint John was over, the steel shipbuilding industry that had been started was closing down. Though Prince Edward Island was by now fairly well adjusted to a quiet but contented farming way of life, and though coal mines and steel mills on Cape Breton Island helped Nova Scotia, the Maritimes on the whole were almost at a standstill.

Thus it was that a movement developed in the 1920's for 'Maritime Rights'. The Maritimes blamed the tariff structure for building up central Canada at their expense, and charged, too, that Dominion governments generally had paid little attention to their special problems. They took a strong stand on the powers of provinces in Confederation, claiming that the Dominion had over-stepped the proper limits of its authority. The King government thereupon appointed a Royal Commission to investigate Maritime grievances, and on its report in 1927 moved to solve the problem in the typical way; by granting new subsidies to the Atlantic provinces. This disposed of the provincial rights question in the East for the time being, but more serious sectional movements were developing in the prairie West.

These movements in part centred around the 'Natural Resources Question', which was pressed by all three prairie provinces. At Confederation the old provinces had kept control of their natural resources—lands, forests, minerals—but in the case of the new provinces of Manitoba, Saskatchewan, and Alberta that had been erected out of the North West Territories, the control of their resources had stayed with the Dominion. This was done to give the Dominion a fund for developing the western country. Through railway land-grants, for example, it had used western land to help pay the Canadian Pacific Railway for building its line. In the 1920's, however, when so much development of natural resources was going on, especially in lumbering and mining, the three prairie provinces demanded control of their own resources. The Dominion gave way, but the whole question helped strengthen sectional feeling.

More important in the long run for the re-emergence of sectionalism was the growth of a western farm movement in post-war politics. Prairie farmers objected generally to the costs of the tariff and railway rates. They felt that the West was paying to

fatten the East. There were besides numerous particular grievances against the eastern powers that handled western trade:
against railway companies, large industrial corporations, banks
and financial houses. After the war, the high price of wheat, the
result of great wartime demands, had dropped sharply. Yet the
debts that the farmer had incurred to expand his wartime production still had to be paid at high rates of interest. The government
Wheat Board, moreover, which had marketed his crops during the
war, was brought to an end in 1920, and the prairie farmer felt he
was completely in the hands of eastern business, which paid him
low prices but fixed high charges in return. The western sense of
grievance grew. Farmers began to organize political parties to
oppose the 'big interests' of the East.

This mounting farm revolt was backed as well by eastern farmers, who shared many of the same grievances against the power
of business. It was, indeed, an eastern farmers' party that first
won political victory in Ontario in 1919. Yet all things considered,
the farm revolt was more deeply rooted in the West. Its effects
were more enduring and more widely felt in the prairies, the
greatest farming region in Canada. Thus the spirit of western
sectionalism loomed large behind the farmers' movement and the
new political parties that developed from it.

2 New Currents in Politics

The rise of new parties in the period between two World Wars
challenged the hold of the two old parties on Canadian political
life for the first time since Confederation. Some of the new
groups tended to fade as quickly as they had grown, and in any
case the Liberals and Conservatives managed to keep to the fore.
They were firmly rooted throughout the Dominion and stood for
national unity. The new organizations were tied more closely to
sectional interests and might be strong in one region but very
weak in others. Hence they never captured national power. Yet
by the 1930's there would be three and even four parties in federal

politics, quite aside from successful new groups in the provincial field. Clearly there were fresh currents stirring in the Canadian political stream, and some of them would have lasting influence.

At the close of the First World War in Canada there was a growing demand for new goals in politics. There was an upsurge of democratic feeling after 'the war to make the world safe for democracy'; there was new hope of progress, and, at the same time, a desire for broad government social policies that would improve the welfare of the people and balance the scales for the ordinary citizen in a world where wealth had so much power. On the whole, before 1914, Canadian politics had been far less concerned with democratic progress or social advance than with the problems of developing half a continent. Canada seemed to have plenty of room to expand, and rather accepted the North American idea of 'go west, young man' as the answer to the troubles of society. The governments, furthermore, had not sought to check the power of private wealth but had worked in partnership with it in order to develop the country. In general, they had given the large business interests a free hand.

By the end of the First World War, however, it was becoming clear that conditions of life in Canada were changing. The era of easy growth was ending; there was very little of the 'last, best West' left for the young man to go to. There were still many lines for development; but most of these lay in industry or the mining North, and took money—which usually returned to business interests or to controlling companies in the United States. More and more Canadians were living in towns and working in factories. Accordingly, as the old open horizons closed down, demands arose for new policies that would, above all, favour the mass of the people more than powerful special groups. The core of these demands was for more state action to serve the public interest. Wider state ownership of necessary services or utilities, such as railways and power plants, heavier taxes on profits and large incomes, old-age pensions, labour laws, health measures: these were but some of the new goals in politics that emerged between the wars.

The rising labour movement supplied another new force in Canadian life. It first became important in this period between the wars. There had been trade unions in Canada long before, and in 1886 a national Trades and Labour Congress had been established. But union membership had been small for many years, since so many factory workers stayed outside, especially among the Catholic, conservative-minded French Canadians. With the growth of industry during the First World War, however, union membership doubled. And afterwards, the unemployment caused by shifting from war to peace production, and the removal of wartime price controls while living costs soared, brought much working-class discontent. There were exciting ideas abroad as well, stemming from the recent Russian Revolution, or from the plan of 'One Big Union' to overcome the power of big business by the massed power of labour. Eastern union leadership remained cautious; but some western unions, impatient at this restraint and aroused by the O.B.U. idea, hoped for a nation-wide strike to overthrow private business. A strike among metal workers in Winnipeg in 1919 actually spread to city-wide proportions, though it was severely repressed by frightened local authorities, backed by the Dominion government, which feared red revolution. These extreme fears were groundless; the great mass of Canadian labour was very far from revolutionary. Yet it was stirring in politics, and this current would run on into the future. One sign of it was the election of several Labour members to provincial legislatures.

Meanwhile the farm discontent was taking shape, in the East as in the West. In 1918 the Canadian Council of Agriculture, the national association of farmers, issued what it called the 'New National Policy'. This was a long, detailed document which attacked the protective tariff as creating powerful privileged groups and demanded tariff reductions, taxes on business profits, the public ownership of utilities, and political reforms to strengthen the power of democracy. Here was a programme which had a wide appeal, not only within farm ranks. It expressed many of the new currents in Canada and it soon led to action. The first move came in Ontario, where the farmers quickly organized themselves for the provincial election of 1919. In that year the United Farmers of Ontario, supported by many besides farmers, swept the polls and installed a U.F.O. government at Toronto under E. C. Drury. In the general mood of excitement and unrest, strong United Farmers parties sprang up in the prairie provinces, and weaker ones in the Maritimes.

Building on all these movements, the Canadian Council of Agriculture called a convention at Winnipeg in 1920. There was launched a new Dominion party, the National Progressive Party, backed by all the United Farmer groups. Its leader was T. A. Crerar of Manitoba, its programme the New National Policy. The next year Progressivism went into a Dominion election, and with wide popular support did so well in its first try that, although the Liberals won, the Progressives displaced the Conservatives as the second largest group in parliament.

Progressivism did not keep up the pace. In 1919 the Liberals under Mackenzie King, who had studied and written on labour and social problems, had themselves adopted a programme to meet the new demands of the time, calling for tariff reductions and social welfare measures. The scheme was not as sweeping as the Progressives', and in office the Liberals were strangely slow in carrying it out. Yet King could argue that his aims were really the same as the Progressives', and they preferred to work with him rather than with the Conservatives. As a result they lost much of their own sense of purpose. A split developed within the party between those who argued that it was better to side with the Liberals and push them onward into reform and those who insisted that Progressivism should stand apart and work solely as a farmers' movement.

Dissension grew, and Progressivism rapidly declined. The electors were discouraged by the new party's failure to achieve anything on its own. The U.F.O. government fell in Ontario in 1923 and the Dominion election of 1926 practically killed the National Progressives as an effective party. The farmers had never linked themselves successfully with labour, Progressivism had never penetrated French Canada, and it had been weak in the Maritimes. But if the Progressive movement faded in eastern Canada it fared better in the West. There the United Farmers parties survived in provincial politics. A U.F.A. Government ruled Alberta until 1935. On the national level, however, many of the remaining Progressive members, including Crerar, were absorbed into the Liberal party.

The period of high prosperity between 1923 and 1929, which revived farm prices, helped also to still the general demand for new social policies, at least for the time being. Yet the spirit of Progressivism remained alive in the prairies. A movement for co-operative societies spread among the farmers as a means of escaping some of the control of eastern business. Spurred on by men like Henry Wise Wood, leader of the United Farmers of Alberta, they organized 'Wheat Pools' among themselves to market their grain jointly and replace the lost Wheat Board. And the enthusiasm for more advanced democratic and social ideas remained strong in this western region.

Then in the 1930's came the blackest depression ever to hit Canada. In its long, hard years the demand for social changes arose with new force all across the nation. Once again it was strongest in the West, which in many ways suffered most from the depression. In Alberta the U.F.A. government fell in 1935 before a more radical movement, that of Social Credit. Social Credit is based on a plan to redistribute the wealth of a community gradually through 'social dividends' paid to its members by the government. Under William Aberhart, Social Credit began in Alberta by promising dividends of $25 a month; but though it failed to fulfil its promise, Aberhart's vigorous leadership and Alberta's firm rejection of both old parties helped to keep a Social Credit government in control of the province. Similarly Social Credit controlled Alberta's block of seats in the Dominion parliament, though for some time it made little headway elsewhere. On the whole, therefore, it remained a distinctly Albertan experiment. Alberta, it is said, likes to be different.

Another important new party, which also developed on the prairies in the depressed early 'thirties, was the Co-operative Commonwealth Federation, or C.C.F. To a considerable extent the C.C.F. was built on old Progressive foundations, since it was backed by the United Farmers of Alberta and other western farmer organizations. Thus far it was another expression of the farm revolt, of the long-felt western grievances against the power of big business that had revived tenfold in the bleakness of depression years. Yet the new party also had strong ties with the labour movement, for working-class groups in the four western provinces shared in its formation. Beyond this, the C.C.F. was new, indeed. It was a socialist party. It stood not only for more government controls but for government ownership of major industries, finance, and utilities, and not only for certain social measures but for over-all social planning.

In one sense the C.C.F., backed as it was by labour organizations, was Canada's version of Britain's Labour party. Its socialist principles came chiefly from British Labour thought. It, too, believed in the British parliamentary system and gradual, peaceful progress to the goal of socialism. It turned its back on communism and the tiny communist party that made only minor and temporary gains in Canada during the depression. But if the C.C.F. followed British Labour in ideas, it was distinctly North American in its descent from Progressivism and its deep-rooted western farm support. Though the party made headway in British Columbia ports and mines and in Ontario factories, its strength continued to centre in the prairies, particularly in Saskatchewan.

It was here at the provincial capital of Regina in 1933 that the C.C.F. issued its definite platform. This, the Regina Manifesto, set forth a short-run programme to meet depression problems and a long-range plan for socialism. The few Progressives left in parliament joined the C.C.F., and the party entered both federal and provincial politics. Its federal leader was J. S. Woodsworth, a Methodist minister turned social reformer, who had sat as a Labour member from Winnipeg after making his name during the Winnipeg strike of 1919 as editor of the strikers' newspaper.

Under Woodsworth, a high-minded, universally respected leader, the C.C.F. firmly established itself in national politics. Yet it did not grow to anything like the size of the two old parties in parliament. One reason for this limited growth was the fact that many trade unionists still rejected socialism, especially in the East, where dwelt the bulk of the working class. While the C.C.F. received a significant amount of labour support, it thus could not make the thorough-going connection with trade unionism that had proved so valuable to the British Labour party. In addition, the C.C.F. made no headway in French Canada, where the powerful Catholic church frowned on socialism. And no national party can really hope to control Canada without some measure of French Canadian support.

French Canada was producing its own new party in the depression of the 1930's. This was a wholly provincial party; and it came on the conservative right rather than on the radical left, when another upsurge of conservative-minded French Canadian nationalism created the Union Nationale in Quebec. The new group practically replaced the Conservative party in provincial politics, for the Quebec Conservatives had never recovered in French Canada from their party's stand on conscription. Yet this latest nationalist movement was somewhat different because it was closely related to the rise of industrialism in the province of Quebec. Since the First World War the spread of industry had been transforming the old rural world of New France into a region of crowded cities and great factories. Quebec was going through the strains of the industrial revolution. And then on top of these were added the problems of trade depression and unemployment.

Out of this troubled background emerged a demand among French Canadians that the financial and industrial control of their province be wrested from the dominant English-speaking business interests. Big business was being denounced in the depression in Quebec as elsewhere, but here the racial division coloured the picture. In the growing clamour a clever politician, Maurice Duplessis, came forward, promising both to modernize and to 'free' Quebec and to carry out a new social programme. His Union Nationale drove the provincial Liberal government from power in 1936. Soon, however, he seemed to have reached his own terms with the existing business interests, although his hold over Quebec's sectional feelings still kept his place secure.

In Ontario meanwhile, the Liberals under Mitchell Hepburn broke up a long Conservative reign in 1934, following a campaign to reduce government spending during the depression that was strongly supported by the old Ontario farm interest. Soon angry quarrels flared between the Hepburn government at Toronto and the Dominion Liberals in Ottawa, for Hepburn took a firm stand on 'Ontario rights'. Here was yet another sectional party. In sum, the trying years of the depression were plainly encouraging a variety of sectional movements at the expense of national parties. This was true of Social Credit under Aberhart in Alberta, of Hepburn Liberalism in Ontario, and Duplessis Nationalism in Quebec. Only the C.C.F. could be called a new national party, and it was only partially so. The political trend of the 'twenties and 'thirties was not only to raise new social demands, it was to weaken national unity. In the depression of the 1930's Canada had to face a testing of her national system as stern as any since the birth of the Dominion.

3 *The Federal System and the Depression*

It might be said that the Liberals governed Canada for much of the inter-war period less through their own strength than through the weakness of their foes. The new parties were still not effective rivals in national politics and the Conservatives were held back by their troubles in Quebec. But in any case the Liberals gave no strong national leadership. That fact was seen in the way the King government set aside the Liberal social programme of 1919 as merely a set of ideals for the future and generally ceased to direct the development of Canada, although the Dominion government had regularly taken the lead in the day of Laurier or Macdonald. Yet in one respect the decline in Dominion leadership could hardly be charged to the King Liberals. They could do little about a change in the whole balance of the Canadian federal system, which made the Dominion government much weaker and the provincial governments far stronger than the Fathers of Confederation had ever intended.

The change in the balance of power had long been developing. It was chiefly the result of legal decisions by the Judicial Committee of the imperial Privy Council. Since the British North America Act of 1867 that established Canadian federalism was a law of the imperial parliament, legal cases concerning the extent of federal or provincial powers under the Act could be referred to the Privy Council justices in London for final decision. And in the decisions that the Privy Council had handed down there had been, at least since 1896, a strong trend in favour of provincial interests over Dominion. Apparently the justices of the Privy Council had their own ideas on federalism, which put considerable stress on provincial rights. Yet the consequence was that the intentions of the men who had shaped the Confederation scheme were ignored.

The Fathers of Confederation had clearly wanted a strong federal state in Canada. The British North America Act, therefore, had given the Dominion a general and superior power in government as well as certain particular powers listed under numbered headings. These 'enumerated powers', the Act declared, were set forth merely 'for greater certainty' and did not limit the general authority of the Dominion to make laws for 'peace, order and good government'. Yet in 1896 the Privy Council ruled that the Dominion could normally use only its enumerated powers, and that the general reserve authority was simply meant for great national emergencies such as war. In effect, Canada was made a weak, not a strong federal state. The Dominion had one set of fixed powers, the provinces another, and the Dominion's reserve of power was set aside. It was only in time of war that the federal government could be really strong, for then it could call on the reserve 'emergency' authority to enact sweeping laws like the War Measures Act of 1914, used in two world conflicts.

Thanks to various Privy Council decisions, the provinces ceased to be the local authorities planned in 1867 and became the near-equals of the Dominion. Of course, the federal government still ranked above them because it represented the whole country, and in many ways its set of powers was still the wider, especially in the field of taxation. But because its reserve of authority had been put aside, the Dominion found it difficult to enter new fields of government to meet new problems. In fact, the widening range of government activities in the years following the First World War led to a number of Dominion-provincial conferences in which the division of new government duties was debated back and forth almost as between independent states.

When it came to expanding the duties of government, the powers already granted to the provinces gave them a good deal of advantage. For example, by the Act of 1867 'property and civil rights' lay with the provinces. When granted in 1867, this power had meant little more than the control of the civil laws that protected real property and personal rights, a task well suited to a local authority. But in the world of the twentieth century, when government was called on to do more and more, this vague term could cover labour laws, pensions, social insurance—a variety of social measures that the new age demanded, all of which naturally affected the property and personal rights of the people. The framers of Confederation could not foresee this development. But if the Dominion had been left with the reserve power to take up new tasks, as had been planned, the problem would not have arisen. As it was, however, the national government could only proceed on various social measures by agreements with the provinces, many of which preferred to go ahead with their own social schemes. Thus the standard of government services was uneven across Canada, varying between the richer and poorer provinces.

Still, all the provinces were forging ahead at their own best rate in the new field of social services. They were also broadening their activities through the highway-building and hydro-electric development of the post-war era, both of which fell in the provincial field. There was a serious difficulty here. In the new age, it seemed, the provinces were the advancing powers; yet they did not really have the financial strength to back their ambitious programmes of services and development. The British North America Act had given most of the taxing power to the Dominion. The provinces could finance their expansion through their limited tax resources only while times were good. But when the depression of the 'thirties arrived, it found the provinces heavily committed to activities that many of them could not really afford, while the Dominion had the money but not the power to take these functions over. Clearly the federal system was badly off balance, and at a critical time for Canada.

By 1930 all parts of the Dominion were swept into the vicious circle of depression. As world trade dropped, unemployment mounted, so that people could not afford to buy, and trade sank lower. Immigration was halted. Canada had trouble enough with her existing population. The industrial East was hard hit, but here the continuing advance of gold-mining in the Shield helped to ease the blow. The far West was also affected by the decline in

Pacific commerce and fishing, but again mining in the Rockies helped British Columbia. As for the Maritimes, because they had never risen so high they had less far to fall, though life in the little fishing outports was hard, indeed. But the prairie West, dependent on one great crop, was especially affected. The collapse of world wheat prices struck heavily at the prairies, and cut the incomes of the railways that served them, to increase Canada's costly problem of railway debts. In addition, drought in the West reduced the wheat crop to an all-time low, often wiping out what little income a farmer might hope to receive. The people of 'Palliser's Triangle' were particularly in distress. Prairie governments were facing bankruptcy as revenues fell and the bills for unemployment relief soared. It was out of this background that the new radical parties, Social Credit and the C.C.F. sprang up in the West.

As these problems swiftly developed, the King government still gave no lead; and so, in 1930, the Conservatives at last came back into office, with a promise to end the depression. The new Conservative prime minister was R. B. Bennett, who had replaced Meighen as party leader in 1927. Bennett was a mixture of undoubted ability, bold energy, and arrogant assurance; in some ways he was his own worst enemy. His first move was along traditional Conservative lines. He raised the protective tariff steeply, higher than it had ever been before. This was partly done to save what was left of the Canadian market for Canadians, and it probably benefited industry to some extent. But in its main purpose, 'to blast a way into world markets' by showing Canada's readiness to meet other nations' tariff increases with those of her own, it was a complete failure.

There was still another kind of tariff measure that might offer hope: imperial preference, first proposed by Canada in Laurier's day. In 1932 the depression led Britain to abandon free trade. A system of empire preference at last became possible, whereby Dominions could give British goods lower rates in their tariffs in exchange for similar preferences in the British tariff. An Imperial Economic Conference met at Ottawa and after hard bargaining reached a series of agreements. Canada's were mainly with Britain. They provided for lower rates on British steel, coal and manufactures entering Canada in return for similar British rates on Canadian wheat, lumber and farm products. The preferences were limited, however, because Canada was by now an industrial nation herself and sought still to protect her own industry. Britain, moreover, did not mean to tie her food market down too much to one supplier. Nevertheless a freer flow of trade in the Commonwealth was an advantage, although it was not large enough to cure the depression.

By 1934, although the worst of the depression had passed, it still hung heavy, and new Dominion policies were plainly needed. The Bennett government re-established a Wheat Board to market the reduced western crop, gave loans and grants to the provinces, particularly to bankrupt Saskatchewan, and reorganized the control of the government's railways. But the main Dominion activity consisted in footing the provinces' bills for relief, and while spending for relief was sorely necessary it was not solving any problems. Accordingly, in 1935 (when a new election was approaching) Bennett suddenly produced a surprising set of sweeping measures that would reduce farm debt, control export trade, regulate business, and establish unemployment insurance and minimum wages—in order, as he said, to reform the capitalist system and restore the nation's health. It was Canada's version of Roosevelt's New Deal, then challenging the depression in the United States.

But these new measures, introduced almost without warning, nearly split the Conservative party. The bulk of the Conservatives were not convinced of the need for such a sweeping programme, and the country as a whole was none too convinced by Bennett's sudden change of policy. And so, although the 'New Deal' laws were rushed through parliament, King and the Liberals were returned in the election of 1935. They could not have been more fortunate: the Conservatives received all the blame for the depression, and trade began reviving as the Liberals came back to power.

King, however, still pursued a very cautious policy. In a typical move for time he referred Bennett's laws to the courts for testing. The Privy Council acted true to form. It declared most of them beyond the powers of the federal government. Apparently a tremendous depression was still not enough of a national emergency to allow the use of the Dominion's reserve authority. This final judgment, however, together with the unbalance of the federal system, glaringly revealed by the depression, led King to appoint a Royal Commission in 1937 to inquire into all the problems of Dominion-provincial relations.

This, the Rowell-Sirois Commission, produced a report in 1940 that was a masterpiece of investigation and proposed what was almost a plan of refederation. Its chief proposals called first for the Dominion to round out its already wide taxing powers by 'renting' much of the provinces' power of taxation. In return the Dominion was to take over provincial debts and pay a series of 'adjustment grants'. These would help finance the provinces, so that the services of all could be kept at one national level. The Dominion would assume the whole burden of unemployment relief and unemployment insurance, while there would be a nation-wide system of social services administered by the provinces and aided in certain cases by the federal government. The problem of the Dominion having money but not power, and the provinces power but not money, would be overcome. Finally, the barriers in the federal system raised by the Privy Council decisions would be avoided since the plan did not attack provincial powers but sought only to proceed by agreement.

The Rowell-Sirois Report was a product of the question of federalism and the depression, but its results lie in a later period. Meanwhile, as the Commission was sitting, trade was recovering in Canada, reflecting a world recovery that was connected with a rising armament boom, as another war loomed abroad. Yet King undoubtedly aided Canada's revival by tariff reductions that increased her trade with both Britain and the United States. More important, in 1935 and 1938, he was able to reach mutual trade agreements with the Roosevelt government of the United States, which did not share the extreme high-tariff ideas of previous American governments. Canada kept her basic policy of protection, and the empire preferences as well, but also reduced the duties on about half of her American imports in return for similar treatment by the United States. The King government could well say that it had brought back the reciprocity principle that had been lost since 1866.

Nevertheless King had not cured the depression any more than had Bennett: it had simply gone away. The Liberals had continued their policy of doing nothing in particular—and did it very well. Yet perhaps King was right in thinking Canada needed such a policy in days of powerful sectional forces. He believed that his own chief task was the preservation of national unity. On the whole he pursued it successfully by not letting major issues come to a head: he appointed Royal Commissions instead. Such a policy, of course, may seem to do very little and still require a great deal of hard running to stay in the same place. At any rate, despite the unrest and friction of depression years, not greatly eased by Bennett, King was able to lead a united nation into the Second World War in 1939. Perhaps the very extent of the problem of federalism and the depression had shown the strength of an underlying belief in Canadian unity that, despite angry criticisms and dark prophecies, simply took it for granted that the national system would survive. Perhaps this is the strongest basis for an enduring nation.

4   Canada Enters World Affairs

Thanks to the achievement of nationhood under Borden and King, Canada entered world affairs in the period between the

SASKATCHEWAN GRAIN ELEVATORS

WEALTH OF THE SHIELD — FORESTS AND WATERPOWER

A Recruiting 'Station' in the war of 1914-18

YELLOWKNIFE, NORTH WEST TERRITORIES
THE NORTHERN MINING FRONTIER

H.M.C.S. SWANSEA, DESTROYER OF TWO U-BOATS, ON
NORTH ATLANTIC CONVOY DUTY, 1944

CANADIANS UNDER FIRE IN GERMANY, 1945

wars. She continued her close relations with Britain and the United States within the North Atlantic triangle. But now to these were added direct contacts with other countries, through the League of Nations and the Commonwealth, and through the gradual spread of Canadian diplomatic posts abroad. For the first time, therefore, Canada was able to carry on her own foreign policy. The question was, what lines should it follow? Certain main lines of policy were already clear for the Dominion: for example, the need to work for the best possible relations between Britain and the United States, and the vital interest that a fairly small nation with a very large overseas trade had in a world at peace. Yet beyond these general considerations the young Canadian foreign policy seemed to be shaped chiefly by a desire to avoid committing Canada to any definite stand in world affairs.

This policy of 'no commitments' was to some extent a reflection of a general North American feeling of isolation; the American continent seemed far from Europe and its troubles, and did not want to be drawn into them. Isolationism, however, was more widespread in the United States. A purely Canadian cause of the desire to avoid advance commitments lay in the difference of the viewpoints of French and English Canada on many world questions. Any very definite line of policy only invited a clash of opinion between the two groups of Canadians, and this King in his concern for unity particularly sought to avoid. On the whole, the French Canadians were firmly isolationist. They feared that English Canada's main aim in foreign policy was the support of Britain, which thus might lead to new entanglements in 'British wars'. English-speaking Canadians were far from being as thoroughly imperialist as the French believed, but there was a strong feeling among them that Canada should back up British foreign policy more or less automatically. And even when English Canadians proposed a course of action on national grounds French Canada suspected that this was disguised imperialism. Accordingly, in an effort to avoid as much friction as possible, King pursued a vague policy of no commitments, expressed in his famous phrase for putting off to the future Canada's decisions on world questions: 'Parliament will decide.'

Even King's campaign to complete Canadian nationhood was in part an effort to avoid the commitments resulting from being bound by British foreign policy. It was not so much a constructive effort as an attempt to withdraw more into isolation. Hence, although the rights of nationhood were a major achievement for Canada, it was the right to say 'no' that she made most use of in foreign affairs. Nevertheless the freedom to say 'no' was important, and on the whole, the nation accepted this negative sort of policy. Furthermore, a small state like Canada (small in world power, for all her great size) could not make a great mark among the nations merely by taking a strong line of policy.

The pattern of no commitments began to appear almost as soon as Borden had won separate membership for Canada in the League of Nations. Article X of the Covenant that established the League called for collective action by all the member-states against any country that endangered world peace by committing an act of aggression. This article was really the keystone of the League plan, since it tried to create a world police-power, based on all the League members, that would prevent any country from threatening the security of the world. It was disliked by many nations because it committed them in advance to actions that might lead to war, and it was never very effectively used. Canada, however, strongly objected to the plan for collective security. Borden protested against such a grave obligation, that could involve Canada in European struggles with which she had little connection when she herself, living in secure America, had no need of aid in return. As a Canadian representative at the League put it, Canada lived in a fireproof house, far from the danger of flames, and thought she should be able to pay a lower insurance rate.

In spite of Borden's protests in 1919, Article X was kept in the League Covenant: but in the following years Canada still sought to limit the commitment that it involved. It was not her efforts, however, but the steadily sinking faith of the leading powers in collective security which really killed Article X. In any case that principle, and the League itself, had largely been built on the belief that the United States would be a member of the League of Nations. Instead, isolationism in that country led it to reject League membership, and the loss of the great American strength was disastrous. Canada, at least, was a member, though not a very effective one, and so found herself with the task of representing North America in a largely European body.

The failure of the League to check the Japanese invasion of Manchuria in 1931 or the Italian attack on Abyssinia in 1935 doomed the principle of collective security. The Canadian delegate at the League did propose oil sanctions that would have cut off Italy's oil supply for the Abyssinian War. But the Canadian government, true to its policy of no commitments, hastily rejected this effective but dangerous measure, stating that Canada's delegate had acted without authority. The League took no effective action. Italy, led by the fascist dictator Mussolini, had proved, apparently, that aggression could pay. As a result, another fascist dictator took heart. Under Hitler, Nazi Germany began the acts of violence and aggression that greatly enlarged German territory, but ended in the Second World War.

The rise of Germany as a storm centre and the steady decline of the League caused Britain and France, the leading European powers, to try to keep the peace by satisfying Nazi demands. Here was the policy to be known as appeasement. Appeasement was as unreal as isolationism, but because European countries were not far enough away to ignore Hitler they tried to come to terms with him. Canada, on the whole, approved of the British policy of appeasement, largely because this too seemed a way of avoiding trouble and commitments. By this time in Canada the country's foreign policy was in dispute among nationalists and imperialists, isolationists and collectivists—or groups which called each other by these names. The collectivists were those who saw the only hope in a return to the idea of collective security through the League. Still King held them all off, and turned aside their insistence on some definite stand with the statement that when the time came for decision, parliament would decide: a rather doubtful statement since he and his party controlled parliament in any case. Yet any other course would surely have split the country.

The time for decision was fast approaching. While still hoping to appease fascist violence the democracies of Europe began to rearm, and in 1937 Canada also began an enlarged defence programme. But meanwhile she was greatly strengthening her position in the North American continent through the improvement of her relations with the United States. Relations with the United States had been satisfactory since at least the start of the First World War, and the citizens of the two countries had been building lasting friendship from the 1870's on. Yet in general the government of the United States had ignored Canada ever since it had dropped any ideas of annexation. There was little thought of a 'good neighbour' policy with Canada in American government circles until Franklin D. Roosevelt came to the presidency in 1932. The Americans had opposed separate Canadian representation in the League in 1919, had sought still to treat Canada as a British colony in the 1920's, and had waged a tariff war with their exceedingly high tariff of 1930. President Roosevelt's general policy, however, was the promotion of close friendly relations throughout the Americas.

In Canada's case, this led to the signing of new tariff agreements and to gestures of friendship such as President Roosevelt's visit in 1938. At the same time his condemnation of fascist aggression and his swing away from extreme isolation pleased anti-isolationist feeling in Canada, which was as yet much stronger than in the United States. In 1938, moreover, Roosevelt on his visit gave a pledge that his country 'would not stand idly by' in the case of an attack on Canada : a much more definite and more acceptable protection for the Dominion than the terms of the Monroe Doctrine. And a few days later Mackenzie King made clear that Canada welcomed this pledge of friendship and common interest, while ready still to do her own part in joint defence and while maintaining her place in the Commonwealth. In consequence, when war did break out in 1939 Canada's position in North America was secure, and she found a cordial and very useful ally in the United States long before that country also joined in the world conflict.

In the last few years before the war, Canada's policy of no commitments was also wearing thin. There was no doubt of Canadians' dislike for Hitler. Defence costs mounted; in the Munich crisis of 1938 King was prepared to back Britain if the crisis led to war; and in general, isolationist forces weakened. There was a growing feeling of Canada's responsibility in the Commonwealth and in the world, a growing recognition that commitments could not be avoided. The visit of the King and Queen as the rulers of Canada in the summer of 1939 strengthened both the pride of nationhood and the sense of Commonwealth ties. And then, in September, 1939, the moment of decision came. Britain and France at last went to war to end the ceaseless spread of a fascist system based on tyranny, fear, conquest, and destruction. This time the British declaration did not bind the full-grown nation of Canada. As King had promised, the Canadian parliament met to decide the issue of peace or war.

It was not for a moment in doubt. Despite the long internal strains of sectionalism and depression, despite the past strength of isolationism and the policy of no commitments, the Canadian parliament voted grimly but overwhelmingly for war. Undoubtedly sentiment for Britain still played a large part, as in 1914. But so did the realization that Canada's national future was bound up with the survival of Britain and the free Commonwealth. And this time, with the memory of the last bloody struggle still strong, there was a new awareness of what the cost might be—in racial discord as well as in men and material. Beyond this too, there was a realization that Canada did not, and could not, live in a fireproof house in the modern world: as the United States again realized for herself in 1941. Canadians saw that they had to do their share to save the free and democratic way of life they believed in. Isolationist, imperialist and collectivist, French and English, they buried their differences in facing the world menace of fascism. There was little excitement. It was an act of sober maturity. With the declaration of war on 10 September 1939, Canada really came of age in world affairs.

CHAPTER 19

THE MATURING NATION,
1939–50

1   *Canada and the Second World War*

When the Second World War began in 1939 it seemed that Canada would mainly be called on as a supply base, to furnish food and raw materials, as before, and also to provide a wide range of industrial products. A division of soldiers was rapidly raised and sent to Britain, the first Canadian contingent sailing towards the close of the year. It was generally believed, however, that Britain and France could win the war against Germany without a heavy use of troops, by means of a blockade that would cut her off from outside supplies and destroy her ability to carry on the struggle. Nineteen-forty doomed that hope. The sudden collapse of France in June, under the lightning German onslaught, brought Italy into the war on Germany's side and left Britain and her Commonwealth partners standing alone. The shock was tremendous, though Britain saved most of her men from France in the miracle of Dunkirk and fought on with no thought of yielding.

In Canada, as everywhere, the whole view of the war was altered. The Dominion now stood as the next strongest nation to Britain in the fight against the German-Italian Axis. All her strength would be needed. Projects for great new industrial developments were laid down, and secret British arms plans were sent out for use in the rising Canadian war factories that were safe from bombing. Canada became an arsenal, and Britain's chief overseas source of war production. At the same time the Dominion organized and equipped new divisions of troops until in all five divisions, two of them armoured, and two armoured (tank) brigades had been sent abroad. This was a full army formation, more than half a million strong. The bulk of it went to Britain, the free world's last great stronghold in a Europe largely conquered by German might.

For a time after Dunkirk, indeed, the Canadian forces under General McNaughton were almost the only troops in Britain fully equipped to resist a German invasion. But the brilliant air victories of the Battle of Britain and the British command of the seas about the island made invasion impossible for Hitler's armies, and plans were soon being laid for a grand assault on German-held Europe. In the next few years the Canadian army was kept in Britain and prepared for the return to Europe, while British and other Commonwealth forces fought in battles all around the world. Canada did send troops to Hong Kong in 1941, when Germany's Axis partner, Japan, unleashed war in the Pacific, but they were captured after the hopeless defence of Hong Kong in December of that year. Japan's entry into the war, however, with a sudden savage thrust at the main American naval base in the Pacific, Pearl Harbour, brought in the giant strength of the United States and made possible a powerful and victorious Allied partnership. Meanwhile the huge Soviet Union had also been brought in by the eastward attack of Germany and her conquered European empire in June 1941.

In August of 1942 came the first Allied return to France, when the Canadians provided most of the troops for a raid in force on Dieppe. The bold Dieppe raid, costly though it was, supplied valuable experience for the western Allies in launching the successful invasions of Germany's 'Fortress Europe' that came later. Then in 1943 a Canadian division was sent to the Mediterranean, and distinguished itself in the conquest of Sicily. After the Allied landings in Italy another division was added to form the First Canadian Corps in the British Eighth Army. The Canadians shared notably in the advance up the peninsula, particularly in the hot fighting around Ortona.

In June of 1944, the great hour struck. A vast Allied armada under the supreme command of America's General Eisenhower descended on the coast of France. American, British, and Canadian divisions battled their way inland. The Canadians worked with the British in clearing the bloody ruins of Caen, the hinge of the whole Allied advance. The forward movement of the British-Canadian front was less sweeping than the American, but the losses were not, for here the main weight of the German armour was massed. When the last-ditch German defence of Caen had fallen the Canadians moved on at last, now formed into the Canadian First Army under Canada's General Crerar. This Canadian-led army contained strong British units—although the Canadians were the principal group—since the rest of the Canadian units were still serving under British command in Italy.

Canadian forces formed one of the pincers that met with the Americans to close the Falaise trap, cutting off some of Hitler's best troops. In the sweep through France that followed, the Canadians again took a major role. Their task was to anchor the northern end of the Allied line as it wheeled ahead, and they had to fight their way through the heavy German shore defences in moving up the French coast to Belgium. Their next duty lay in clearing the approaches to the big Belgian port of Antwerp, which was essential to the Allies as the only port capable of handling the huge amount of war material necessary to mount an invasion of Germany itself. Again, while the biggest battles and most spectacular advances went on on other fronts, the Canadians pressed through the costly struggle to take the Walcheren Islands, which the Germans strove to hold to the end in order to block the use of Antwerp and prevent the attack on their homeland.

When the job was done, and the Allies again swept forward, the First Army opened the attack on Germany's Rhineland, working closely with Britain's Second Army. Then it turned north to liberate all the Netherlands. In this last stage it became a wholly Canadian formation, since the units from Italy were transferred to it. At last, as Russians and Americans met in central Germany over the ruins of Hitler's empire, the Canadian Army in the Netherlands received the surrender of the German armies in that region. Allied victory came on 8 May, 1945. Canada's share had cost her 41,700 in dead and missing. The cost in lives was lower than in the First World War because Canadian troops had only been heavily engaged in the final year of the Second War, but then they had suffered a high rate of losses. And Canada's soldiers, who had distinguished themselves in rapid advances in the First War, had won no less credit in the Second for their record in bitter, sustained fighting.

The Royal Canadian Navy also distinguished itself in the hard work of war, without much chance of great battles and victories. Its main job lay with the North Atlantic convoys that were vital to the whole Allied war effort if the stream of men and materials from the North American arsenals were to reach embattled Britain and enter the fight against the Axis. For most of the Canadians at sea the war was an endless round of grey days and black nights with the precious convoys; of storms, ice and northern cold, of drudgery and monotony that might suddenly be shattered by a torpedo blast and death. There were submarine alarms, tense U-boat hunts and running battles at sea to bring periods of suspense and victory, but the main victory lay in getting the convoys through. At times the long, wearing Battle of the Atlantic rose to violent heights, as U-boat wolf-packs sank ships faster than they could be replaced. But each time new methods and weapons, particularly in the use of aircraft at sea, brought the menace under control. The little ships and their heavy-laden charges sailed on to final success.

At the start of the war the small Canadian peacetime navy contained only 5,000 men, but it was expanded to nearly twenty times that number until it was the third largest naval force in the world. Most of its strength, of course, lay in small anti-submarine craft, for it was clear from the start that Canada's chief contribution at sea should be to the all-important convoy system and in ships that she could quickly build and man. In 1943 Canada took over naval control of the north-west Atlantic. In the next year the bulk of Allied convoys sailed from America under Canadian escort—four-fifths of them, in the closing stages of the war. At the same time Canadians served around the world with the Royal Navy, or fought in the Mediterranean in motor boat squadrons; went into battle off the French coast in Canadian destroyers, or sailed on the Murmansk run to Russia. A Canadian fleet unit, newly equipped with cruisers and aircraft carriers, had entered the Pacific war when in August, 1945, Japan, the eastern foe, surrendered.

In the air Canada raised her forces from 4,000 to 200,000. She sent 45 Royal Canadian Air Force squadrons overseas and provided men besides for the air crews of the R.A.F. Canadian fighter pilots fought in the Battle of Britain and in the sweeps over France; bomber crews joined in the nightly Battle of Germany, and by 1944 one-quarter of the air-crews attacking Germany under British command were Canadian. Canada's airmen flew over Malta, in North Africa, Italy, India, Burma, in Britain's Coastal Command and in the Fleet Air Arm. They ferried aircraft over the Atlantic and patrolled the Arctic North. They worked in Alaska with the Americans and at sea with the Allied navies. In this Second War, as in the First, Canada set up an outstanding record in the air, but this time her own R.C.A.F. achieved much of it.

One of the chief Canadian contributions to the air war was made through the British Commonwealth Air Training Plan, a scheme to provide the large number of skilled airmen who were necessary for the air offensive on Germany. Agreements for the multi-million dollar Plan were signed late in 1939 between Britain, Canada, and other Commonwealth countries. The broad reaches of the Dominion, far from the war fronts, served as a training ground. Air bases, schools and workshops were erected across Canada, and a flow of candidates came there from many parts of the Commonwealth. More than half the men trained under the

Plan, however, were Canadians. The whole complex scheme was a monument to Commonwealth co-operation. It showed that the member-nations could work closely and effectively together in a fellowship that was real, however slight its formal bonds.

Indeed, the whole conduct of the war showed once more the value of Commonwealth ties in meeting a common danger. The member-nations, thanks to their common background, ideas and institutions, agreed on the greatest questions. The passage of the war actually made formal Commonwealth ties even slighter—if that were possible. Thus full-scale Imperial Conferences ceased, and there was no return to an Imperial War Cabinet. But this in part was due to the very success of informal relations. Modern communications by air and radio made 'continuous consultation' a reality, although not in the old sense of framing a joint imperial policy. Instead Commonwealth ministers and officials could meet and consult with one another as need arose. This development, together with the practice of holding Commonwealth prime ministers' meetings, made the old formal Imperial Conferences seem unnecessary.

Yet while nothing essential was lost in Canada's relation to Britain and the Commonwealth, major changes occurred in Canada's relations with the United States. The war, in fact, saw increasingly close connections between the United States on the one hand and Britain and the Commonwealth on the other. But Canada's ties with the republic grew especially strong because of their common need to defend North America. An attack on one was a threat to the other. That realization led to the signing of the Ogdensburg Agreement between Canada and the United States in the black year of 1940, by which a Permanent Joint Defence Board was established to plan the protection of North America. Here was a binding military alliance without limit, and one of weighty significance. Under the Board joint Arctic defences were planned against a northern attack by air. Chains of Canadian-American air bases and radio posts were stretched across the northern wastes.

The Alaska Highway was pushed through the wilderness for 1,500 miles, from the 'end of steel' in British Columbia across the Yukon to Alaska, in order to link that outflung region to the south by land. This measure seemed particularly necessary when the Japanese invaded the islands off the Alaskan coast in 1942. Besides these joint military measures, the Hyde Park Agreement of 1941 tied the Canadian and American economies much closer together, and after the United States had entered the war there was a good deal of joint planning of production on a continental basis. These were significant steps for the future, from which there could be no easy thoughts of return. They were an expression of the closely entangled interests of the two neighbouring North American nations in a dangerous new world. Canada had to seek the fullest co-operation with the United States, while trying still to preserve the Canadian identity in North America that she had struggled so long to establish.

The Canadian war effort produced equally significant developments in industry and finance. The First World War had left Canada a vigorous industrial nation; the Second made her fourth in world importance. Mining and steel-making, tank- and shipbuilding, machine and automobile production were all greatly expanded, until by the close of the conflict Canada's industrial exports much exceeded her staple products in value. Hydro-electric development was striking: in Quebec it led to a great new aluminium industry, whose raw materials came by sea from Greenland and British Guiana. In northern Ontario, similarly, wartime needs led to major developments in iron-mining, and, on the prairies, to a successful search for oil which brought on a post-war oil boom. Meanwhile the West was flourishing again under heavy wartime demands for food. Shipbuilding and war traffic brought prosperity to the Maritimes and to British Columbian ports. Quebec and Ontario factories worked to capacity. So at last did the railways. In fact, they were overloaded.

The increased wealth of Canada produced twelve billion dollars in victory loans and war taxes to finance the war effort. The nation was able as well to lend to Britain during and after the war sums that in proportion to population greatly exceeded United States loans. Canada, moreover, did not take American Lend-Lease aid but carried out her own Lend-Lease system of supplying war materials worth four billion dollars to her allies under the name of Mutual Aid. And though the wartime boom mounted, as in the First World War, this time an efficient overall system of government controls and rationing kept price levels down most successfully until the conflict was over. Nevertheless Canada faced internal troubles during the struggle. As before they largely revolved about the question of conscription.

2 War and Post-War Politics

In the First World War Canada had had eight million people and had placed over 600,000 of them under arms. In the Second War, with twelve million, she raised armed forces of over a million men and women. This in itself was a substantial achievement, when so great an industrial expansion was going forward, and especially since most of it was accomplished on a volunteer basis. But inevitably the conscription question arose once again. Since Canada's chief allies applied national conscription from the start, her own efforts appeared to fall short of total war. When the neighbouring United States entered the conflict with full conscription, Canadians questioned their own case more, although they had already been at war for over two years. In addition, those whose sons, husbands and relatives were fighting overseas naturally resented the thought that other Canadians could escape the same hard burden. Yet, whether it be reason or excuse, the presence of French Canada again made conscription a dangerous and destructive measure in a country composed of two such distinct peoples.

The French Canadians accepted the Second War and a large-scale war effort far more fully than they had the First. For them to forget their old resentment at being swamped by the English-speaking majority in 1917 was not easy. But in general the French Canadians showed a new willingness to depart from their isolationism. They overthrew the nationalist Duplessis government in Quebec and put in a Liberal administration; they followed the lead given by Ernest Lapointe, King's chief French Canadian lieutenant, in his appeal for national unity; and they volunteered for military service in larger numbers than in the First War. Still they were determined not to have conscription, which had become for them more a symbol of English-Canadian domination than a plain question of war policy. Indeed, King and Lapointe had largely gained the support of French Canada in their appeals for national unity in the war by the promise that the Liberal party would not introduce conscription.

When the war took its grave turn with the fall of France, however, the realization grew that Canada could not escape with only a partial effort. Freedom would not come cheaply. English-speaking Canada was already supplying the greater number of troops and it now began to call for conscription. This demand was readily taken up by the Conservative party. The Conservatives had already lost a wartime election in the spring of 1940, thanks partly to their continued weakness in Quebec. They had little to lose in French Canada by pursuing their old policy of conscription, and much to gain in the rest of the country. The King government took strong steps to expand the war effort but still sought to head off the conscription cry by enacting compulsory military service for home defence only. This measure somewhat quieted the conscriptionist demand without arousing French Canada too far, because the critical question for the French was conscription for overseas service. Yet the American entrance into the war on the basis of conscription swelled the demand in Canada again. It grew so powerful that in April, 1942, a national plebescite was held on the question, in order to see whether the Liberal government should be released from its pledge not to introduce conscription. The question as put to the voters was skilfully worded so that the government merely asked whether it should be left free to bring in compulsory service if necessary. A large majority voted 'yes', in a sharply racial division; there was an almost solid French Canadian 'no'. King had still avoided the final issue, pleasing neither side, but leaving both in a mood of grumbling acceptance of his indefinite policy.

In the autumn of 1944, however, when the Canadian losses in Europe began to mount, the problem of securing sufficient reinforcements to keep the army up to strength loomed larger and larger. English Canada would wait no longer. Colonel Ralston, the Minister of Defence, insisted on conscription as utterly necessary for the army. When King accepted his resignation the crisis reached a peak. The Prime Minister still delayed, making every effort to find reinforcements on a volunteer basis. Then, as he knew he must in the final emergency, he gave way to the English-speaking majority. Sixteen thousand home-service conscripts were ordered overseas as replacements. Quebec cried out angrily. The racial crisis of 1917 had apparently repeated itself, the tragic result of Canada's greatest internal problem and her great external need.

But would the racial storm continue? Strangely enough, it did not. In the special session of parliament that was then called, the government lost Quebec votes temporarily, but the great majority of them soon returned to the support of the ministry in the House of Commons. Not that French Canada had come to approve of conscription; it simply realized it could not hope for a more favourable government than that of Prime Minister King. He had held out against compulsory service to the last and had yielded finally to the necessity of majority rule. He had not pressed conscription forward as had Borden. In consequence, there was less trouble in Quebec over the drafting of men overseas than there had been in the First War, although King and Canada were most fortunate in that the war, and hence the need of replacements, ended as soon as it did the next year.

The Liberal leader had saved both national unity and his party. Never had his policy of delay and indefiniteness been used more cleverly nor to so constructive an end. It was not a noble policy; but given the problems of Canada it was a highly successful one. Nor had it been easy. Behind the appearance of drifting before the currents of public opinion lay King's concern for unity, careful calculation, and the readiness to act at the right political moment. Perhaps, ironically, Mackenzie King's handling of the conscription question was his greatest achievement in politics.

Largely because of his success in avoiding a racial division, the ageing Liberal leader won victory once more in the general election which he called in the summer of 1945. The C.C.F. and Social Credit still had only a limited appeal, while the Conservatives had not made the gains that they had expected from their conscriptionist stand. It was in vain that they had acquired a new and respected leader in John Bracken, former premier of Manitoba, and under his influence had changed their name to 'Progressive Conservatives' and adopted a full programme of social measures. There was a feeling that the Liberal government had proved its efficiency in the war effort, and the Conservative social programme was not so different as to win the voters away from the experienced Liberals.

The Conservatives under George Drew had, indeed, replaced the Liberals in the great English-speaking province of Ontario during the war, while in Quebec in 1944 French Canada safely released its racial feelings by turning out the Liberal provincial government and restoring Duplessis and the Union Nationale. Yet the Liberal party was undoubtedly still in the ascendant in Canada. The C.C.F. which had advanced during the war, becoming, for example, the official opposition in Ontario as well as in British Columbia, slipped back to some extent in the post-war years. In the general wave of prosperity that continued without very much break from the wartime period, Canadians on the whole did not seem interested in socialism. It was only in Saskatchewan that the C.C.F. achieved striking success. Coming to power in that province in the war years, it continued in office afterwards. Under Premier Douglas socialist measures were carried as far as seemed possible within a single province, although they stopped far short of full socialism.

During the war the problems of federalism and sectionalism greatly declined. The Dominion government was able to exercise wide powers in the wartime emergency, and patriotism and prosperity both helped to weaken sectional forces. In 1941 it is true, a Dominion-Provincial Conference held to consider the Rowell-Sirois recommendations had foundered on the opposition of wealthy Ontario and British Columbia, which felt they had little to gain, and Alberta, which wanted to go its own Social Credit way. But temporary tax-renting agreements somewhat as the Report proposed were reached between the Dominion and provinces for the war period. Dominion unemployment insurance was also carried into effect. After the war, moreover, there was no swift return to a formal state of peace, for no peace treaty was signed with Germany. Hence the broad wartime federal powers could still operate. Furthermore, the steady post-war boom worked against any strong revival of sectionalism, while rising new international dangers again took most of Canada's attention as the mid-century mark drew near.

When the wartime tax arrangements came to an end in 1946, the Dominion was able to make new five-year agreements with each of the provinces except Ontario and Quebec. Thus the scheme of redistributing the financial load could be carried out, for the time being at least, in the very parts of Canada where it was most required. And, as time went on, almost all the provinces seemed willing to reach a fuller, more permanent settlement of the financial question with the Dominion. Meanwhile, further changes were occurring in the constitutional field. Canadian citizenship, apart from the general status of British subject, was established in 1947 as a natural accompaniment of nationhood.

Appeals to the Privy Council were abolished in 1949 and it was enacted that at least in matters relating wholly to federal powers the Dominion parliament could itself carry through amendments to the constitution. The right to make amendments that would affect provincial powers still remained with the Imperial parliament, but Dominion-provincial discussions were set afoot to try to reach agreement on how this too might be transferred to Canada.

Following the war, federal social legislation advanced with the adoption of a system of family allowances, although the steady rise in living costs after wartime price controls were removed offset the value of these payments to the Canadian people. Immigration meanwhile began again, both of European displaced persons and immigrants from Britain, some of them brought by air. Another immigrant tide was swelling, which would bring nearly half a million new citizens within six years of the war.

In 1948 Mackenzie King retired from political life, an undefeated champion, indeed. The new prime minister, Louis St Laurent, was a leading French Canadian lawyer who had only entered politics during the war, when he became Minister of Justice on Lapointe's death. After serving briefly at the close of the war as Secretary of External Affairs, St Laurent was chosen by a Liberal convention in 1948 to be King's successor as party leader. This choice of a distinguished French Canadian, fluent in both tongues, seemed to recall the great days of Laurier Liberalism. In the election that followed in 1949, St Laurent and the Liberals were easily returned over their nearest rivals, the Progressive Conservatives, now led by George Drew. The new government, however, had to face an ever-darkening world situation, and when Mackenzie King died in July, 1950, perhaps his passing marked the end of another era for Canada.

3   *Canada in a Two-Power World*

The coming of the Second World War had made clear to Canadians the ineffectiveness of a policy of no commitments in the modern world. No nation could stand aloof. If it did not share in making world decisions, world decisions would be forced on it in any case; the war had proved that. Hence Canada's best course was to try to influence world decisions along lines that she wanted, as far as it was possible for a small nation to do. A world organization promised the best means for smaller nations to be heard, and though the League had failed, a new association firmly based on the principle of collective security still seemed the only hope for a lasting world peace.

During the war Canada had gained a good deal of experience in world affairs. The need for maintaining a joint Allied war effort had brought her into close touch with Britain and the United States through 'combined boards' of all three countries in London or Washington, which dealt at the highest levels with such matters as military and naval strategy, allied food resources, air transport, prisoners of war, and so on. Two great conferences of allied war leaders had been held on Canadian soil at Quebec in 1943 and 1944. In addition Canada had shared with Britain and the United States in the secret development of atomic energy. She held one of the world's chief supplies of uranium, the raw material for atomic power, deep in her North West Territories and built one of the first atomic piles to study the new energy at Chalk River, Ontario.

Besides these close contacts with her two main allies, Canada had also developed contacts with many other allied nations, China and Russia, for instance, through a much expanded Department of External Affairs. Her Mutual Aid administration also transferred war materials to these countries in the general interest. There was nothing narrowly national in this—except that Canada had come to realize that the truest national policy was the building of a strong and healthy free world in which she could live at peace. It was in accord with this policy that at the close of the war she became a leading member of UNRRA, the United Nations Relief and Rehabilitation Administration, whose massive task it was to restore and rebuild those countries torn by war.

Canada became a leading member of UNRRA because she was one of the few nations at the war's end with a large surplus of food and industrial goods for the work of restoration. This fact raised a problem in Canada's newly active relations with the world. Was she a small or a great power? Beside the militarily strong and well-populated states like the Soviet Union, the United States, or Britain, she was obviously small and could not exert much influence. But in terms of her major war effort, her world importance as a source of food and materials, and her industrial and financial strength, Canada was plainly not small. She was, in effect, a middle power, and one of the objects of Canadian foreign policy now became to win recognition of that fact. Other middle powers like Australia or Brazil also made similar efforts to win that standing.

The question came up at the San Francisco Conference of 1945, held to draft a plan for a world organization. This solemn meeting to create 'one world' produced the Charter of the United Nations, the new international body that was to keep the peace and protect human rights. Canada's delegation to San Francisco included Prime Minister King and the leaders of the opposition parties. Their work at San Francisco might seem to recall that of Borden in Paris in 1919, except that this time Canada had already won the rights of nationhood, and that this time, also, the peace treaties with the defeated enemy powers were to be left for the future—where they long remained, unsettled and unsigned.

At the Conference Canada made efforts to have the status of middle powers recognized. Thus it was that, in various special international authorities set up under the United Nations, Canada was given a leading role when her importance warranted it. Hence, for example, she became a principal member of the Atomic Energy

Commission, the World Food Board, and the International Civil Aviation Authority, whose headquarters were established in Montreal. But in the United Nations itself, whose first concern was world security, Canada could not hope to rank with the great powers on whom world peace depended. She did not therefore gain a permanent seat in the all-important Security Council, although in 1947 she was elected for a two-year term to one of the non-permanent seats.

This arrangement of the Security Council with a few permanent members exposed a new and unpleasant truth about the post-war world. World peace really depended on a few great powers, and on two above all: the United States and the Soviet Union. Britain still exercised an important influence in world affairs, but by the end of the Second World War it was clear that final power had passed from western European countries to the two great land-masses, the American and Russian, with their large populations and extensive resources. Canada found herself in what was basically a two-power world.

The Second World War had much advanced Canada's own power, international standing and sense of responsibility. Yet more important was the fact that Canada had come of age in a cold new world, where Britain's power could no longer serve to protect her, where even the broad oceans could not ensure security against air attack and the atom bomb, and where the Arctic wastes were no longer an impassable barrier but a frontier to be defended. Instead of having her back securely to the Pole, Canada found herself looking north on the air highways of the world. The shortest air routes between the main continents crossed her Arctic regions. This meant new stature for Canada, but it also spelt new dangers.

The dangers seemed to grow as the United Nations did not fulfil its early hopes and as the world gradually divided into two huge camps of communism and democracy, led by the Soviet Union on the one hand and the United States and Britain on the other. Canada lay in an exposed position between the two main rivals. As quarrels grew in the United Nations over the Soviet Union's use of the veto power to block action by the Security Council, as crises repeatedly appeared in Europe and the Far East, or in Palestine and the Arab lands, Canada faced world problems of utmost gravity. She still could not decide these problems. But she had to use her influence on them in any way possible, and particularly at the United Nations in trying to remove international trouble spots. Beyond this, however, it was necessary to strengthen the defences of the free world. Hence Canada took a leading part in forming the North Atlantic Treaty Organization in 1949, which built on the old North Atlantic Triangle to include western European nations in a pact for the joint defence of the Treaty partners. Canadian rearmament began, and military supplies were sent to Treaty countries.

In this two-power world, Canada found herself tightly linked as well with the United States in the common defence of North America. The die had already been cast by the Ogdensburg Agreement of 1940, but in any case, since there was no thought of siding with Russian communism in Canadian minds, Canada was committed by position, inclination, and a need for protection to the United States. At the same time the common ideas and interests of Britain and the United States, the common stake that they and the Commonwealth had in a free world, also drew Canada's Commonwealth partners together with the American republic. In a vague and general, but real, way the difficult new two-power era was bringing the whole English-speaking world more closely together than it had been since the American Revolution.

Nevertheless, since Canada was largely and even basically bound to American policy, she had to make her own world views plain as never before; for her great neighbour tended to take the smaller northern country for granted and often assumed that their interests were wholly the same. But Canada still had her own identity to preserve and did not necessarily believe that American policies were correct, though she might have to back them in the last analysis. It was necessary, therefore, for Canada still to shape her own course, to take her own military responsibilities, and on occasion to remind some American authorities that she was a nation with her own mind to make up.

In this effort, two great world associations allowed Canada to stand outside the pull of American foreign policy, the United Nations and the Commonwealth. In the first she worked for mediation and compromise, and by no means simply followed an American line. Through the second she kept up informal 'family' consultations with Commonwealth countries, sought through loans and agreements to restore Britain's financial strength, which was still so vital to Canadian trade, and joined in the Commonwealth Conference at Colombo in 1950 to draft plans for developing the backward lands of Asia in order to save them from communism. But in these Commonwealth matters Canada was working outside the United States, not against her. Indeed, her hopes in the two-power world turned on the United States, the Commonwealth, and the United Nations all put together.

Yet, as the mid-century mark drew near and the vital question was undoubtedly whether peace and a free world could be preserved the relations of Canada with the United States revived historic arguments at home. Some Canadians dusted off the old labels 'colonial' and 'imperialists' for those in their midst who freely criticized American policies that affected Canada. Others warned again of the threat of American dominance, as the United States loomed ever larger. It was striking how Canadian history tended to repeat itself, even in the two-power world.

4 *Canada Gains a New Province*

On 1 April 1949, the original plans for the Union of British North America were finally fulfilled. Newfoundland joined Canadian Confederation. Thus ended a period of over eighty years since

Newfoundland first rejected the Quebec Conference scheme, during which time the island had followed its own course of history, although still much influenced by Canada. It had built up its own proud identity, but serious weaknesses in Newfoundland's economy led it at last to merge itself in the larger nation of the mainland as the tenth province of the Dominion.

In 1867 when the Dominion was formed, Newfoundland had a population of 142,000, some of it concentrated in St John's and other towns of the eastern Avalon peninsula, but most of it scattered in tiny fishing outports around the rocky coasts. The interior of the island was still almost unknown. Two problems remained from an earlier age to trouble Newfoundland's all-important fisheries: the fishing monopoly of France on the western 'French shore', which also blocked the effective use of that coast, and the more limited right of the Americans to fish in coastal waters. The first problem dated back to the Treaty of Utrecht of 1713 and the second to the Treaty of Versailles of 1783. They both caused storms in Newfoundland politics, especially when the island's powers of responsible government seemed to be overridden by agreements reached between the imperial authorities and France or the United States.

The first few years after 1867 were prosperous ones for Newfoundland, as its anti-Confederation government strove to show that the island could, indeed, thrive on its own. Yet good times were largely dependent on a healthy fishery. Although sealing, whaling and lobster-fishing were also developed, the island was tied above all to the great cod catch; in fact, the word 'fish' simply meant cod to the Newfoundlander. Hence a poor run of cod catches or low world prices—for the island sold most of its product abroad, especially in the West Indies and the Mediterranean—could spell disaster for Newfoundland and strain the limited finances of its government. This set an enduring pattern for the island. The government, in order to lessen the total dependence on the fishery, would put money into new developments in good times, which then in bad times it could not afford to keep up; leading to a rising burden of public debt and, finally, to bank-ruptcy.

As part of a policy of development, the government-backed Newfoundland Railway was begun in the 1880's, and a large dry-dock was opened in St John's in 1884 to improve on the fine natural advantages of that world port. Farming was encouraged as the railway opened up the land, but the small population made the railway costs heavy and, along with poor soil, limited the growth of farms. Meanwhile the Great Depression that had struck Canada also affected the island, lowering the world prices for its fish. Railway-building and other development produced brief flashes of prosperity, but in general, Newfoundland ceased to advance very rapidly. Then in the early 'nineties came a series of calamities. A great fire in St John's in 1892 destroyed the larger part of the city. Though the loss of life was not large, the cost of rebuilding was enormous. There was a poor catch in 1893, and in 1894 a serious bank failure overturned the island's finances. Newfoundland was in deep distress.

In this emergency the island considered Confederation with Canada once more, since it might no longer be able to afford inde-pendent responsible government. Generous aid from Canada in the St John's disaster promoted good feelings, which seemed to promise that Newfoundlanders would consider Confederation without the old suspicion that had worked so much against it in the 1860's. Yet in the Ottawa conference of 1895 the Dominion itself, pinched for money in the depression, would not meet New-foundland's financial terms. The Confederation talks fell through, and the island faced the future on its own once more. Fortunately the world trade revival after 1896 greatly improved Newfound-land's position.

Improving conditions in the fishery were helped along by the settlement of the two old grievances of Newfoundland, the French shore and the American claims. In 1904 France gave up her rights to land and dry catch on the western coast through an agreement with Britain whereby she gained a strip of territory in West Africa instead. This removed a serious trade rival from Newfoundland and also permitted the extension of the Newfoundland Railway to the western coast. In 1905 a dispute began over an island attempt to prevent American fishermen taking bait fish. It was settled finally by the International Court at the Hague in 1910, which decided that the American fishing claims were an undue limitation of Newfoundland's right to command her own territory and resources. At last the island was in full control of its own fisheries.

In the prosperous early years of the twentieth century, and largely under the capable prime minister, Sir Robert Bond, Newfoundland enjoyed something like the Laurier boom in Canada. While the fisheries flourished and railway branch lines spread, valuable progress was made in lessening Newfoundland's 'one-crop' dependence on fishing exports. Mining and lumbering produced new wealth. The iron mines of Bell Island that reached out under the sea fed the Maritimes' steel industry. Lead, copper and zinc were mined in the interior. At Grand Falls, near the north-eastern coast, the Anglo-Newfoundland Development Company began in 1909 to produce quantities of newsprint for Lord Northcliffe's newspaper empire in Britain. Newsprint became a leading Newfoundland export, and the pulp and paper mills raised populous modern towns at Grand Falls and later at Corner Brook on the west coast.

The prosperity and new development still did not change the basic reliance on fishing, and led indeed to programmes of public works and social services which, though limited, were really beyond the island's strength. Moreover, Newfoundland's vigorous efforts in the First World War left it at the end with a debt of nineteen million dollars and greatly inflated prices that quickly collapsed. Newfoundland had sent its men into British naval and land forces and suffered casualties at a greater rate than any other

Dominion. The Royal Newfoundland Regiment maintained by the island earned a gallant name at Gallipoli and at Beaumont-Hamel in 1916, where its strength was cut down in one day's action from 753 to 68. It was a fitting recognition of the island's war effort that it was afterwards raised to the rank of a full Dominion in the Commonwealth. But the heavy drain in men and money had ill prepared the new Dominion for the future.

Consequently, Newfoundland did not share to the full in the world prosperity of the 1920's. The debt burden remained, railway costs increased, and the fisheries were affected by the decline of the world dried-fish market and the increasing competition of frozen fish produced by wealthier Canadian and American concerns. In 1927 came the award that finally settled the indefinite Quebec-Labrador boundary and gave Newfoundland a large inland addition to Labrador in which vast iron resources would later be found. But in the 1920's Labrador was still only valuable to the island as a mainland coastal strip with whaling and fishing stations. It had a population of less than 5,000, a quarter of it Eskimo.

The grim depression of the 'thirties struck Newfoundland far harder than Canada. World fish prices sank so low that Newfoundland fishermen were flung on relief. Their boats rotted in harbour while a hard-pressed government tried in vain to feed the fishing people, keep the railways running, and meet the debt. Reduced to bankruptcy, the government in despair turned to Britain for aid. A Royal Commission was appointed, which recommended the suspension of Dominion status and a return to colonial control until the island could support itself again. In 1934 responsible government was replaced by a Commission government appointed by Britain, consisting of three Newfoundlanders and three Englishmen under a British governor. In return for this Commission rule under the imperial parliament, Newfoundland received funds from Britain's taxpayers and began to recover from the worst stages of financial collapse.

The colony was still far from self-supporting when the Second

World War broke out, but this time Newfoundland did not maintain its own separate forces and thus its contribution to the British and Canadian armed services did not cause the same drain. And the new conditions of this Second War gave Newfoundland great importance because of its position as that part of North America closest to Europe. The air age turned the island into a busy airport, a centre for the air ferry services to Britain, a base for patrolling over the surrounding oceans. The extension of submarine warfare across the whole Atlantic made the port of St John's in particular a powerful naval base, where from 'Newfyjohn' the convoys approaching and leaving America received guidance and protection. The problems of North American defence also brought Canadian and American troops and money to the island. They built a chain of fortifications to guard this exposed corner of North America lest it might serve as a bomber base for an enemy attacking the continent. The British-American bargain of 1940, that gave Britain old but much-needed United States destroyers in exchange for naval bases, established the Americans at Argentia and other points in the island on ninety-nine year leases. At the same time Canada worked to build up the huge airports of Gander in the island and Goose Bay in Labrador. The war had changed the whole life and destiny of Newfoundland.

At its close, the island was self-supporting at last, and prospering nicely. Canadian and American money in Newfoundland, and the wartime demand for labour for military construction, had helped to create prosperity. So had heavy demands in mining and lumbering; and in the fishery, the whole catch could be sold at good prices. Furthermore, the building of filleting and fish-freezing plants adjusted the fishery to world competition. It was a stronger and healthier Newfoundland, with a large bank balance, that turned again in 1946 to the question of what to do with its government.

In that year the British government called a popularly elected Convention in the island to consider some new form of representative government. But it soon became clear that the only choice in the Convention lay between independent responsible government or responsible government as a part of the Canadian union. The old plan of Confederation, never forgotten, was put forward again; for there were fears that the island would not in the long run be able to maintain its post-war prosperity and would not prove strong enough to stand alone. On the whole, the outport regions were most in favour of union with Canada. They looked to the wealthy federal government for marketing aids and social services that the island could not supply itself. They also hoped for useful subsidies in provincial fields such as education, which in Newfoundland had been but partly provided through Catholic, Methodist, and Anglican schools. On the other hand, St John's and the eastern towns opposed union because they feared that without the Newfoundland protective tariff larger Canadian firms would take over much of their business.

The question of 'Confederation or Responsible Government' was sharply debated in the island for over a year, while the fervent oratory of Joseph Smallwood, the Confederation leader, set the outports afire. The final result was a close popular vote in favour of Confederation at the referendum of July 1948, with the outports almost solidly on that side and St John's and its neighbourhood as firmly on the other. A deep pride in Newfoundland's own past lessened any rejoicing over the victory of Confederation, even in unionist circles. Yet the new knowledge of Canada and Canadians acquired through wartime co-operation also decreased the old feelings of suspicion and strangeness.

In December 1948, terms of union were signed in Ottawa, to come into effect in April 1949. Newfoundland was granted sizeable subsidies, which took into consideration its particular need of improved social services and its special financial problem. The new province received six members in the Canadian Senate and seven elected representatives in the federal House of Commons, and in addition, of course, its own provincial government. Provincial elections were held in the summer of 1949, and that autumn the first parliament in Newfoundland in fifteen years met in St John's under Premier Joseph Smallwood. The Smallwood government at once entered on a programme of road building, hospital improvement and tourist trade development. Newfoundland's new position in Confederation could not immediately be evaluated, but undoubtedly her 'fishing poor' of the outports proceeded to benefit. And Canada gained by the addition of this tenth province of great strategic importance and as yet undeveloped resources, especially in Labrador iron and hydro-electric power. Besides, the inclusion of over 300,000 staunch Newfoundlanders in the Dominion provided another resource of no small value.

5 The Life of a Maturing Nation

By 1950 Canada was close to maturity; still young, still with vast empty regions and room for development, but much more like other adult western nations in her ways of life than a raw pioneer community. The old simplicity of the work of forest and field had been replaced by the highly complicated patterns of modern industrial living. The typical Canadians were no longer the settlers and pioneers seeking new homes in the wilderness but farm-owners and wage-earners searching for security in a country that was already well built up. This did not mean that the people of Canada had ceased to look for broad horizons. They still remembered their past of nation-building and did not expect that process to stop. The 'true North, strong and free' was always at their backs. Even if it were only for a summer holiday, there were always the wilds of lake and forest at hand. There were still bush clearings in New Brunswick, hardy French Canadians pioneering in little colonies in the forests of the Shield, or new Canadians on frontier farms in northern Ontario's Clay Belt; and frontier settlement was still going on in the Peace river country of Alberta. The lure of the far North West or of the mighty Rockies continued to beckon the mining prospector. There were colourful boom towns like Yellowknife and Eldorado in the North West Territories and unknown mountains and hidden valleys in the heart of British Columbia. The cowboys and ranchers of the western foothills or the fishermen of the rugged coasts were not mild white-collared citizens, and the northern bush flyer ranged as free as the *coureurs de bois* or the Nor'Westers had ever done.

Yet most Canadians lived in a world of towns, factories, automobile highways, and fenced-in farms. In the east the countryside had acquired an old, settled look with tall elms standing in close-cropped fields, lilacs sheltering the farmyards, and orchards rounding the gentle slope of hills. Even in the prairies the growth of groves of trees as windbreaks and the varying of crops began to alter the landscape. In the towns, the bustle of life, the electric signs, and the noisy traffic seemed much the same as in any large city of the United States or western Europe. The bigger cities with their towering skyscrapers looked about as prosperous as those below the border. Canada, apparently, had achieved material success. But was she succeeding in other ways? Were Canadians building in the realm of the mind and the spirit?

To a large degree they were. Canada had advanced considerably in all the arts and sciences since Laurier's day. In the field of medicine, the discovery of insulin as a cure for diabetes was the work of two Canadians, Sir Frederick Banting and Dr Charles Best in the 1920's. In scientific research Canada came to the fore in the Second World War, when her National Research Council became a partner of Britain and the United States in developing radar and the knowledge of atomic energy. Scientific education seemed well supported in Canadian universities.

In the realm of the arts, Canadian literature had become much more analytical and self-critical since the rosy nationalism of the turn of the century, but this in itself was a sign of maturity. Poetry largely turned from the landscape to the people of Canada, to tell stories, to deal with social problems and satire, the minds and emotions of individuals, the everyday world they lived in. The depression of the 'thirties, in particular, strengthened the mood of self-examination. E. J. Pratt, a Newfoundlander by origin, broke new paths in Canadian poetry. A. M. Klein, A. J. M. Smith, Dorothy Livesay and many others carried on the work in English-speaking Canada, and the same kinds of current moved among French-Canadian poets.

In the novel, the writings of Frederick Philip Grove closely observed the problems of ordinary life in the West, Mazo de la Roche traced the history of a family in the rich Oakville country-side of southern Ontario in her 'Whiteoaks' series, while Morley Callaghan's novels caught the spirit of the cities. By the 1940's younger writers like Bruce Hutchison, Hugh MacLennan and William Mitchell were striving to express the essence of Canada and the Canadian scene; Hutchison on the Pacific coast, Mac-Lennan in Nova Scotia and Quebec, and Mitchell on the western prairies. Their efforts were the sign of a more mature nationalism, no longer so self-confident, but filled with a deeper consciousness of Canada. Again the same process was going on in French Canada. In 1916 a French novelist, Louis Hémon, wrote *Maria Chapdelaine*, which described French Canadian country life with great charm and simplicity; but in time there was a revolt against this romantic portrait, expressed, for example, in Ringuet's *Thirty Acres* (1938) or Roger Lemelin's *The Town Below* (1949), a novel of the poorer classes in Quebec city.

In painting too, and sculpture, Canadians were making distinct-ive contributions. The work of the Group-of-Seven artists con-tinued across the 'twenties and 'thirties, and long was dominant; although in time their bold, graphic style came to seem not revo-lutionary at all, but almost the accepted way to paint in Canada —which was not entirely good. In sculpture men like Alfred Laliberté and Walter Allward left their mark. The latter designed the magnificent Vimy Ridge memorial to the Canadian dead of the First World War, which was unveiled in 1936. In music, ballet, and drama Canadians were also active, although the people as a whole displayed a habit left over from colonial times, a preference for music and plays from outside and a tendency to think native Canadian products not worth too much attention. The stage did not thrive in Canada, though a strong amateur theatre movement and, in particular, the Canadian Broadcasting Commission provided valuable outlets for acting and writing talents.

The Canadian Broadcasting Commission, which was first established in 1932, was in fact, one of the chief mediums for encouraging and spreading the work of Canadian writers. In this broad country with its small and scattered population radio played a great part in linking the regions together and making them conscious of one another. Canada in radio adopted a typical compromise between British and American practice by setting up a government broadcasting commission but permitting private local radio stations as well. Despite the attacks that a compromise is bound to meet from either side, the C.B.C. proved a valuable instrument for national unity and national education. Its development gave further signs that Canadians were beginning to develop a culture of their own.

Of course, the growth of any national culture was greatly weakened by the racial division in Canada, and by powerful influences from the United States. Canadians lived in surroundings much like those of the Americans, spoke the same language and lay on the edge of the vast American market. Hence, inevitably, when the anti-American feelings declined, books, magazines, radio programmes, motion pictures, and later television from the United States readily poured into Canada. The external features of Canadian life seemed to resemble American more and more. Canadians ate the same nationally-advertised breakfast cereals as the Americans, read the same kinds of newspapers, played the same kinds of sports, dressed and talked in much the same way. 'Americanization' was discussed and deplored; in fact, in 1949 a Royal Commission was set up to study means of promoting a truly Canadian culture.

Yet, while Americanization went on, differences continued. Canada, indeed, seemed to grow more conscious of herself. After all, she was rather a patchwork, made up of regions that had long been divided from each other and had often been in closer contact with Britain or the United States than with one another. Nevertheless, a Canadian consciousness was growing. It could be seen on the C.B.C., in Canadian writing and art, in the Canadian universities, and in the rise of a Canadian publishing world centred in Toronto. Canadians, to Europeans, might seem much like Americans—perhaps on the basis that all foreigners, or in this case, North Americans, look alike. Both Canadians and Americans, however, sensed differences between themselves that were small but significant, extending sometimes even to dress and speech.

At the root of these differences, besides the great fact of Quebec's presence in the centre of Canada, there was the fact that Canada still represented a middle ground between Britain and the United States in ideas and institutions. By the mid-twentieth century she was, as a North American nation, closer to the United States in a number of ways; but she kept a largely British system of law and government. Furthermore, in comparison with the rich and restless republic, Canada was a cautious and conservative country: cautious because her path was harder, and conservative because of her closer bonds with the Old World and the stronger power of traditions brought from Britain and France. Other factors that made for difference lay in Canada's continuing decision to stay in the Commonwealth and not to join the Organization of American States, seeking to offset the pull of the United States. And finally, there was the thoroughly Canadian influence of the great north country, which was all her own. The North was a reservoir of national strength for the future, for new Canadian growth. All these things marked Canada off from the United States and gave her reason for her separate and still developing national identity.

CHAPTER 20

CANADA IN THE LATEST AGE

1 *The Mid-Century Boom*

During the nineteen-fifties the post-war boom in Canada rose to dazzling heights. New resources were developed rapidly and on a giant scale; the population jumped from not quite fourteen million to nearly eighteen million within the decade; and the rate of growth in national wealth and well-being seemed to give all Canada the bright glow of success. The boom, of course, was well under way before the 'fifties opened, after only a short period of business readjustment following the Second World War. It went on expanding with only brief lulls into 1957, and in some respects its passing was not fully plain until the beginning of the 'sixties. These mid-century years thus formed an era of exceptional advance, though they also shaped grave problems for the future. It would take complex and detailed analysis to explain their high prosperity. Yet certain main contributing factors do stand out.

First and foremost was a state of world trade that markedly favoured Canada. Her foodstuffs, raw materials, and manufactures were in wide demand for years after 1945, to help feed, re-stock, and rebuild the many countries that had been damaged or devastated by war. In particular, British recovery and Europe's resurgence under the American-sponsored Marshall Plan provided ready markets for Canadian goods, while the fact that the German and Japanese economies had been shattered meant that two large industrial competitors were temporarily out of the running. As a result, Canada's exports, by which the country must basically live, enjoyed an almost open field around the world.

Second, Canada had already greatly developed her producing and manufacturing capabilities during the Second World War, and at the same time her people had piled up savings in that period when ordinary goods were scarce. Hence there was a big demand waiting to be filled at home when peace returned and the means became available to fill it. Consequently, Canadian production was converted from war to peacetime purposes with surprisingly little letdown, certainly without the sharp post-war depression that many economists had feared. Government measures to re-establish returning soldiers and enlarge social welfare services (in part, to offset the depression that did not come) probably also served to 'prime' the economy, and to set off the great post-war buying spree that ran on through the flush times of the 'fifties.

Third, there was the new wealth created by the opening up of more and more of Canada's natural resources in this era of strong world demand. For example, the tapping of new oil reserves in Alberta in 1947 did much to launch a soaring increase in petroleum and natural-gas development that made many more jobs and provided more varied products for Canada to market. It was notable that these advances particularly affected forest and mineral industries. While in the years 1926 to 1929 farm products had formed more than half of Canadian exports, by the period 1951 to 1954 forest and mineral products had come to hold first and second place respectively. Still, western wheat, which had once been Canada's leading export, did benefit from good post-war harvests and ready overseas markets that helped erase the farmers' bitter memories of drought-ridden and depressed pre-war years.

Fourth, and highly significant in the long run, was the flow of foreign capital into the country, to invest not only in developing raw materials but also in manufacturing. It was only natural that foreign investments should flow in, since prosperous Canada offered wide opportunities for rich returns, and had so many valuable resources still waiting to be exploited. Moreover, the governments and people of Canada generally welcomed the influx of capital, because it enabled large productive enterprises to be undertaken that they could not have financed themselves. The money, however, came chiefly from the United States, which needed new sources of basic materials close at hand to keep up its own high rate of growth, and which had long held many interests in the Canadian market. One result was to make the Canadian economy increasingly dependent on the American. Another was to lengthen and continue the boom in Canada. For when Canadians in the flush of wealth began spending more abroad than they were selling, the inflow of American money balanced the national accounts and kept up the good times. This, of course, meant that Canadian prosperity was increasingly riding on outside capital, while a massive problem of debt was being built up for the future.

Finally, but still important, there was the remarkable rise in Canada's population during the mid-century years. Much of this was due to immigration. By 1956 over a million immigrants had entered Canada since the war, and nearly two million had arrived by the start of the nineteen-sixties. Some still came for political reasons, uprooted as they had been by Nazi military tyranny or harried by the ruthless power of Communism in post-war eastern Europe: for instance, Hungarians who fled their country when their anti-Communist uprising of 1956 failed. But more came to escape the drab austerity of Europe after the war, and to find new prospects in rapidly expanding Canada. Among them were Dutch, Germans, Estonians, and Poles. About one-third of the total arrived from Britain and another third from Italy – although proportions varied from year to year.

One evident result was to enlarge the non-British, non-French segment of the Canadian population. True, most of the European immigrants tended to associate themselves with the English-speaking Canadian community, thereby keeping French Canada still decidedly in the minority. It would be years more, nevertheless, before immigrants of many tongues and cultures were fully integrated with their new surroundings. For the present, they had made Canada an obviously more cosmopolitan country. In cities like Toronto and Montreal, large close-knit foreign-language communities emerged to add colour and variety, as well as to pose new problems in Canadian life. New Canadians also brought with them valuable knowledge, skills, and more capital. They further added to the labour force, and helped to keep up the vigorous home demand for goods.

Immigration, however, was only partly responsible for Canada's big population increase. It was caused as much or more by a high wartime and post-war birth-rate: Canadians were simply raising larger families. This increase alone would inevitably have spurred on other developments, because of the ever-larger numbers that had to be fed, housed, and provided with goods and services. More than that, it helped produce a striking expansion of cities. Both native Canadians and immigrants flocked to the booming urban factories, and to the expected comforts and excitements of city life. Urbanization, the crowding into towns with all its attendant problems, became one of the outstanding features of the mid-century boom. Skyscrapers and apartment blocks shot up; suburbs sprawled out, eating up fertile country-side; traffic threatened to choke the towns and impelled costly highway, subway, and expressway construction. To cope with the complex problems of managing these ungainly new urban 'agglomerations', a new level of governmental authority was set up over Toronto and its suburbs in 1954 – metropolitan government, which largely pioneered for similarly troubled Canadian cities.

The impressive growth in the main Canadian centres of the south must not hide the way in which frontiers in the north were steadily pushed back during the boom years. In order to provide warning against air and missile attack on North America from across the Pole, chains of radar bases, radio-stations, and weather-stations were strung across the Arctic and sub-Arctic wilderness. Their establishment meant the opening of new far-northern air-fields, the construction of supply depots, houses, and sometimes veritable settlements, in areas where everything from bulldozers to building timber might have to be flown in. By 1959, the Distant Early Warning or DEW Line of radar posts stretched across the top of the continent. In the eastern Arctic, Frobisher Bay was developed as a main Canadian base. In the western Arctic, Aklavik, the port on the Mackenzie river, was moved to a completely new site, while traffic mounted on the great river route, and on the Mackenzie Highway built to connect it with transportation systems to the south. Still farther north, ice-breakers of the Royal Canadian Navy probed for shipping lanes through the frozen waters of the Arctic Archipelago; oil-prospecting reached into the distant Queen Elizabeth Islands; and a permanent weather-station was established at the very tip of Canada's Arctic territory at Alert Bay, beyond 82° north latitude.

In the desolate interior of Labrador-Ungava, enormous iron-ore deposits were opened up in the early 'fifties to supply steel mills in Canada and in the United States, whose own mid-continent fields were beginning to show signs of depletion. Rails were laid from the port of Sept Iles, on the Lower St Lawrence, three hundred and sixty-five miles northward to the newly built mining town of Schefferville, while the abundant hydro-electric power resources of Grand Falls on the Hamilton river were tapped to the benefit of both Quebec and Newfoundland. On the other side of the continent, up the mountainous coast of British Columbia, an equally gigantic project to produce aluminum also brought another new industrial community into being, the planned city of Kitimat. This whole enterprise involved reversing the flow of a river inland beyond the Coast Range and tunnelling it under the mountains, in order to obtain the great amounts of hydro-electric power needed in aluminum refining.

These leaps forward in iron and aluminum production, two of

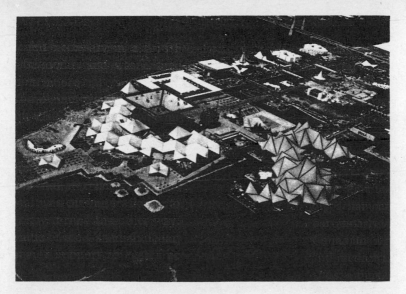

Expo 67

Toronto in the Nineteen-seventies

A PEACEFUL STRETCH OF CANADIAN COUNTRYSIDE

the vital ingredients of modern industrialism, were manifestly important aspects of resource development in Canada during the boom years. Uranium, the source of atomic energy, also played a prominent part. It was already being produced at the Eldorado mine on Great Bear Lake, taken over by the government in 1944. But after the war, the demands of the United States atomic energy programme (not to mention Canada's own major atomic research centre at Chalk River near Ottawa) brought on a rising fever of activity in uranium prospecting and mining. New fields were opened on Lake Athabaska. Uranium City was laid out in northern Saskatchewan in 1951. Still bigger expansion came with the discovery of the Algoma field in Ontario, in 1953, above the northern shores of Lake Huron. Here another sizeable new town soon appeared, Elliot Lake, though its future largely rested on the continuance of uranium-ore contracts with the United States and Britain.

The most striking resource development of all came in oil and natural gas. At the war's end, Canada had had only a small petroleum industry, chiefly for processing imported crude oils. By 1957 she supplied a major part of her own demand and was a large exporter besides – for if her own consumption had grown three times as large, her production had risen more than twenty-fold! This 'oil revolution' really started in Alberta with the blowing in of the well Imperial No. 1 at Leduc in 1947. Hitherto Canadian oilfields, centred in Alberta, had been small and were declining in yield. The find at Leduc marked the start of a cycle of oil discoveries and proving of fields not only across Alberta but in Saskatchewan and Manitoba as well, and on into the North West Territories. The whole western plains region became a real or potential oil and gas reservoir. Alberta remained by far the leading oil province, and benefited most from the new wealth and industry brought by oil, including the royalties that oil producers paid to its government. But all three Prairie Provinces gained from the cheap sources of fuel at hand for local industrial development or for sale outside. The farming West's old dependence on the grain crop was considerably reduced.

To reach outside markets effectively, however, pipe-lines had to be built to carry oil and gas from western fields. By 1953 the world's longest oil pipe-line ran east from Edmonton to the petrochemical centre of Sarnia 1,765 miles away, and to the main Ontario market. The same year another line was opened across the western mountains to the Pacific, 718 miles from Edmonton to Vancouver, and soon extended into the United States. Gas lines came a little later: to Vancouver and the American border, to Emerson, Manitoba, and the border again, and eastward on to Niagara Falls, Toronto, and Montreal. But the arrangements made by the federal government with the Trans-Canada Pipe Lines Company (essentially to aid the firm in building long unprofitable sections of the gas line to the East) brought violent clashes in parliament in 1956. Their political significance will require more comment later.

At any rate, during the 'fifties, the heavy outlay on these pipelines created new links in the national system of communications that bound Canada from east to west. The era equally witnessed a great increase in air services, and the coming of the age of television to Canada: the C.B.C. began transmission in 1952, and in 1958 completed a microwave relay system from coast to coast. Still further, the construction by federal-provincial agreement of a first-class Trans-Canada Highway (not opened until 1962) marked an era of outstanding improvement in national communications that recalled the building of the C.P.R. or the other transcontinental railways during the Laurier boom. Perhaps the greatest single improvement in communications, however, came on the old east-west main line of Canada – on the St Lawrence–Great Lakes waterway that had been the backbone of Canadian development from the very start.

Here, the decade of the 'fifties saw the realization of the long-sought project for a deep-water seaway through the St Lawrence system, one that would open the heart of the continent to the bulk of the world's shipping. Another main objective of the project was hydro-electric power, to be obtained at dams that would harness the upper St Lawrence and overcome its rapids. Much of the industrial heartland of central Canada depended on hydro-electricity. Despite further large-scale power developments at Niagara Falls, on the Ottawa, and on neighbouring Quebec rivers, only the upper St Lawrence could promise a giant new supply of energy to the region.

Opposition from United States seaboard interests, which feared the competition of a St Lawrence seaway, had blocked American signature of an agreement to permit joint Canadian-American development of the river through the rapids of its international section. But now American Great Lakes steel mills wanted Labrador ore easily available at their docks; American lake ports like Chicago sought direct ocean trade; and American power interests faced a shortage of their own in neighbouring New York State. These influences, combined with the undoubted readiness of a thriving, confident Canada to build a seaway on her own side of the international section, managed to convince a hesitant United States Congress to endorse the project.

The necessary American legislation was signed by President Eisenhower in May, 1954. In Canada, the federal and Ontario governments were only waiting to begin digging. Five full years of construction followed, until at St Lambert, Quebec, in June of 1959, Queen Elizabeth and President Eisenhower together formally opened a St Lawrence seaway, twenty-seven feet deep, from the port of Montreal to Lake Erie. It was a fitting climax to a decade of momentous achievement. By now, however, the Canadian boom was fast disappearing. Already the problems it had produced were becoming quite as evident as its positive accomplishments.

2 *Political Affairs from St Laurent to Diefenbaker*

Throughout the peak years of the boom, the Liberals remained in power at Ottawa under the leadership of Louis St Laurent. They had won a sweeping victory in the election of 1949. That of 1953 gave them a smaller but still substantial majority. No doubt the good times worked to the government's advantage; still, the Liberal regime actively identified itself with the vigorous national expansion, and also carried forward a moderate enlargement of social-welfare measures. For example, it put through the Old Age Security Act of 1951, thus rounding out a federal social insurance structure that included family allowances, old-age pensions, and unemployment insurance, though not medical or hospital care. (A number of provinces, however, developed hospital insurance plans, and Saskatchewan would later add a government medical care system.) The St Laurent cabinet itself seemed to inspire public confidence. Leading ministers like C. D. Howe had had years of government experience during the long reign of Mackenzie King. The Secretary for External Affairs, L. B. Pearson, won wide admiration as Canada's spokesman at the United Nations and in international affairs generally. And Prime Minister St Laurent, benign and courtly, – Good Uncle to the nation – seemed to represent the amicable concord and confident strength of Canada in her era of success.

It was also true, however, that the rivals of Liberalism remained weak. The Conservatives led by George Drew had still not escaped from their reputation for repeated failure. Quebec still distrusted them, and there was little yet to swing significant numbers of Canadians elsewhere over to them. Certainly, they offered no real alternative to the Liberals, whose policy was essentially middle-of-the-road and far from radical. On the other hand, the programme of the socialist C.C.F., which had been largely shaped during the pre-war depression, had only limited appeal in a prosperous, contented Canada – especially when Liberals had been judiciously taking over and enacting small, soothing instalments of it for years. As for the followers of Social Credit, they remained a somewhat ineffectual fringe, with little strength beyond Alberta.

Nevertheless, the opposition parties continued to hold firm bases outside federal politics in provincial spheres. Though Liberals dominated the Maritimes, and the French sectionalist Union Nationale controlled Quebec, the big province of Ontario was solidly under the Conservative government of Leslie Frost, while T. C. Douglas and the C.C.F. held Saskatchewan, and Ernest Manning and Social Credit ruled Alberta. Here, indeed, Social Credit had changed remarkably. The Manning government piled up surpluses (thanks largely to oil royalties), gave cautious, careful administration, and directed Social Credit more along the paths of right-wing conservatism than of the radical monetary theories of its early days.

In fact, this newer and clearly right-wing version of Social Credit was soon successfully exported to British Columbia. There, in 1952, Social Credit forces under W. A. C. Bennett defeated the existing coalition government of Liberals and Conservatives. This coalition, however, had largely served to keep the C.C.F. out of power in the Pacific province; for socialism had been quite strong among the dock workers, lumbermen, and fishermen of the Coast. Accordingly, the Social Credit victory in British Columbia virtually replaced a weak and worn-out conservative ministry with a new and vigorous one; another indication that broadly throughout Canada the trend was to conservative-minded governments of some sort – perhaps even in the only moderately socialist regime of Saskatchewan. At any rate, it was plain that all across booming Canada there was but limited desire for ardent left-wing enterprises.

In the federal realm in the earlier 'fifties, the sense of nationalism seemed strong, and sectional, dividing issues made little stir. Certainly, French Canada still continued Maurice Duplessis in control of his Quebec provincial empire, from where he thundered periodically against the 'centralizing' menace of the Ottawa authorities. But his sectional regime had lost its aggressiveness; it was growing old in office, and was really content to maintain the *status quo*. Moreover, French Canadians readily supported St Laurent as national leader, showing little objection to his government's policy of active Canadian participation in world affairs, and to decided military commitments abroad such as Mackenzie King would never have dared to make before the war.

A further sign of nationalism was the appointment of the first Canadian Governor-General in 1952: Vincent Massey, a distinguished diplomat and patron of the arts. He had, in fact, headed the Royal Commission on the Arts, Letters and Sciences, which reported in 1951 after an exhaustive inquiry into the state of Canadian culture. Its report led to the founding of the Canada Council to aid and develop national cultural activities. A valuable and historic social document, the Massey Report expressed Canada's desire to shape her own identity without being swamped by the mighty influence of the neighbouring United States. It clearly recognized that if Canada wanted to be a distinct nation culturally no less than economically or politically, she must pay for it. What, indeed, would be the worth of a costly transcontinental system of communications, or the gradual evolution of Canada to the rights of political nationhood, if there were no real Canadian culture and character to give meaning to the country's separate existence on the continent or in the world?

Everything changes. The mood of national unity and comparatively good feeling that helped maintain the long-established Liberal regime could not last forever. The very strains produced by rapid growth, together with growing evidence that all was not rosy in the boom, would surely have brought complaints and criticisms to trouble the national government. Still more than that, the country began to feel that the Liberals were growing complacent and out of touch with the people. Perhaps they had been in power too long. Nothing can be more destructive of political power than that feeling. In 1956 the Liberals' course in parliament seemed to give reason for it.

The government sought to pass a bill giving effect to arrangements it had made for the construction of the natural-gas pipeline from Alberta to the East. This multi-million-dollar measure was only introduced in parliament in the middle of May, although it had to be carried into law by June 7, if the government's agreement with Trans-Canada Pipe Lines was to be honoured. Apparently the ministry felt confident that it could push the bill through in this comparatively short time, because of the big Liberal majority in parliament. Yet the Pipe Lines Bill drew loud and determined opposition criticism, largely over the dominance of American interests in the company that would control this major Canadian undertaking. Faced with vigorous resistance, the government used the power of its majority to close off long debates and speed the bill forward. This allegedly high-handed use of 'closure' roused still more angry criticism. Opposition speakers charged that the cabinet was overriding the rights of parliament, that Liberals had grown arrogant and dictatorial after too many years in office. The bill passed in time; but only after the strongest government pressure and after violent protests in the House. Public sentiment swung significantly from the party in power to the 'underdog' opposition forces. It was really the turning of the ways for Liberalism.

The change was plainly shown in the subsequent election of 1957. The Liberals took only 104 seats to the Conservatives' 109, while the C.C.F. won 25 and Social Credit 19. It was not a clear victory for the Conservatives, but it was an obvious rejection of the Liberals; and it stood to reason that in this rejection a conservative-minded Canada would largely turn toward the official Conservative party, now led by John Diefenbaker of Saskatchewan. George Drew had had to resign as party leader because of ill-health, but Diefenbaker, a vigorous western Conservative who had played a prominent part in the struggle over the Pipe Line Bill, displayed an aggressive fighting spirit that made him a first-rate campaigner as he fierily denounced the sins of Liberal despots and bureaucrats.

There were other causes, of course, for the Liberal defeat. Maritimers felt that their section had not shared sufficiently in boom developments, and that the government had not paid sufficient attention to the special problems of Atlantic Canada. Western farmers, who had been piling up wheat surpluses in recent years, thought that not enough was being done to dispose of their stored-up wheat. Furthermore, many industrial and financial interests in both East and West objected to the government's 'tight money' policy, which was designed to check inflation, but also seemed to be dampening business enterprise at a time when the boom was showing signs of slackening.

In the next parliamentary session, the new Diefenbaker regime moved promptly to provide cash advances for stored wheat and grants for power developments in Atlantic Canada. It also increased old-age pensions and eased measures restricting the supply of money. This was something for nearly everybody. When Diefenbaker called another election in 1958, to try to obtain a firm majority for his government, the people responded beyond his wildest expectations in their desire to give the new ministry a proper chance. The Liberals, now led by Lester Pearson, were reduced to a mere 49, the C.C.F. took only 8 seats, Social Credit none. And the Conservatives won 208 places, the greatest sweep so far in Canadian history.

The reconfirmed Diefenbaker government applied itself to more nation-building projects: more northern development, the huge South Saskatchewan dam and irrigation scheme, and more aid to improve the position of Atlantic Canada. Despite very heavy government expenditures that brought a succession of budget deficits, the Canadian economy did not seem to be growing at its former rapid pace. One increasingly grave problem was unemployment, which rose even while many boom developments were still going forward. Part of the trouble was seasonal unemployment, a condition hard to avoid in a northern country like Canada where weather governs many activities, though here the government's winter-work programme offered help. Part of the unemployment was 'technological', the result of advanced modern methods of industrial production that stressed highly skilled labour, or even automation, and thus threw the less skilled out of work. Here government programmes to teach unskilled workers new trades promised some assistance, though pockets of people in out-of-date industries – unwilling to move or too old or uneducated to be retrained effectively – remained an enduring problem.

Yet much of the unemployment was due as well to Canadian producers losing some of their markets to foreign competitors. Japan and Germany had recovered, while Europe generally had revived so far that its efficient, modernized industries were now taking sales away from Canadians at home and abroad. In some fields Canadian products were in danger of pricing themselves out of the market, and were being undersold by more cheaply produced foreign goods. Perhaps Canada had been living too high, and beyond her actual means.

The difficulties that faced the Diefenbaker government, therefore, were largely not ones that it had created or could solve easily and in a short time. Yet its policies did not seem to achieve any truly significant success, and its opponents might argue that it did not squarely face up to fundamental problems. Instead, it went on much as if the boom really were continuing, priding itself on achievements that might be commendable but did not touch Canada's increasingly urgent needs: achievements such as the appointment in 1959 of the first French-Canadian Governor-General, General Georges Vanier, another distinguished diplomat, and the passage of a Canadian Bill of Rights in 1960. The latter was an American-model addition to the Canadian constitution that was not previously felt necessary in a British structure of law and parliamentary freedoms, and was limited only to rights under federal jurisdiction.

In any case, it was natural that complaints would more and more be voiced against the government that had won overwhelmingly in 1958. Canada was so obviously slipping from boom into something approaching a depression. An unedifying quarrel in 1961 between the Governor of the Bank of Canada and the cabinet over national financial policy did not help Canada's standing in investment circles. Capital was ceasing to flow into the country. In fact, the movement now turned the other way. This threatened a critical fall in the value of the Canadian dollar, and beyond that would remove a major support of economic growth.

The upsetting changes were soon reflected in politics. The Liberals were newly active. They regained power in Quebec in 1960, a year after its old Union Nationale master, Duplessis, had died. The same year they came back in New Brunswick, which had only briefly turned Conservative, although the Conservatives still kept their other provincial gains of the 'fifties – Nova Scotia and Manitoba. Social Credit, moreover, began making headway in back sections of French Canada. There was renewed activity on the left as well, stimulated by the spread of economic troubles. The powerful Canadian Labour Congress decided to join with the C.C.F. in founding a broad party of the left backed by unionism, somewhat like the British Labour Party. The combination produced the New Democratic Party in 1961, under the leadership of 'Tommy' Douglas, who left another successful re-election in Saskatchewan in order to enter national politics. Consequently, when the Diefenbaker government decided to go to the country again in 1962, it was bound to be vigorously attacked, left, right and centre.

The results showed how sharply the feelings of the people had changed since the last election. It was almost 1957 over again.

This time the Conservatives had fallen drastically. They had still won the largest number of seats, 116, but they did not have an actual majority. The Liberals had climbed back to 100; the N.D.P. had taken 19 seats and, most surprisingly, Social Credit had obtained 30: 2 in Alberta, 2 in British Columbia, the rest in Quebec! The results were obviously indefinite. There would have to be another election. Still, thus far one fact seemed obvious: Canadians had revealed a striking loss of confidence in both the major parties in succession, without turning strongly to any other one. In short, as Canada's troubles had mounted, the votes of her people had largely been negative. No one party had yet inspired a broad, positive belief in its policies.

Moreover, sectional differences had reappeared. Their significance, and that of forces generally that had produced the election results of 1962, would grow increasingly evident as the new decade proceeded. Hence they may best be dealt with when that period comes under discussion. It is sufficient now to say that Canada had entered the 'sixties politically confused and considerably disunited.

3 *External Relations in the Mid-Century Years*

Generally speaking, Canadian concerns in the world at large continued much as they had been in the immediate post-war years. There were three major fields of interest, though they often overlapped or fused together. First, concern for international security and a peaceful, freely developing world – which largely shaped Canada's activities at the United Nations and in the North Atlantic Treaty Organization. Second, security and prosperity in North America – which essentially meant close relations with the United States, together with a firm defence of Canadian viewpoints. And third, continued ties with Britain and the Commonwealth of Nations – which involved important markets overseas and valuable contacts with emerging nations in Asia and Africa.

Canada took a significant role in NATO, the North Atlantic Treaty Organization established by the free nations of western Europe and North America, in 1949, for joint defence against the threat of Soviet armed power, which had already subdued eastern Europe. A Canadian army brigade was stationed in Germany, with R.C.A.F. squadrons in support in France. Canadian naval units operated under NATO command, while airmen from NATO countries were trained in Canada. Canadians, however, had hoped to see the North Atlantic community developed as an economic and cultural partnership of peoples who had still more in common than their urgent need for joint defence. Hence Canada's representatives at NATO meetings had tried to stress the non-military aspects of the organization from the drafting of the Treaty onward. Although their success was limited, it did become evident that NATO partners in Europe were moving into closer economic co-operation, which might be the necessary first step toward a broader North Atlantic relationship.

Canada was equally active in the United Nations. Here her stand against Communist fomenting of international disorders often took her to the same positions as her closest associates, the United States or Britain. But not necessarily so: basically, Canada followed her own course as she strove to reduce world tensions and uphold the principle of collective security through the United Nations. Hence she sent troops to the Korean War of 1950-3, in order to support the U.N.'s declaration that North Korea's attack on South Korea was aggression that must be halted – not to fight a largely American war against the Communist Chinese who backed their North Korean allies. In general, Canada won recognition in the U.N. as a nation with her own mind. This was all-important in enabling her to do valuable work in helping to ease clashes between Communist and non-Communist forces around the world. In 1954, for example, she was chosen along with Poland and India to supervise the armistice arranged in Indo-China between the Vietminh Communists and the non-Communist Vietnamese. Canadians had no direct interests in Indo-China or South-East Asia, but they knew that local wars anywhere threatened the security of the world.

An equally difficult situation arose in the Middle East in 1956, where, after years of border strains and clashes, Israeli troops invaded Egypt, while British and French forces moved to re-occupy the Suez Canal which Egypt had just nationalized. Again Canada pursued her own course. As she had not previously followed the United States in bristling antagonism to Communist China, so now she did not endorse Anglo-French armed inter-vention at Suez. Instead she sought once more to find a means of peaceful adjustment through the United Nations. The Canadian External Affairs Minister, Lester Pearson, introduced a resolution in that body calling for a U.N. Emergency Force to go to the Middle East and supervise a cease-fire. The force was sent; Canadian troops formed part of it; and the danger at Suez came under control as the Israeli, French, and British withdrew. Although the trouble-spot was not removed, it was now under orderly policing by international authority. Here was construc-tive achievement through Canadian policy – for which Pearson won the Nobel Peace Prize in 1957.

Another international police force was established when the Congo erupted into civil war and anarchy after gaining inde-pendence from Belgium in 1960. Once more Canada sent a contingent with the supervising U.N. expedition, as she con-tinued firmly to uphold the principle of collective action to save world peace. In the interests of world security – which meant her own – Canada by the opening of the 'sixties thus had units abroad in western Europe, the Middle East, South-East Asia, and Africa. This did not include her numerous representatives on United Nations health, food, and welfare agencies at work in many parts of the world to improve standards of living, so as to reduce the suffering, poverty, and ignorance that may lead to violence and war. To this end she also spent sizeable sums on foreign aid – though some said she could afford more.

Security still had to be safeguarded at home, in North America. During the 1950's, Canada's co-operation with the United States in joint continental defence grew notably, and particularly to meet the common danger of attack across the Arctic. They shared in maintaining the Pine Tree Line, part of the radar warning system, not far above the American border. Canada set up the Mid-Canada Line along the 55th parallel, and under an agreement of 1955 the United States built and manned the DEW Line from Alaska across the Canadian Arctic. This last project was thus a permanent American military installation on Canadian soil. But Canada could not have met its enormous cost, while the United States was deeply anxious to have it. In a common cause and need, Canada accepted this new binding commitment to the United States, still reserving her future right to take over the DEW Line. Military commitment went still further when an agreement of 1958 established a joint United States and Canadian command for North American air defence. The command, called NORAD, had already been organized provisionally the year before, under an American supreme commander and a Canadian deputy at headquarters in Colorado Springs.

NORAD sharply underlined the political question whether Canada still had any real scope for her own decision in matters of peace or war, or was simply bound to follow her much bigger partner in the continental command. Yet arrangements for NORAD had been begun under the Liberals and concluded under the Conservatives. Both major parties, evidently, had shared in the process that tied Canada closely to ultimate American military direction. There was really a further question, still debated by Canadians: was anything else possible when the danger was that of nuclear attack and the issue actual survival?

In spheres other than defence, Canada found room to bargain with and sometimes disagree with the United States, though any disagreements were still within the framework of their intimately friendly relations. Quite apart from the fact that even the strongest friends will still have their own viewpoints and interests, there were two additional reasons why Canada might well try to assert her own policies. First, she sought to preserve her national lines of development against the inevitably great weight of American influences. Second, she had to speak up when the big republic threatened to ignore and override her views. Sometimes traditional anti-American emotions may have affected her response, but it would be foolish to ascribe Canada's attitude merely to this. When one shares close quarters with a giant however well-intentioned, one is wise to keep pointing out that one is there – to avoid being stepped on.

Accordingly, Canada protested the United States 'grain giveaway' programme that cut into Canadian wheat markets abroad. She sold goods, within limits, both to Communist China and to newly Communist Cuba, doubting that American attempts to wholly isolate these states were really wise. And she negotiated firmly with the United States on the question of the waters of the Columbia river, in order to secure a treaty that would give the northern nation a fair share of the water-supply and hydro-electric power to be derived from this mighty stream that ran through the Far West of both countries. Final passage of a Columbia River Treaty was delayed till 1963 by disagreements within Canada herself between the federal and British Columbia governments. But one excellent example of an agreement reached by the two nations for joint development was that which brought about the St Lawrence Seaway. Here, undoubtedly, Canada's expressed willingness to proceed alone, while being no less ready to co-operate, did much to bring the United States to act in 1954. It was an indication that a firm, frank, self-respecting policy might earn respect from Canada's continental partner.

Beyond the continent, and around the world, Canada still maintained her significant Commonwealth relationships. Under the Colombo Plan of 1950, for example, she provided valuable technical aid to help develop Asian countries that had just risen to full Commonwealth membership. The 'Canada Dam' was built in Pakistan; Canadian scientists guided the construction of an atomic energy plant in India; and Canadian technical knowledge was applied to improve Ceylon's fisheries. Moreover, concern for the Negro national movements that were creating new self-governing states in Africa brought Canada to officially deplore the policy of *apartheid* maintained by the white-ruled Union of South Africa, a policy that kept the Union's large Negro population segregated and subjected. South Africa, in fact, withdrew from the Commonwealth largely because of the antagonism to *apartheid* made clear by Canada as well as Asian and African members at the Commonwealth Prime Ministers' Conference of 1961.

The next year brought a far more serious problem in international relations, when Communist Cuba based Soviet atomic missiles on its territory, thus opening the United States to possible close-range nuclear attack. Canada was directly involved as America's defence partner in NORAD, when in October, 1962, President John F. Kennedy announced a naval 'quarantine' of Cuba until the missiles were removed. The Diefenbaker government in Canada supported Kennedy's stand, as the weight of Canadian opinion seemed to do. Nevertheless, a good deal of dissent was evident, notably in the New Democratic Party, and the government itself did not indicate its support for forty-eight hours, later noting that there had not been prior consultation, the proper precondition for joint action. The very real threat of an atomic world war passed when the Soviet Union undertook to remove the missiles; but for Canada the brief, tense Cuban crisis only underlined the grave question of how fully and fatally the country might be committed to American military decisions through its defence agreements.

There was, if anything, a reaction against such a commitment, reflected in the question of whether Canada should equip her own forces with nuclear armaments. The Diefenbaker government had indeed agreed to do so, in 1958 and in 1959. The United States now pressed hard for Canada to carry out those agreements. This produced an argument that split the Canadian government, already greatly weakened by the election of 1962, and in February, 1963, the Conservative regime was defeated in parliament. In the ensuing April election, the Liberals under Lester Pearson came to power, though without gaining a sure majority themselves. Pearson now urged that Canada honour its nuclear commitments, but looked forward to phasing them out. The Liberal ministry signed new agreements with the United States in 1963, providing nuclear warheads for Canada's short-range defensive missiles and aircraft, only to be used under joint control. Generally, however, it still sought to offset American influence over Canadian external affairs by trying to bring home to United States authorities points where Canadian foreign policies differed from the attitudes, or assumptions, of its huge American defence partner. Also, the Pearson regime still sought to support international collective action in dealing with world trouble spots. Thus in 1964 a Canadian contingent was sent with United Nations forces to Cyprus, to supervise that Mediterranean island torn by violent clashes between its Greek and Turkish inhabitants.

A far greater area of violence, however, had emerged in Asia, in South Vietnam, where in 1964 the United States government sharply increased its armed intervention against Communist Viet Cong insurgents supported by North Vietnamese forces. While Canada was not herself engaged in this tortured, bloody struggle, she was inevitably connected; partly through her membership in the now all-but-impotent Vietnamese supervisory commission; but above all through her defence partnership with the United States. This also meant that she provided limited quantities of arms to the Americans through reciprocal defence supply agreements. Thus, as the war grew longer and harsher, and discord over it spread within the United States itself, Canadians inevitably responded with their own protests and divisions of opinion. Prime Minister Pearson, indeed, took a critical stand on American Vietnam policy, speaking in Vermont in 1965; but the evident resentment of United States authorities at this intervention in an American foreign question led to a general position that neither country should take public stands contributing 'unnecessarily to public division'.

Hence little progress was really being made on the vital issue of the close involvement of Canada with American international decisions. Gaps between the two countries were simply being papered over, although Canada still tried to explore ways leading to the settlement of the tragic, dangerous Vietnamese conflict. The external issues for Canadians had not changed greatly, then, as their country approached its centenary of Confederation in 1967. True, the Pearson government had successfully sponsored a national, maple-leaf flag for Canada in 1964, increased expenditures on external aid and reduced those on defence (as well as undertaking to unify the three armed services into one streamlined force in 1965-7). Furthermore, it strongly backed Canada's great centennial exposition that opened in Montreal in April, 1967. The beauty and wonder of Expo 67 undoubtedly helped to give the world a sense of Canadian achievement, as well as deep pride to Canadians themselves. But these far from insignificant accomplishments of the Pearson ministry by no means altered the fact that Canada still lived in a perilous world that was poised on a veritable balance of atomic terror between the United States and the Soviet Union – and deeply involved herself with the former super-power. Indeed, in March, 1968, the NORAD agreement was renewed for a further five years, leaving that involvement essentially unchanged.

4 *'Troubled Canada' in the* 1960's

However important external issues were for Canada's very survival, internal problems loomed far larger for most Canadians in the troubled decade of the sixties. They gave less attention to wars and nuclear dangers, or even to the opening of the startling new era of space exploration, than they did to problems much more familiar and close at hand. Above all, as the decade opened, they worried over the ending of the mid-century boom and the growth of unemployment. Had Canada run into the doldrums? Was a new depression taking shape?

One could contend that Canada's boom-time growth had been so rapid and spectacular that when she reverted to a more normal rate, the situation, by contrast, looked far worse than it was. Whether this be true or not, it does seem clear that the boom had been an abnormal period, and like all good things was bound to end. It had largely depended on highly favourable post-war markets for Canadian products, combined with the great inflow of capital. Market conditions alter, however, and the capital flow had eventually died off, leaving Canada with much larger productive capacities, but facing the need to adjust her production and prices to a strongly competitive new era. Though the process could be painful, for a land with Canada's basic resources it scarcely had to be fatal. Growth had not stopped, nor was this the deep depression of the 'thirties.

Perhaps a more serious long-run problem was the way in which Canada had become tied into the American market during the very years of boom development. Of course, north-south trade ties had long been powerful in Canada, and her forest and mineral exports depended largely on American sales. Nevertheless, economic integration with the United States advanced much further during the capital influx of the mid-century years. United States corporations multiplied their branch plants across Canada or bought out Canadian firms. American investors acquired ownership or control of a very large part of Canada's productive capacity, especially in newer fields of power and mining development. Much of the northern country's resources in raw materials and energy had been channelled to feed industries below the border, and at the same time, Canadians had come increasingly to accept American goods, styles, and price levels. They traded proportionately more with the United States and less now with the world overseas; they were still buying more from the Americans than they were selling. In almost every way, then, whether by control of production, ties of debt, markets, or buying habits, Canada was being more and more bound in with the United States. The great paradox of the boom was that, in enlarging her economy, it had also made her much more dependent.

This says nothing of military integration, or the constant influence of American mass media on the northern country through movies, periodicals and press, and above all, television. It was small wonder that some Canadians grew disheartened in the state of doldrums and talked again of their country's inevitable absorption by the United States, or that others reacted with newly sensitive and suspicious nationalism against that possibility.

Still further to trouble the 'sixties, sectionalism was manifestly rising again. Once more the boom had something to do with it. Many of the mid-century economic developments had a strongly regional or sectional basis: western oil and gas, for example. Even though pipe-lines or seaways might be built across the country, the new resource developments tended to serve north-south lines of trade more than they did the national east-west economic pattern. The regional nature of these interests became still clearer when the national mood of harmony dwindled with the passing of the boom. Furthermore, all regions of Canada had not enjoyed the same high degree of prosperity. The Atlantic provinces had still suffered from their relative lack of resources to develop and from their limited population, and they also feared that the St Lawrence Seaway would divert trade from Maritime ports. Similarly, Saskatchewan or Manitoba farmers in the later stages of the boom faced problems either of grain surplus or of prices too low for profit, and felt that they were not keeping up to the economic level of other sections of the country.

Thus the sectional differences grew anew. Atlantic Canada sought special grants and aids. Newfoundland under Joseph Smallwood quarrelled with the federal Conservative government, because he charged that additional payments promised under the terms of union with Canada had not been properly maintained. And western farmers demanded and got special subsidies to help them. Revived sectional feeling became clearly apparent in the federal election of 1962. In fact, it was a major reason for the failure of any party then to gain a majority.

Big, industrialized Ontario, angered by Conservative financial policies that had not prevented a sharp fall in the value of the Canadian dollar on the very eve of the election, went strongly Liberal. It also returned a significant number of New Democrats, as did British Columbia; in part, no doubt, because of the issue of unemployment. The farming West and the Maritimes stayed firmly with the Conservatives who had given them the regional aid they wanted – except for a Liberal and resentful Newfoundland! The most notable fact of all, however, was the rise of Social Credit in Quebec, much reducing the expected Liberal gains there. And the unique developments in this most distinctively different portion of Canada deserve special comment themselves.

Quebec had undergone a new awakening since the death of Duplessis in 1959. It was as if an iron clamp had suddenly been released from French-Canadian society, and educational and social reforms, new energy, ideas and hopes, came bursting forth together. It would only be fair to note that changes were already proceeding under the short-lived Sauvé and Barrette Union Nationale regimes that succeeded Duplessis. Nevertheless, the rapid sweep of change, the virtual social revolution in Quebec, must be strongly identified with the Liberal provincial government of Jean Lesage that was elected in 1960 and re-elected late in 1962. Quebec's education, and its universities especially, were greatly aided; the trade-union movement felt new freedom; and a plan to 'nationalize' provincial power production went quickly forward. Lesage was quite as much a believer in Quebec provincial autonomy and an opponent of Ottawa centralization as Duplessis had been; but he achieved a fairly successful basis of agreement with the federal authorities as his province surged ahead.

The natural result of the changes, however, was to stimulate the French Canadians' idealism and pride in themselves. French Canada's own nationalistic sentiment was readily encouraged, as Quebec sought to build for itself. In Lesage and the majority of *Québecois*, this spirit did not preclude working in partnership with the rest of Canada, though many said the partnership must be made more equal than it had been, and some looked for changes in the federal constitution to recognize French Canada's rights more fully. Some others went far beyond this. In a mixture of heady optimism, idealistic nationalism, and long-endured resentments, they talked of a separate French-Canadian nation – a Quebec taken out of Confederation and removed from the dominance of English Canada.

Separatism had a mounting impact on French Canada though it took varied forms: from small underground activist groups, seeking 'liberation' through scattered acts of violence, to a vague, broad feeling that, after all, it provided a final alternative if Canada could not meet French Canadians' desires to live and develop in their own language and culture. In any case, it was still one more of the forces that were cutting across the existing Canadian national structure – if potentially the most extreme of them all.

The forces of regionalism, sectionalism, and Quebec-regarding French Canadian nationalism were all the more clearly evident in the federal election of 1963. While the defence question and the increasing failure of John Diefenbaker to give a firm lead on policy then helped to bring down the Conservatives, the confused and divided state of the country did much more. The Pearson

ministry that took office faced the same condition. Although 129
Liberals were returned, to 95 Conservatives, 24 Social Credit
members and 17 New Democrats, the Liberals had no majority
of their own. In short, troubled Canada had produced another
minority government, Liberal instead of Conservative this time.
The new regime was bound to be weak, open to constant attack in
parliament and the continual danger of defeat there.

Nevertheless, the Pearson government managed to put through
some significant measures; for example, in 1964 the redistribution
of parliamentary seats to suit changing population patterns and
particularly urban growth. It mounted a re-examination of
Canadian defence policies and proposed wide-ranging pension
and medicare schemes as part of a 'war on poverty' proclaimed in
1965. Furthermore, improving trade conditions and enlarged
demands for most of Canada's basic products eased economic
problems after 1963, giving the ministry some glow of financial
success. Indeed, by 1966 the emerging problem was that of rapidly
advancing prices and the need to control inflation. Canada was
growing buoyantly again in many areas, by the year of Expo,
especially in the big urban centres of Montreal, Toronto, Vancouver, Edmonton, and Calgary. And the stream of immigration
rose anew.

Despite the better times and its own constructive work, however – and despite its leader's dedication and diplomatic experience – the Pearson cabinet repeatedly found itself in trouble. It
was, of course, under relentless opposition attack, notably from
John Diefenbaker, but it was also involved in administrative
blunders and party scandals. These did not really implicate it in
wrong-doing, but they did suggest a fumbling in its direction,
which did not help the government when it went to a new election
in November, 1965, hoping to strengthen its position. Instead, it
was left virtually where it had been, with 131 Liberals elected, to
97 for the Conservatives, 21 for the N.D.P., and 14 for Social
Credit, now split into French and English factions. Pearson had

not gained a clear majority. If anything, his old foe Diefenbaker had had more satisfaction, for he had crushed rebellious followers in his own party and carried it intact through his own strenuous campaign.

Still, the Liberals remained in power, to benefit from the rising sun of Expo and the better national mood it temporarily produced. And as for Diefenbaker, the discontented elements in Conservative ranks, who felt he was too negative a leader and too out of touch with the newer aspects of Canada, finally managed to displace him at the party leadership convention of September, 1967. Robert Stanfield, successful premier of Nova Scotia, became Conservative leader in his stead. The next year, Lester Pearson himself retired as Liberal leader and prime minister. His successor, Pierre Elliott Trudeau, was chosen at a Liberal convention in April, 1968.

Minister of Justice in Pearson's final cabinet, Trudeau had earlier been a lawyer, left-wing magazine editor, and university professor; but above all he was a man of keen intellect and independent cast of mind. A much younger man, a world traveller, and a 'new' French Canadian, he seemed to represent a fresher generation in outlook for all Canada. Undoubtedly he was so taken up by the public, and given a swinging image in the press during the election campaign that followed. His personal appeal, and revived hopes of strong federal leadership, overcame much of the divisive forces in Canada of the sixties. In the election of June, 1968, the Liberals won a clear majority, with 155 seats, the Conservatives dropping to 72, the N.D.P. holding 22, and English-speaking Social Credit being eliminated—though the French-speaking 'Créditistes' under boisterous Réal Caouette rose from 8 to 14. In general, the Liberals had swept both Ontario and Quebec, particularly in the urban areas, gained in the Prairies, and more than doubled their holdings in British Columbia.

Hence the new Trudeau regime was strongly based, and in the

first months enjoyed something of a honeymoon as it set about planning to achieve its objective of the 'just society' for Canada. It showed energy and purpose as it moved to reorganize governmental machinery, complete social measures projected under Pearson, and effect new reforms of its own. But, by 1969 the honeymoon was inevitably wearing thin, and by 1970 it was over, for the forces of division in Canada had plainly reasserted themselves. Trudeau faced questions of underdevelopment, proportionately lower incomes, and higher unemployment in the Atlantic provinces and much of Quebec. A new piled-up wheat surplus in the western provinces and Ottawa's failure to handle it roused angry resentment. British Columbia, still under the durable Mr. Bennett, was a booming world, but almost a world of its own; Ontario's Conservative government, firmly ruled by John Robarts since 1962, represented a still more powerful provincial empire. Yet Quebec was the continuing centre of the greatest problem, since here the vital issue of French-English relations was focussed; and this had come to involve the structure of the Canadian constitution itself.

The constitutional question had come to the fore again in the 1960's, as the Lesage government in Quebec sought to expand provincial power, especially financial, to enable it to build the powerful and modern French Canadian realm it was striving to achieve. As this affected the federal system, Pearson Liberals and Lesage Liberals well might disagree over Quebec demands for wider authority, especially as pressed by René Lévesque, Lesage's vigorous Resources Minister, whose views at times seemed close to separatism. But generally the Pearson government adopted a policy of 'co-operative federalism', which permitted Quebec to enlarge its control considerably over areas such as taxation and pension plans. Furthermore, in order to inquire into French Canadians' claims that they did not receive equal treatment as French-speaking citizens of the nation, the Pearson government had appointed a Royal Commission on Bilingualism and Biculturalism in 1963, whose reports over the decade did much to make both Canadas aware of the problems of trying to deal with two major language groups in one transcontinental state. But Quebec itself, where separatists were increasingly vocal – and even political parties like the Union Nationale wanted some sort of special status for their province in Confederation – was more and more looking for changes in the constitution to recognize the national rights of French Canada.

In 1966, in fact, the Lesage government was defeated in an election by a reinvigorated Union Nationale party led by Daniel Johnson, who demanded 'equality or independence'. By 1967 René Lévesque had moved on to advocate outright separation of Quebec from Canada, while the Johnson government sought a wholesale reconsideration of the structure of Confederation, on the grounds that the plan laid down in 1867 was thoroughly out of keeping with the needs of modern Canada and Quebec. Now began a series of full-scale federal-provincial conferences on the constitution, where provincial premiers like Liberals Louis Robichaud of New Brunswick and Ross Thatcher of Saskatchewan, and Edward Schreyer, N.D.P. premier of Manitoba, brought still more positions on federal-provincial problems to add to those of the federal ministers, Quebec's Johnson and Bertrand, and Robarts of Ontario. It was at such a conference, in February, 1968, that Trudeau (then Minister of Justice) took a strong stand against Johnson's demands for constitutional change, asserting that none were needed, but that guaranteed language rights for any French-speaking individual in all parts of Canada would remove all need for special powers for Quebec. This was the policy Trudeau as prime minister established for the federal government in 1969. But federal-provincial constitutional discussions nevertheless proceeded, though with little achievement yet beyond the airing of opinions.

In the meantime, Johnson's sudden death placed the Union

Nationale government in the hands of a successor, Jean-Jacques Bertrand, while Lévesque went on to form the Parti Québecois out of various separatist organizations. As the 1960's ended, it was too soon to say how far separatism yet might grow in French Canada, or where either the Quebec Liberal or Union Nationale parties would finally plant themselves on the basic constitutional question. Nor was it clear how strong the very real sentiment in Quebec for federal Canada would prove itself to be. One thing only was plain. The 1970's would surely produce more decisive changes in the internal structure of Canada than the sixties, which had brought talk rather than action – however necessary the former might be as a prelude.

Thus the latest age left Canada in internal affairs much as it had in external: with grave questions shaped for the future but little yet decided. They also included questions of American economic penetration, of the cost and congestion of urban living, of city slums and rural poverty – of native peoples, Indians, Métis, and Eskimo, also demanding recognition in the would-be just society. There was sudden awareness of the drastic problem of pollution, in its many forms; there was a growing radicalism in the ranks of the young that yet might change the older conservative cast of Canada. The outlook was not wholly troubled. A country that had grown and thrived mightily was still growing. Its cultural life had broadened with enlarging recognition of its arts and artists – like Borduas, Riopelle, Smith, Shadbolt, and Gladstone. In fact, what lay ahead were still more challenges. And when Canadians had effectively responded to so many others through all their history – did it necessarily follow that they would fail this time?

INDEX

440